STUDIES IN MEDIEVAL AND RENAISSANCE HISTORY

Volume VII

(Old Series, Volume XVII)

STUDIES IN
Medieval and Renaissance
History

Volume VII
(Old Series, Volume XVII)

EDITORS:
J.A.S. EVANS
R.W. UNGER

AMS PRESS
New York

Published by

AMS PRESS, INC.
56 EAST 13TH STREET
NEW YORK, NY 10003

ISSN 0081-8224
ISBN 0-404-62850-8 (Set)
ISBN 0-404-62857-5 (Vol. VII)

Library of Congress Catalog Card Number 63-22098

Manufactured in the United States of America

CONTENTS

INTRODUCTION

Studies in Medieval and Renaissance History is a series designed for original major articles in all fields of medieval and renaissance history. Volumes will appear approximately once a year.

Studies in Medieval and Renaissance History was formerly published by the University of Nebraska Press, and the impetus for the creation of the series came from the belief that there was a need for a publication that would accommodate the study that was too long to be included regularly in scholarly journals, but too short to appear as a book. The editors will consider articles in all areas of history from approximately the third to the sixteenth centuries — economic, social and demographic, political, intellectual and cultural, and studies that do not fit neatly into a single traditional category of historical investigation.

While the series is devoted primarily to the publication of major studies, it contains occasional bibliographic essays, and briefer articles dealing with unpublished archival and manuscript resources. The *Studies* also makes available in translation original articles by scholars who do not write in English or French.

Studies in Medieval and Renaissance History is published by AMS Press for the Committee for Medieval Studies at the University of British Columbia, and the editors welcome submissions from all scholars doing research in medieval and renaissance fields, including those whose interests are not strictly historical.

J.A.S.E.

GEOFFREY GREYMANTLE, COUNT OF THE ANGEVINS 960–987: A STUDY IN FRENCH POLITICS

Bernard S. Bachrach
The University of Minnesota

GEOFFREY GREYMANTLE, COUNT OF THE ANGEVINS, 960–987: A STUDY IN FRENCH POLITICS*

Geoffrey Greymantle, count of the Angevins from 960–987, pursued the kind of career from which medieval people fashioned their legends. In the eleventh century a Latin prose epic detailed Geoffrey's heroic exploits. By the twelfth century "Gefreid d'Anjou," as he was sometimes called in the vernacular, was well established in literature as a figure of importance among the great magnates of France. In the *Song of Roland* he is given the high honor of serving as Charlemagne's standard bearer.[1]

Modern scholars, however, have tended to neglect the epic-making career of Geoffrey Greymantle. The magisterial studies by Halphen and Guillot deal with the Angevin counts in the eleventh century and not unreasonably they devote only a few pages to Geoffrey's reign as an introduction to their main subject.[2] In this they follow the pattern established by Kate Norgate, who almost a century ago provided some interesting observations concerning Geoffrey in an introductory chapter to her monumental treatment of the Angevin house.[3] The prevailing reason for this tendency to begin the "serious" study of Angevin history with the reign of Fulk Nerra, Geoffrey's son, appears to have been best expressed by Sir Richard Southern when he wrote: "By 987 the family was ready to emerge from its legendary and epic age onto the stage of history."[4]

Yet to consider Geoffrey Greymantle a part of the "prehistory" of the Angevin house runs counter to the dramatic results produced by K. F. Werner's brilliant application of prosopographical techniques to the *Frühzeit* of the *französisches Fürstentum* during the ninth and tenth centuries. Werner showed that we no longer need to consider the familial and political policies of Geoffrey's father, grandfather, and even great-grandfather to be shrouded in legend. Yet, by contrast with the activities of his ancestors, Geoffrey's career appears to be so well-documented that it did not require the extensive application of Werner's innovative methods. Thus, in what must be

3

considered the most important study of the French aristocracy since Dhondt's ground-breaking work on the principalities appeared in 1948, Werner does not examine the reign of Geoffrey Greymantle.[5]

The purpose of this study is to provide a comprehensive treatment of Geoffrey Greymantle's political activities. It is hoped thereby that the gap between Werner's fine treatment of Geoffrey's predecessors and the works of Halphen and Guillot which focus upon his successors will be filled. Further, it will be suggested here that Geoffrey Greymantle is a transitional figure in Angevin history. He began his career by following the broadly-gauged policies of aggrandizement that had been initiated by his grandfather. These were aimed to pursue family advantage throughout France wherever opportunity might be found. Geoffrey, however, ended his career by outlining a design for Angevin territorial contiguity which was to be refined and developed by his son and successor Fulk Nerra.[6]

I

The Defense of Angers and Its Environs

Geoffrey Greymantle's grandfather, Fulk the Red, had been settled at Angers and had been given extensive rights and possessions in the area as well as the comital title so that he might defend the city and its environs from the ravages of the Vikings. Faithful to their charge, the Angevin counts frequently fought against these raiders and later against their Norman successors. Ingelger, Geoffrey's uncle, was killed in battle during one of these many combats.[7]

In order to pursue their mandate to defend the region it was necessary for the Angevins to have a strong if not impregnable base from which to operate. This defensive strongpoint at Angers was the *aula comitis.* For almost four decades before Geoffrey Greymantle succeeded as count in 960, his grandfather and father had enjoyed the security provided by this citadel which from its position on a steep promontory some thirty-five meters above the river Maine dominated the walled *urbs* of Angers.[8] The old Roman defenses of Angers, which had been built during the later third and early fourth centuries and which had been repaired frequently thereafter, provided an elaborate defensive bastion for the local population. The walls of the *urbs* which had a perimeter of approximately 1,200 meters and enclosed an area of nine hectares stood about ten meters in height, were up to four meters thick at the base and benefited from the reenforcement of towers. At the end of the city opposite the *aula comitis* was the old imperial *praetorium* or citadel which was held by the bishop whose cathedral stood just beside it.[9]

Like the Angevin-dominated fortifications at Loches and Nantes, Angers was defended by a garrison that was comprised of both *milites* and *pedites*. Geoffrey Greymantle provided *beneficia* to at least some of these *milites*.[10] For example, among his *fideles*, the *miles* Hilgerius held lands within the walls of the *urbs* of Angers and Griferius' *beneficium* lay just beyond the walls. These *milites* were men of considerable importance who had military followers of their own. Thus we find Geoffrey giving permission for Hilgerius to give a part of his *beneficium* to his own *vassalus*, Archinulfus, and Griferius is seen to benefice Arnulfus whose brother, Amalbertus, was also one of the count's *vassali*.[11]

While men such as Hilgerius and Griferius along with their own *vassali* may be considered to have comprised the elite defense forces at Angers, it was contemporary military thinking in light of the prevailing technology that for each yard or meter of perimeter wall that had to be defended in time of attack one able bodied man was required for the defense.[12] The proper defense of Angers's 1,200 meter perimeter would have required a force of no less then 1,000 men — effectives are rarely as numerous as planning requires — who were moderately skilled in the use of the cross bow, short bow, and perhaps the sling.[13] In order for a force of such size to be available regularly for the defense of the walls of Angers it seems likely that the majority of effectives were local levies drawn from the city and its environs. Indeed, this type of local defense obligation was well established in the barbarian successor states of the Roman Empire in the West and continued to flourish in the lands of the erstwhile Frankish empire well into the eleventh century.[14]

Geoffrey Greymantle also made provision for the defense of the region beyond the walls of the city. For example, the security of the left bank of the Loire River as far east as Saint-Rémy-la-Varenne (*v* map I) was entrusted to Cadilo, who also held a *beneficium* down river at Blaison. Among the other *beneficia* held by Cadilo, who is seen to have attested Geoffrey's charters more frequently than any other of the count's *fideles*, was the office of *praepositus* of the monastery of Saint-Lézin. Geoffrey granted half of the monastery's tithes to Cadilo and six of the eighteen prebends which are styled *honores* in the count's act. Each of these *honores* obligated Cadilo to perform six weeks of service to the count who as archabbot of Saint-Lézin disposed of its resources as he saw fit.[15]

Along the right bank of the Loire in the area of the Roman road that ran west from Tours to Angers, Geoffrey established one of his more important *fideles*, the *miles* Walter, at Limelle.[16] Eight kilometers further to the east southeast, Ascelinus, another of the more frequent witnesses to Geoffrey's charters, was established at Brain-sur-l'Authion.[17]

About twenty kilometers north of Brain-sur-l'Authion at Jarzé, Geoffrey established members of the Bouchard clan. This family played an important role in the administration of the cathedral and numbered among its members various *nobiles* and *milites*. One of these Bouchards Geoffrey made abbot of the newly restored monastery of Saint Serge outside the walls of Angers and another was made castellan of Briollay by Fulk Nerra.[18]

At Seiches on the right bank of the Loir only ten kilometers west of Jarzé, Geoffrey established another of his *fideles*, a *miles* named Éon. Éon was not a local magnate but was recruited from Brittany. He was a member of the viscomital family of Rennes and seems to have held that title for a time after leaving Geoffrey's entourage. Geoffrey recruited Éon no later than 966, and by 969, the count also had recruited the *miles* Joscelin of Rennes. The latter, who very probably was Éon's close relative, perhaps his brother or son (Éon and Joscelin were the *Lietnamen* of the viscomital family of Rennes), succeeded him in possession of Seiches and later was established as castellan at both Baugé and Beaupréau.[19]

Only four kilometers south of Seiches at a particularly narrow turn in the Loir we find the *miles* Alveus holding a *beneficium* at Corzé. Part of this *beneficium* he granted to Arnulfus and to the latter's brother Amalbertus, the *vassalus* of Geoffrey Greymantle who was mentioned above as holding lands near Angers from Griferius with the count's permission.[20]

North of Corzé, Count Geoffrey's *fideles* were established at Vaux, Prignes, Boudré, and Noyau. The first three-mentioned places were held by a magnate named Renaud, and Noyau was held by one of the count's *fideles* named Fulcoius. Both of these names are prominent in the *Namengut* of the Renaud-clan whose leading members, father and son both named Renaud, Geoffrey made viscount and bishop of Angers, respectively. One of the main holdings of this clan, Thorigné from which Viscount Renaud obtained his sobriquet, *Thoringus*, is located less than twenty-five kilometers west of Prignes.

About sixteen kilometers west of Prignes, Geoffrey granted the exceptionally large and valuable *curtis* of Champigné-sur-Sarthe that had the capacity to support numerous *milites* and *vavassores* to Albericus of Orléans. Like Éon and Joscelin, Alberic was an outsider and he appears to have been affiliated with the viscomital family of Orléans.[22]

To the southwest of Champigné-sur-Sarthe was Renaud's *villa* of Thorigné, discussed above, and further to the west was the important *castellum* of Rochefort-sur-Loire. Robert, who was also probably the lord of Buzançais and a long-time supporter of the Angevin counts, held this stronghold until early in 970, when Geoffrey arranged for his *vassalus* Renaud, the future viscount of Angers, to be established there as castellan.[23]

East of Rochefort, Fredericus held the earthen fortification *(fossa)* at Morin where the river Maine runs into the Loire.[24]

An examination of map I which plots the location of the beneficies held by Geoffrey's *milites* who have been discussed above would seem to indicate that the Angevin count had established this group of important supporters, i.e. men who are styled in various contemporary documents as the count's *fideles, proceres, nobiles*, and *potentissimi milites*, in a perimeter that extended no more than twenty-five kilometers from the *urbs* of Angers in any direction but virtually encircled it.[25] The deployment of these important *milites*, men who had personal armed followings of their own, would seem to suggest that Geoffrey had a sound understanding of the strategy and tactics that were necessary for the security of Angers. For example, many of these *milites* were placed in key locations along the land and water routes to Angers: Blaison and Saint-Rémy-la-Varenne were on the Loire to the east of the city while Rochefort-sur-Loire and Fosse Morin were on the river to the west. Brain-sur-l'Authion and Limelle were within sight of the Roman road that ran west from Tours, and Corzé, Seiches, and Prignes were located at strategic points along the Loir.

Each of the *milites* whose benefices are depicted on Map I was in position to reach the city of Angers, itself, in a ride that would take two hours or less. Conversely, Count Geoffrey could muster his own entourage of *milites* at Angers and ride to the defense of his *fideles*, their lands or dependents at any of the locations on the defensive perimeter in the same amount of time that it took for the journey in the other direction. In addition, any of Geoffrey's *milites* who were established near the *villa* or *curtis* or a fellow supporter of the Angevin count who was threatened by an enemy attack could ride to the support of the neighbor who was in danger even more rapidly than the count could come from Angers. For example, the six kilometers from Blaison to Saint-Rémy-la-Varenne could be negotiated by a force of mounted fighting men in less than a half hour as could the eight kilometers from Brain-sur-l'Authion at Limelle.[26]

Although very little archaeological work has been carried out in Anjou on the fortifications of this period, there is sufficient data available to suggest that at least some and perhaps many of the benefices held by Geoffrey's *milites* could be defended by or at least could provide for the safety of a portion of the local population until help arrived to drive off the invaders. For example, Rochefort-sur-Loire is clearly indicated in a contemporary documentary source to have been fortified with a *castellum*. However, few others are so obvious. Thus the *podium* at Sazé which overlooked and probably guarded the two *curtes* at Saint-Rémy-la-Varenne and which also served as the location for a comital court might well have been a *motte*. Yet, confirmation for this hypothesis can only come from the archaeologist's spade. Less problematical is the *fossa* at Morin. The term *fossa* in this region during the tenth and early eleventh centuries is as unambiguous an indication of a fortified place, albeit a primitive one, as any location called *castrum* or *castellum*. It is possible that Saint-Rémy-la-Varenne which is reported to have had an aula in the sixth century was maintained as a fortified position into the tenth century. Blaison, which had been part of the royal fisc and housed various elements connected with the monastery of Saint Maur, is said to have been fortified after the Viking attacks of the ninth and early tenth centuries. Finally, Limelle is known to have been the location of a Roman *villa*, and more than one such historic site was converted into a stronghold during the early Middle Ages. Until, however, each *fosse* and *motte* has been catalogued and studied scientifically and each ruin has been systematically excavated we will remain greatly handicapped in our attempt to appreciate fully the strength of Geoffrey's defensive system which boasted at least some fortifications to support his internal lines of communication and transportation.[27]

For the defense of the region around Angers, Geoffrey relied in large part upon important men, i.e. *proceres, fideles, potentissimi milites,* and *nobiles*, who were drawn from old local families. For example, Hilgerius, Cadilo, the two Renauds, Alveus, and Fulcoius appear to have been relatives of men who are seen to have served in the entourage of Fulk the Red.[28] A second group of supporters, e.g. Albericus of Orléans, Éon of Rennes, and Joscelin of Rennes was recruited from important (i.e. viscomital) families in somewhat distant regions where Geoffrey either already had a substantial interest or was seeking to establish a position (*v* below).

Although the Angevin counts possessed substantial resources in the environs of Angers, Geoffrey Greymantle frequently rewarded his *milites* with lands and other *beneficia* that belonged to the fisc of the cathedral church of Saint Maurice or from the holdings of local monastic establishments such as Saint Aubin, Saint Lézin, and Saint Serge. For example, Griferius held a *beneficium* "from the largess of the count" but *ex rebus Sancti Maurici Andegavensis*. Similarly, Geoffrey's *fidelis* Walter held a *beneficium ex rebus Sancti Albani* and Alveus's *beneficium* was *ex potestate Sancti Sergii*. Cadilo, as mentioned above, held many *honores* from the fisc of Saint Lézin which Geoffrey who was also *archiabbas* of the monastery had granted to him. These and other examples of the use of ecclesiastical and monastic lands highlight the stipulation that Geoffrey included in the charter for the "reform" of Saint Aubin in which it is made clear that the monks were expected to provide *auxilium* to the count from their resources for military purposes. This old

Carolingian practice so effectively employed by Charles Martel, Pepin, and Charlemagne did not die with the dissolution of the empire.[29]

II
The Western Frontier

We turn now from the strategy used by Geoffrey Greymantle to defend the heartland from which he ruled the complex of lands and lordships that had been accumulated by his ancestors to examine the policies that he pursued to maintain control of these dominions scattered throughout France. As mentioned earlier, Geoffrey's family had originally been established at Angers in order to help defend the *regnum Francorum* against the Northmen. From a diplomatic and military point of view, the defense and the expansion of their western frontier dominated the policies of the Angevin counts more than any other single problem. Throughout the early Middle Ages, the lower valley of the Loire river served as a conduit for raids inland. Thus the counts at Angers were threatened with attacks from the sea which encompassed all the logistic advantages that a vigorous naval capacity provided in a period of inadequate land transport. The Saxon raiders of the fifth century who exploited the collapse of imperial river defenses were no less successful in despoiling the region than were the Vikings who sailed up the Loire during the twilight of the Carolingian empire. Indeed, the safety of Angers and the defense of the western frontier depended in large part upon control of the formidable fortified *urbs* of Nantes.[30]

Nantes was defended by a perimeter wall of 1,600 meters that enclosed an area of sixteen hectares. The walls were strengthened by perhaps as many as thirty towers and within the *urbs* at the southeastern corner was the old Roman *arx* that served as the count's residence and internal citadel. Nantes was only 100 kilometers down river from Angers and therefore was of great strategic importance to anyone who would desire to control access from the west to the middle Loire valley. From a defensive point of view the count at Angers could ill afford to permit Nantes to be in enemy hands. It is equally clear that whoever might be in a position to keep raiders from passing Nantes could also halt the activities of merchants and traders. Therefore the control of Nantes had economic as well as military significance.[31]

Geoffrey Greymantle pursued a policy of dealing with Nantes that differed little from that of his predecessors. During the early tenth century Fulk the Red, Geoffrey's grandfather, held the title count of Nantes. This title was lost, however, and Alan Barbe-Torte emerged as the ruler of much of Brittany including Nantes. Alan was an ally of Theobald the Trickster, count of Blois, Chartres, Châteaudun, and Tours, who exercised successfully a claim to be overlord of Rennes and was one of the most powerful magnates in the West of France. The alliance between Theobald and Alan was sealed by the latter's marriage to the sister of the former.[32]

When Alan died in 952, Theobald saw an opportunity to move Fulk the Good, Geoffrey Greymantle's father, into the Blésois orbit and further weaken the network of Capetian power in the West.[33] To this end Fulk, who was eager to secure control of Nantes, and Theobald arranged for the Angevin count to marry Alan's widow; she was Theobald's sister. Thus, Fulk assumed domination of Nantes as well as of Herbauge, Tiffauges, and Mauges; these regions Alan had acquired from Count William of Poitiers ca. 941.[34] Shortly after his marriage to Alan's widow, Fulk is reported to have had Alan's son and heir, Drogo, murdered.[35] It seems unlikely for Drogo to have been Theobald's nephew because by ca. 956 ties between the count of Blois and the Angevins were drawn even closer when Geoffrey Greymantle, Fulk's son, married Adele of Vermandois who was the sister of Count Theobald's wife, Leudegarde.[36]

In 960, Duke Richard of Normandy and Theobald the Trickster went to war. Fulk the Good died at this time, and Geoffrey Greymantle supported his ally Theobald and King Lothair in this conflict against the Normans. As part of this campaign, the Normans along with allies drawn from Scandinavia attacked Nantes. Fulk the Good had appointed Hoël, one of Alan's bastards, as count of Nantes. However, when Geoffrey Greymantle, who was occupied elsewhere, was unable to provide forces to help defend Nantes, Hoël apparently defected and joined with the Normans.[37]

Geoffrey's western frontier was now exposed to attack from the Normans and from a count of Nantes who had nothing to gain by recognizing Angevin overlordship. In order to strengthen Angevin defenses in the lower Loire valley, Geoffrey looked to Renaud of Thorigné, a magnate of distinguished ancestry, who held important lands in the valley of the Sarthe and many alods in the Mauges region. In fact, Geoffrey seems to have developed a plan to entrust to Renaud the defense of the left bank of the Loire between Nantes and Angers. The largest segment of this riparian expanse fell within the Mauges region which was bounded on the west by the Eavre river and on the east by the Hyrome. In 970, as mentioned above, Geoffrey arranged that Robert, one of his supporters, transfer possession of the stronghold of Rochefort-sur-Loire with all that pertained to it to his *vassalus* Renaud.[38]

Geoffrey Greymantle seems to have been well-satisfied with Renaud's performance. Thus, before September 973, Geoffrey appointed Renaud's son, also named Renaud, as bishop-designate of Angers. To secure this appointment the elder Renaud promised that many and perhaps all of his alods in the Mauges region would pass into the possession of the comital fisc after the death of the younger Renaud. Through this agreement Geoffrey saw to it that a firm territorial base in the Mauges region would be part of the inheritance that he left to his heir. In the future the Angevin counts would not have to rely upon the support of the Renaud clan for control of this region. Geoffrey's concern for the future, however, should not lead us to conclude that he had doubts concerning the loyalty of Renaud; indeed, the latter was given the title viscount of Angers no later than 976.[39]

With Nantes in enemy hands, Geoffrey took steps to strengthen his position at Rennes. Judicâel Berengar, count of Rennes, was a supporter of Count Theobald of Blois,[40] Geoffrey's ally and brother-in-law, thus the Angevin count sought to establish closer ties that would provide for greater security since Rennes was a traditional enemy of Nantes. Éon, a potential heir to the viscomital office of Rennes, as mentioned above, was recruited by Geoffrey for his entourage no later than 965, and by 969, as we have seen Geoffrey had also acquired the services of Joscelin of Rennes, a close relative of Éon.

During the early part of 971, Geoffrey sought still further to improve his position in the West and obtained an alliance with Conan, the new count of Rennes who had just succeeded his father. It was arranged for Geoffrey's daughter to marry Conan. In mid-May of 971 we find Bishop Auriscandus of Rennes at Angers negotiating with Geoffrey. When the prelate left he issued a charter in which he indicated that his mission had been a success. Geoffrey is styled by the bishop as "magnificentissimus et decentissimus comes." Before 977, Hermengarde gave birth to a son who was named Geoffrey Berenger in honor of his two grandfathers. While an Angevin heir at Rennes certainly was a good sign that Geoffrey Greymantle's plans were working, more concrete evidence is provided by the fact that Conan was almost constantly at war with Count Hoël of Nantes during this period.[41]

With the cooperation of Count Theobald of Blois, Count Conan of Rennes, Viscount Renaud and the viscomital family of Rennes, Geoffrey Greymantle was able to compensate for the loss of Nantes and to protect his western frontier. During the late 970s, however, Geoffrey's relations with the counts of Blois gradually deteriorated. In 974, Geoffrey's wife Adele, the sister of Theobald's wife, died. By January 977 Theobald was dead, and his son Odo I had succeeded him. In March 977, Odo aggressively challenged Angevin control of the estates at Pèlerine and at Cru.[42] Geoffrey remarried sometime between the spring of 978 and March of 979. Whatever positive role family ties played in encouraging Angevin-Blésois cooperation since 952 may be thought to have come to an end with Geoffrey's marriage to Adele of Chalons.[43]

Since the early 970s, Geoffrey had made significant inroads into Poitou at the expense of William Iron Arm (*v* below). William, count of Poitiers and duke of Aquitaine, was married to Emma of Blois; she was the daughter of Theobald the Trickster and the sister of Odo I. The importance of the family ties that had been developed between the Angevin counts and the house of Blois, particularly to Countess Leudegunde who began a war in 960 because of a family feud, should not be underestimated. The death of Leudegunde's sister, Adele, followed by Geoffrey's remarriage, and his mistreatment of Emma's husband (both Leudegunde and her son Odo I were very close to Emma) may well have sufficed to turn the dowager countess of Blois into a dedicated enemy of the Angevin count.[44]

As Geoffrey Greymantle's relations with the count of Blois deteriorated, he sought to strengthen his ties with his *senior* Hugh Capet. In addition to appearing in Hugh's entourage with increasing frequency, Geoffrey acted in 977, shortly after the death of Theobald and the accession of Odo I, to better his relations with one of Hugh's closest friends, Bouchard of Vendôme; the Angevin count made Bouchard's stepson, Theobald, abbot of Cormery. In 980, Geoffrey fought at the side of Hugh Capet in northeastern France at Montreuil-sur-Mer against forces to which Odo I was friendly.[45]

As noted above, Geoffrey Greymantle sought to develop his position at Rennes, so that it was not solely dependent upon the Blésois connection, by maintaining close relations with Count Conan and with the viscomital family. In 981, however, the entire picture changed radically. Count Conan succeeded in killing Count Hoël and was on the verge of conquering Nantes.[46] At this point, Count Guerech of Nantes, Hoël's successor, was faced with Conan's advance and sought Geoffrey Greymantle's aid. Guerech very probably promised that he would recognize the overlordship of the Angevin count in return for support against Conan (see below). Geoffrey thus had to choose between Guerech and Conan. If Conan would agree to recognize Geoffrey as his overlord for Nantes then clearly there would be no problem. Geoffrey could claim control of Nantes, maintain good relations with his son-in-law, and not worry too greatly about the western frontier. Conan, however, recognized Odo I as his *senior* and held Rennes from him. The count of Rennes thus had to choose between the domination of his father-in-law whose lands bordered on his own and loyalty to Odo I, Geoffrey's enemy, whose territory was separated from eastern Brittany by the Angevin lands and lordships.

It became clear to Geoffrey that Conan would not withdraw from the Nantais and that he would not recognize him as overlord of the region when the count of Rennes's forces invaded Angevin territory. After expelling the invaders, Geoffrey launched his own forces against Conan's men and in support of Guerech. In 982, Geoffrey's and Conan's armies met in what has come to be called the first battle of Conquéreuil. Conan was decisively defeated. With Geoffrey's support, Guerech was able to extort a treaty from William Iron Arm by which the latter recognized Nantais domination over the districts of Herbauge, Tiffauge, and Mauges. This pact, in effect, recognized the concession made by the count of Poitiers ca. 941 and reconstituted the territorial agglomeration that had come into the hands of Count Fulk the Good, Geoffrey's father, when he married the widow of Count Alan in 952.[47]

Count Guerech, however, apparently was not happy under Geoffrey Greymantle's domination. In 984, he journeyed to the court of King Lothair; there the Breton count recognized that he held the Nantais from the king. By establishing this direct relationship with Lothair, Guerech, in effect, intended to avoid recognizing that he held Nantes from Geoffrey Greymantle. Guerech sought to substitute a distant *senior* whose relations with Geoffrey Greymantle were very poor at this time (see below) for a lord whose vital interests were intimately involved with what took place in Nantais.

Guerech underestimated the importance that control of Nantes played in Angevin strategy and failed to understand that Geoffrey Greymantle would even oppose the king in this matter if that were necessary. Thus when news of Guerech's arrangements with Lothair reached Geoffrey, the Angevin count acted quickly and decisively. The story is related by the chronicler of Nantes in the following manner:

> After Guerech had gone to the court of King Lothair and thence was returning through Angevin territory, he was captured by Count Geoffrey who prepared ambushes for him on all the roads. Seeing little chance to escape from captivity unless he first received from him [Geoffrey] the city of Nantes and that part of Brittany that Count Fulk the Red had held . . . [Guerech] did as Geoffrey asked.[48]

Two charters issued by Count Geoffrey illustrate Guerech's fate as outlined in the *Chronicle of Nantes.* In August of 985, Guerech was in Geoffrey's entourage, a prominent prisoner, as the Angevin count traveled from the stronghold of Nouâtre to Angers in the company of his ally Count Bouchard of Vendôme. At this time Guerech apparently had not yet consented to recognize the Angevin as his *senior*, and thus Geoffrey deprived him of his title; Guerech appears in the witness list simply as *Guarecus*, a *bonus homo*.[49] A half-year later, however, Guerech had already agreed to Geoffrey's demands. Thus he appears in Geoffrey's entourage later bearing the title count and is considered among the Angevin count's *fideles*.[50]

Although Geoffrey's demands on Guerech seem to have been slight, the count of Nantes repeatedly tried to define an independent course of action. Very shortly after being forced to recognize Angevin domination, Guerech had a stronghold built at Ancenis only thirty-five kilometers up river from Nantes. The author of the *Chronicle of Nantes* depicts an elaborate charade that Guerech is alleged to have undertaken apparently for the purpose of limiting Geoffrey's rights at Ancenis. According to this source, Guerech had his wife Aremberga build the stronghold; she in turn gave the lordship over it to their infant son Alan.[51] Thus, theoretically Geoffrey's legal rights over this new stronghold would seem to have been of a less direct nature than they would have been had Guerech himself held the lordship of the stronghold.[52]

Guerech also took advantage of his position as lord of the Mauges region to force Renaud of Thorigné, who held alods in the area, to recognize him as his *senior*.[53] When Renaud asked Guerech for the stronghold of Champtoceaux the latter at first refused but later agreed under pressure from the Angevin court.[54] Champtoceaux, only twenty-five kilometers east of Nantes, was about five kilometers west of Ancenis and thus was positioned to strengthen the Angevin defenses on the western frontier.

While Guerech remained an unhappy but apparently loyal supporter of Geoffrey Greymantle, there was no rapprochement between the Angevin count and his son-in-law Conan of Rennes. It had been traditional for the counts of Rennes to regard the Mayenne river as their eastern frontier, and while Geoffrey and Conan cooperated, the latter seems to have expressed no desire to extend his control east of Chateaubriant. Conan devoted his energies toward defeating his and Geoffrey's enemy, Count Hoël of Nantes. However, the hostilities that took place in 982 demonstrated clearly to Geoffrey Greymantle the vulnerability of Angers to attack from the direction of Rennes.[55]

Three key locations: Pouancé, Segré, and Candé that control the approaches to Angers from Rennes through Chateaubriant have been shown to have been provided with relatively primitive fortifications of the *fossa* variety at the least before the eleventh century. In light of Geoffrey's problems with Conan it is likely that these fortifications either were constructed by the Angevin count or placed in defensible condition at his direction sometime after 982.[56] In addition, Geoffrey took steps to secure the frontier further to the north by placing his long-time *fideles* of the Suhard-Warinus clan at Craon fifty-five kilometers north-northwest of Angers on the west bank of the Oudon.[57] These precautions should not lead us to conclude that Geoffrey Greymantle had given up all hope that a rapprochement with Conan could one day be accomplished through the influence of Hermengarde or that when her son Geoffrey succeeded to the countship friendly relations once again could be established between Anjou and Rennes.[58]

III
Angevin Eastern Interests

The interests of the Angevin counts extended well beyond the walls of Angers, its environs and the western frontier. During the second half of the ninth century, Geoffrey Greymantle's great-grandfather Ingelgarius, obtained control of Château-Landon. This stronghold located only sixty-five kilometers east-northeast of Orléans and about eighty-five kilometers almost due south of Paris, was in Capetian territory. When Geoffrey Greymantle came to power in 960 not only did he inherit possession of Château-Landon, but he also had control of the monastery of Saint-Pierre-de-Ferriers-en-Gâtinais which was located only nine kilometers to the southeast of the abovementioned stronghold. Geoffrey's brother Guy was abbot of Saint Pierre, and the two men saw to the reform of the house. This reform, however, did not entail the surrender of control over Saint Pierre's fisc; the Angevin count retained the power to grant lands from the monastery's holdings to his *vassali*. This control of the monastic fisc seems to have been absolute, and the count was in a position, if he wished, to bankrupt the house.[59]

From a military point of view, Geoffrey's stronghold at Château-Landon dominated the eastern part of Gâtinais and the count's ability to use the resources of Saint Pierre helped to provide the support for his *vassali* so that the region could be kept under Angevin control. The Gâtinais was a large forested area which stretched westward from Château-Landon toward Orléans; during the early 990s it was organized under a count. Geoffrey sought to strengthen his position in Gâtinais by cultivating a friendly relationship with the viscomital house of Orléans. In 966, Viscount Alberic of Orléans supported a charter given by Geoffrey at Angers in which the Angevin count detailed his reorganization of the monastery of Saint Aubin. Geoffrey rewarded another Alberic from Orléans, very probably a relative of the viscount, with a substantial *beneficium* at Champigné-sur-Sarthe. Geoffrey also obtained a very large *beneficium* in Orléanais from Hugh

Capet. Although Bishop Arnulf of Orléans managed to recover substantial church lands from Geoffrey through the later intervention of Hugh Capet, the Angevin count remained a formidable power in the region.[60]

Also, through their close connection with the family of Hugh Capet, the Angevin counts were able to establish their influence as far north and east as Soissons and to form an important alliance with the counts of Amiens who were also counts of Valois and Vexin. In 937, Hugh the Great established Guy of Anjou, the son of Fulk the Red and the uncle of Geoffrey Greymantle, as bishop of Soissons. During the early 960s Bishop Guy worked with Geoffrey and with the latter brother, also named Guy, to reform several monasteries that were under Angevin control. Probably at about the same time that the elder Guy became bishop of Soissons, his sister Adele was married to Walter I, count of Amiens, Valois, and Vexin.[61]

Walter was a potential ally to the Angevin counts because Vexin bordered Rouenais, and the Normans were a long-time foe of the Angevins. Indeed, Ingelgarius, Fulk the Red's eldest son, was killed fighting the Normans. It is also probably no coincidence that when Geoffrey Greymantle married Adele of Vermandois during the early 950s she brought as her dowry to the future count substantial lands in the region of Beauvais just south of Vexin. In this context of curbing Norman aggression it might be well to point out that Geoffrey Greymantle cultivated close relations with the house of Bellême, an old and well established family in Normandy, that did not rely directly upon the Norman dukes for their position.[62]

Thus, through the arrangement of a marriage alliance with Count Walter I, by gaining control of the bishopric of Soissons, and through the acquisition of dowry property, the Angevin counts established a presence on the eastern frontier of Normandy. The continued good relations between the Angevins and Count Walter I is evidenced by the fact that the latter and his wife Adele named their sons Walter, Guy, Radulf, Geoffrey, and Fulk. Obviously Walter was named for his father and he succeeded as count of Amiens, Valois, and Vexin. Radulf was named for his paternal grandfather, but Guy, Geoffrey, and Fulk were all named for their mother's relations. In this context it is noteworthy that Guy succeeded his mother's brother, Guy, as bishop of Soissons and that Geoffrey was later made count of Gâtinais.[63]

In the region of Paris, the Capetial heartland, the Angevins also possessed substantial territory and they had blood relations living in the region as well.[64] It is clear that the Angevins' eastern interests were closely tied to their long-time cooperation with the Capetians. The resources that Geoffrey Greymantle and his ancestors had obtained through his nexus seem to have been not inconsequential, but it should also be appreciated that the Amiens alliance had strategic importance well beyond the relations of the Angevins with the Capetians. The establishment of an Angevin presence in Vexin and Valois could help to curb the expansionist aims of the Normans. With a discernible Angevin threat to eastern Normandy established in Vexin, the "pirate" dukes might well be dissuaded from harassing the western frontier of the Angevin lands.

IV

Angevin Penetration of Aquitaine

The Loire river formed a natural boundary separating Neustria from Aquitaine and provided the southern frontier for the Angevin *pagus*. The Angevin counts, however, had for three generations before the accession of Geoffrey Greymantle developed their family holdings in the southeastern Touraine and northwestern Berry; these areas may be considered to have been important parts of northeastern Aquitaine. The valley of the lower Indre river for eighty-five kilometers was in Angevin hands. The lords of Buzançais who were proverbially loyal to the Angevin counts anchored the southern limits of this area of Angevin penetration with their family stronghold at Buzançais. To the north of Buzançais, the counts themselves held the strongholds of Châtillon-sur-Indre and Loches. Further north substantial estates at Courçay as well as the monastery of Cormery were under Angevin control. [65]

East of the Indre on the direct route from Loches to Bourges the Angevin counts were in possession of the monastery of Villeloin, the villa of Valençay and, nearby, the stronghold of Villentrois. Further to the east the lords of Graçay may well have already been part of the Angevin entourage at this time. West of the Indre on the chain of rivers — Claise-Creuse-Vienne — the Angevins had access to the stronghold of Preuilly-sur-Claise; Hatto the lord of Preuilly was one of the count's men. The Angevins also held the stronghold of La Haye directly and they had close ties with Guenno of Nouâtre whose stronghold was situated just north of the confluence of the Creuse and the Vienne. Saint-Épain, nine kilometers north of Nouâtre, was also held by the Angevin counts. [66]

The Angevin presence in this northeastern part of Aquitaine was centered on the stronghold of Loches. There Geoffrey improved the fortifications substantially by building a tall rectangular stone tower within the walls of the *castrum*. [67] This stronghold Geoffrey garrisoned with *milites*; some of these were styled *ingenui milites* in the sources and there may also have been some *servi milites* within the garrison. In this context it should be emphasized that at Loches both *viri nobiles* and *viri ignobiles* are known to have held *res* from the comital fisc. These men, however, could not dispose of their holdings without the permission of the count.[68] Among Geoffrey's more important *fideles* who seem to have had a strong interest in affairs at Loches were Adalhardus, Marcoardus, Wido, Ulgerius, and Fulculfus all of whom are namesakes of important men found in the entourage of Fulk the Red.[69]

The extensive Angevin penetration into southern Touraine and northeastern Berry, which as noted above was centered upon the stronghold of Loches, bordered Poitou on the east. North of Poitiers and in Poitou, itself, Fulk the Good, Geoffrey's father, had seized possession of Méron. Further to the east, Fulk had gained control of Mauges, Tiffauge, and Herbauge through his marriage to the widow of Count Alan.[70] Fulk's interest in penetrating further south of the Loire is perhaps best illustrated by his opportunistic alliance with Stephen, count of Gévaudan and Forez, the most powerful magnate in eastern Aquitaine. To cement these arrangements, Adelaide, Fulk's daughter, was married to Stephen.[71] Thus, just as Fulk the Red allied with the count of Vexin to out-flank the duke of Normandy, Fulk the Good arranged a marriage alliance in order to out-flank the duke of Aquitaine.

Geoffrey Greymantle pursued the Angevin policy of extending the family interest south of the Loire. In the area of Méron, which the Angevin counts had seized perhaps as early as the reign of Fulk the Red and certainly as early as that of Fulk the Good, Geoffrey had Abbot Widbold of Saint-Aubin establish Hilgerius, who as noted above, was a *fidelis* of the count and also held a *beneficium* from him at Angers.[72]

Not far from Méron at le Caudray-Macouard, Geoffrey established another of his *fideles*, the *miles* Walter, with a *beneficium* from the monastic fisc of Saint-Aubin (*ex rebus ecclesiasticis*). In addition, Geoffrey saw to it that this *fidelis* Walter, who also held a *beneficium* at Limelle, and his brother Constantius were granted land by Abbot Albert of Saint Aubin in the suburb of Angers and more importantly they were granted a *fossa*. This *fossa* was to serve as a *configium* in the *villa* of Montaglan which was in the area of Méron and le Caudray-Macouard. The *fossa* was a moat which circled a wall built from the earth that had been extracted when the ditch was dug. Abbot Albert also granted to Walter and Constantius twelve arpents of arable land at Montaglan to provide them with income so that they would have the means to construct a stronghold on the hill (*Mons Samarenda*) of Montaglan which probably was within the wall that was circled by the *fossa*. Finally, the brothers were provided with meadow land at the villa of Trezé at Méron.[73]

With a *point-d'appui* in the area of le Caudray-Macouard and Méron, Geoffrey seems to have focussed his primary attention upon undermining the position of Count William Iron Arm in Poitou itself. To this end Geoffrey cultivated the friendship of Viscount Aimery II of Thouars and granted to him extensive holdings at Chavagné near the monastery of Saint Maixent astride the road from Niort to Poitiers, at Faye-l'Abesse near Bressuire, and at Missé on the outskirts of Thouars. When Aimery died, Geoffrey used his influence with King Lothair and saw to it that Viscount Herbert II of Thouars obtained these same lands. Herbert, who became involved in a feud with William Iron Arm because of the latter's attentions to the viscountess of Thouars, proved to be a useful supporter of the Angevin counts as was his son Viscount Aimery III. The stronghold of Thouars was long recognized as being of great strategic importance and it was already fortified in pre-Roman times. Throughout the early Middle Ages this stronghold, located on a promontory overlooking the Thouet River, dominated the most important approach to Poitou from the west.[74]

Geoffrey Greymantle advanced his policy of encroachment into Poitou also through the force of arms. Before 973, he defeated William decisively at the battle of les Roches. It seems likely that as a result of this battle Geoffrey seized the stronghold of Loudun and perhaps the territory of Mirebeau as well. William, however, came to terms with the Angevin count. Thus Geoffrey gained *de jure* title to Loudun as a *beneficium* and recognized William as his *senior*.[75]

Shortly after Geoffrey gained control of Loudun and no later than 975, Abbess Hermengarde and the nuns of the convent of Sainte-Croix recognized that they could no longer expect Count William to protect their interests and thus they retained the Angevin count as their advocate. Geoffrey agreed to defend the lands of Sainte-Croix that were under his jurisdiction in the region of Loudun and to pursue the interests of the convent in the royal court and in certain other, though unnamed, places. In return for rendering the abovementioned services, Geoffrey was given the *curtis* of Preuilly and the *curtis* of Arcé. In addition, Geoffrey was given a *fedum* so that he could defend the lands of Sainte-Croix that were located in the region of Loudun. This *fedum* consisted of the right to obtain fodder (*farragina*) for his animals, the right to take piglets (*porcella*) to feed his men, and the right to demand fifteen days of service twice each year from all of the lands and dependents of Sainte-Croix in Loudunais for military support service (*bidannum*).[76]

The early medieval fortifications located at Loudun were very important to Geoffrey because they dominated his southern route from Angers to Loches and Buzançais which ran from Thouars through Nouâtre and la Haye. Loudun also lay on the direct route north from Poitiers to Anjou. The *bidannum* obtained from Sainte-Croix's extensive holdings in Loudunais may well have been of importance in providing the labor that was necessary for the new construction of a stone tower by Geoffrey and to keep these fortifications in defensible condition.[77] Geoffrey seems to have entrusted command of Loudun to one of his *fideles*, a man named Roger who was a *miles*.[78]

As discussed earlier, Geoffrey had strengthened the Angevin position in the Mauges region before 973 and insured that his successor would obtain substantial alodial property there in the future. Further to the east, Geoffrey sought to win the friendship of Arnustus abbot of Saint-Jouin-des-Marnes. This monastery, located on the Dive river about midway between Thouars and Mirebeau, was a favorite of Viscount Renaud who was *praepositus* there.[79] Thus in April 976 we find Count Geoffrey holding court at Poitiers and restoring lands to Saint-Jouin that had been held unjustly by previous Angevin counts, Fulk the Red and Fulk the Good. Among those who witnessed this act were Viscount Renaud, Bishop Renaud, and three members of the viscomital house of Thouars: Radulfus, Aimery, and Savaricus. Conspicuous by his absence is Count William Iron Arm of Poitou.[80]

In Aquitaine, beyond Poitou, Geoffrey Greymantle worked diligently to strengthen the Angevin position. Count Stephen died in 961, and Adelaide played a key role in ruling the counties of Gévaudan and Forez for their sons William, Pons, and Bertrand.[81] In 975, through the influence that he had with King Lothair, Geoffrey obtained the appointment of his brother Guy to the bishopric of Le Puy; there the prelate also exercised comital powers.[82] Le Puy was strategically located between Forez to the north and Gévaudan to the south. These three counties now joined together under Geoffrey's sister and brother, who cooperated effectively to suppress local opposition, constituted a formidable enclave in southeastern Aquitaine.[83]

Sometime between the spring of 978 and March 979, Geoffrey married Adele, the widow of Count Lambert of Chalons, and exercised comital powers there.[84] It may be suggested that Geoffrey's heroic performance in defending King Lothair's interests against Otto II in 978—the stuff from which legends were made—led the monarch to support the marriage of the Angevin count to the widow of the count of Chalons.[85] In 957, King Lothair had exercised substantial power in the Chalonnais when he established Lambert there as count, and the monarch seems to have retained this power after Lambert's death. In broader terms, we cannot overlook the possibility that at this time King Lothair had an interest in supporting the creation of an Angevin enclave on the western border of Capetian burgundy (Duke Henry of Burgundy was Hugh Capet's brother).[86]

Angevin penetration of Aquitaine continued with the marriage of Adelaide's daughter, Adalmode, to Aldebert who was count of both la Marche and Périgord. This alliance, which was to prove so very important to the Angevins in 995–996, helped to bring two important counties in central Aquitaine within the Angevin family circle. La Marche bordered directly on Poitou's southeastern frontier.[87]

During this period Geoffrey Greymantle also continued to penetrate Poitou directly. In 981, for example, when he was returning from Montreuil-sur-Mer through the region of Paris he recruited one of his relatives, a man named Alberic, and gave to him all of the land of Vihiers, the church of Saint Mary at Loudun, and a long list of other properties that the monk who drew up the notice in which this information survives did not see fit to record. Vihiers, forty kilometers south of Angers and about mid-way between Thouars and the eastern frontier of the Mauges region at Chemillé, became of greater strategic importance to Geoffrey as his relations with Count Odo I of Blois deteriorated.[88]

Vihiers became the western terminus for securing Geoffrey's southern line of communications with Loches and Buzançais through le Coudray-Macouard, Méron or Thouars to Loudun, Nouâtre, and either to Ligueil and Loches or to la Haye and Preuilly-sur-Claise to Buzançais. This route, protected by strongholds such as Thouars, Loudun, and Nouâtre, was necessary because the more northerly line of communications through the Loire valley was controlled by Odo's strongholds at Saumur, Chinon, and Île-Bouchard.[89]

Early in 981, as the fifteenth birthday of King Louis, Lothair's recently crowned son, approached, the process of finding a wife for him commenced. Thus Geoffrey Greymantle had some of his loyal supporters suggest to Queen Emma, who apparently was in charge of the search, that Adelaide, Geoffrey's widowed sister, would be a suitable wife for young King Louis. It was probably at this time that Geoffrey's friends outlined the advantages that this projected match between the adolescent heir to the throne of *Francia Occidentalis* and a countess old enough to be his mother would have for the Carolingian dynasty.[90] Thus they exposed Geoffrey's plan to have Louis established as king in Aquitaine with the Angevin Adelaide as queen.

Queen Emma, and certainly through her King Lothair, would be reminded by Geoffrey's men that the Angevins controlled Chalons, Forez, le Puy, and Gévaudan directly and that they were closely allied by marriage to Count Aldebert who ruled la Marche and Périgord. In addition, it could be pointed out to the queen that William Iron Arm, count of Poitou and duke of Aquitaine, the man most likely to oppose the marriage and the establishment of King Louis V in Aquitaine, was not in position to provide effective opposition. Geoffrey Greymantle, William's powerful neighbor to the north, controlled Nantes, Mauges, and Loudunais. In addition, Geoffrey was closely allied with the viscount of Thouars, the second most powerful man in Poitou, who was personally hostile to William because of the Poitevin's affair with the viscountess of Thouars. Further, William could not rely upon the support of Count Odo I of Blois, his brother-in-law, because of this same amorous escapade with the viscountess.[91]

Louis's parents would also have had little difficulty in understanding that the establishment of their son in Aquitaine would enclose the lands of Hugh Capet between the realms of two Carolingian monarchs, Lothair and his son. It was at this very time when the marriage was being discussed that King Lothair had become convinced that Hugh Capet, who had gone to Italy contrary to the monarch's wishes, was an enemy of the Carolingian dynasty.[92] Hugh who was in Italy while these negotiations were being carried out would have had great difficulty opposing the project actively because his most powerful "friend" in the West of France, Geoffrey Greymantle, was the instigator of the plan and its prime mover. Any ardor that Duke Henry of Burgundy, Hugh's brother, might have had to interfere in this plan would have been cooled by the realization that a solid phalanx of powers closely tied to Geoffrey Greymantle lined his western frontier.

The political situation in Aquitaine as outlined above may well have helped to convince King Lothair that Geoffrey's plan to have his sister Adelaide marry young King Louis was a sound one. Thus by early July 981, Lothair decided not only to pursue the marriage alliance and to have his son established as the ruler of Aquitaine, but also he took action to win over Duke Guifred of Roussillon to the plan. A large train led by King Lothair and King Louis headed south, probably late in the spring of 982 when the roads had dried out. Adelaide and Louis were married at Vieux Brioude in the heart of Angevin Aquitaine. On the same day as the wedding, Adelaide was crowned queen by at least two bishops. One of these prelates almost certainly was her brother Guy.[93]

Although Lothair may have seen the marriage and the establishment of Louis and Adelaide as king and queen at Vieux Brioude as steps toward asserting Carolingian rule in Aquitaine, Geoffrey Greymantle would seem to have had a somewhat different picture of the situation. It requires little imagination to conclude that Geoffrey set in motion this entire project in the hope of expanding Angevin power in Aquitaine under the guise of enforcing royal prerogatives. Geoffrey may well have been aware that although Louis had reached marriageable age, the newly crowned king was according to a contemporary report a childish and self-indulgent adolescent. As Adelaide's husband, Louis spent his time dressing up in the costumes of the local inhabitants and other activities that can be characterized as juvenile. The royal couple not only did not share the same bed, but they lived under separate roofs. In public they had little contact with each other and according to the same contemporary source cited above they had nothing to say to one another.[94]

At Vieux Brioude where the royal court was located, Louis exercised no political power. He was deprived of control of financial resources and commanded no armed forces. In fact, he was deprived of all authority and even of any show of power that might imply that he was a monarch.[95] It may be suggested that whatever was done in the royal name from the court at Vieux Brioude was carried out not primarily in the interest of the Carolingian dynasty but in the furtherance of Angevin family policy.

By the end of 983, when King Lothair finally learned from a variety of sources that his son's position was not what was expected, he went with a significant armed force to Vieux Brioude and brought the boy back to the north. The marriage to Adelaide was abruptly put to an end. Fearing for her safety, Adelaide fled to Arles. Aquitanian chroniclers loyal to the house of William Iron Arm took this opportunity to attack the Angevins and spread the rumor that Adelaide had poisoned Louis.[96]

The bad feelings created by the failure of the marriage led to a distinct cooling of relations between King Lothair and Geoffrey Greymantle. As discussed above, Lothair agreed to Count Guerech's plan to undermine Geoffrey's authority as overlord of Nantes. In addition, Herbert the Old of Vermandois died at this time and since he had no direct heirs, King Lothair determined who would receive the count's vast holdings. Fulk Nerra, Geoffrey Greymantle's son, had a sound claim to inherit his uncle Herbert's honors through Adele, his mother, the old count's sister. King Lothair, however, decided to establish Odo I of Blois, Herbert's nephew through his sister Leudgarde who had been Odo's mother, as the heir.[97] Geoffrey, as we will see below, drew much closer to Hugh Capet as a result of these problems with King Lothair.

Geoffrey's major accomplishment during the brief period of Angevin ascendancy in Aquitaine seems to have been the alteration of the line of succession to the countship of Chalons. Sometime after November 980, but while Geoffrey was acting as count of Chalons, Hugh, son of the deceased Count Lambert of Chalons, entered the clergy. This would seem to suggest that at this time his future career was not intended to be as count but rather that his opportunities lay elsewhere. That Hugh should be moved from what might be considered the normal line of succession suggests that some one was already on the scene who was considered a more suitable heir to the comital honor. Thus it is probable that Adele of Chalons had given birth by about the year 980 to a son, Maurice, who was fathered by Geoffrey Greymantle.[98] Parenthetically, it might be pointed out that Geoffrey Greymantle acted in a considerably less decisive manner than did his father in a not dissimilar diplomatic situation; indeed, as we have seen, after Fulk the Good married the widow of Count Alan, he had the latter's son, Drogo, murdered.

Despite the dissolution of Adelaide's marriage to King Louis and the hostility demonstrated by King Lothair, Geoffrey Greymantle did not abandon his policy of Angevin aggrandizement in Aquitaine. For example, it was arranged that Adelaide marry William of Arles, count of Provence, a man of substantial wealth and power in the south. Geoffrey, himself, continued to exercise power as count of Chalons and was at Chalons in October 984 looking after family interests. On 18 October 984, Geoffrey and Adele lent their support to a substantial gift made to Abbot Maiolus and the monks of Cluny. In fact, this was not Geoffrey's first show of favor toward Cluny, but ever since he became count of Chalons he had been generous to this initial house. Aside from giving substantial parcels of land to the monks and their revered Abbot Maiolus, he gave to Cluny the monastery of Saint Marcellus at Chalons.[99]

The importance of Abbot Maiolus who was a close friend of Hugh Capet[100] to Geoffrey's plans in eastern Aquitaine should not be underestimated. Geoffrey's successful effort to have Hugh of Chalons made a cleric and thus to alter the comital succession could well have been undermined by Abbot Maiolus whose influence, especially in religious matters, was considerable. During the period after Geoffrey's break with King Lothair and his return to close relations with Hugh Capet, the abbot of Cluny may well have been of help to the Angevin count. In this context, it is also of importance to emphasize that Maiolus was a very close friend of William of Arles. The latter had rescued the abbot in 972 after he had been captured by Saracen raiders.[101] This same William became Adelaide's third husband after she was given refuge at Arles in the wake of King Lothair's advance into Aquitaine to rescue his son from Angevin-imposed squalor at Vieux Brioude. Abbot Maiolus is the only known link between William and the Angevins before the count of Arles's opportune intervention on Adelaide's behalf saved her from the king's wrath. It may well be that Maiolus's good will which was probably a precondition necessary to sustain Geoffrey Greymantle's plans at Chalons led the abbot to take an active part in supporting Angevin interests. Abbot Maiolus would seem to have been the only person on the scene in 984 who could have arranged for William of Arles to protect Adelaide. When Adelaide and William were married shortly after her rescue, their union was probably considered to be tainted by adultery.[102] However, no ecclesiastical action was taken against the couple, and once again we may perhaps see the influential hand of Maiolus protecting Angevin interests.[103] Indeed, it takes little imagination to visualize the kind of trouble Maiolus could have made in this circumstance had he been so inclined.

V
Penetration of Maine and the Vendômois

By the twelfth century it was widely believed in Anjou that Geoffrey Greymantle had been granted the county of Maine by a grateful king of France in return for important military services. It is generally agreed that this account, in its twelfth-century form, was developed, in part at least, to justify Angevin domination of the region and that it has little or no value for understanding the situation in Geoffrey's reign. Although the formal aspects of this account are undoubtedly fictionalized, it is not improbable that King Lothair or perhaps Hugh Capet, who claimed overlordship of Maine, either individually or in combination, gave Geoffrey license to seize lands from Count Hugh of Maine. They may even have conceded such a "blank check" to Geoffrey in return for important military service as suggested in the twelfth-century source. Geoffrey did support Lothair vigorously in the Norman war which began in 960 and again heroically against Otto II in 978. The Angevin count campaigned with Hugh Capet in 980 at Montreuil-sur-Mer and in 987 against the supporters of the count of Blois.[104]

Indeed, whether Geoffrey Greymantle had the formal blessing of either King Lothair or Hugh Capet for encroachment into Maine is clearly of less moment than the fact that the Angevin count pursued a policy of territorial aggrandizement at the expense of his northern neighbor. Fulk the Good, Geoffrey's father, apparently began extending Angevin domination into the valley of the Sarthe when he seized control of lands at Précigné and Parcé-sur-Sarthe that belonged to Saint Martin of Tours and imposed *malae consuetudines* on them.[105]

By ca. 970, Geoffrey Greymantle had become deeply involved in the affairs of Maine. Seginfredus of Bellême wanted to become bishop of Le Mans and sought Geoffrey's support. Seginfredus promised Geoffrey the episcopal *vicus* of Coulaines and the villa of Dissay-sur-Courcillon with its fiscal rights which included an income in excess of 1,000 lbs. of *solidi* per year if the Angevin count would obtain the bishopric for him from King

Lothair. Geoffrey did use his influence with Lothair in this matter and was successful. Seginfredus, in his turn, proved to be a resourceful enemy of the count of Maine. This success in securing the bishopric for Seginfredus illustrates Geoffrey's influence with King Lothair ca. 970–971, and the willingness of the monarch to support the Angevin count's policy of encroachment into Maine. Seginfredus's request for Geoffrey's support, moreover, was based upon the count's involvement with a family alliance in Maine and its environs whose interests lay in weakening the count of Maine. Seginfredus's predecessor as bishop of Le Mans was Mainard, the brother or perhaps the brother-in-law of Viscount Radulf of Le Mans. Radulf, who appears in a charter of 967 closely alligned with Geoffrey Greymantle, appears to have been married to the sister of Ivo of Bellême who probably was the brother of Bishop Seginfredus.[106]

Geoffrey Greymantle's aim in penetrating Maine was two-fold. He sought to dominate the southwest, especially along the Sarthe to protect the approaches to Angers and he wanted apparently to secure the Loir river as a northern frontier in the expansion of the Angevin heartland. With regard to the former intention we have already mentioned that Geoffrey seems to have sought to control the approach to Angers along the Oudon-Mayenne rivers. As we have seen he secured possession of the stronghold of Craon and placed it in the possession of his supporters from the Suhardus-Warinus clan. In the valley of the Sarthe itself, Geoffrey sought to build upon Angevin domination of Précigné-sur-Sarthe which lay about ten kilometers to the south of the important stronghold of Sablé and also on Parcé which was situated about ten kilometers east of Sablé.

Geoffrey, the lord of Sablé, was one of the sons of Viscount Radulfus of Le Mans and probably a nephew of Bishop Seginfredus of Le Mans. Coincidentally, since ca. 970, at about the same time that Geoffrey Greymantle played a key role in obtaining the bishopric for Seginfredus, a *nobilis* named Geoffrey appears very frequently among the count's *fideles*. Geoffrey appears frequently with the Angevin count thereafter and is considered one of his most powerful *milites* as well as a *procer*. On several occasions Geoffrey is given the distinguished position just after the count in the witness list of a charter. It is especially noteworthy in the context that in a document concerning Le Lude in Maine, Geoffrey appears ahead of a bishop and two viscounts. It seems likely that we should identify this *nobilis miles* with Geoffrey of Sablé since to refuse to do so would be to assume that there was at least a second very important man named Geoffrey in the count's entourage who otherwise is completely unknown.[107]

Although Geoffrey Greymantle already possessed le Lude and Chenu when he acquired Dissay-sur-Courcillon ca. 970, he seems to have had little inclination to expand his holdings eastward into the valley of the middle Loir. Geoffrey's lack of ambition in this direction was probably due to the strong position enjoyed by Count Bouchard of Vendôme who controlled most of the Loir valley east of Dissay-sur-Courcillon. Bouchard, moreover, was not only count of Vendôme, but also count of Corbeil, Melun, and Paris. Further, he was Hugh Capet's very close friend and loyal supporter. Although, on occasion Geoffrey acted in a manner that did not please Hugh who was his *senior*, their relations usually were good. Thus it would have been difficult for Geoffrey openly to have attempted to advance his interests in the Loir valley at the expense of Bouchard. Geoffrey certainly appears to have recognized the importance of Vendôme as early as 977 when he established Bouchard's step-son, Theobald, as abbot of Cormery.[108]

By the spring of 985 much had changed for Geoffrey. As the hostility of King Lothair toward Geoffrey grew, the Angevin count drew closer to Hugh Capet. Geoffrey's efforts to strengthen his position with the Capetian faction at this time could be greatly enhanced by arranging a marriage for his son and heir, Fulk Nerra, who was nearing his fifteenth birthday. Thus it was a propitious coincidence that Bouchard of Vendôme's only son, Renaud, was a cleric in the entourage of Hugh Capet and clearly destined for ecclesiastical preferment. Ultimately, the county of Vendôme would pass either to Renaud's sister Elizabeth, who was of marriageable age by ca. 985, or to her heir.[109]

By the spring of 985 or perhaps even earlier, Geoffrey had bound Fulcradus, the viscount of Vendôme, to him as a *fidelis* with the grant of a *beneficium*.[110] This technique of securing a favorable relationship with the viscomital house in a county that he sought to penetrate was a favorite with Geoffrey who as we have already seen used it in Orléanais, Poitou, Rennes, and Maine.

During the first three weeks of August 985, Geoffrey Greymantle and Count Bouchard spent considerable time together, apparently visiting various areas under Angevin control such as the stronghold of Nouâtre. Fulk Nerra was in the entourage that accompanied the two counts as were Viscount Fulcradus and many members of Geoffrey's entourage. It seems likely that during this period two important decisions were taken by Geoffrey and Bouchard which bore fruit following this meeting. The marriage of Fulk Nerra and Elizabeth was arranged and took place not too long after. Also, Fulk Nerra was associated with his father in the Angevin countship. This took place by early March 986, and probably was done at least in part to assure Bouchard that Fulk would succeed his father. Thus, Maurice, Fulk's half-brother, was denied the right to succession.[111]

The alliance with Bouchard heightened Geoffrey's interest in the Loir valley since he could expect that the Vendômois one day would be a part of the agglomeration of Angevin lands and lordships. Thus it should not surprise us to find Geoffrey besieging the strong hold of Marçon in July 987. Marçon controlled access through the Loir valley between Dissay-sur-Courcillon and the holdings of count Bouchard to the east, and at that time it was in the hands of Odo the Red, a supporter of Count Odo I of Blois. Indeed, almost from the time that he had succeeded his father Theobald as count in 977, Odo I had been hostile to his *senior* Hugh Capet and to Geoffrey. That Hugh Capet was in the field with Geoffrey Greymantle at Marçon suggests not only that the duke of *Francia* strongly supported the alliance between Bouchard and Geoffrey but that the interests of the Angevin count were increasingly in conflict with those of the count of Blois.[112]

VI
The Middle Loire From Angers to Amboise

Since the later ninth century the family of Geoffrey Greymantle had been one of the major powers of the middle Loire region between Angers and Amboise. They possessed both of these formidable strongholds as well as the *castrum* of Saumur. At one time Geoffrey's grandfather, Fulk the Red, held the titles viscount of Angers and viscount of Tours and also served as the treasurer of Saint-Martin's at Tours. Fulk the Good, Geoffrey's father, used his influence to gain control of various lands belonging to Saint-Martin of Tours in this region. Indeed, Fulk the Good and his brother Guy were both canons of Saint-Martin of Tours and Herveus I of Buzançais, a loyal supporter of the Angevins, was treasurer of Saint-Martin. In this office, Herveus controlled the extensive fisc of Saint-Martin from ca. 966 to ca. 980.[113]

Probably only the Robertians (i.e. the family of Hugh Capet) were more powerful than the Angevins in this region of the middle Loire during the first third of the tenth century. To strengthen the Capetian position, however, Hugh the Great established Theobald of Blois as viscount of Tours. An able man of many talents, Theobald developed his own position in this region until it rivaled that of the Angevins. His major accomplishments were gaining control of the stronghold of Saumur (probably ca. 952), establishing the monastery of Saint Florent at Saumur ca. 955, acquiring the title count of Tours ca. 958 and establishing Arduin, one of his supporters, as archbishop of Tours in 960. All of this was done more or less peacefully and, ironically, with the cooperation of Fulk the Good who considered his alliance with Theobald essential to the protection of the western frontier and control of Nantes.[114]

Geoffrey Greymantle continued his father's policy of maintaining the alliance at least until Theobald's death in 977. Thus a quarter-century of cooperation between the Angevin counts and the count of Blois had permitted the latter to gain control of the middle Loire valley from Tours in the east to Saumur in the west and to dominate the valley of the lower Vienne from Île-Bouchard through Chinon. In addition, the monastery of Saint Florent which Theobald and Odo I dominated acquired substantial territory in this region of the middle Loire and controlled the area south of the Loire between Saumur and the eastern frontier of the Mauges region. In the Mauges region itself Saint-Florent-le-Vieil, the old home of Saint Florent, was still of some importance and served as a potential *point d'appui* for further Blésois movement to the west.[115]

Originally, Hugh the Great had brought Theobald into Touraine to curb the Angevins. This plan, however, did not work and the Blésois power developed at the expense of both the Capetians and the Angevins, but with the cooperaction of the latter. When the Blésois-Angevin alliance floundered following the death of Theobald, Hugh Capet lent his support to Geoffrey Greymantle so as to undermine the growing power of Odo I, Theobald's son. In this context it must be remembered that Odo was given substantial support by King Lothair who became hostile to Geoffrey Greymantle and sustained the Blésois claim in Vermandois which thereby posed an additional threat to the Capetians from the east. Indeed, by ca. 985, Hugh Capet's role in Touraine had been so reduced that he now merely held the balance of power between his two *fideles*, Geoffrey Greymantle and Odo I.[116]

Substantial areas north of the Loire valley remained in Angevin hands to counter-balance Blésois advances in the valley itself. As we have seen Geoffrey Greymantle wisely maintained and, indeed strengthened, his line of communications between Angers and Amboise along a route from Seiches in the east through Jarzé, Baugé, Semblançay, and Morand. He also established Éon and later Joscelin of Rennes at Seiches. Jarzé was in the hands of the Bouchard family. Baugé was held directly in comital hands as was Noyant which Geoffrey obtained from Saint-Martin of Tours, perhaps with the aid of the treasurer Herveus, and upon which he imposed *malae consuetudines*. Both Semblançay and Morand were held directly by the count. These important locations were spaced no more than thirty kilometers apart, about an easy day's travel and clearly were positioned to provide Geoffrey with whatever logistical support he may have required while moving from Angers to Amboise. This route to Amboise was important because the Old Roman road through the Loire valley was vulnerable to attack from Saumur.[117]

We have already seen that Geoffrey's position in the southern part of the middle Loire region was weak. For example, in order to secure his communications with the east he had to go south to Vihiers and then travel east through le Coudray-Macouard, Méron, or Thouars, to Loudon, Nouâtre, and either to Ligueil and Loches or to la Haye, Preuilly-sur-Claise and Buzançais. Sometime between August 985 and July 987, Walter, Count Geoffrey's *fidelis* who held le Coudray-Macouard, sold his *beneficium*, with the permission of his *senior*, to Saint Aubin to whom it originally had belonged.[118]

Clearly, the deterioration of relations between Count Geoffrey and Odo I placed this *curtis* in danger; it was only ten kilometers south of Saumur, and it could not easily be defended. Even after returning le Coudray-Macouard to Saint Aubin, Geoffrey retained the vicarial rights there and could still expect to gain some revenue from the *curtis*.[119] He could also hope that by placing the *curtis* in the possession of Saint-Aubin, Gelduin, Odo I's man at Saumur, would refrain from ravaging it. Further, Geoffrey's relations with Saint-Aubin certainly would not suffer by this restoration to the monastic fisc. Finally, Geoffrey's close relations with the viscount of Thouars lessened the strategic importance of le Coudray-Macouard which had become a military liability.

Geoffrey apparently found the device of placing potentially endangered lands in the possession of monastic foundations to be effective and he used it not only with Saint Aubin but also with Saint Julien of Tours and Cormery. Through the right of *vicaria*, Geoffrey retained the ability to enter these lands, to obtain various fees of justice, requisition various kinds of military support, and to obtain hospitality. At the same time he strengthened his ties with the monastery that received the grant. Finally, it seems that Geoffrey may have believed that his spiritual well-being and that of his family was enhanced by providing religious institutions with material aid.[120]

The eastern terminus of Geoffrey's lands and lordships in the middle Loire valley was the *castrum* of Amboise. The main fortifications of Amboise as they stood throughout the ninth and tenth centuries probably had been built during the later Roman empire and were an important element in the defense of *Francia Occidentalis* against the Vikings. Ingelgerius, Geoffrey Greymantle's great-grandfather, had obtained this key stronghold from Archbishop Adalard of Tours and established Robert of Buzançais there to help in its defense. When Geoffrey Greymantle became count about a century later there were two important strongholds within the walls of Amboise. One of these was held directly by the count and the other was defended by the family of Buzançais.[121]

The strongholds held by Geoffrey and the lords of Buzançais were within the old Roman walls of Amboise. However, a new fortification was constructed outside the old stronghold, and with the exercise of very little imagination it came to be called *Novum Castrum* (Fr. Châteauneuf).[122] Apparently, Amboise's strategic location between the Loire and the Masse, where it dominated the fording places, and the peaceful cooperation between the Angevin counts and Theobald the Trickster in the Region for a quarter-century had resulted in demographic and economic expansion which brought new settlement outside the old walls.

It may be hypothesized that the need to fortify this new area of settlement was engendered by the break between Geoffrey Greymantle and Odo I. Thus it is probably to the latter part of Geoffrey's reign, and certainly post-977, that we should date the establishment of Landry in Châteauneuf by Geoffrey. The need to provide for the effective defense of *Novum Castrum* led Geoffrey to give to Landry, who seems to have been recruited from the locality of Dun in Berry, a fortified *domus* and many *casamenta* in the southern part of Châteauneuf. At least some of these *casamenta* it may be assumed were distributed by Landry to his *homines* so that they could provide the armed support necessary to defend the stronghold.[123]

By ninth-and tenth-century standards, the defenses developed by the Angevin counts at Amboise — two internal strongholds to strengthen the old Roman defenses and a third stronghold to protect the new suburb — were the most elaborate of any in the West of France at any time for a *castrum*. The Angevin investment in this elaborate system of defense which contnued to be maintained and improved for more than a century after Geoffrey's death may well be seen as a measure of the strategic importance attributed to Amboise by Geoffrey and his family as the eastern base for their position in the middle Loire valley.[124]

VII

Conclusions

Geoffrey Greymantle pursued a broad spectrum of policies; some of these he inherited and some he initiated. In general, however, whether Geoffrey inherited a particular policy or initiated it, all were intended through one means or another to strengthen his family's position or to aggrandize its holdings. Two of the major policies that Geoffrey followed throughout his career, the defense of the western frontier which focused upon control of Nantes and the deep penetration of Aquitaine, he seems to have inherited from his father; and these policies may even have been initiated by his grandfather, Fulk the Red. Both of these policies Geoffrey pursued with vigor and diplomatic skill and in both he enjoyed a substantial measure of success.

Through the arrangement of the marriage of Fulk Nerra to Elizabeth of Vendôme and through *conventiae* with Renaud of Thorigné, Geoffrey Greymantle set in motion a course of events that would, if the plans worked, vastly increase the agglomeration of Angevin lands and lordships to the northeast and southwest of the Angevin heartland, respectively. With these two acquisitions for future possession kept in mind, the vague outline of a rather large territorial expanse with some natural boundaries may be seen to take shape. Looking eastward from the stronghold of Craon, which Geoffrey's *miles* Suhard held, to the *vicus* of Bazouges, where Fulk Nerra would build the stronghold of Château-Gontier, to the fortifications at Sablé, which were held by Geoffrey, the count's man and a brother of the count's ally Viscount Radulf of Le Mans, we can perhaps discern the makings of a frontier which also served the purpose of dominating access to Angers through control of the valleys of the Oudon, Mayenne, and Sarthe at strategic points. If we continue eastward along the valley of the Sarthe to the Angevin-held villa of Parcé-sur-Sarthe and then turn due south to another Bazouges, this one on the Loir and in the hands of Hugh I of Lavardin, a son-in-law of Viscount Radulf of Le Mans, we can trace the Angevin presence to le Lude, Dissay-sur-Courcillon, thence to Hugh's main holding at Lavardin and finally to Vendôme itself.[125]

From the stronghold of Vendôme in the northeast, the eastern frontier ran south to Morand, which Fulk Nerra later fortified, to Amboise, Loches, and then along the Indre to Châtillon-sur-Indre and Buzançais. From the stronghold of Buzançais in the southeast the southern limits can be vaguely discerned to move westward to Preuilly-sur-Claise, then northwest to La Haye and Nouâtre, due west to Loudun through the *fosse* at Montaglan to Vihiers and then into the Mauges region. From this area which the Angevins had not yet begun to exploit, the frontier was established on the Loire at Rochefort-sur-Loire and ran north into the valleys of the Mayenne and Oudun to Craon.[126]

It may seem difficult to believe that Geoffrey Greymantle contemplated the creation of a territorial entity within the boundaries outlined above. Indeed, to accomplish such a goal Geoffrey would have to drive the count of Blois from the strongholds of Saumur, Chinon, and Île-Bouchard, gain control of Saint Florent (the richest monastery between Saint-Aubin in the west and Fleury in the east), dominate the monastery of Saint-Peter at Bourgueil, seize the fortified city of Tours and dominate its local politics including control of the office of archbishop. This was certainly a formidable agenda, but for a man such as Geoffrey who not only had contemplated the domination of Aquitaine but actually worked for two decades to attain this goal, a vision that called for the conquest and domination of the middle Loire valley could hardly be considered a fantasy.

It must be remembered that Geoffrey Greymantle had pursued policies that had been developed by his father and some that may even have been initiated by his grandfather. Geoffrey was aware that the aggrandizement of the dynasty was a long-term affair. Thus, for example, he knew it was likely that the *conventiae* with Viscount Renaud which would bring the Mauges alods to the Angevin fisc probably would not be realized until the reign of Fulk Nerra. Geoffrey also knew that Vendôme very probably would not come under Angevin control during his own lifetime.

The Angevins did, however, have a traditional interest in the middle Loire valley and particularly at Tours. Geoffrey's grandfather had held the title viscount of Tours. His father and his uncle Guy had been canons of Saint-Martin. By 985 when the Vendôme marriage was arranged, Geoffrey may be assumed to have concluded that there would be no rapprochement with Odo I whose own clearly demonstrated aim was expansion into the Loire valley at the expense of both the Angevins and the Capetians. The stance taken by Odo I meant that Hugh Capet could defend his own interests in the West only with the friendship of Geoffrey and Bouchard of Vendôme. Thus Geoffrey also could probably rely upon Hugh's support at least in the short term. In addition, as we have seen, Geoffrey had close ties with Herveus I of Buzançais, the treasurer of Saint-Martin and with Hatto of Preuilly-sur-Claise whose family had once been viscounts of Tours but ultimately had been displaced by men loyal to Odo. Also Geoffrey endeavored to maintain good relations with Saint Julien of Tours and with Marmoutier, two other powers that played an important role in the politics of Tours and its environs.

Angevin advancement into Touraine to develop a coherent geographical unit was clearly strengthened as a result of the need to develop and to maintain lines of communication between Angers and the eastern frontier strongholds of Amboise, Loches, and Buzançais. What we have delineated as the potential southern frontier also served as a communication route. Such a dual purpose, frontier and communication route, is hardly unique in the development of strategic thought in Western civilization. Indeed, the Roman *limes* served a similar dual military strategy and political aim. By contrast, the northern line of communication from Angers to Amboise through Baugé, Noyant, Château-la-Vallière, Semblançay, and Morand provides evidence of well-developed penetration of Touraine between the valleys of the Loir and the Loire.[127]

Beyond the limits of the Angevin geographical unit delineated above, Geoffrey had secured the overlordship of Nantes on the western frontier. He penetrated Maine on the northern frontier where he may have put forth an unrealized claim to overlordship. He did, however, see to it that his man was chosen bishop of Le Mans. To the south, Geoffrey recognized William Iron Arm as his *senior* but the political realities made the duke of Aquitaine the *de facto* inferior of the Angevin count in northern Poitou. In addition, Geoffrey was count of Chalons, his brother was count-bishop of Le Puy, his nephews ruled Gévaudan and Forez, his sister was countess of Arles, and his nephew-in-law was count of both Périgord and La Marche. Within Poitou, the viscount of Thouars was Geoffrey's man.

Geoffrey Greymantle's strong position on the borders of the potential Angevin territory, delineated above, as well as on the borders of the lands of his enemies—we cannot ignore in this latter context the position in Gâtinais, connections with the house of Bellême and the alliance with Walter I who was count of Vexin, Valois, and Amiens—provided buffers and positions of strategic importance which would inhibit his enemies' ability to obstruct Angevin advances.

This examination of Geoffrey Greymantle's wide-ranging diplomatic activity during a reign of twenty-seven years has not only permitted us to grasp the outlines of his policies but allows us to observe some of the techniques that he employed to accomplish his goals. When Geoffrey sought to take control of an area or to create an alliance with a powerful family, he frequently arranged a marriage between one of his very close relatives, a daughter, sister, son, niece, or even himself with someone likely to have a supportable claim to rule the coveted region or with someone who was actually in power. In arranging such alliances Geoffrey sometimes sought immediate goals. The marriage of his daughter to Conan of Rennes, of his niece to Aldebert of La Marche and Périgord, of his son to Elizabeth of Vendôme, of his sister to Louis V and to William of Arles, and his own marriage to Adele of Chalons all created new political alliances and by extension, military alliances or strengthened already existing older alliances. The Rennes, Vendôme, Chalons, and royal marriages, however, were intended to have long range significance as well. Geoffrey could look forward to the possibility that one of his grandsons would become count of Rennes, that his son or another grandson would become count of Vendôme, that another son would become count of Chalons, and that a nephew would become king of France. Not all of these possibilities were to become actualities and even those that did cannot be said always to have worked out in a manner that Geoffrey could have foreseen or approved. But these long range goals, like the arrangement to acquire the Mauges alods, were distinct, perhaps even probable, eventualities in Geoffrey's way of thinking. Indeed, it would be an injustice not to emphasize that Geoffrey understood the long range potential of his actions and consciously pursued these policies.

Geoffrey, however, did not rely solely upon marriage alliances when he pursued his diplomatic goals. When he sought the peaceful penetration or domination of a region, he frequently worked to win the support of important families that ranked second to that of the count. For example, he granted *beneficia* to the viscomital family of Rennes and of Vendôme before arranging the marriages of his daughter and son, respectively, to the heirs of these counties. Geoffrey also granted a substantial *beneficium* to a member of the viscomital family of Orléans probably with the intention of securing support for Angevin policies in Gâtinais.

When Geoffrey sought to penetrate an area where substantial hostility might be expected from the ruling house and where he might even find it necessary to go to war, he also sought out important families within the region for support. Thus Geoffrey granted *beneficia* to the viscounts of Thouars to facilitate Angevin advances in Poitou, he worked closely with the viscomital family of Le Mans and their allies from the house of Bellême to pursue his interests in Maine, he rewarded the Renauds handsomely so that he could dominate the Mauges region, and he cultivated Hatto of Preuilly who was descended from a viscomital family of Tours. In a slightly different variation of this theme it would be incautious to omit mention of Geoffrey's substantial gifts to Cluny as a result of which the ambitious Angevin count may well have hoped to win the moral and perhaps even the diplomatic support of Abbot Maiolus for the establishment of Angevin control at Chalons and for Adelaide's marriage to Louis V.

When diplomatic maneuvering failed, Geoffrey was not unwilling to go to war — although he appears to have done so very infrequently. He soundly defeated William Iron Arm at Les Roches when the latter apparently was intent upon resisting Angevin advances into Poitou. However, Geoffrey made an effort to mask his differences with William and recognized him as his *senior*. Seen in context, this action by Geoffrey cannot be understood to indicate that he would serve William or obey his commands in a manner that might limit the pursuit of Angevin policies. In fact, as we have seen, Geoffrey pursued his interests in Aquitaine to William's detriment during the period after he had recognized the Poitevin as his *senior*. Yet Geoffrey's act in recognizing William as his *senior* was not meaningless. Not only was William provided with a face-saving device — in diplomatic exchanges it is always useful to placate a loser with something of nominal value — but much more importantly, Geoffrey's usurpations and conquests in Poitou were given *de jure* recognition as *beneficia*.

Geoffrey's use of the institution of lordship as a tool in his dip-
lomacy was quite varied. We have seen, for example, how he forced Count
Guerech to recognize him as his *senior* and thus he reestablished the right of
the Angevins to dispose of Nantes to someone who could be relied upon to
serve the family's interest. Geoffrey recognized Hugh Capet as his *senior*
and publically acknowledged that he held the title "comes Andecavorum"
from him. Yet Geoffrey did not permit this state of affairs to thwart his
policies when Angevin interests were in conflict with Capetian interests as
was the case with the marriage of Adelaide to Louis V. Similarly, Geoffrey
served King Lothair loyally for two decades. But when he saw the opportunity to advance Angevin interests at royal expense, Geoffrey exploited
the situation and reduced Louis V to a squalid state. Geoffrey's relations
with the greater powers of the West and even with the king illustrate on
balance that he acted on the premise that the Angevins had no permanent
friends, only vital dynastic interests.[129]

Geoffrey's policies both at home and on the diplomatic front were
made possible in part through his effective exploitation of various rights
which during the century and a half following the death of Charlemagne
had come to be considered prerogatives of the count. Geoffrey presided
over the disposition of a broad spectrum of judicial matters that provided
him with both income and with power over people and land. Frequently, he
imposed new customs to increase his gains; these were often labeled *malae
consuetudines* by those who were burdened with them. When Geoffrey saw fit
to reward a loyal supporter with control over judicial rights or when he
granted immunities he was careful to reserve jurisdiction over major crimes
for himself. In addition, such grants were not made generally on a heritable
or permanent basis and the count retained the option not to regrant these to
the successor or heir of the original recipient. Geoffrey also exercised a wide
variety of rights related to the defense of his lands and lordships. These included control over the building of fortifications, the requisition of labor for
the construction of fortifications, and the requisition of labor for the repair of
such fortifications. Geoffrey also secured fighting men for the defense of the
lands he controlled and requisitioned logistic support for his armed forces.[130]

Geoffrey's activities were supported in part by the comital fisc
which included lands within the Angevin heartland and extensive resources
in the region of Orléans, Château-Landon, Amboise, and Loches. These
lands along with the rights pertaining to them provided a wide variety of income and enabled Geoffrey to grant *beneficia* to useful supporters who could
demand and enhance Angevin interests. In addition to the comital fisc,
Geoffrey also had at his disposal the economic resources of several important ecclesiastical institutions. We have seen how Geoffrey granted lands *ex*

rebus Sancti Mauricii to his *fideles* and how Bishop Nefingus also used the resources of the diocese of Angers to grant *beneficia* to the count's *homines*. Even the monastery of Saint Serge, which nominally was under episcopal control, had as its abbot one of Geoffrey's *fideles*, Abbot Bouchard.

Geoffrey's reputation as a monastic reformer should not leave the impression that he surrendered anything of economic significance when he helped his brother Guy institute the Benedictine rule at Saint-Aubin, Villeloin, Cormery, and Saint-Pierre de Ferriers or when they replaced the canons who had dwelt in these houses with monks. We have seen, for example, how after the reform of Saint Aubin, Geoffrey continued to appoint the abbot and had the latter's continuing cooperation in providing the count's *homines* with *beneficia* from the monastic fisc. The situation with regard to the use of the resources of the other reformed monasteries was no different from that at Saint Aubin.[131] In this context it may be emphasized that when Geoffrey initiated the program of monastic reform in concert with his brother Guy, he placed comital authority behind the goal of restoring to these religious institutions all of the lands that legally belonged to them but were in the hands of laymen.[132] With the return of these properties to the monasteries, their fiscs were substantially enlarged with lands to which previously Geoffrey had not had access. However, once the monasteries had possession of the lands that had been in the hands of canons or of other important laymen, Geoffrey could see to it that these same lands were granted to his own *homines*, for example, *ex rebus Sancti Albini*. Indeed, as we have seen, in the very charter by which Geoffrey "reformed" Saint Aubin he made it clear that the monks were required to use their wealth to provide *auxilium* to the count for military purposes. Thus the process of monastic reform carried out by Geoffrey Greymantle may be viewed from the economic and political perspective as substantially increasing the resources at the count's command.

However, through his participation in the reform of Saint Aubin, Cormery, Villeloin, and Saint Pierre as well as in the reconstruction of Saint Serge and Saint-Mary at Loches, Geoffrey helped to develop the image of the Angevin counts as supporters of the church. Fulk the Red had contributed to Saint-Aubin, Saint-Lézin, and Saint-Martin at Angers. Fulk the Good had been influential at Saint-Martin of Tours and supported Saint-Florent. Indeed, while enhancing this image Geoffrey seems to have employed a somewhat theatrical air which led him to publicize in a charter, quoted in part below, the pilgrimage that he made to Rome in 969:

> I set out for Rome . . . to seek foregiveness. There I was led into the
> honorable presence of the magnificent Pope John who spoke to me and

to my companions . . . for five days. . . . On the sixth and seventh days he ordered that we spend our time on the highest devotions with fasts, prayers, and vigils and by giving alms to the poor so that we might merit that our sins be washed away. When we had been fortified . . . , and sustained by God, we entered the basilica of Saint Peter and there the pope heard my confession of each and every sin that I could remember. While I spoke, tears burst forth from his eyes and from mine. . . .

He ordered me to build a church in the name of our Lord Jesus Christ . . . so that God might take pity on the soul of my father, Fulk . . . and so that He would wipe away the stains of my sins. . . . Moreover, so that He would learn that I have accepted this order [to build the church] joyfully, the pope with eighty-two bishops in holy council supported this and by the authority of God and the holy canons of Saint Peter the Apostle anathematized and banned from Christian life all who might dare to oppose this order. . . . [133]

The publicization of Geoffrey's pilgrimage to Rome and his successful audience with the pope cannot have hurt the image of the Angevin counts as supporters of the church and as leaders favored by the Lord and his saints. In this context it is important to note that Geoffrey customarily approved the use of formulae in the documents drawn up by the ecclesiastical recipients of his largess which suggested that God played a role of some significance in comital power. For example, we find phrases such as "Gauzfredus, gratia Dei, Andecavorum comes," and "Gauzfredus, misericordia Dei, Andegavensium comes."[134]

Geoffrey's concern about the way people thought of him is also evidenced by the fact that he acquiesced in having himself lavishly praised in local charters. For example, we see him styled *magnificentissimus et decentissimus comes* and *fortissimus comes*.[135] On one occasion Geoffrey permitted Bishop Nefingus to use the formula *fortissimus dux ac nominatissimus in universo mundo comes*.[136] This last-mentioned formula may perhaps suggest that Geoffrey was having tested the possibility tht he might assume the title *dux*. The success that Geoffrey had in image building may perhaps be gauged by his introduction as an important figure into the cast of characters who came to populate medieval French epic poetry. That Geoffrey came to be the hero of a Latin epic devoted to his career may be considered an additional measure of his success in this context.

While it is clear that Geoffrey Greymantle saw the value of being perceived as a supporter of the church and as a *fortissimus comes*, he also paid careful attention to the more tangible bases of his power. In a charter issued during the last decade of his reign, Geoffrey subscribed to the dictum that he owed his powerful position as count to the *generositas* of the Angevin *milites*. This formulation is somewhat surprising because it seems to depart from Geoffrey's frequent practice of recognizing *gratia Dei* as the source which provided the basis for his position. In addition, Geoffrey is known to have recognized that he held the position *comes Andegavorum* through the "largess" of his *senior* Hugh Capet. However, Geoffrey's pronouncement concerning the key role of the *milites* should not be understood to mean that he was rejecting divine support or that he had abandoned his *senior* Hugh Capet; this form of extreme action would clearly have been out of character. Rather, it appears that Geoffrey was making explicit for the ultimate benefit of his two sons, Fulk and Maurice, who were present when the charter was given, that the real strength of the count lay in his excellent and/or brave *milites*.[137]

By conveying this admonition to his sons in the *arenga* of the charter, Geoffrey seems to have made an effort to compensate for several admissions that he makes further along in the document which seem to have been forced upon him by circumstances that remain obscure. Geoffrey makes clear in the document that he is tied very closely in companionship to his *optimates*, but he is constrained to admit that he consented to many crimes (sins) which they had perpetrated and that, indeed, he had done much that was sinful in concert with them and at their request. These *crimines* carried out by Geoffrey for the members of his entourage and with the members of his entourage may perhaps be linked with the *malae consuetudines* he frequently imposed upon ecclesiastical lands, his extensive use of church property to provide for his own needs, and his practice of rewarding various of his followers *ex rebus ecclesiae*. It also might be instructive to note that according to this document Geoffrey's sins and those of his *socii* were "washed away" through prayer, confession, and a liberal gift to the pope.[138]

That Geoffrey should want his sons to know that the effective exercise of comital power and indeed the strength of their dynasty rested upon the support of the comital entourage (despite or perhaps because of the fact that he found it necessary in the very same document to repudiate some of his actions that involved these men) seems to have been well-grounded advice. The members of Geoffrey's entourage, who in contemporary documents are styled *fideles, proceres, viri nobiles, optimates, vassali, socii, homines, milites, potentissimi milites,* and *viri ignobiles,* held *beneficia* from the count or through him from various ecclesiastical establishments. These men formed the backbone of his army and garrisoned his strongholds. Many of these men—Adalhardus, Alveus, Arduinus, Durandus, Fulculfus, Hildemannus, Herneisus, Herveus, Marcoardus, Norbertus, Odulgarius,

Rainaldus, Sieffredus, Ulgerius, Warinus, and Wido—appear as we have already seen to have been descended from supporters of Geoffrey's father and grandfather. The men of Geoffrey's entourage recognized him as their lord, but more importantly they shared common interests, and the success of the count was calculated to redound to the credit and fortune of his followers.

Titles of superiority and subordination, legally constituted rights, and moral preachments had the value that the men of the time could make of them. The Angevin position did not rest upon abstract ideas. Rather, the power Geoffrey Greymantle exercised, the lands that he controlled, the policies that he pursued, the men who followed him, and the allies who furthered his aims in consonance with their own, comprised a complex of delicately balanced interests, a living organisim of human relationships with the greymantled count at its heart.

NOTES

*The research for this study was made possible by grants from the American Council for Learned Societies and the Graduate School of the University of Minnesota; I am grateful for their generosity and support. In addition, I would like to thank Mlle. Poirier-Coutansais, director of the Archives de Maine-et-Loire, for her many kindnesses, and the staffs of the Archives de Maine-et Loire, the Bibliothèque Municipale d'Angers, and the Bibliothèque Nationale for their help. I would also like to thank Professor Steven Fanning of the University of Illinois, Chicago who read the entire manuscript and made several useful suggestions for its improvement.

[1] The best work on Geoffrey is found in Ferdinand Lot, "Geoffroi Grisegonelle dans l'épopée," and "Traditions sur Geoffroi Grisegonelle et sur Helgaud de Montreuil." *Romania,* 19 (1890), 377–393 and 46 (1920), 376–381, respectively. These studies by Lot are much superior to those by G. d'Espiney, "La légende des comtes d'Anjou," *Mémoires de la Société d'agriculture, sciences et arts d'Angers,* 3rd Ser., 25 (1883), 49–112 and 4th Ser., 7 (1893), 3–96. F. Amory, "The Viking Hasting in Franco-Scandinavian Legend," in *Saints, Scholars and Heroes: Studies in medieval culture in honour of Charles W. Jones,* ed. M. King and W. Stevens (Collegeville, Minn., 1979), II, 275–276, adds nothing new. *La Chanson de Roland,* ed. J. Bédier (Paris, 1937), l. 106: "Gefreid d'Anjou, le rei gunfanuner, . . ."

[2] Louis Halphen, *Le comté d'Anjou au XIe siècle* (Paris, 1906), pp. 1–9; and Oliver Guillot, *Le comte d'Anjou et son entourage au XIe siècle,* 2 vols. (Paris, 1972), I, 2–15.

[3] Kate Norgate, *England under the Angevin Kings,* 2 vols. (London, 1887), I, 118–126. For a critique of Norgate's treatment of the early Angevins see Bernard S. Bachrach, "The Angevin Strategy of Castle Building in the Reign of Fulk Nerra, 987–1040," *AHR,* 88 (1983), 533–534.

[4] *The Making of the Middle Ages* (New Haven, 1953), p. 83.

⁵ K. F. Werner, "Untersuchungen zur Frühzeit des französischen Fürstentums (9.-10. Jahrhundert)," *Die Welt also Geschichte*, 18 (1958), 264–286. J. Dhondt, *Études sur la naissance des principautés territoriales en France (IXᵉ-Xᵉ siècle)*, (Bruges, 1948), also does not deal with Geoffrey.

⁶ I have made some observations concerning Fulk Nerra's policies in the following articles: "The Angevin Strategy of Castle Building," pp. 533–560; "Toward a reappraisal of William the Great, duke of Aquitaine (995–1030)," *Journal of Medieval History*, 5 (1979), 11–21; "Fortifications and Military Tactics: Fulk Nerra's Strongholds circa 1000," *Technology and Culture*, 20 (1979), 531–549; "Robert of Blois, Abbot of Saint-Florent de Saumur and Saint-Mesmin de Micy (985–1011): a study in small power politics," *Revue Bénédictine* 88 (1978), 123–146; "A Study in Feudal Politics: Relations Between Fulk Nerra and William the Great, 995–1030," *Viator*, 7 (1976), 111–122; and "Enforcement of the *Forma Fidelitatis*: The Techniques used by Fulk Nerra, Count of the Angevins (987–1040)," *Speculum*, 59 (1984), 796–819. In the following articles I have commented on various aspects of Geoffrey Greymantle's reign: "The Family of Viscount Fulcoius of Angers: Some Methodological Observations at the Nexus of Prosopography and Diplomatics," *Medieval Prosopography*, 4.1 (1983), 1–9; "Fulk Nerra and His Accession of Count of Anjou," in *Saints Scholars and Heroes*, 2, 331–342; and "The Idea of the Angevin Empire," *Albion,* 10 (1978), 293–299.

⁷ Werner, "Untersuchungen zur Frühzeit," pp. 264–286, is now the basic study of Geoffrey's predecessors.

⁸ *V* Norgate, *Angevin Kings,* I, 132–134, and more recently Carlrichard Brühl, *Palatium and Civitas: Studien zur Profantopographie spätantiker civitates vom 3. bis zum 13 Jahrhundert, I Gallien* (Vienna, 1975), 158. For the topography *v* George H. Forsyth, Jr., *The Church of St. Martin at Angers* (Princeton, 1953), pl. 181.

⁹ Brühl, *Palatium and Civitas*, pp. 153–154. By 976 Geoffrey Greymantle would seem to have made some additions to this wall, at least, and perhaps he even increased the entire circuit. *V* in this context *Cartulaire de Saint-Aubin-d'Angers,* ed. Bertrand de Broussillon (Angers, 1896), 3 vols., nos. 3, 4. We do not know the nature of its circuit in great detail (*V* Forsyth, *St. Martin*, p. 141, n. 242 but cf. pl. 181 and Brühl, *loc. cit.* map of Angers facing p. 160) nor its dimensions and therefore its military significance remains obscure. *V* also *Atlas historique français: Anjou*, ed. R. Favreau, et al. (Paris, 1973), map XLIX, 1A. Cf. J. Mallet and H. Enguehard, "L'enceinte gallo-romaine d'Angers," *Annales de Bretagne,* 71 (1964), 85–100; and J. Mallet, "Les enceintes médiévales d'Angers," *Annales de Bretagne,* 72 (1965), 237–262, who argue that there is no sound evidence for "Geoffrey's wall." However, in their treatment of earlier archaeological studies both Mallet and Enguehard tend to be hypercritical and, in addition, they do not give sufficient weight to the written evidence such as the *acta* cited above.

¹⁰ *Chronica de Gestis Consulum Andegavorum,* p. 49, in *Chroniques des Comtes d'Anjou et des seigneurs d'Amboise (CCASA)*, ed. L. Halphen and R. Poupardin (Paris, 1913), as this episode is dated to Geoffrey's reign by Norgate, *Angevin Kings,* I, 137. The *Gesta Consulum,* however, can only be considered suggestive on this point. For

the comparison with Nantes *v Chronique de Nantes,* ed. R. Merlet (Paris, 1896), ch. XLIV, and Richer, *Histoire de France* (888–895), ed. R. Latouche, 2 vols. (Paris: 1930–1964), Bk. IV, chs. 81–82; and concerning Loches, Jacques Boussard, "La charte de fondation de Notre-Dame de Loches," *Mémoires de la Société des antiquaires de Touraine,* 9 (1975), *p.j.,* I, pp. 7–9. Also of some use in understanding how the defenses of major strongholds were organized by Geoffrey's contemporaries *v* the *Consuetudines Bucardi Comitis* in *Cartulaire de La Trinité-de-Vendôme,* ed. Ch. Métais (Paris 1893–1897), 4 vols. and (Vannes, 1900), 2 vols., no. 2, as dated by J. Boussard, "Le comte d'Anjou au XIᵉ siècle," *Journal des Savants,* (1975), 135–136, to the reign of Bouchard the Venerable.

[11] Concerning Hilgerius and his *vassalus v Cartul. de Saint-Aubin,* nos. 2, 18, 34, 38, 131; *Cartulaire noir de la Cathédrale d'Angers,* ed. Ch. Urseau (Angers, 1908), no. 18; and "Fragments de chartes du Xᵉ siècle provenant de Saint-Julien-de-Tours," ed. C. de Grandmaison, *Bibliothèque de l'Ecole des Chartes,* 46 (1885), 47 (1886), no. 23. For Griferius and his *vassalus v Cartul. de Saint-Aubin,* nos. 2, 18, 21, 38; and *Cartul. noir,* nos. 18, 21. For Amalbertus *v Cartul. noir,* no. 19.

[12] These calculations are easily available in Patrick Wormald, "The Ninth Century," in *The Anglo-Saxons,* ed. James Campbell (Ithaca, N.Y., 1982), 152–153.

[13] Concerning these weapons and their use for the defense of fortifications *v* Bachrach, "Angevin Strategy," pp. 557–558. To these references may be added the materials collected by C. Morton and H. Muntz in their edition of *The Carmen de Hastingae Proelio of Guy, Bishop of Amiens* (Oxford, 1972), pp. 112–115. However, their reference to the "arcubalistis" in the *Miracula* of abbot Martin of Vertou should be dated to the late tenth century. For this date *v* Richard Hogan, "The *Rainaldi* of Angers: 'New Men' or Descendents of Carolingian *Nobiles?,*" *Medieval Prosopography,* 2.1. (1981), 49, n. 7.

[14] A selection of texts drawn from the early sixth century through the late eleventh century illustrates this point: *Vitae Caesarii episcopi Arelatensis libri duo,* ed. B. Krusch, *MGH, SRM,* III (Hannover, 1896), Bk. I, chs. 28–31; Procopius, *B.G.,* I, ix, x *passim (Opera Omnia,* 2nd ed., eds. J. Haury and G. Wirth, 4 vols. [Leipzig, 1962–64]); *Les Annales de Flodoard,* ed. P. Lauer (Paris, 1905), pp. 9, 30, 52; Richer, *Hist.,* Bk. III, ch. 5; Bk. IV, chs. 16, 26, 27, 77; and *Urkunden zur Geschichte der Stadt Speyer,* ed. A. Hilgard (Strassburg, 1885), no. 11, ch. 7. In Anjou as early as Fulk Nerra's reign we have substantial evidence for the use of *homines* living near fortifications being called upon to defend them. Guillot, *Le comte,* I, 381–391, reviews the evidence but tends to date several key texts far too late. On this *v* Bachrach, "The Angevin Strategy of Castle Building," p. 557, for a discussion of Fulk Nerra's "ancient custom". There is no reason to believe that Fulk was an innovator, and it is more than likely that the use of local levies persisted in the region from the Carolingian period. Indeed, Geoffrey certainly used the *bidannum* (Bachrach, *loc. cit.* and concerning fighting men *v* Boussard, "Notre-Dame de Loches," *p.j.* I).

[15] *Cartul. noir,* no. 21; *Cartul. de Saint-Aubin,* nos. 20, 21, 131, 281; and Ambrose Ledru, *La maison de Maillé,* 3 vols. (Paris, 1905), II, *p.j.* no. 4, who published the

document concerning the prebends; this should be read with the correction provided by Guillot, *Le comte*, II, no. 104. The family of Cadilo was an old one in the Angevin *pagus* and one of substantial importance. Cadilo's own association with the monastery of Saint-Lézin and the fact that his son, Theobald (the Old) I, was lay abbot there (*Cartul. de Saint-Aubin,* no. 178) should perhaps be connected with the fact that Theobald, count of the Angevin *pagus* in 848 (Dhondt, *Principautés territoriales,* pp. 91–92) was also lay abbot of Saint-Lézin (see Guillot, *Le comte,* I, 138, n. 39). This Theobald was succeeded as abbot by Waracus (*Cartul. noir,* nos. 36, 38) a man with obvious Breton links as illustrated by his name. In this context it is important to note that Cadilo is a name of Breton origin and that Cadilo's great grandson Éon (Ledru, *loc. cit.*) also bore a Breton name. It may be of further importance that the main estates possessed by Cadilo and his successors were at Blaison (cf. Halphen, *Le comté,* p. 164, n. 2) which had been a part of the royal fisc earlier in the Middle Ages (*Atlas historique: Anjou,* map V.1). Cf. Guillot, *Le comté,* I, 132, n. 18 and 138, n. 39 who recognizes the role of Count Theobald at Saint-Lézin but takes the matter no further in trying to understand the origins of this important family in Geoffrey's entourage. The hypothesis concerning this family's origins and early history has an analogue in the better documented family of Viscount Renaud as shown by Hogan, "The *Rainaldi* of Angers," pp. 35–62. For Cadilo family involvement at Saint-Rémy-la-Varenne *v Cartul. de Saint-Aubin,* no. 30.

16 *Cartul. de Saint-Aubin,* nos. 18, 26, 138, 285; and *Cartul. noir.,* no. 18.

17 *Cartul. de Saint-Aubin,* nos. 20, 23, 131, 211, 281, 821; perhaps "Fragments de Chartes," no. 23; and *Livre des serfs de Marmoutier,* ed. A. Salmon (Paris, 1845), no. 1. For the family at Brain-sur-l'Authion *v Cartulaire du Ronceray,* ed. P. Marchegay (Angers, 1856), nos. 93, 95, 96, 314.

18 *Cartul. de Saint-Aubin,* no. 281 as dated by Bachrach, "Fulk Nerra and his accession as count," pp. 331–333. For Bouchard of Briollay at Jarzé as a family possession *v Cartul. noir,* no. 98 bis. Bouchard of Briollay was archdeacon of Saint-Maurice by 1025 and treasurer by 1028. He held the former position into the 1040s (Halphen, *Le comté,* pp. 112, 157, 162–163 and Guillot, *Le comte,* I, 319, 322, 393). In the period from ca. 966 to ca. 970, the position of archdeacon was also held by a cleric named Bouchard (*Cartul. de Saint-Aubin,* no. 18 and *Cartul. noir,* nos. 18, 21). The combination here of *Leitname,* office political loyalty, and the geographical proximity of lands under their influence strongly suggests that the two men named Bouchard who held the archidiaconate of Saint-Maurice during the later tenth and early eleventh century were related. For additional references to the Bouchard clan *v Cartul. de Saint-Aubin,* nos. 18, 21, 38, 131; and *Cartul noir,* nos. 18, 27. *V,* in addition the reference to Abbot Bouchard, Geoffrey's *fidelis* (*Cartul. de Saint Aubin,* no. 281 and Bachrach, *loc. cit.,* pp. 331–333, for the date) where he is distinguished from Bouchard *laicus.* Abbot Bouchard flourished as late as 1000 (*Cartul. noir,* no. 22). However, Guillot, *Le comte,* I, 139, misdates *Cartul. de Saint-Aubin,* no. 281 and assumes with no evidence at all that Bouchard was a layman and lay abbot of Saint-Aubin between 960–964. Guillot, *loc. cit. ,* p. 179, n. 214, assumes that the Renaud, abbot and

monk, who appears in a charter dated 2 June 994 (Bib. nat., n.a. Lat. 1930, fols. 23v–24r, v.) was abbot of Saint Serge. There is no compelling evidence, however, that Renaud became abbot of Saint Serge before 1005 (Bib. nat. Coll. Com. Housseau, vol. 2.1, no. 347) and there was a monk named Renaud who was abbot of Saint-Aubin from 988 until 996–997 (*Cartul. de Saint-Aubin*, nos. 23, 677). The interest of the Bouchard family in the monastery of Saint-Serge was maintained by Archdeacon Bouchard II, lord of Briollay and possessor of Jarzé, who personally favored that monastery with gifts and encouraged his men to do so as well (*v*, e.g., François Marie Tresvaux du Fravel, *Histoire de l'église et du diocèse d'Angers* (Paris, 1859), I, 465–467, who provides an edition of a grant indicating Bouchard's feelings toward Saint-Serge.

[19] *Cartul. du Ronceray*, no. 127; *v* also *Cartul. de Saint-Aubin*, no. 281, dated by Bachrach, "Fulk Nerra and his accession as count," pp. 331–333. *Cartul. de Saint-Aubin*, nos. 20, 21, 34, 131, 224, for a list of Éon's attestations. It is of great importance to note from a methodological perspective that the Breton name Éon at this time was very rare in Anjou, and that the individual under discussion here appears in Angevin documents of Geoffrey's reign only in acts in which the count himself plays a juridicial role. In a notice, that survives only in a thirteenth-century copy, Geoffrey Greymantle gave to *Vicecomes Heudo*, "qui ex Britannia venit," the land of Seiches except for a mill and the church of Seiches (*Cartul. du Roncerary*, no. 127). It is likely that Éon obtained the title of viscount after his service in Geoffrey's entourage, and that the thirteenth-century copy cited above listed him with his highest title. This type of anachronism was common practice (*v* Halphen, *Le comté*, p. 19, n., who deals with a similar problem in relation to the title of treasurer held by Sulpicius of Buzançais). Further, it is clear that during this period Angevin writers refer to the viscounts of Rennes as viscounts of Brittany (viz. "Gozolinus vicecomes Britanniae" who was viscount of Rennes as he appears in Bib. Nat., Coll. Dom Housseau, vol. 2.1, no. 445. Concerning Joscelin see *Cartul. du Ronceray*, nos. 126, 295, and Halphen, *Le comté*, p. 156, no. 1. Joscelin, unlike Éon, appears to have been a rather more common name among the magnates of Anjou during the period under consideration. Thus there is some difficulty in identifying which of those who appear in Geoffrey Greymantle's entourage are to be identified with Joscelin of Rennes. As Éon's close relative, the possessor of a substantial *beneficium* at Seiches, and a man of prominence also during the early reign of Fulk Nerra (cf. the treatment of Joscelin by Halphen, *Le comté*, pp. 156, 163, and Guillot, *Le comte*, I, 288, 298), Joscelin might well be seen to have witnessed many of Geoffrey's charters and shared the type of titular honors held by Cadilo, Bouchard, and Éon. *V Cartul. Noir*, no. 21 and *Cartul. de Saint-Aubin*, nos. 131, 281. In *Cartul. de Saint-Aubin*, no. 34, there may be two men named Joscelin in Geoffrey's entourage but the fact that the second entry is prefaced by the word "item" may lead us to conclude that the same man is being referred to a second time. In *Livre des serfs de Marmoutier*, no. 1, two Joscelins are mentioned, but this act includes men from the entourages of both Count Geoffrey and Count Bouchard of Vendôme. *Cartulaire de l'abbaye de Redon*

en Bretagne, ed. A. de Courson, (Paris, 1863), nos. 290, 293, 294, 300, provide examples of the *Leitnamen* of the viscomital family.

[20] *Cartul. de Saint-Aubin,* nos. 2, 18, 20, 131; and *Cartul. noir,* nos. 18, 19. In light of the relatively few documents that survive in this context note should be made of the frequency with which Geoffrey's supporters are mentioned as holding *beneficia* from various religious institutions (*v,* below for further discussion on this point).

[21] *Cartul. de Saint-Aubin,* nos. 937, 938, 940; *v* also no. 38 but cf. no. 224. The identification of the Renaud mentioned above with a supporter of the Angevin count is shown by the following *acta:* Archives Indre-et-Loire, H 24, no. 8; Bibl. nat. ms. lat. 17127, pp. 157–159; and Bib. nat., Coll. Dom Housseau, I, no. 282. These *acta* show that the Renaud who held Prignes, among other *beneficia,* which is also called Luché-Prigné, held *Ciconia* which is within the Prignes complex of lands, and gave *Ciconia* to Saint-Peter-of-Bourgueil with Fulk Nerra's support in 999. *V* M. Dupont, *Monograhie sur le cartulaire de Saint-Pierre-de-Bourgueil* (Tours, 1962), pp. 176, 210; and cf. Guillot, *Le comte,* II, no. 13. Concerning Viscount Renaud's holdings see Hogan, "The *Rainaldi* of Angers," pp. 37–38. With regard to Fulcoius *Cartul. de Saint-Aubin,* no. 394; and *Livre des serfs de Marmoutier,* no. 1. *V,* also, Bachrach, "The Family of Viscount Fulcoius of Angers," pp. 1–9.

[22] Concerning Champigné-sur-Sarthe see *Cartul. de Saint-Aubin,* nos. 85–106, with special attention given to no. 85. But also no. 2, where Viscount Albericus of Orléans participates in Geoffrey's "reform" of Saint-Aubin.

[23] *Cartul. noir,* no. 18. It seems very likely that the Robert who held the stronghold at Rochefort is to be identified with Robert I of Buzançais for several reasons which, when taken together, provide a stronger basis for drawing this conclusion than would any single reason. The name Robert is an exceedingly rare one in the entourage of Geoffrey Greymantle and it only appears in special circumstances (see below). Robert, however, is a *Leitname* in the family of the lords of Buzançais whose ties to the Angevin counts extended at least into the later part of the ninth century. Rochefort was an exceptionally important stronghold, from a strategic point of view, and for some one who was not very close to the count of the Angevins to hold it would appear to be unthinkable. In addition, the chronology of the house of Buzançais fits this situation well. Robert I was an older contemporary of Geoffrey Greymantle and Robert's sons Archembaudus and Sulpicius were older contemporaries of Fulk Nerra (Guy Devailly, *Le Berry du Xe siècle au milieu du XIIIe siècle* [Paris, 1973] p. 130). Finally, we encounter Robert in Geoffrey's entourage on important occasions such as in 966 when the Angevins reformed the monastery of Saint-Aubin (*Cartul. de Saint-Aubin,* no. 2); at Poitiers in 976 (*Cartul. de Saint-Aubin,* no. 821) which may well have been in the wake of Geoffrey's victory at Les Roches (see below); and finally at Cluny following Geoffrey's marriage to Adele of Chalons (*Recueil des chartes de l'Abbaye de Cluny,* ed. A. Bruel, 6 vols. (Paris, 1876–1903), no. 1474). It may be noted, in addition, that in the last two mentioned examples, above, we find a man named Sulpicius as a witness and this is very likely to have been Robert's young son. *V Gesta Ambaziensium Dominorum,* p. 87 (in *CCASA*).

[24] The name Fredericus is very unusual in Anjou at this time. *Cartul. de Saint-Aubin*, vol. III, 62, (Index) for example, lists only two references to the name in a volume of 218 pages averaging fifty-five names per page. Fredericus appears only once in Geoffrey's entourage (ibid., no. 821) and once in Fulk Nerra's entourage very early in his reign (ibid., no. 395) where he is seen to possess Fossa Morin as a *beneficium* from the count.

[25] For the various terms used to describe these men *v* the documents cited in nn. 10, 11, 15-24, above.

[26] Concerning the movement of mounted troops *v* Bachrach, "Angevin Strategy," pp. 541-542, nn. 27, 28.

[27] For Rochefort *v*, above, n. 23; *Cartul. de Saint-Aubin*, no. 178, for the *podium* at Sazé and concerning *mottes* in general *v* M. de Boüard, *Manuel d'archéologie médiévale* (Paris, 1975), pp. 90-103; for the *fossa* at Morin *v* above, n. 24, and Boüard, *loc. cit.*, pp. 82-90, 104-105; and concerning Blaison, Saint-Rémy-la-Varenne, and Limelle, respectively *v* C. Port, *Dictionnaire historique, géographique et biographique de Maine-et-Loire*, 3 vols. (Paris-Angers, 1878), I, 355; III, 460; and II, 518.

[28] E. Mabille, *Introduction aux chroniques des comtes d'Anjou* (Paris, 1871), *p.j.*, nos. 1, 2; and *Cartul. de Saint-Aubin*, no. 36. In light of the very few charters that survive from the reign of Geoffrey's grandfather it is likely that an even larger number of supporters could be identified were there more documents. *V*, e.g., the identifications made by Boussard for the region of Loches ("Notre-Dame de Loches," pp. 1-10).

[29] *V*, above, the documents cited in nn. 15-23. With regard to early Carolingian and Merovingian policy *v* Bernard S. Bachrach, "Charles Martel, Mounted Shock Combat, The Stirrup, and Feudalism," *Studies in Medieval and Renaissance History*, 7 (1970), 66-72; and for the later period F. L. Ganshof, *Feudalism*, trans. P. Grierson (New York, 1957), pp. 16-61.

[30] Concerning the activities of the Saxons in the Loire valley *v* J. Lair, "Conjectures sur les chapitres XVIII et XIX du livre II de l'*Historia Ecclesiastica* de Gregoire de Tours," *Annuaire-Bulletin de la Société de l'histoire de France*, 35 (1898), 2-29 and W. Junghans, "Histoire critique de règnes de Childeric et de Chlodovech," (translated and augmented by G. Monod), *BEHE*, 37 (1879). On the Vikings *v* Walther Vogel, "Die Normannen und das fränkische Reich bus zur Gründung der Normandie (799-911)," *Heidelberger Abhandlungen zur mittleren und neueren Geschichte*, 14 (1906), 92, 137, 139, 145, 153, 197, 218, 231, 234, 238-244, 250, 257, 260, 349, 354. Concerning the use of concepts such as "lands and lordships" and "dominion", I have adopted the very useful ideas of John Le Patourel, *The Norman Empire* (Oxford, 1976), *passim* and especially p. 322, and also his "The Plantegenet Dominions," *History*, 50 (1965), 289-308.

[31] On the fortifications of Nantes *v* Adrien Blanchet, *Les enceintes romaines de la Gaule* (Paris, 1907), pp. 56-60; Albert Grenier, *Manuel d'archéologie galloromaine* (Paris, 1931), 5 (1931), p. 422; and Bernard S. Bachrach, "Some Observations on Early Medieval Fortifications in the 'West' of France," *Technology and Culture*, 16 (1975),

544. It is of some importance to note here that the Carolingian rulers of the mid- and later-ninth century understood the strategic interdependence of Angers and Nantes. Thus they frequently tried to link them in a unified command. *V* Dhondt, *Principautés territoriales*, pp. 83–92.

32 *V* the discussion by Werner, "Untersuchungen zur Frühzeit," pp. 266–269 and Guillot, *Le comte*, I, 8–10. The most complete single source for relations between Nantes and the counts of Anjou is *Chron. de Nantes*, chs. xxxvii, xxxviii, xlii. Although Theobald recognized Hugh the Great and later Hugh Capet as *senior* (Ferdinand Lot, *Les derniers carolingiens, Lothaire, Louis V, Charles de Lorraine: 954–991* [Paris, 1891], pp. 13, 34), he worked to dominate the Touraine and Berry at their expense. Theobald's brother, Richard, and then Theobald's son, Hugh, were archbishops of Bourges (Devailly, *Le Berry*, p. 138) and the arch-bishop of Tours, Ardouin (960–985), was one of his supporters (Jacques Boussard, "Les évêques en Neustrie avant la réforme grégorienne (950–1050 en-viron)," *Journal des savants* (1970), 172–173. *V* also for background R. Merlet, *Les comtes de Chartres, de Châteaudun et de Blois aux IXe et Xe siècles* (Chartres, 1900); Fer-dinand Lot, "L'origine de Thibaud le Tricheur," *Le Moyen Age*, 20 (1907), 169–189 (repr. *Recueil des travaux historiques de Ferdinand Lot* (Geneva-Paris, 1973), III, 103–123); F. Lesueur, *Thibaud le Tricheur, comte de Blois, de Tours et de Chartres* (Blois, 1963); and Jacques Boussard, "L'origine des comtés de Tours, Blois et Chartres," *Actes du 103e congrès national des sociétés savantes: 1977* (Paris, 1979), 85–112.

33 *Chron. de Nantes*, ch. xxxvii.

34 Ibid., also indicates Theobald's share in this arrangement and his arrangement with the count of Rennes, Judicaël Berengar.

35 *Chron. de Nantes*, ch. xxxvii. Scholars vigorously disagree concerning the death of Drogo. For example, some like Merlet in his edition of *Chron. de Nantes*, p. 110, n. 1, consider the murder to be a legend. However, Lot, *Derniers carolingiens*, p. 347 and Halphen, *Le comté*, p. 5, lean toward accepting the murder account. Guillot, *Le comte*, I, 10, n. 5, accepts it. I am inclined to give full acceptance to this story. It is certainly not inconsistent with what is known about medieval political behavior. Even later in the Middle Ages rulers such as King John and King Richard III of England did not shrink from murdering their own blood relatives. The child under discussion here was in no way related to Fulk. We must not let the epithet "Good" that has become attached to Fulk's name lead us to believe that he was incapable of political murder.

36 For this marriage *v* Michel Bur, *La formation du comté de Champagne: v. 950–v. 1150* (Nancy, 1977), p. 513. Bur does not deal with the date. However, Hermengarde, the eldest child of Adele and Geoffrey, was married to the count of Rennes no later than 971. Fifteen years of age was about the earliest time for marriage among the girls of the great families during this period. Therefore it is unlikely that Hermengarde was born much later than 956 and the marriage of her parents probably took place by ca. 955. For some observations on Angevin marriage policy *v* Bachrach, "The Idea of the Angevin Empire," pp. 203–299. For a good

example of close relations between Fulk the Good, Theobald, and various important Bretons see Bib. Nat., Coll. D. Houss., II.1, no. 181.

[37] Lot, *Derniers carolingiens*, pp. 34, 346–357, for a discussion of the war and of the marriage of Hugh Capet to the sister of the Norman duke. Hugh was Geoffrey's *senior* (*Cartul. de Saint-Aubin*, no. 2). *Chron. de Nantes*, chs. xxxviii–xxxix, makes clear that the Normans attacked while Fulk still lived and indicates that he was responsible for establishing Hoël at Nantes.

[38] Hoël, however, does not seem to have recognized Geoffrey as his *senior* and warred continuously with Geoffrey's son-in-law, Count Conan of Rennes (*Chron. de Nantes*, ch. xxxix). Hogan, "The 'Rainaldi' of Angers," pp. 35–62, outlines the history of the family. *V* Guillot, *Le comte*, I, 205–208, for a discussion of the boundaries of the Mauges region. *V* Boussard, "Les évêques en Neustrie," p. 166, for the holdings in the Sarthe and more generally Boussard, "Le comte d'Anjou," pp. 137–138.

[39] *Cartul. de Saint-Maurice*, no. 25, provides notice of the *conventiae*. Cf. Guillot, *Le comte*, I, 219 ff. It may perhaps have been at this time that the so-called *beneficium vicecomitalis*, located just beyond the walls of Angers on the other side of the Maine, was established and given to Renaud (*Cartul. de la Trinité de Vendôme*, no. 73. Halphen, *Le comté*, p. 99, no. 1, who is followed by Guillot, *Le comte*, I, 202, n. 26, maintain that Renaud held the viscomital title no later than 964 and perhaps as early as 960. This dating, however, is based upon *Cartul. de Saint-Aubin*, no. 281, which should be dated ca. 985–986 as shown by Bachrach, "Fulk Nerra and his Accession as Count," 331–333. *Cartul. de Saint-Aubin*, no. 18, which is dated 966, and in which Renaud appears as a witness was interpolated and the viscount's name and title were inserted between the confirmation clause of the principal, Bishop Nefingus, and his *subscriptio*. Finally, *Cartul. noir*, no. 21, which also has a suspect *datum*-clause lists Renaud as viscount in 969. However, more important is the exceptionally informative charter which mentions Renaud's wife that is dated 970 and in which the viscomital title is not used by Renaud; he is styled there as a *vasallus* (*Cartul. noir*, no. 21). In addition, the Renaud who appears in *Cartul. de Saint-Aubin*, nos. 2, 38, among the magnates of Anjou is likely to have been the Renaud under discussion here. In these acts dated 966, and 966–973, respectively, Renaud is not styled viscount.

[40] *Chron. de Nantes*, ch. xxxviii.

[41] Arthur le Moyne de la Borderie, *Histoire de Bretagne* (Rennes-Paris, 1898), II, 423 and for the charter *Cartul. de Saint-Aubin*, no. 906. Concerning the naming of the heir *v Chron. de Nantes*, ch. xlv. Geoffrey succeeded his father as count of Rennes in 992 and was old enough at that time to lead his own military forces. This would seem to indicate that he was at least fifteen years of age by 992. For Conan's wars with Hoël *v Chron. de Nantes*, chs. xxxix–xli.

[42] For the death of Adele *v Cartul. de Saint-Aubin*, no. 3; and for the death of Theobald, *v* Boussard, "L'origins des comtés," p. 92, with the literature cited there. Concerning Odo's challenge to Geoffrey *v Cartul. de Saint-Aubin*, no. 3, with the discussion of the diplomatic problems by Guillot, *Le comte*, II, no. 2.

[43] Geoffrey's marriage to Adele must post-date the death of her husband Count Lambert of Chalons (he was still alive on 22 February 978 — *Chartes de Cluny*, ed. Bruel, no. 144 *bis*) and pre-date a charter in which Geoffrey and Adele participate together as husband and wife in March 979 (*Chartes de Cluny*, ed. Bruel, no. 1474). Boussard, "Notre-Dame de Loches," p. 2, provides an excellent discussion of the date. We must not underestimate the importance of the marriages — first the one by Fulk the Good to Theobald's sister and then that of Geoffrey Greymantle to Theobald's sister-in-law. Clearly, the first marriage could be interpreted to indicate a temporary alliance between Blois and Anjou — no children were likely to be born from it. However, the second marriage, that of Geoffrey to Adele, provides substantial evidence that both Theobald and Fulk the Good were intent upon ensuring good relations between their respective houses and aimed to create a long-term alliance.

[44] Alfred Richard, *Histoire des comtes de Poitou, 778–1204*, 2 vols. (Paris, 1903), I, 102, no. 3; the marriage took place in 968 and Emma was fifteen years of age. *De Moribus et Actis primorum Normannisa Ducum, auctore Dudone Sancti Quintini decano*, ed. J. Lair (Caen, 1865), p. 263, and accepted by Lot, *Derniers carolingiens*, p. 347. Now for a reevaluation of Dudo as a source see Eleanor Searle, "Fact and Pattern in Heroic History: Dudo of St.-Quentin," Humanities Working Paper, 91. Division of the Humanities and Social Sciences, California Institute of Technology (1983). Evidence for very close relations between the members of the house of Blois can be seen in their family involvement in monastic reconstruction. On this *v* Guy Oury, "La reconstruction monastique dans l'Ouest: l'abbé Gauzbert de Saint-Julien de Tours (v. 990–1007)," *Revue Mabillon*, 30 (1964), 69–124. *V* also *Cartulaire de Saint-Père-de-Chartres*, ed. B. Guérard, 3 vols. (Paris, 1840), no. 8.

[45] Between 970 and 974, Geoffrey is not seen to appear in Hugh Capet's entourage. In 975 (*Recueil des historiens des Gaules et de la France (HF)* new ed., ed. L. Delisle (Paris, 1874), IX, 485); 975–979 (*Recueil des actes de Lothaire et de Louis V, rois de France*, eds. L. Halphen, and F. Lot (Paris, 1908), no. 69); and in 978–980 ("Fragments de chartres," no. 27), Geoffrey actively cooperates with Hugh. For Abbot Theobald *v* Guillot, *Le comte*, I, 23. For Geoffrey's military action *v* Lot, *Derniers carolingiens*, p. 116, and *Cartul. de Saint-Aubin*, no. 85.

[46] *Chron. de Nantes*, ch. xl.

[47] Concerning this conflict *v* Halphen, *Le comté*, p. 6, and the perceptive observations of Norgate, *Angevin Kings*, I, 137, in which she reconciles Fulk le Réchin, *Fragmentum Historiae Andegavensis*, p. 233 (*CCASA*) with *Gesta Consulum*, p. 49. It should be noted that Halphen, "Étude sur l'authenticité du fragment de chronique attribué à Foulque le Réchin," *Bibliothèque de la Faculté lettres de Paris*, 13 (1901), 18–20, reviews all the evidence and is properly cautious. Cf. *Chron de Nantes*, ch. xli and p. 119, n. 1 on this point. But concerning Guerech's activities and those of Count Alan see *Chron. de Nantes*, ch. xli. With regard to Geoffrey's position vs. William Iron Arm *v* below.

[48] *Chron. de Nantes*, ch. xlii. This effort to develop a direct tie with King Lothair in order to subvert the power of Geoffrey suggests that the count of Nantes had

previously recognized the Angevin count as his overlord. It is in this context that we should view the aid provided by Geoffrey to Guerech in 982, above, n. 47. The history of Angevin overlordship is complicated. The two surviving versions of the chronicle disagree concerning the basis of Geoffrey's claim. Both trace it to Fulk the Red but one version calls Fulk Geoffrey's father while in the other Fulk is simply called *comes*. Geoffrey's father was Fulk the Good so that if the claim rested on the latter's holding of Nantes from 952 until ca. 960 our text is in error in denoting him as Fulk the Red. This, moreover, cannot be considered a crippling error. However, Fulk the Red, Geoffrey's grandfather, held the title count of Nantes (see above, note 48), and the text that reads "quam Fulco Ruffus comes tenuerat" cannot be disputed as a fact (cf. Merlet, *Chron. de Nantes*, who in an editorial note, p. 122, n. 1, is clearly in error when he writes: "Foulques le Roux, grand-père du même Geoffroi, n'eut jamais aucun droit sur la Bretagne ni sur Nantes." The fact that Fulk the Red was count of Nantes, however, does not prove that it was upon this basis that Geoffrey Greymantle made his claim of overlordship. It might well be that the disagreement in the surviving versions of the *Chronicle of Nantes* reflect an ambiguity insofar as Geoffrey made his claim on the basis of the positions held both by his grandfather and by his father. Note the observations by Werner, "Untersuchungen zur Frühzeit," p. 267.

[49] *Livre des serfs de Marmoutier*, no. 1. The stronghold of Nouâtre was in the hands of a certain Guenno who actively supported Fulk Nerra during his reign (*Gesta Consulum*, p. 48). That Geoffrey issued a charter at Nouâtre would seem to suggest that he was on good terms with Guenno and perhaps the *bonus homo* who was one of the witnesses to the above-cited act and is recorded in an eleventh-century copy as Gemmo can be identified with the castellan of Nouâtre.

[50] *Cartul. de Saint-Aubin*, no. 281 with a discussion of the date by Bachrach, "Fulk Nerra and his accession as count," pp. 331–333.

[51] *Chron. de Nantes*, ch. xlii. On the stronghold itself *v* E. Orieux and J. Vincent, *Histoire et géographie de la Loire-Inférieur* (Nantes, 1885), II, 412.

[52] This elaborate scheme may perhaps permit the inference that Geoffrey, as Guerech's *senior*, had the right to occupy the latter's strongholds but that Geoffrey's rights over the strongholds held by those subject to Guerech were less well-defined. It is perhaps worth noting that Geoffrey's neighbor to the south, William Iron Arm (and his son William the Great) had some considerable difficulty in enforcing the right to occupy the strongholds of their *fideles*. This was particularly true for William the Great. See Bachrach, "William the Great," p. 15. It is clear that Fulk Nerra claimed the right to occupy the strongholds of his *fideles*. *V* Jane Martindale, "Conventum inter Guillelmum Aquitanorum comes et Hugonem Chiliarchum," *The English Historical Review*, 84 (1969), 548.

[53] *Chron. de Nantes*, ch. xlii, recounts a story in which Renaud recognizes that Guerech controls hunting rights in the Mauges region. This is a rather obscure way of indicating the count of Nante's lordship there. Considerable debate has been generated concerning the precise legal relationship that existed between Renaud and Geoffrey and Guerech and their respective rights in the Mauges

region. On this *v* Halphen, *Le comté*, p. 13, notes 1, 2; Boussard, "Le évêques en Neustrie," pp. 165–166; and pp. 170–171; and Guillot, *Le comte*, I, 207–208. The question of legal rights (provided that they existed with some precision at the time and provided that modern scholars could ascertain their precise nature) seems somewhat beside the point. In short, the relative power of the individuals involved in a particular situation would seem to have been of considerable greater moment than were putative rights. Guerech's ability to have his way with Renaud in this context would seem to highlight this point as does Geoffrey's ability to enforce his will on the count of Nantes (*v* above, n. 47).

[54] *Chron. de Nantes*, ch. xlii.

[55] Guerech had nowhere to go for help against Geoffrey. Conan was intent upon taking Nantes and he was supported by his lord Odo I, count of Blois. Hugh Capet, the only other major force in the West, north of the Loire, was an ally of Geoffrey Greymantle. Further away in Normandy, the duke tended to favor Rennes. To the south, William Iron Arm was not in a position to oppose Geoffrey Greymantle (Bachrach, "Feudal Politics," pp. 112–113). For the policy of the counts of Rennes *v Gesta Consulum*, p. 49, and Halphen, *Le comté*, pp. 16–17. For Châteaubriant *v* Orieux and Vincent, *Hist. et géog.*, II, 319.

[56] *V* the basic survey by O. Desmaizières, "Essai d'inventaire des camps, enceintes, buttes, mottes, et retranchements anhistoriques ou sans origine précise du départment de Maine-et-Loire," *Congrès préhistorique de France*: Tours, 1910 (Paris, 1911), pp. 1065, 1067, who provides evidence that there were fortifications at the above-mentioned locations before the eleventh century. However, much of this material must be reworked and investigated with modern archaeological methods. Until such thorough studies have been carried out our observations concerning Geoffrey Greymantle's role in regard to these fortifications must remain conjectural. Later counts of Anjou built formidable strongholds at these locations. *V* Guillot, *Le comte*, I, 290, 420, for Pouancé; 294–295, for Segré; and 300, 466, for Candé.

[57] A stronghold was built at Craon during the ninth century as noted by Guillot, *Le comte*, I, 310. Exactly when the Suhard-Warinus clan was established there cannot be ascertained with any precision. Suhard is a very uncommon name during this period. A Suhard (the old) appears in Geoffrey Greymantle's entourage by 965 where he is considered one of the count's *fideles*. After this he is found frequently with Geoffrey to the end of his reign and is described variously as a *miles* and a *potentissimus miles* (*Cartul. de Saint-Aubin*, nos. 34, 48, 131, 281, 821). Like Suhard, Warinus appears in Geoffrey's entourage and is styled as one of the count's *fideles* (*Cartul. de Saint-Aubin*, no. 38). But whereas Suhard I (the old) remains with Geoffrey until the end of his reign, Warinus does not appear after 973. During this relatively short period of time Warinus, nevertheless, is styled *nobilis, miles*, a *potentissimus miles* (*Cartul. de Saint-Aubin*, nos. 20, 821 and *Cartul. noir*, no. 18). For the subsequent history of the Suhard-Warinus clan *v*, e.g., *Cartul. de la Trinité de Vendôme*, no. 98, from which we can see the alternation of the *Leitnamen* Suhard and Warinus. See also Guillot, *Le comte*, I, 335–336, for the later history of the family.

[58] It must be remembered that Geoffrey Greymantle had maintained good relations with the count of Rennes for more than two decades before the break with Conan in 981–982. In addition, Fulk the Good through his marriage to the sister of the count of Blois had maintained good relations with Theobald, the lord of the count of Rennes, since 952. That relations between the counts of Rennes and the Angevin counts were to remain poor for more than a half-century following Geoffrey's break with Conan should not lead us to interpret Geoffrey's actions as though he had foreknowledge of such circumstances. Indeed, it is an all too common error on the part of historians to evaluate a particular situation with the benefit of perfect hindsight. Thus, in the mid-980's the experience of the past thirty years would probably have suggested to Geoffrey that a rapprochement with Rennes was certainly not impossible. Indeed, he appears to have acted as though this were the case.

[59] *Geste Consulum*, pp. 38–39, 49. *V* the discussion by Halphen, *Le comté*, p. 1, n. 3 and Werner, "Untersuchungen zur Frühzeit," p. 271. For Saint Pierre *v* Guillot, *Le comte*, I, 166–167, and Abbo, *Epist.*, no. 1 (*Patrologia Latina*, ed. J-P. Migne [Paris, 1880], 139), which shows Fulk disposing of the wealth of Saint-Pierre at will and with absolutely no restrictions. The reform of this house as emphasized by Guillot, *loc. cit.*, is exaggerated.

[60] For the passing of Château-Landon into the hands of Geoffrey Greymantle's cousins *v* Werner, "Untersuchungen zu Frühzeit," p. 272, and with regard to the long standing presence in the Orléanais *v* pp. 273–274. With regard to Viscount Alberic *v* in *Cartul. de Saint-Aubin*, no. 2, and concerning the viscount's probable relative *v ibid.*, no. 85. The extent of Angevin penetration with the help of Hugh Capet is suggested by a useful collection of acts that have been published in *Cartularie de l'église cathédrale Sainte-Croix d'Orléans*, ed. J. Thillier and E. Jarry (Orleans, 1906), nos. 20, 40, 63, 64. *V* Guillot, *Le comte*, I, 3–4.

[61] Philip Grierson, "L'Origine des comtes d'Amiens, Valois, et Vexin," *Le Moyen Age*, 49 (1939), 96–97, and the genealogy. *V* also the treatment of Guy's career in Flodoard, *Hist.*, pp. 78, 99, 113, 116–120, 154, and *Cartul. de Saint-Aubin*, nos. 2, 38; *v* the discussion by Guillot, *Le comte*, I, 140–141, for the reform activity.

[62] Werner, "Untersuchungen zur Frühzeit," p. 271, for Ingelgarius. *V* also *Cartul. de Saint-Aubin*, no. 3; for the dowry, and for the house of Bellême see Le Patourel, *Norman Empire*, p. 10, and below.

[63] Grierson, "Comtes d'Amiens, Valois, et Vexin," pp. 96–97, and concerning the subsequent history of this family, *v* the material above in n. 61.

[64] *Cartul. de Saint-Aubin*, no. 85.

[65] *Liber Castri Ambaziae* (in *CCASA*), p. 21; *Gesta Consulum*, pp. 30, 46; *Gesta Ambaz. Dominorum*, pp. 80, 83, 86, 87, for Buzançais; for Châtillon-sur-Indre, Devailly, *Le Berry*, pp. 128–129, 166–167, 172 and cf. Guillot, *Le comte*, I, 466, n. 2, who is not willing to admit that the Angevins controlled the stronghold at Châtillon-sur-Indre; for Loches, Halphen, *Le comté*, pp. 4, 15 and Guillot, *Le comte*, I, 283–284; and the estates held at Courçay are to be found in an unpublished act, Bib. nat., Coll. Baluze, vol. 76, fol. 256. Finally, for Cormery *v HF.*, X, p. 577 and Guillot, *Le comte*, I, 168–169.

[66] A charter issued in 965 at Tours which survives in an 18th-century copy (Bib. Nat. Coll. D. Houss., I.1, no. 189, and there is no complete edition) makes clear that Villeloin was a daughter house of Cormery and under Angevin control. *V.* Guillot, *Le comte*, I, 163–166, and the effective analysis by Dom Guy Oury, "La situation juridique des monastères de Cormery et de Villeloin sous l'abbatiat de Guy d'Anjou (v. 954–975)," *Bulletin de la Société archéologiue de Touraine*, 9 (1975), 551–563. Concerning Valençay, *v Cartulaire de Cormery*, ed. J. Bourassé (Tours, 1861), no. 47; and *v Gesta Consulum*, p. 33, which provides the evidence on Villentrois. From small fragments of a lost charter (L. Raynal, *Histoire du Berry* (Bourges, 1844), I, 350, 424) it is clear that Renaud, lord of Graçay, was one of Fulk Nerra's supporters no later than October 1000 and perhaps much earlier. *V* also the observations of Devailly, *Le Berry*, p. 167, n. 2, where he points out Halphen's failure to identify Graçay correctly in his edition of *Gesta Ambaz. Dominorum*, p. 80. Concerning Preuilly *v* Jacques Boussard, "L'Origine des familles seigneuriales dans la région de la Loire moyenne," *Cahiers de civilisation médiévale*, 5 (1962), 304. For Hatto in Geoffrey's entourage where he is styled *miles v Cartul. de Saint-Aubin*, no. 281, and for the date Bachrach, "Fulk Nerra and his accession as Count," pp. 331–333. For relations of the Hattoclan and the Fulconians going back to the early tenth century (Boussard, "L'origine des comtés," p. 95). *V* below, n. 89 for additional material on the family. For La Haye *v* Halphen, *Le comté*, pp. 4–5. *V* concerning Guenno of Nouâtre, above, n. 49; and for Saint-Épain, Halphen, *loc. cit.*, p. 15.

[67] André Chatelain, *Donjons romans des pays d'Ouest* (Paris, 1973), p. 157, wants to date this construction to the reign of Fulk Nerra and it is clear that it cannot be later than the later tenth or early eleventh century. However, since Loches is not mentioned by Fulk le Réchin, *Hist. Andeg.*, pp. 233–234, among his grandfather's more important construction projects, it is likely that Fulk Nerra did not build this tower at Loches but that Geoffrey Greymantle did. Cf. P. Heliot, "Le château de Loches et les fortresses des XIe et XIIe siècles," in *Actes du colloque médiéval de Loches (1973), MSAT*, 9 (1975), 33–40. In addition, the complex military organization and social structure revealed in the charter cited below in note 68 suggests that in Geoffrey's reign Loches was very well developed.

[68] Boussard, "Notre-Dame de Loches," pp. 7–9, provides a model critical edition of the act where these men are mentioned.

[69] *Cartul. de Saint-Aubin*, nos. 36, 38, 177; *Cartul de Sainte-Maurice*, no. 18; *Chartres de Cluny*, ed. Bruel, no. 1474; and Boussard, "Notre-Dame de Loches," p. 4, for Geoffrey's men and *v* Mabille, *Introduction, p.j.* nos. 6, 8, for Fulk's men.

[70] *Cartul. de Saint-Aubin*, no. 224. *V* Alfred Richard, *Histoire des comtes de Poitou*, 778–1204, 2 vols. (Paris, 1903), I, 115; Halphen, *Le comté*, p. 14, n. 1; and Marcel Garaud, *Les Châtelains de Poitou et l'avènement du régime féodal, XIe et XII siècles* (Poitiers, 1964), p. 3. Concerning Fulk's marriage *v* above, n. 48.

[71] Lot, *Derniers carolingiens*, pp. 81, 127, 367; Marius Balmalle, "Les comtes de Gévaudan et de Brioude," *Almanach de Brioude* (Brioude, 1964), pp. 251–252; and Bachrach, "Feudal Politics," p. 113. While it is clear that Fulconian connections with the greater families of *Francia* were well established as early as the reign of

Charles the Bald (Werner, "Untersuchungen zur Frühzeit," pp. 246–289) the lines of contact between the Angevins and the house of Gévaudan are obscure. Thus in trying to search out the possible source for these contacts it should be noted that Odo, abbot of Cluny (926–942) and a neighbor of Gévaudan, was of Touraine origins and that at one time Fulk the Red had been viscount of Tours and Treasurer of Saint Martin at Tours. According to a generally accepted tradition found in John of Salerno, *Vita Odonis*, (Bk. I, chs. 11, 18, 21, ed. Migne, *Patrologia Latina*, vol. 133) Odo went to Saint Martin where Fulk the Red provided the future abbot of Cluny with a cell in which to live, a prebend for his support, and sent him a large sum of money. Under these circumstances it would seem highly likely that Odo was acquainted with Fulk's sons, Fulk the Good and Guy, who were both canons of Saint Martin. It would seem likely that an Angevin interest in matters in the east of Aquitaine might well have been developed through contacts with Odo when he was abbot of Cluny. It might also be added that Hugh Capet, the lord of Geoffrey Greymantle, was a close friend of Maiolus (943–994) who succeeded Odo as abbot (Ferdinand Lot, *Etudes sur le règne de Hugues Capet et la fin du Xe siècle* (Paris, 1903), pp. 183–184).

[72] *Cartul. de Saint-Aubin*, no. 224.859, and, above, note 11.

[73] *Cartul. de Saint-Aubin*, no. 211, and Bachrach, "Fulk Nerra and his accession as count," pp. 334–335, for the date and above n. 16 concerning Limelle. Concerning Montaglan *v* Port, *Dict . . . Maine-et-Loire*, II, 695, and *Cartul. de Saint-Aubin*, no. 695. For discussion on this type of fortification *v* Boüard, *Manuel d'archéologie médiévale*, pp. 76–84, and the works he cites in n. 271. Also *Cartul. de Saint-Aubin*, no. 40 and no. 232, which indicate that Abbot Gunterius granted lands to Albuinus and his son Narbertus also at Trezé within the jurisdiction of Méron. A man named Norbertus is found in the entourage of Fulk the Red (*Cartul. de Saint-Aubin*, no. 36).

[74] *Recueil des actes de Lothaire*, no. 62. This act is considered inauthentic by the editors, Lot and Halphen, but only formally so. They agree that the content is accurate. Guillot, *Le comte*, I, 6, n. 28, agrees and makes a compelling argument for accepting the accuracy of the material in the document. This charter is dated "anno dominicae incarnationis DCCCCLXXIII, XIIII kalendas februarii, anno regnante domno Lothario glorissimo rege XXI." The 19th of January of the 21st year of Lothair's reign was 975 and not 973. It seems likely that either in the original or in Bouhier's copy (Bib. Nat. ms. lat. 17709, p. 150) made from the original in 1721 there was a transposition of the numbers from XIX to XXI. Such errors are very common in both medieval documents and in early modern copies. This appears in the same act, *Recueil des actes de Lothaire*, no. 62. Note the discussion by George Beech, *A Rural Society in Medieval France: The Gâtine of Poitou in the Eleventh and Twelfth Centuries* (Baltimore, 1964), pp. 129–130, concerning the extent of Angevin holdings in this part of Aquitaine. Pierre de Maillezais, *Relatio*, fol. 247v., 249v.-r. (Bib. nat. *ms.* lat. 4892; the edition in *HF*, X, is incomplete). This is the basic source for this story of William's affair with the viscountess of Thouars. Unfortunately, this author has a reputation for being somewhat of a romantic. Although some scholars regard this story as true, either

wholly or in part, a more sceptical approach might be safer. The story has many of the elements of a vulgar romance and it may well have been a popular oral tradition in Aquitaine during the eleventh century. Yet, even if the historical accuracy of this tale is to be discounted completely, it may be hypothesized that the romance developed as a popular means of explaining why there were some hostilities between the counts of Poitou and the viscounts of Thouars during the reign of William Iron Arm. For a discussion of this problem see H. Imbert, *Histoire de Thouars* (Niort, 1871), p. 33–34 and Richard, *Comtes de Poitou*, II, 480–486. On the continued loyalty of the viscounts of Thouars to the Angevins through ca. 993–994 *v* Bachrach, "Feudal Politics," p. 113. This is made clear by the observations of George Beech, "The Origins of the Family of the Viscounts of Thouars," *Études de civilisation médiévale: mélanges offerts à Edmond-René Labande* (Poitiers, 1974), 26.

75 Fulk le Réchin, *Hist. Andeg.*, p. 233, provides the information concerning Geoffrey's victory and the seizure of Loudun and Mirebeau. Adémar de Chabannes, *Chronique*, Bk. III, ch. 36, ed. J. Chavanon (Paris, 1897), for the *beneficium* at Londun. By January 975, Geoffrey had recognized William as his *senior* (*Recueil des actes de Lothaire*, no. 62). The relation of these two texts to one another has been much debated because Fulk le Réchin clearly favors Geoffrey Greymantle and Ademar favors William. *V* Norgate, *Angevin Kings*, I, 139–140; Halphen, *Le comté*, p. 7, 55; Richard, *Comtes de Poitou*, I, 115–116; Garaud, *Les châtelains*, p. 3; and Guillot, *Le comte*, I, 5–8, who would seem to give too much weight to legal matters.

76 "Documents inédits pour servir à l'histoire de l'abbaye Sainte-Croix de Poitiers et de ses domaines jusqu'à la fin du XIIIe siècle," ed. P. de Monsabert, *Revue Mabillon* (1913), no. I. This act must post-date the death of Bishop Pierre of Poitiers in 975. Cf. the reading of this act by Guillot, *Le comte*, I, 6, no. 27, and the discussion by Bachrach, "Feudal Politics," p. 14, n. 11.

77 Louis Charbonneau-Lassay, "Les châteaux de Loudun après les fouilles archéologiques de M. J. Moreau de la Ronde," *Mémoires de la Société des Antiquaires de l'Ouest*, 3rd ser., 8 (1915), 76–93, 143–173, and Bachrach, "Early Medieval Fortifications," p. 550, for a discussion of the various stages of fortifications at Loudun from the late third century A.D. onward. Concerning the *Bidannum*, cf. Guillot, *Le comte*, I, 383, who believes that this service was first taken by Fulk Nerra. The term *bidannum* or *bianum* as it is found in the charter cited in note 76, above, evolved no later than the third quarter of the tenth century and probably derives from the duty of the count to provide for the defense of the region under his jurisdiction. When the Carolingians were forced on the defensive, Charles the Bald finally placed the central authority behind insuring that fortifications would be kept in repair. With regard to the policies of Charles the Bald see the study by F. Vercauteren, "Comment s'est-on défendu dans l'Empire franc contre les invasions normandes," *Annales du XXXe Congrès de la Fédération archéologique et historique de Belgique* (1935–1936), 117–132. For a not very satisfactory examination of some *bidannum*-texts see R. Grand, "Une curieuse appellation de certaines corvées au moyen âge: le 'bian,' 'biain," ou 'bien,'" *Mélanges dediée à la mémoire de Félix Grat* (Paris, 1946), 288–300.

[78] Roger is referred to as *senior* of Loudun sometime between 988 and 994, probably closer to the former date (Bib. Nat., n.a. lat. 1930, fol. 116 and published by Halphen, *Le comté*, pp. 345–346, from a nineteenth-century copy. Roger of Loudun is perhaps to be identified with Geoffrey's *fidelis* of that name who was also a *miles* and considered to have been one of the count's *proceres* (*Cartul. de Saint-Aubin*, nos. 211, 281). By 972 we find a Roger in Geoffrey's entourage who is considered *nobilis* (*Cartul. de Saint-Aubin*, no. 20). In 973 Roger is considered among the count's most powerful *milites* (*Cartul. de Saint-Aubin*, no. 131). In both of these acts Roger heads the witness list directly after the count; this may perhaps be an indication of his importance.

[79] *Cartul. de Saint-Aubin*, no. 821. *Miracula Martini Abbatis Vertavensis*, ed. B. Krusch, *MGH, SRM*, 3 (Hannover, 1886), where one finds considerable information on the Renaud clan and Renaud the *praepositus* of Saint Jouin who is identified with the viscount; p. 574 mentions the Abbot Renaud who headed the house during the late ninth century; and p. 575 deals with *dux* Renaud who administered the territory of Maine, owned lands near the monastery, donated some of his own lands to the house, and was killed in 885. *V* Hogan, "The *Rainaldi* of Angers," pp. 37–40, who deals with these materials and effectively answers Halphen's criticism of this source (*Le comté*, p. 98, n. 1).

[80] *Cartul de Saint-Aubin*, no. 821.

[81] Lot, *Derniers carolingiens*, pp. 81, 367. There seems to be considerable discussion as to whether William was Adelaide's son or the son of Stephen's first wife. Marius Balmelle, "Les comtes de Gévaudan et Brioude," *Bulletin de la Société des lettres, sciences et arts du département de la Lozère*, n.s. 9 (1963), 107, takes the latter position and follows E. Fournial, "La souveraineté du Lyonnais au Xe siécle," *Le Moyen Age*, 62 (1956), 48–49. In a charter of either 1010 or 1011 (*HGL*, III, 242), Count Pons refers to William who is by that time long dead (see below) as his brother. (*HGL* for *Histoire Générale de Languedoc*, ed. C. DeVic and J. Vaissete, 16 vols., rev. edit. (Toulouse, 1872–1904). There is some discussion as to when William died. Fournial, loc. cit., pp. 447–448, accepts the date of 1010, because the earliest datable act in which Pons appears with the title count can be placed in that year. But *Chronicon Sancti Petri Aniciensis*, pp. 152–154 (in *Cartulaire de l'abbaye de Saint-Chaffre-du-Monastier*, ed. U. Chevalier [Paris, 1884]), makes it clear that William was gone from the scene by 975 when Guy, Adelaide's brother, became count-bishop of Le Puy. By 975 Adelaide is the dominant figure in the lives of her surviving sons, Pons and Bertrand, who share the comital title and are already in their majority, i.e. over fifteen years of age (*HGL*, IV, 134). A further reason for believing that William was Adelaide's son is the fact that her brother Guy associated William's son Stephen with him in the episcopal office (*HGL*, III, p. 242, n. 10). The study by Oury cited in note 66, above, and his "Le frère de Geoffrey Grisonelle: Guy II d'Anjou. Moine et évêque du Puy (av. 998)," *MSAT*, 9 (1975), are of no help here.

[82] Lot, *Derniers carolingiens*, pp. 81, 82, n. and *Chron. S. Petri Aniciensis*, pp. 152–153, where Bishop Guy is characterized as an adviser of King Lothair. The king is

reputed to have made clear to Guy that he expected him to be a most faithful administrator (*fidelissimus procurator*) for Lothair as well as for his flock. Guy is identified "cui erat frater germanus noblissimus comes Gaufridus, cognomento Grisagonella."

83 On the joint action of these Angevins v *Chron. S. Petri Aniciensis*, pp. 52, 54. Guy is generally considered to have been the man who introduced the peace of God into Aquitaine at this time. *V* H.E.J. Cowdrey, "The Peace and the Truce of God in the Eleventh Century," *Past and Present*, 46 (1970), 43.

84 *Chartes de Cluny*, ed. Bruel, nos. 1474, 1701, 2484, and *Cartulaire du prieure de Saint-Marcel-lès-Chalon*, ed. M. and P. Canat de Chizy (Chalon, 1894), no. 6. *V* also Boussard, "Notre-Dame de Loches," pp. 1–10, for Geoffrey as count and the marriage. Lot, *Derniers carolingiens,* pp. 328–329.

85 Lot, *Derniers carolingiens*, pp. 92–108, deals with the year 978 in considerable detail and pp. 105–106 he examines Geoffrey's role in the conflict with Otto II. Lot examined the epic material in the two articles cited in note 1, above. Guillot, *Le comte*, I, 4–5, argues that Fulk was not a *fidelis* of King Lothair but Boussard, "Le comte d'Anjou," pp. 134–135, shows that he is in error.

86 *Cartulaire de prieure de Paray-le-Monial*, ed. U. Chevalier (Paris, 1890), no. 2. *V* Georges Duby, *La société aux XIe et XIIe siècles dans la région mâconnaise* (Paris, 1953, reprinted 1971 [all citations here are to the latter]), p. 91. By contrast, it should be noted that Dhondt, *Principautés territoriales*, pp. 51, 165, 166, sees Lambert as tied to the Capetian house in Burgundy as does Duby, *Région mâconnaise*, p. 93. The latter, however, also maintains that Lambert "jouit en réalité dans son comté et dans ses domaines de l'Autunois méridional d'une entière liberté d'allure . . ." in 980. As we have seen (note 43 above) Lambert was already dead by 22 February 978. This fact somewhat disturbs Duby's all too smooth chronology of events which moves by decades and which he does not confuse by mentioning Geoffrey Greymantle. Geoffrey's appearance at Chalons can best be explained by Lothair's continued power to dispose of the county as he had done in 957. Duby's objections to the exercise of royal power in this matter are ill-conceived. It might be recalled in this context that King Lothair disposed of the vast holdings of Herbert of Vermandois as late as ca. 984 (Bur, *Comté de Champagne*, pp. 114–116) and that Hugh Capet granted Corbeil to Bouchard of Vendôme when the latter married Elizabeth, the widow of Count Aimo (Lot, *Derniers carolingiens*, p. 123, n.).

87 Bachrach, "Feudal Politics," p. 113 and Cf. Richard, *Comtes de Poitou*, I, 147.

88 *Cartul. de Saint-Aubin*, no. 85, for the recruitment of Alberic and for Geoffrey's difficulties with Odo I which can be seen clearly as early as March 977 *Cartul. de Saint-Aubin*, no. 3. For Odo's support for Conan of Rennes and the latter's invasion of Anjou seem to have taken place while Geoffrey was in the eastern part of *Francia* and awaiting the king (*Gesta Consulum*, p. 49, and the discussion as already developed in note 47, above, has the Angevin count at Orléans waiting for the king when the Bretons attack Angers). A modern scholarly study of Odo I is badly needed. Until one appears we must rely upon works that focus on his

son such as H. d'Arbois de Jubainville, *Histoire des ducs et comtes de Champagne depuis le VIe siècle jusqu'au milieu du XIIe siècle* (Paris, 1859), I, 187 ff.; J. Landsberger, *Graf Odo I von der Champagne (Odo II von Blois, Tours u Chartres)*, Inaugural dissertation (Berlin, 1878), pp. 17 ff; and Léonce Lex, *Eudes, comte de Blois, de Tours, de Chartres, de Troyes, et de Meaux (995–1037), et Thibaud son frère (995–1004)*, Troyes, 1892), pp. 205 ff. Some very useful material is to be found in Lot, *Derniers carolingiens*, pp. 432–433, for references and Lot, *Études sur le règne de Hugues Capet et la fin du Xe siècle*, pp. 471–472, for additional references.

[89] It should be noted that the viscounts of Thouars were of the same family as the castellans of Loudun during the early tenth century. This family held lands in and around both strongholds as well as along the twenty-five kilometer route between them. *V* Beech, "Viscounts of Thouars," pp. 28–29, who develops the prosopography here. In 937, Viscount Hatto of Tours came to an agreement with Hugh the Great by which the former gave up substantial holdings in Touraine in return for impressive holdings at Preuilly-sur-Claise where he had the right to build a stronghold. (Bib. Nat., Coll. Dom Housseau, vol. II.1, no. 166). In 1008, Acfredus who held the stronghold at Preuilly was one of Count Fulk Nerra's men (*HF*, X, p. 600 and Guillot, *Le comte*, I, 456). It is certainly possible that the *miles* Hatto who was one of Geoffrey Greymantle's *fideles* was related to Viscount Hatto and perhaps also to Viscount Acfredus (for Hatto in Geoffrey's entourage see *Cartul. de Saint-Aubin*, nos. 34, 38, 231). Port, *Dict . . . Maine-et-Loire*, II, 487, for Saumur and Halphen, *Le comté*, p. 19, for Chinon and Île-Bouchard.

[90] Lot, *Derniers carolingiens*, pp. 54, 108, notes that Lothair and Emma were married in late 965 or early 966. Louis, their first born, was thus barely thirteen years of age when he was associated in the kingship with his father. Louis would reach his fifteenth birthday late in 981 or early in 982; the exact date is not known. Concerning the role played by the queen in the arrangements see Richer, *Hist.*, Bk. III, ch. 93, with note 3 (p. 117) by the editor Latouche and the observations made by Lot, *Derniers carolingiens*, p. 126, n. 3. Richer, loc cit. permits the inference that negotiations were indirect. Adelaide was the mother of four children before her first husband Stephen died in 961 or shortly thereafter. If we assume that she was married at the earliest time favored by custom among the aristocracy at that time, i.e. when she was fifteen years of age, that during the next four years she had her four children she would have been about nineteen when the last one was born. The youngest child could have been born after Stephen's death in 961 and perhaps as late as 962. Taking all this into consideration it is unlikely that Adelaide was any less than thirty-eight years of age when Geoffrey Greymantle set his scheme in motion to have his sister marry young King Louis V. We do know that Adelaide was still fertile at this time (Lot, *Derniers carolingiens*, pp. 367–369) and indeed for several years thereafter. It would seem that if Lothair were to agree to the marriage he too would have to have been convinced that Adelaide was fertile. Cf. Fournial, "Lyonnais au Xe siècle," p. 448, n. 113. On the plan *v* Lot, *Derniers carolingiens*, pp. 126–127.

[91] *V* n. 74 above.

92 Lot, *Derniers carolingiens*, p. 127, concerning Lothair's plan. For Hugh *v* Richer, *Hist.,* Bk. III, chs. 89, 90, and the observations by the editor Latouche, p. 115, n. 1.

93 *Recueil des actes de Lothaire*, nos. 45, 46. Cf. Lot, *Derniers carolingiens*, p. 126, n. 3. for relations with Guifred. For the wedding Richer, *Hist.*, Bk. III, chs. 92–94, with the corrections by Lot, *Derniers carolingiens*, pp. 127–128, 367–368. However, Lot, loc. cit., p. 127, suggests that one of the bishops was Hugh, archbishop of Bourges; Hugh was the brother of Count Odo I and it would seem unlikely that Odo I's brother would be cooperating with Geoffrey.

94 Richer, *Hist.*, Bk. III, chs. 94–95. Cf. Lot, *Derniers carolingiens*, p. 197, for a somewhat different appreciation of Louis's character. Astronomer, *Vita Hludowici Imperatoris*, ed. G. Pertz, *MGH, SS*, II (Hannover, 1827), Bk. I, ch. 4, may provide the *topos* on dress. *V* Richer, *Hist.*, Bk. III, ch. 94, for the conjugal relations.

95 Richer, *Hist.*, Bk. III, ch. 95.

96 Ibid., and Lot, *Derniers carolingiens*, p. 129. For the poison see Ademar, *Chron.*, Bk. III, ch. 30, and the discussion by Lot, *Derniers carolingiens*, p. 166, n. 3, who nevertheless fails to see the fundamental anti-*Franci* bias in these southern sources.

97 Bur, *Comté de Champagne*, pp. 114–116, for the details. Bur, however, does not call attention to King Lothair's *parti-pris* in relation to the failure of the marriage.

98 *Chartes de Cluny*, ed. Bruel, no. 1537 (30 November 980) Hugh is not yet a cleric. In *Cartul. de Saint-Marcel*, no. 6, in which Hugh appears with Count Geoffrey, the youth is designated as a cleric. The chronology concerning Geoffrey's activities is provided by Boussard, "Notre-Dame de Loches," p. 8. In dating Hugh's removal from the succession and his apparent replacement by an Angevin it is of importance to remember that King Lothair had demonstrated both in 957 and in 978–979, when Geoffrey Greymantle married Adele and ruled the county, that the king had a role to play in legitimizing the succession. Thus it seems clear that some type of royal authority would have been exercised to support Geoffrey's plan to have Maurice recognized as heir in place of Hugh. By early 984 the marriage of Louis and Adelaide was ended, and King Lothair was hostile to the Angevins. Therefore the change in succession and the ordination of Hugh probably took place before the break between King Lothair and Geoffrey. *V Chartes de Cluny*, ed. Bruel, no. 1794, in which Maurice is styled *comes* but clearly is not yet fifteen years of age.

99 Lot, *Derniers carolingiens*, p. 129. C. Bouchard, "The Origins of the French Nobility: A Reassessment," *AHR*, 86 (1981), 516, n. 42, confuses Adelaide's marriage (*v*, above, n. 81). *Chartes de Cluny*, ed. Bruel, nos. 1474, 1701, 2484, and *Cartul. de Saint-Marcel*, no. 6, with regard to Geoffrey's gifts.

100 Lot, *Derniers carolingiens*, p. 234, n. 3.

101 René Poupardin, *Le royaume de Bourgogne (888–1038): étude sur les origines du royaume d'Arles* (Paris, 1907), pp. 97–100.

102 Richer, *Hist.*, Bk. III, ch. 95. We have already seen that the Angevin counts enjoyed a very close relationship with Abbot Odo (*v* above, n. 81). It may be added in this context that Odilo, Abbot Maiolus' close confidant and successor, had

close ties through his brother, Berardus, with Le Puy (*HGL*, III, 243) where
Adelaide's brother Guy was bishop. I think that it would be a mistake to underestimate the support that Cluny may have provided for the Angevins in the east
of Aquitaine.

[103] Poupardin, *Le royaume de Bourgogne*, p. 100, n. 3, makes clear that close relations
between William and Maiolus continued even after the former's marriage to
Adelaide. Constance, the daughter of Adelaide and Count William, never had
her legitimacy challenged although she became queen of France and was much
hated (*Miracula Sancti Benedicti*, ed. E. de Certain (Paris, 1858), Bk. VI, ch. 16,
and the discussion by Lot, *Derniers carolingiens*, pp. 338-369.

[104] Achille Luchaire, "Hugh de Clers et le 'de senescalcia Franciae'," *Bibliothèque de la
Faculté des lettres de Paris*, 3 (1897), 1-38; and Lot, *Hugues Capet*, pp. 197-198 for
the critique and in defense *v* Norgate, *Angevin Kings*, I, 140-142, who maintains
that the author of this text believed that Geoffrey had been given "a sort of carte-
blanche to take and keep anything he could get." The coincidence of Geoffrey's
close relations with King Lothair—the monarch supported the Angevin candi-
date for the see of Le Mans—and Geoffrey's close relations with his *senior*, Hugh
Capet, may well have operated so as to provide the Angevin count with the opportunity to advance his interests in Maine. For Geoffrey's relations with Lothair
v, above nn. 82, 85, and for his cooperation with Hugh Capet at Marçon in 987,
v Fulk le Réchin, *Hist. Andeg.*, p. 233 and Guillot, *Le comte*, I, 21.

[105] Bib. nat., coll. Balluze, vol. 76, fol. 256, and Bib. nat. coll. Dom. Housseau,
II.1, no. 358, provides an extract of the original.

[106] *Actus Pontificum Cenomannis in urbe degentium*, ed. G. Busson and A. Ledru (Le
Mans, 1902), p. 352, for the agreement where the Angevin count is called
"Fulco". This must be an error, however, because Count Fulk the Good died in
960 and his son Geoffrey Greymantle was count from 960-987. Seginfredus
became bishop of Le Mans no later than February 971 but not before 13
November 968. R. Latouche, *Histoire du comté du Maine pendant le Xe et le XIe siècle*
(Paris, 1910), p. 134, for Seginfredus and pp. 80-81, for the wars. *Actus Pont.*, p.
350, provides some important data on the relations. "Fragments de chartes," no.
21, has a witness list that includes some of the most important magnates of northern France. The first twelve witnesses following Hugh Capet and Girard, the
man who ordered the charter to be drawn up, are divided into four groups of
three men each, and Viscount Radulf is placed in Geoffrey Greymantle's group.
In addition, see Steven Fanning, "Les origines familiales de Vulgrin, Abbé de
Saint-Serge d'Angers (1046-1056) et Évêque du Mans (1056-1065) petit-fils du
vicomte Fulcrade de Vendôme," *La Province du Maine*, 82 (1980), 243-255, who
explores the family of Viscount Fulcradus of Vendôme, a *fidelis* of Geoffrey
Greymantle, who married his daughter to Hubert, one of the sons of the viscount
of Le Mans. The exact ties between the viscounts of Le Mans and the lords of
Bellême are less clear. *V* Jacques Boussard, "La seigneurie de Bellême aux Xe et
XIe siècles," *Mélanges d'histoire du moyen âge dédiés à la mémoire de Louis Halphen*
(Paris, 1951), 43-54, with the works cited there. For the strategic significance

of the house of Bellême on the frontiers of Normandy *v* Le Patourel, *Norman Empire*, p. 10.

[107] Latouche, *Comté du Maine*, p. 62, n. 13. It can be noted here that Geoffrey of Sablé is seen to be very influential in supporting Fulk Nerra's interests very shortly after Geoffrey Greymantle's death (*Cartul. de Saint-Aubin*, no. 85). For Geoffrey of Sablé's relationship to the viscount of Le Mans, i.e. his father and brother, who were viscounts of Le Mans, respectively, *v* Latouche, *Comté du Maine*, p. 128. Concerning Geoffrey of Sablé's place in the count's entourage *v*, *Cartul. de Saint-Aubin*, nos. 20, 34, 131, 281, 821; *Cartul. de Saint-Maurice*, no. 18; and "Fragments de chartes," no. 26. It is important that although Geoffrey certainly is not an uncommon name in Anjou during the later tenth and early eleventh centuries, two *fideles* named Geoffrey never appear in Count Geoffrey's entourage at the same time.

[108] Halphen, *Le comté*, p. 15, for le Lude and Chenu. The basic source, *Vie de Bouchard le Venerable comte de Vendôme, de Corbeil, de Melun et de Paris par Odo, moine de Saint-Maur-des-Fosses*, ed. Charles Bourel de la Roncière (Paris, 1982), was written about a half century after the count's death. The introduction by la Roncière is the best scholarly examination of the count's career but a new more detailed study is badly needed. With regard to relations between Geoffrey and Hugh Capet *v* Lot, *Derniers carolingiens*, pp. 126–127, and concerning Theobald see, above, note 45.

[109] Bachrach, "Fulk Nerra and his accession as Count," pp. 334–335. Renaud was made chancellor by Hugh Capet in 988 and bishop of Paris in 992. Lot, *Hugues Capet*, p. 229, n. 2 and *V. Domni Burcardi*, intro., p. xii. Bouchard was an aging and very pious widower at this time and it is not likely that he contemplated yet another marriage. *V* the discussion by Guillot, *Le comte*, I, 21–22 and esp. n. 7.

[110] For Viscount Fulcradus *v*, in general, Fanning, "Les origines familiales de Vulgrin," pp. 250–253. The name Fulcradus was not a common one in Anjou and its environs during the period of Geoffrey's countship and it was sometimes the case that a person's title such as that of viscount was omitted in a particular document. It is perhaps possible that the *nobilis* Fulcradus who appeared in Geoffrey's entourage as early as 972 or the very powerful *miles* who appears in 973 (*Cartul. de Saint-Aubin*, nos. 20, 131) is to be identified with the count's *fidelis* Fulcradus who appears with him in 978 or the count's *procer* who appears almost a decade later ("Fragments de Chartes," no. 26 and *Cartul. de Saint-Aubin*, no. 211). If this important man named Fulcradus (perhaps there was more than one, but two men named Fulcradus never appear in Geoffrey's entourage at the same time) is not to be identified with the viscount then he may perhaps have been one of the viscount's relatives.

[111] *Livre des serf de Marmoutier*, no. 1. Those members of Geoffrey's entourage who have been discussed already or will be discussed below who accompanied the count were: Joscelin (of Rennes), Ascelinus, Guenno (of Nouâtre), Odulgerius, Fulcoius, Frotmundus, Burchardus, Erneisus, and Witbertus. For the marriage and for the association *v* Bachrach, "Fulk Nerra and his accession as Count," pp. 331–342.

[112] For Geoffrey at Marçon *v* the evidence cited by Halphen, *Le comté*, p. 8, n. 6, and for the identification of Odo the Red as one of Odo I's men *v* Guillot, *Le comte*, I, 21–22; and for Hugh Capet at Marçon, *Cartulaire blésois de Marmoutier*, ed. Ch Métais (Chartres-Blois, 1891), no. 4, shows Odo I restoring a *villa* to Marmoutier and among his *fideles* listed there is Count Geoffrey. It is not impossible, only unlikely that in the year 985 Odo I and Geoffrey were still maintaining peaceful relations. However, it is far more likely that the witness list, like the *datum*-clause, of this document which only survives in a nineteenth-century copy (Bib. nat., Coll. D. Houss., vol. I,1, no. 231) was poorly transmitted. Geoffrey, viscount of Châteaudun, was a close supporter of Odo I and is the likely *fidelis* mentioned here.

[113] Werner, "Untersuchungen zur Frühzeit," pp. 269–270, and *Gesta Consulum*, p. 30, *Historia Sancti Florentii Salmurensis*, pp. 230, 276, ed. P. Marchegay and E. Mabille in *Chroniques des églises d'Anjou (CEA)*, (Paris, 1869), provides two traditions concerning Saumur and both seem to be in error: 1) Count Theobald of Blois is said to have held Saumur as early as 937 and 2) Theobald's family is said to have held Saumur from the early sixth century. Halphen, *Le comté*, p. 14, n. 2, accepts the former and n. 3, rejects the latter. As late as 958, however, Count Fulk the Good seems to have exercised substantial power at Saumur (Archives de Maine-et-Loire, H. 3715, fols. 27v–28r which is a thirteenth-century copy from a lost original and may not have been transmitted in a perfectly accurate manner). According to this document the monks of Saint Florent examined several royal charters and learned that they had an exemption from vicarial rights that were being exercised by both Fulk and Theobald. At the instigation of Fulk, who ordered that the charter cited above be made, the counts ostensibly agreed to recognize the abovementioned exemptions. It must be remembered in this context that Saumur was well within both the Carolingian *pagus* of Anjou and within the dioceses of Angers (Michel Dupont, *Monographie du cartulaire de Bourgueil* (Tours, 1962), p. 6). For the titles Werner, "Untersuchungen zur Frühzeit," pp. 283, 285. *V* also, *V. Odonis*, Bk. I, chs. 11, 18, 21. Of this text Oury, "La situation juridique," p. 554, says: "la valeur historique est hors de conteste" and goes on to use the data concerning Odo's relations with Fulk the Red as the basis for this discussion. For Fulk's land acquisitions *v* Bib. nat. Coll. Baluze, vol. 76, fol. 256. For the brothers as canons, *v* Guillot, *Le comte*, I, 70; the more general observations by Southern, *Middle Ages*, pp. 82–83; and concerning the office of treasurer Jacques Boussard, "Le trésorier de Saint-Martin de Tours," *Revue d'histoire de l'église de France*, 47 (1961), 76.

[114] *V* the extent of the evidence developed by Werner, "Untersuchungen zur Frühzeit," p. 264 ff., which demonstrates the great variety of Angevin possessions. Concerning Count Theobald *v* above n. 32. Cf. Mary S. Woodward, "Archbishop and Count: Rivals for the Touraine in the Tenth Century," Ph.D. dissertation (Syracuse University, 1977), pp. 45 ff., who sees the conflict as existing between Theobald (count, but earlier viscount) and the archbishops of Tours. Her researches do not give sufficient attention to Bib. nat., n.a. lat. 1930, which indicates *passim* the cooperation of Archbishop Arduin and the counts of

Blois. *V* Boussard, "L'origine des comtés," pp. 104–112, who takes good advantages of these documents. On the basis of the material discussed in note 113, above, I would suggest the hypothesis that Fulk the Good gave possession of Saumur to Theobald in ca. 952 in exchange for the hand of the latter's sister in marriage and control over the territory of Nantes that went with it (*v* also above notes 33–36). In a previous study (Bachrach, "Abbot Robert," p. 123) I accepted the arguments of Oury, "Reconstruction monastique," p. 70, n. 5. He relies on *Hist. S. Florent.*, p. 241, n. 1, in which the editor Marchegay relies upon *Gallia Christiana*, 14, col. 621, which is itself based upon a conjecture. Concerning Theobald's acquisition of the comital title at Tours *v* the texts cited by Woodward, "Touraine in the Tenth Century," p. 51, n. 13; and with regard to the establishment of Arduin see Boussard, "Les évêques en Neustrie," pp. 172–173.

115 Except for the Angevin stronghold at Amboise, the count of Blois was very strongly positioned between Tours in the west and Blois in the east. *V* Boussard, "L'origine des comtés," pp. 98–104. Concerning the westward thrust, for example, the document published by Halphen, *Le comté*, pp. 345–346. With regard to matters at Saint-Florent-le-Vieil see René de Lamothe-Dreuzy, "Saint-Florent-le-Vieil des origines à 1500," *Bulletin de l'Académie des Sciences et Belles-Lettres d'Angers*, ser. 9, 2 (1968), 69–77, who provides a useful introduction to some of the important problems. It should also be emphasized here that Theobald's sister was countess of Nantes (*v*, above, n. 34).

116 Concerning the balance of power in the Touraine cf. Woodward "Archbishop and Count," pp. 45 ff.

117 Halphen, *Le comté*, p. 16, discusses developments at Baugé and *v* Boussard, "Le trésorier de Saint-Martin," p. 76 and Bib. nat., Coll. Baluze, vol. 76, fol. 256 with regard to Noyant. Concerning Morand and Semblançay Halphen, *Le comté*, p. 15, and *Gesta Consulum*, p. 48. *V* also Dupont, *Monographie*, pp. 2–3, discusses the route from Angers to Tours. *Hist. S. Florent.*, p. 275, provides a fair idea of the strategic importance of the stronghold of Saumur.

118 *Cartul. de Saint-Aubin*, no. 211 and Bachrach, "Fulk Nerra and his accession as Count," p. 334, for the date.

119 Geoffrey always indicated exemptions by charter and without a charter no exemption was valid. (*V*, e.g., *Cartul. de Saint-Aubin*, nos. 21, 22). Even when Geoffrey had already given a blanket exemption as in the grants cited above for lands already in the possession of the beneficiary, the grant of a new holding necessitated a new act in which the exemption was recorded. (*Cartul. de Saint-Aubin*, no. 34), and clearly the beneficiary saw the need for a new document. These exemptions it may be noted were made and held at the count's pleasure and could be revoked as he saw fit (compare *Cartul. de Saint-Aubin*, nos. 21, 22 with nos. 23, 24, 25). However, compare the remarks by Guillot, *Le comté*, II, 277–278.

120 In addition to the example discussed above see *Cartul. de Saint-Aubin*, no. 224. For Geoffrey's policy on this point concerning St. Julien *v* "Fragments de chartes," no. 26. Note that Geoffrey made these grants or more accurately confirmed

these grants in January 978 after his alliance with the count of Blois may be considered to have broken down. With regard to Geoffrey's position concerning Cormery see *Cartul. de Cormery*, no. 47. For the nature and exercise of vicarial rights see Jacques Boussard, "Le droit de *vicaria* à la lumière de quelques documents angevins et tourangeaux," *Études de civilization médiévale: mélanges efferts à Edmond-René Labande* (Poitiers, 1974), 39–54, who provides a useful overview of *vicarii* and vicarial rights with a comprehensive review of the important scholarly literature. Concerning spiritual matters *v Cartul. de Saint-Aubin*, no. 244, where Geoffrey Greymantle sees the restoration as benefiting the souls of his parents and his brother as well as his own soul and *Cartul. de Cormery*, no. 47, where Geoffrey indicates that those who provide material aid to the holy places in this world will receive their rewards by being the heirs of God's kingdom. *N.b.* we know that the monastic recipients of these acts were responsible for drawing up the charters, but we must assume that the sentiments expressed above would not have met with strong objection from the count.

[121] R. Ranjard, *La touraine archéologique*, 5th edit. (Tours, 1971), pp. 129–130 and Frederic Lesueur, *Le château d'Amboise* (Paris, 1935), pp. 7–9, provide a survey of the early history. For the Angevin presence see *Gesta Consulum*, pp. 30–31. Werner, "Untersuchungen zur Frühzeit," p. 273 and Devailly, *Le Berry*, p. 130. The military topography is provided by *Gesta Consulum*, pp. 30–31.

[122] For Châteauneuf see *Gest Consulum*, p. 45.

[123] Ibid. Halphen, *Le comté*, p. 158, asserts that Landry was from Châteaudun. In *Gesta Consulum* (p. 47), however, Châteaudun is rendered *Castrum Dunum*. Landry is styled *Dunensis* which is more likely to be Dun-sur-Auron (Lat. *Dunensis*) in Berry which from later sources we can identify as within the Angevin *mouvance* (Devailly, *Le Berry*, p. 610, for references). Châteaudun by contrast with Dunsur-Auron was firmly in Blésois hands.

[124] *Gesta Ambaz. Dominorum*, pp. 87–132, provides a useful repository of information on the fortifications.

[125] Concerning these fortifications and strategy *v* Bachrach "Angevin Strategy," pp. 555–556.

[126] Ibid., p. 556.

[127] Ibid., p. 541.

[128] It should be made clear in this context that the use of marriage alliances was not in any way an Angevin innovation and certainly not an innovation by Geoffrey Greymantle whose family had employed this technique long before his accession to the countship. *V* Bachrach, "The Idea of the Angevin Empire," pp. 295–296.

[129] Thietmar of Mercerburg's remark (Bk. VII, ch. 30) concerning Otto-William of Burgundy, Geoffrey's later contemporary: "Willehelmus comes . . . miles est regis, nisi is, dominus in re . . ." would serve as a fitting description of the Angevin count in relation to King Lothair after 984 and generally in regard to William Iron Arm (*Chronicon.* ed. and trans. W. Trillmich [Darmstadt, 1957]).

[130] Guillot has taken the position that Carolingian institutions survived in Anjou through the tenth century and that Geoffrey Greymantle was "un personage

encore carolingien" (*Le comté*, I, 2). But Guillot does not develop the evidence in detail that might support this assertion. When scholars have examined the evidence in great detail within the framework of particular institutions (Duby, "L'Evolution des institutions judicaires," *Le Moyen Age*, 52 [1946], 149–194; and 53 [1947], 15–38. Robert Fossier, *La terre et les hommes en Picardie* [Louvain, 1968], pp. 480–510; and J. Yver, "Les premières institutions du duché de Normandie," *SSCI* [1968], 299–366), they have not been very successful in proving continuity. The notion that tenth-century counts (and dukes) took over Carolingian institutions "at once and more or less intact" to use Le Patourel's wording "is a process which cannot be demonstrated and, in the conditions of the early tenth century, is scarcely credible" (*Norman Empire*, p. 4, n. 1). That Geoffrey Greymantle exercised powers that modern scholars have been able to identify as similar to powers exercised by a Carolingian count is not the issue — it is clear that he did — but this is not the same as proving that these powers were perceived by contemporaries as being Carolingian powers, as being possessed as the result of a continuous process, and as legitimate. Nor does this prove that Geoffrey Greymantle was obeyed because perhaps some people may have believed that Geoffrey was "un personnage encore carolingien." Cf. Werner, "Kingdom and Principality in Twelfth-Century France," in *Medieval Nobility*, ed. and trans. Timothy Reuter (Amsterdam: Elsevier, 1978), pp. 241–290.

The case for continuity in Geoffrey's lands is no worse than for that in many other parts of the Carolingian empire but it is clear that Geoffrey did a great deal more with what was at his disposal than did many of his contemporaries. To lose sight of the individual who influences the course of events, indeed the man who may cause events to happen, is to ignore the essential part of history.

[131] Cf. Guillot, *Le comte*, I, 149–150.

[132] *Cartul. de Saint-Aubin*, no. 38.

[133] Boussard, "Notre-Dame de Loches," pp. 7–8.

[134] *Cartul. de Saint-Aubin*, no. 2; *Cartul. de Cormery*, no. 47; and "Fragments de chartes," no. 26.

[135] *Cartul. de Saint-Aubin*, no. 20.

[136] Ibid., no. 131. Walther Kienast, *Der Herzogstitel in Frankreich und Deutschland (9. bis 12. Jahrhundert)*, (Munich-Vienna, 1968), apparently did not find this example.

[137] Boussard, "Notre-Dame de Loches," pp. 7–8, with Boussard's discussion of Fulk and Maurice as being present when the act was given. The use of the term *generositas* enabled Geoffrey to emphasize two important points with a single word. The general meaning of *generositas* as nobility or high standing (by birth) is confounded with the notion of excellence, boldness, and courage. In short, *generositas* embodies many of the positive characteristics that a leader might desire in one of his followers without being so specific as to exclude a worthy supporter who was not of high standing by birth but nevertheless was a bold and brave *miles*. The use of the term *ingenui* to modify *milites* in a particular context in the same act would appear to convey a different meaning and may suggest that Geoffrey had *milites* in his entourage who were not of the highest class.

[138] Boussard, "Notre-Dame de Loches," pp. 7–8.

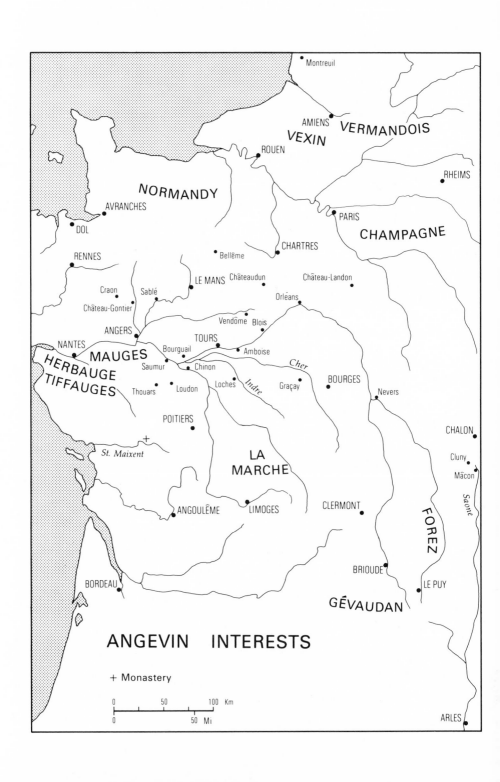

Montreuil

AMIENS VERMANDOIS
VEXIN
RHEIMS
ROUEN
NORMANDY
AVRANCHES
PARIS CHAMPAGNE
DOL
CHARTRES
RENNES Bellême
LE MANS Châteaudun Château-Landon
Craon Sablé Orléans
Château-Gontier Vendôme Blois
ANGERS TOURS
NANTES Bourguail Amboise
MAUGES Saumur Chinon Cher
HERBAUGE Thouars Loudon Loches Indre Graçay BOURGES
TIFFAUGES Nevers
POITIERS CHALON
+ Cluny
St. Maixent Mâcon
LA
MARCHE
Saône
ANGOULÊME LIMOGES CLERMONT FOREZ
BRIOUDE
BORDEAU LE PUY
GÉVAUDAN

ANGEVIN INTERESTS

+ Monastery

0   50   100 Km
0   50 Mi

ARLES

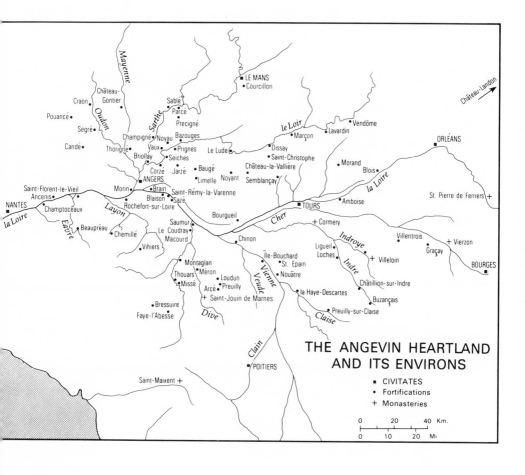

THE ANGEVIN HEARTLAND
AND ITS ENVIRONS

■ CIVITATES
• Fortifications
+ Monasteries

0   20   40 Km.
0   10   20 Mi

THE FLORENTINE RULING GROUP UNDER THE *"GOVERNO POPOLARE,"* 1494–1512

Roslyn Pesman Cooper
University of Sydney

THE FLORENTINE RULING GROUP UNDER THE *"GOVERNO POPOLARE,"* 1494–1512*

In recent years, a number of studies have been devoted to an analysis of the structure and composition of the ruling circles in Florence in the late fourteenth and fifteenth centuries.[1] These studies suggest that the victory of the *arti maggiori* in the 1380s rather than the triumph of the party of Cosimo de' Medici in 1434 was a major watershed in Florentine political and social history.[2] In 1382 the members of the *arti minori* were relegated to a minority position in Florentine government and to a diminishing presence in the ruling group.[3] Thereafter, two trends emerge: the one towards expansion at the base of government with an increasing number of citizens from the *arti maggiori* being rendered eligible for major office, the other towards contraction at the apex.[4] This latter trend, manifest in the growing presence of elite groups within and without the framework of the formal government structure, culminated after 1480 in the Medicean *Consiglio dei Settanta*, if not in the handful of men around the head of the regime.[5]

Fourteen years after the introduction of the *Settanta*, the Medici were driven from Florence.[6] The extent to which the anti-Medicean revolution of November-December 1494 altered the basic configuration and patterns of Florentine politics is one of the central problems of the historiography of the closing decades of the Republic, and of the transition to the principate. The present study confronts the particular problem of the impact of this revolution on the composition of ruling circles. It has usually been argued that the dismantling of the Medicean régime and the establishment of the *governo popolare* resulted in a significant change both in the composition of the ruling group and in the distribution of power.[7] A more comprehensive analysis of council membership and office holding over the period 1495–1512 suggests that this view requires radical revision. The constitutional reforms of December 1494 led to little change in the composition of the Florentine political class or in its inner circles of position and influence.

71

Far from opening up the class of politically enfranchised citizens to new men, the introduction of the *Consiglio Maggiore* was in effect a *serrata*. These conclusions have implications for our understanding of both the political struggles of the period and the contemporary vocabulary of political and social classification. They also provide a new perspective on the issue of political mobility in fifteenth-century Florence.

The eventual outcome of the rejection of Piero de' Medici was indeed the largest and most open régime that Florence had hitherto experienced. Sovereignty was vested in a new institution, the *Consiglio Maggiore*, and some three-and-a-half thousand citizens were eligible for membership of that Council.[8] Whereas by the late fifteenth century the traditional Councils of the *Comune* and the *Popolo* had been rendered ineffectual, and major legislative enactments finished in the Medicean innovation of the *Consiglio dei Cento*, after 1494 all bills, including those pertaining to taxation and state finance, required the assent of two thirds of those present in the *Consiglio Maggiore*.[9] Whereas under the Medici the selection of major officeholders had been manipulated and controlled, the electoral processes of the new régime rendered all members of the *Consiglio Maggiore* equally eligible for office.[10] The dismantling of the Medicean institutions allowed the traditional offices of government headed by the *Signoria* to reassume their customary authority, initiative and independence. And, perhaps most important of all, with the abolition of the *Consiglio dei Settanta*, there was no longer an institutional place for an elite to hold a monopoly over effective power.[11]

Many of those involved in the coup against Piero de' Medici had not intended that their action should result in such extensive constitutional change.[12] Their aims had been fulfilled by the more moderate and restricted reforms of 2 December 1494 which amounted to the abolition of the Medicean innovations and a return to the situation which was thought to have prevailed before 1434. Further reform embodied in the legislation of December 22–23 had been forced upon the architects of the coup by popular pressure and by their own quarrels and disagreements as to what form of government best met their individual ideologies, private interests, and ambitions.

There seems little doubt that some redistribution of power took place with the establishment of the *governo popolare*. Certainly one aspect of the political struggles after 1494 was the attempt on the part of some citizens to reform the constitutional structure in a more oligarchic direction, to render it *più stretto*. Contemporary commentators presented these struggles in social terms as between *nobili* or *grandi*, and *popolani, primi cittandini* and *cittadini mediocri* or *mezzani*, *uomini di più cervello* or *qualità* and *uomini di meno cervello* and *qualità*.[13] But the crucial problem is the extent of the redistribution of power and among which social groups and families, their branches and members it took place.

The answer to the problem of whether or to what extent the establishment of the *governo popolare* resulted in the entry of new social groups and families into the governing circles of Florence depends in some measure on what is understood by ruling group. The model adopted by historians to define and describe the Florentine political community is that of a series of concentric circles or levels of participation and power.[14] The widest circle of the formal political structure, the *uomini da reggimento*, has been identified with those citizens who were eligible for the offices of the *tre maggiori*, that is the Signoria and its two advisory Colleges, the *Dodici Buonuomini* and *Sedici Gonfalonieri*.[15] Within this circle there was an inner group of *uomini principali*, those who occupied the important offices of decision making and administration. But the officeholding and power were not necessarily coincident and contemporaries and later historians concur in the view that always in Florence effective power rested with a much smaller elite group, at its outer perimeter institutionalised for the first time in the Medicean *Consiglio dei Settanta*. This model has been adopted in the present study which proceeds to an examination of the composition of the ruling group after 1494 in three parts. The political class of enfranchised citizens is identified with the membership of the *Consiglio Maggiore* and the inner oligarchy with the membership of the *Consiglio degli Ottanta*, the smaller council established alongside the *Consiglio Maggiore* in December 1494. While the *Consiglio degli Ottanta* was intended by some of the citizens involved in the drawing up of the new constitutional structure as an elitist institution, it did not develop as such. The last section of this paper is concerned with the problem of the identification of those who occupied a position at the centre of Florentine government and politics. At all three levels discussion is confined to the members of the *arti maggiori*.[16]

The *Consiglio Maggiore* — The Political Class

I

The political class is identified with the members of the *Consiglio Maggiore*. All and in effect only members of the Council were eligible for office.[17] By laying down fixed criteria for membership of the Council, the laws of December 22–23, 1494 served legally to define the Florentine political class for the first time in its history. They also rendered its structure more oligarchic. In the past, eligibility for office had been determined in periodic scrutinies.[18] While the scrutiny procedures had been increasingly weighted in favour of continuity in the composition of the political class,[19] it was only with the creation of the *Consiglio Maggiore* that membership became by law both permanent and hereditary. It also became visible.[20]

In seeking a new constitutional structure at the end of 1494, the Florentines had looked to the example of Venice for guidance and inspiration,[21] and with the introduction of their *Consiglio Maggiore*, they were following in the footsteps of the Venetians in creating a legally defined and hereditary political class. As will be suggested later, they were also effecting their *serrata*. Florence had indeed been moving in this direction for over a century. For this reason the Venetian example was particularly relevant. There were differences, however, between the Florentine and Venetian Councils, most obviously in the presence in the former of the artisans and tradesmen of the *arti minori*, albeit in a disadvantaged position in respect to officeholding although not to legislation. The presence of the *arti minori* derived from the criteria for membership of the Council, criteria which were the product of Florentine traditions and Florentine experience.[22]

The criteria for membership of the *Consiglio Maggiore* were that a citizen be of legitimate birth, be over 29 years of age, free of tax debt, and possess the *beneficio*, that is, either he himself or an ancestor in the direct male line over three generations had been *seduto* or *veduto* for the *tre maggiori*.[23] The *seduti* were those citizens who had occupied a position in the *Signoria* or *Collegi*, the *veduti* were those whose names had been drawn but who were disqualified from taking up the office because of arrears in taxation payments, youth or the *divieto* regulations which disallowed successive occupancy of office or the presence of more than a specified number of members of a family in office at the same time.[24] The *seduti* and the *veduti* and their political heirs, the *beneficiati*, had come in the fifteenth century to constitute a privileged inner circle within the political class.[25] They received preferential treatment in the scrutinies and provided the personnel for various special councils. Their position was confirmed and amplified in 1494 when they were given a monopoly over formal political participation. In this respect, the establishment of the *Consiglio Maggiore* was a restrictive step, in that participation in government was now confined to citizens who had enjoyed a privileged position in the fifteenth-century ruling group and their descendants. Thus membership of the ruling group after 1494 was based on an hereditary principle, and it was his family's past record which gave a citizen his entrée.

The membership of the *Consiglio Maggiore* will be discussed in terms of families, understood as *consorterie*. Recent work on earlier regimes has emphasised "that the constitution, laws and electoral machinery which defined and regulated the ruling group assumed that the basic entity of

Florentine political life was the *consorteria.*"[26] The laws governing electoral procedures in the *Consiglio Maggiore* forbade those drawn as electioneers to nominate "nè loro nè alchuno loro consorto" and required abstention from voting by all members of a *consorteria* when one of their number was nominated for office.[27] The traditional *divieto* provisions continued to apply after 1494, and thus no more than two members per *consorteria* could sit simultaneously in the *Consiglio degli Ottanta* — a regulation which was rigorously applied.[28] Some aspects of the *divieto* regulations worried one of the more conservative reformers in 1494. Piero Capponi, himself a member of one of the largest *consorterie*, was critical of practices which prevented a citizen from accepting election to an important office because of the presence of his relatives in minor ones.[29] He was further disturbed by the possibility that, given the original decision to divide the Council into three sessions should the number of *beneficiati* exceed 1500, any one session might include all members of a *consorteria*. To remove this possibility, the legislation establishing the Council laid down that "nella tracta di tali consigli s'abbia riguardo che non vi concorra in una casa o famiglia più che il terzo o metà."[30] In view of this evidence it does seem legitimate to discuss the composition of the *Consiglio Maggiore* in terms of family blocs.[31]

When the lists of citizens eligible for the *Consiglio Maggiore* were drawn up, there appears to have been surprise at its size — some 3,500 citizens.[32] The size of the Council is not so surprising to later historians who, unlike contemporaries, have access to the results of the scrutinies. It has been estimated that by the mid-fifteenth century those eligible for the *tre maggiori* already numbered between 2,500 and 3,000 citizens.[33] Thus while the political class after 1494 was the largest that Florence had hitherto experienced, the increase in size was proportionally not very great. At the time when discussions for the new constitutional structure were taking place in Florence, some of the more conservative participants had wanted membership of the new Council restricted to the *seduti* and their descendants in the belief that this would be a smaller and more homogeneous group.[34] And it has been suggested that it was the admission of the *veduti* and their *beneficiati* which enlarged the ruling group and altered its social composition.[35] But it appears that the restriction of membership of the Council to the *seduti* and their *beneficiati* would have reduced its size by less than ten percent.[36] Nor were the most recently arrived individuals and families conspicuous among those whose *beneficio* came from merely being *veduti*. The *veduti* and their *beneficiati* came from a wide variety of families who in most cases also had *seduti* in their ranks. Thus it seems likely that at the level of the family the *seduti* and *veduti* were virtually the same group despite the Medicean practice of having names drawn "solo per far verdere."[37]

While new families continued to be qualified for the *tre maggiori* after the mid-fifteenth century, the main factors in the increase in the size of the ruling group with the creation of the *Consiglio Maggiore* appear to have been the admission of *all* the *beneficiati* of the *seduti* and the *veduti* and the extension of the *beneficio* back over *three* generations. Although the growth in the size of the ruling group in the fifteenth century was largely the product of the qualification of more members of established families, the observation made by Piero Guicciardini on the 1484 scrutiny that larger families suffered some discrimination has been borne out by studies on the results of the scrutinies.[38] No such discrimination operated for the *Consiglio Maggiore*. Whereas the Rucellai had 22 members qualified in the scrutiny of 1433, there were 41 Rucellai in the *Consiglio Maggiore* in 1508.[39] The membership of the Altoviti had risen from 13 in 1433 to 43 in 1508, that of the Pitti from 22 to 41, and of the Albizzi from 22 to 41.

Contributing also to the size of the *Consiglio Maggiore* was the decision to admit those whose *beneficio* derived from as far back as their great-grandfathers. This decision was the result of the desire or need to meet the claims to membership in the Council of the enemies of the Medici, and particularly of the families of the "vecchio stato," subject to exile and political discrimination from 1434.[40] The full reabsorption of these families served to enlarge the size of the ruling group.[41] Thus while the Strozzi had only one member qualified in the scrutiny of 1453, there were 44 Strozzi in the *Consiglio Maggiore*. The Baldovinetti who had one member qualified in 1453 and the Ardinghelli, who had no success at all, each had eight members in 1508. Designed to encompass the families of the "vecchio stato," the acceptance of a *beneficio* which derived from as far back as three generations also served to include in the membership of the *Consiglio Maggiore* the descendants of any citizen who had been *venduto* or *seduto* during the preceding century, including those whose presence in the ruling group had been fleeting or who came from families in decline.

One source from which the increase in the size of the political class did not flow in any significant way was the admission of new members to the Council after its establishment. The periodic scrutinies of the previous regimes had provided the opportunity for citizens whose families had not participated in the ruling group in the past to be nominated and qualified for the *tre maggiori*. If they were then drawn for a position in the *Signoria* or *Collegi*, they entered the ranks of the *veduti* and *seduti*, and their descendants, the ranks of the *beneficiati*. The establishment of the *Consiglio Maggiore* was followed by the abolition of the scrutiny as an institution in 1495 when it was decided to fill the new *borse* with the names of the members of the Council only.[42]

While possession of the *beneficio* was the prerequisite for entry into the *Consiglio Maggiore*, the legislation which set up the Council did provide for the admission of *non beneficiati* both at the time of its introduction and in the future.[43] Thus in theory membership of the Council was not closed. However, the implementation of these provisions does suggest that with the establishment of the *Consiglio Maggiore*, the Florentines were in fact closing their ruling group.[44]

The admission of certain groups of citizens at the beginning of 1495 was essentially a tidying-up process.[45] The intention was partly to preserve continuity with the past by admitting those citizens without the *beneficio* who had been successful in the 1484 scrutiny or who had been selected for the Councils of the *Comune* and the *Popolo* at the beginning of December 1494 before the more sweeping reforms later in the month replaced these Councils with the *Consiglio Maggiore*. In addition, the first two Signorie of 1495 were empowered to admit citizens from lists prepared by the *Sedici Gonfalonieri*.[46] This measure was designed to provide for the inclusion of citizens who had lost the *beneficio* "per antichità o altra cagione." Piero Vaglienti, among those admitted by the Signoria, argued that this group was confined to "chi avessi paghato cento anni o più le graveze di Firenze,"[47] and the majority of those admitted appear to have been from families established in Florence as taxpayers for a very long period. Just over one third were members of old magnate families, and all but about twenty of the remainder had relatives with the *beneficio*.[48]

The establishment of the *Consiglio Maggiore* was not a single event but a process worked out over four years.[49] Thus there was further legislation on its membership. The direction of this legislation appears to have been towards restricting the entry of new families into the ruling group. In February 1497, when Francesco Valori was *Gonfaloniere*, the *Signoria* moved to expel the *non beneficiati* from the *Consiglio Maggiore*, including those groups specifically admitted by the legislation of 22–23 December 1494.[50] This step was, however, directed only against new men, the *non beneficiati* who enjoyed the "beneficio di chi fussi seduti a tre maggiori nella loro famiglia o consorteria" were exempted from the purge.[51] To further ensure the exclusion of the Medici protegees, those *non-beneficiati* who had been successful in the 1484 scrutiny or who had been members of the Councils of the *Comune* or the *Popolo* had to show evidence that their ancestors had been taxpayers in Florence for at least fifty years.[52] The dismissed members could apply for readmission to the Council, success depending on an acceptance vote from half those present plus one. Between the following March and June, 36 citizens applied for readmission of whom 29 were successful, 20 from the *arti maggiori*.[53] In that the *Consiglio Maggiore* itself was now deciding whether those without the *beneficio* admitted prior to its establishment should remain, the Council was assuming control over its own membership.[54] Whereas in the immediate past, mobility had been controlled from above, it was now being controlled from below, by the whole political class.

The legislation on the admission of *non beneficiati* in December 1494 had declared that their position would be the same as that of other members of the Council, and those readmitted in 1497 were to enjoy "tutti quegli beneficii e privelegi come hanno gli altri cittandini fiorentini habili al consiglio in tutto et per tutto."[55] In July of the following year, however, the *non beneficiati* were placed in a disadvantaged position. The regulations for the new *borse* from which offices were to be filled decreed that those whose *beneficio* was "nella consorteria per linea traversale et non per linea recta" were to be given only one *polizza* regardless of their age and that those who had been "habilitati a decto consiglio et non hanno tale beneficio non sieno imborsati per poliza alcuna."[56] If the *non beneficiati* were subsequently elected to and occupied a position in the *tre maggiori*, they were then to be accorded the number of *polizze* commensurate with their age. The replacement of election by sortition for the filling of the *tre maggiori* in 1499 meant that the *non beneficiati* were permanently placed at a disadvantage or disqualified from office holding, and presumably too, that their descendants would be excluded from the Council.[57]

The laws which established the *Consiglio Maggiore* also set up the procedures for the admission of new members in the future. Every three years, beginning in 1497, 45 citizens from the *arti maggiori* and 15 from the *minori* could be nominated and voted upon in the Council for admission.[58] In February 1497 another avenue was opened up for citizens who merited membership, "o per la qualità degli antichi loro o per loro virtù."[59] In March or April every year, 28 citizens drawn as electioneers could each propose a citizen to the Council for membership. A favourable vote from half the members plus one was necessary for acceptance. But this *provvisione* also served to restrict the group of potential members. In the past to be eligible for office a citizen had to show evidence that either he himself or certain members of his family had been taxpayers in Florence for thirty years.[60] The requirement placed on the *non beneficiati* admitted to the Council via the 1484 scrutiny or membership of the Councils of the *Comune* and the *Popolo*, that they themselves or their direct ancestors have paid taxes for fifty years, was now applied to all aspiring members of the Council.

Under the laws of 22–23 December 1494 and 1 February 1497, it was theoretically possible for over seven hundred *non beneficiati* to enter the Council between 1497 and 1512. Only 39 were admitted of whom 28 were from the *arti maggiori*.[61] The records suggest that on two occasions only did new members enter the Council under the legislation of December, 1494. The remainder were admitted under the tighter provisions of 1497 which appear to have virtually replaced the earlier legislation on the admission of new members. Just under half of the *non beneficiati* accepted from the *arti maggiori* were from the magnate houses of Adimari Bardi, Buondelmonte, Cavalcanti, Manelli, Rossi and Tornaquinci. Six were from families with other members in the Council.[62] Only ten appear to be from families without the *beneficio*, of whom three had had members in the Signoria in the past for the *arti minori*.[63] After 1505 only one new family was accorded membership of the Council for the *arti maggiori*.

Jacopo Pitti argued that one reason why so few citizens were elected to the Council was the low quality of the candidates proposed for admission; *clientelismo* and hostility towards the régime often led to the nomination of base persons.[64] But whatever the motivation behind the nomination of citizens for the Council, the failure of more than a handful to be accepted does suggest that by the first decade of the sixteenth century, the political class in Florence was virtually being closed to newcomers.

If the *Consiglio Maggiore* was reluctant to admit new members, it was equally unwilling to open the Signoria to families who had not had priors elected in the past. Selection for a position in the Republic's highest magistracy marked the political arrival of a family, and Florentines dated their participation in the public life of the Republic from the time of the presence of the first member of the family in the Signoria.[65] Between 1495 and 1501 five citizens, two from the *arti maggiori* and three from the *minori*, were the first of their families to sit as priors.[66] After 1501 no citizen without previous priors in his family entered the Signoria. Mobility into the Signoria was in fact far more restricted during the period of the *governo popolare* than it had been even in the later years of the previous regime. Between 1478 and 1494, some fifty-one priors were the first in their families to sit in the Signoria.[67] The restored Medici regime, 1512–1527, was to admit some twenty new families.[68] That no citizens from families without previous priors entered the Signoria after 1501 suggests that access to the Republic's highest magistracy was also being closed under the *governo popolare*.

II

The *Consiglio Maggiore* has rightly been described as the "quintessential embodiment of the fifteenth century *reggimento*."[69] Thus its membership provides evidence on some aspects of political and social developments in Florence. An analysis of the compositior of the *Consiglio Maggiore* when taken in conjunction with Dale Kent's work on the *reggimento* in 1433 can provide a more long term perspective on the modifications that had taken place in the political class during the sixty years of Medicean hegemony. A consideration of the backgrounds of the families who entered the *reggimento* for the first time after 1434 serves to place the argument that the establishment of the *Consiglio Maggiore* was in effect a closure of the political class in a wider context, and leads to the further suggestion that the Florentines had been moving towards this closure from at least the late fourteenth century. It is to these issues that this paper now turns.

In 1433 the members of the *arti maggiori* qualified in the scrutiny for the *tre maggiori* numbered some 1757 citizens from 334 *case*.[70] The 1508 roll of the members of the *Consiglio Maggiore* suggests a membership for the *arti maggiori* of just over 3,000 citizens from 516 *case*.[71] Although the number of families in the ruling group had increased over this period by just over fifty percent, only slightly more than half the families in the *Consiglio Maggiore* in 1508 had members qualified for the *tre maggiori* on the eve of the Medicean coup. But political mobility in Florence was a highly complex process, comprising not only the decline and disappearance of old families and the rise of new, but also movement in and out of the ruling group reflecting the volatility of political and economic fortunes.[72] Of the 516 *case* in the *Consiglio Maggiore*, about 137 or just over one quarter appear to have entered the political class for the first time between 1434 and 1494, of whom twenty-five had moved up from the ranks of the *arti minori*, and thirty-six had not yet had members selected for the Signoria.[73] A number of these families, however, were of considerable antiquity and social status and by no means necessarily new to participation in politics and government. Nine came from the ranks of the old magnate families. Others like the Cancellieri were nobles from the *contado* or like the Sassetti and the Gondi had long been active in the economic and public life of the Republic. While claims to a long lineage are often difficult to substantiate, some fifteen or so families appear to be genuinely old.[74]

The 137 families in the *Consiglio Maggiore* do not of course account for all the families successful in scrutinies for the *tre maggiori* for the first time after 1434. Much of the mobility into the political class in Florence was ephemeral, the fleeting appearance of citizens who failed to consolidate their own place or to pass it on to their descendants.[75] The post-1434 families in the *Consiglio Maggiore* had entered not only the political class under the Medici but also the inner privileged circle of the *seduti, veduti* and *beneficiati*. This evidence would support the view that after 1434 mobility into the ruling group continued at a considerable rate and one that was comparable to that under the previous regime.[76] It does seem, however, that the rate of mobility may have begun to slow down in the later years of the

Medici regime. The records for the three scrutinies after 1453 do not appear to have survived, but the 1508 list of members of the *Consiglio Maggiore*, taken together with Dale Kent's tables on the results of scrutinies between 1382 and 1453 in the quarter of Santa Maria Novella, does provide some limited evidence on mobility after 1453 at least into the group of the *seduti, veduti* and *beneficiati*. In 1508 in the *Consiglio Maggiore* for Santa Maria Novella there appear to be fifteen families who entered the ruling group for the first time between 1434 and 1453 and thirteen who entered between 1454 and 1494.[77] Thus slightly more new families appear to have achieved the ranks of the *seduti, veduti* and *beneficiati* in the first twenty years of Medicean rule than during the last forty.

If the post-1434 families account for just over a quarter of the families in the *Consiglio Maggiore*, they provided only fifteen percent of the members. This lower figure is consistent with the view that the Medici in no way swamped the ruling group with newcomers and that a balance between mobility and continuity was preserved.[78] The ruling group after 1494 shows the same predominance of large old families as it had done in the past.[79] Five alone, the Rucellai, Strozzi, Altoviti, Albizzi, and Pitti, account for just over seven percent of the members of the *Consiglio Maggiore*. The 107 families with nine or more members provided over half of the total membership. Of the 107, nine had entered the ruling group after 1434 of whom only four can be regarded as genuinely new.[80]

Mobility is not only, however, a process of ascent but also one of decline. Thus some 61 families represented in the *reggimento* in 1433 did not have members in the *Consiglio Maggiore*.[81] The low number of majorities obtained by most of these families in the 1433 scrutiny suggests that they were already then on the fringe of the political class.[82] The composition of the *Consiglio Maggiore* also provides some evidence of the more long term fate of the families of the "vecchio state" who had lost the battle with the Medici faction for control of the Florentine government in 1434 and who were subsequently subject to exile and discrimination.[83] When the Medici returned to Florence in 1434, members of some 58 families who were considered enemies of the new régime were punished.[84] In 1444 more citizens, including the *accoppiatori* of 1433, were deprived of their political rights for ten years.[85] The evidence provided by the membership of the *Consiglio Maggiore* suggests that many of the major families of the "vecchio stato" had indeed been politically ruined.[86] Only the Ardinghelli, Baldovinetti, Gianfigliazzi, Peruzzi, Serragli, Strozzi, and Altoviti had a considerable presence in the *Consiglio Maggiore*.[87] The last three families had increased their representation but whereas other large families had doubled their presence in the political class between 1433 and 1508, the Strozzi with forty members qualified in 1433 had only added four to have 44 members in the *Consiglio Maggiore*. Nevertheless, the Strozzi were the second largest *consorteria* in the *Consiglio*. If the 1434 and later proscriptions did not result in the political liquidation of the families of the "vecchio stato," they had reduced them with a few exceptions to the fringe of the political class. In that many of these families had already by 1434 passed the peak of their prosperity, the Medicean proscriptions may have only accelerated their eclipse.[88]

A further perspective on mobility in the fifteenth century is provided by some consideration of the backgrounds of the families who entered the *reggimento* in the fifteenth century. After the establishment of the *Consiglio Maggiore*, one Florentine citizen, Piero Vaglienti, complained bitterly that citizens whose families had paid taxes in Florence over a long period were not eligible for office.[89] Vaglienti's bitterness is understandable. His family had been goldsmiths and silk merchants in Florence, unsuccessfully nominated in scrutinies from 1382. He himself, as noted earlier, had been among the *non-beneficiati* admitted to the *Consiglio Maggiore* at the beginning of 1495 and subsequently expelled, and his had been one of the few applications for readmission which was rejected. Vaglienti argued that citizenship, by which he appears to understand eligibility for office, should be restricted to those whose families had resided in Florence and paid taxes for at least a century. In fact, almost all the families in the *Consiglio Maggiore* would have met Vaglienti's conditions. Of the 137 families admitted to the ruling group under the Medici, all but twenty-seven had had members nominated as major guildsmen in scrutinies by at least 1433. Of the twenty-seven, fifteen had been successfully or unsuccessfully nominated as minor guildsmen.[90] Given that by the early fifteenth century the period of tax payment for eligibility for office has been extended to thirty years, it is evident that all but a handful of families in the *Consiglio Maggiore* had been established in Florence as taxpayers from at least the late fourteenth century.[91]

On the basis of this evidence, two trends in social mobility in Florence from the late fourteenth century can be noted, the one towards restriction, the other towards expansion. The rise of an individual or family in Florence passed through three stages; immigration to the city; the acquisition of citizenship and eligibility for consideration for office-holding after entry into a guild and a defined period of residence and taxpayment; and finally qualification by the scrutiny councils.[92] While from the mid-fourteenth century migration into Florence no longer took place on the same level as in the past, it had continued at a significant level. On the basis of the *Catasto*, it has been suggested that in 1427 just under twenty percent of the heads of households in Florence were of immigrant origins, although this does not necessarily mean that they were permanent residents of the city.[93] The majority of the immigrants were certainly from the poorer elements in rural society but the city did continue to attract men of some substance who might aspire to rise in the urban hierarchy.[94] The road was, however, being blocked to them. From the late fourteenth century the requirements for citizenship in terms of periods of residence and taxpaying were extended, and eligibility for office was restricted and curbed.[95] Julius Kirshner's suggestion, on the basis of his work on citizenship and office-holding in the late fourteenth and early fifteenth century, that only a few members of families who acquired Florentine citizenship after the mid-fourteenth century reached the most prestigous offices in Florence is reinforced by the presence of no more than a handful of them in the *Consiglio Maggiore*.[96] The extension of the period of taxpaying in the family to fifty years for aspiring members of the *Consiglio Maggiore* in 1497 reflects a further hardening in the attitude to newcomers. Equally significant, too, is the fact that as few as five persons may have been granted Florentine citizenship in the years of the *governo popolare*, all five before 1499.[97]

If social mobility at the primary level of the admission of immigrant families to eligibility for office had almost ceased by the late fourteenth century, at the level of the acceptance of established families into the ruling group, it had continued at a considerable rate. The suggestion has been made that the opening of the ruling group to a large number of citizens in the last decades of the fourteenth century was, in part, the attempt to include all those who could be accommodated.[98] It seems, however, that this process of absorption took virtually a century to work itself out. And it included not only families who had arrived in Florence in the fourteenth century but also those whose pedigrees were much longer and who had stood apart from the political life of the Republic in the past. By the end of the fifteenth century the process appears to have been completed and the Florentines were ready to close their ruling group.[99]

Part of the process of absorption was the full reintegration of the old magnate families into the ruling group. From the late fourteenth century, a growing number of members and branches of magnate families were granted *popolano* status.[100] Then in 1434, the Medicean *Balìa* virtually eliminated the magnates as a social category.[101] Thereafter, an increasing number of citizens from magnate families returned to the ruling group or were qualified for the first time for the *tre maggiori*.[102] The introduction of the *governo popolare* in no way altered this trend; in fact it was accelerated. In the projects for reform called for by the Signoria in December 1494, special attention was paid to the incorporation of the magnate families, and as we have seen their members were the most prominent group elected to the *Consiglio Maggiore* between 1497 and 1512.[103]

Clearly by no means all those established in Florence by the late fourteenth century had been successful in their quest for a place in the ruling group. The scrutiny lists contain the names of many who were never successful and the appearance of others was brief. Failure is difficult to explain but the attempt can be made to seek out some of the factors in success.

Wealth appears to be the most important factor in the ascent of the families who entered the ruling group in the fifteenth century although it took time for this wealth to be crowned with political recognition.[104] On the basis of the Tables compiled by Lauro Martines of the 150 wealthiest households in each Quarter in the 1427 *Catasto*, Dale Kent has suggested that some 268 of the highest taxpayers were from families with no representation in the scrutiny of 1433.[105] At the beginning of the sixteenth century, the descendants of 154 of these 268 taxpayers were in the *Consiglio Maggiore*.[106] They came from 96 families of whom about 53 had entered the ruling group after 1434. In addition to the 53 post-1434 families among the Republic's highest taxpayers in 1427, another nine were included by Benedetto Dei in his list of the "magiori ricchi di Firenze dell'Anno 1472," and two more were on his list of "setaiuoli grossi."[107] While in some cases wealth may have stemmed from the Medici connection, just under half of the families admitted to the ruling group after 1434 belonged to the wealthiest strata in Florentine society, the majority having arrived there by the second decade of the fifteenth century. Legal and notarial careers, particularly in the service of the state, were another important factor in the backgrounds of the families who entered the ruling group in the fifteenth century.[108] Seventeen of the post-1434 families included lawyers in their ranks. As Professor Martines has shown, the presence of lawyers was rarely the source of a family's rise but rather its reflection.[109] The Gaddi and the Borromei were both in the wealthiest strata in Florence in the 1420s, the Pucci owed their rise to a Medici connection, and the Tanagli, Uguccioni, Palarcioni and Ubaldini were old families.[110] Four families, however, do appear to owe their success to legal origins, the Salvetti, Redditi, da San Miniato (Vaio) and Buongirolami. Messer Bartolmeo di Andrea Redditi was the son of a blacksmith first admitted to the Signoria as a minor guildsman in 1463.[111] His older brother, Ser Filippo, was a notary in the second Chancery. The Buongirolami were a dynasty of lawyers who had come to Florence from Gubbio and the first member of the da San Miniato to be elected to the Signoria was the grandson of a lawyer.

Notaries had been conspicuous among the immigrants and *gente nuova* of the fourteenth century, and some of the most prominent families in fifteenth century government like the Pandolfini, Serristori, and Sernigi had notarial origins.[113] In the late fourteenth century when attitudes and policies were hardening towards immigrants, official policy was more flex-ible towards notaries whose services were required to staff the burgeoning bureaucracy.[114] Of the 137 families in the *Consiglio Maggiore* who had been first qualified for the *tre maggiori* after 1434, just under a third had notaries in their background.[115] About seventeen of these had provided notaries to the Signoria and seven more to other offices of government and administra-tion.[116] Also among the post-1434 families were those of lawyers and notaries who had occupied high positions in the Chancery; of the Chan-cellors, Coluccio Salutati, Pietro Sermini, Poggio Bracciolini and Carlo Marsuppini, of the notaries of the Riformagioni, Filippo Balducci and Bar-tolomeo Guidi da Pratovecchio and his son, Giovanni.[117] Bartolomeo Scala was also a member of the *Consiglio Maggiore* until his death in 1497.[118]

The rise of notaries and Chancery officials was cleary resented by patricians like Piero Guicciardini.[119] But the hostility was probably even sharper at the grass roots level. In his letter to the Signoria, Piero Vaglienti complained about the ascent of notaries and added that "non stava bene ammetterre alla cittadincia chi fosso stato famiglio di alcuno magistrato o arte".[120] After the flight of Piero de'Medici, the *provveditore del Monte*, An-tonio di Bernardo Minati, was hanged in a popular demonstration, and at the end of December a number of officials in the Chancery, including Bar-tolomeo Scala, were dismissed.[121] The introduction of the *Consiglio Maggiore* provided a vehicle for general resentment to express itself. Thus in 1497 the Council expelled from its midst the descendants of citizens who had been public officials and had gained the *beneficio* after 1453. In what may well have been an expression of general hostility towards notaries, in March, 1496, the Council passed legislation requiring them to choose whether they were to be eligible for the offices belonging to notaries or those of ordinary citizens.[122] Notaries who chose the former were not, however, deprived of their membership of the Council or of their right to participate in elections.[123] At the end of the 1508 roll of members of the *Consiglio Maggiore*, there is a separate list of 170 notaries who had chosen the professional of-fices, and it appears that almost all notaries had taken this option. However, the reaction against the notaries and public officials was exagger-ated in terms of the few who had been successful.[124] Notarial careers, even in the public sector, were by no means a certain path to mobility. The ma-jority of the notaries to the Signoria from the late fourteenth century did not have descendants in the *Consiglio Maggiore*, and others were present only in the ranks of the *arti minori*. Even among the officials permanently em-ployed in the Chancery at the end of the fifteenth century, the families, in the *Consiglio Maggiore* did not extend beyond those of Bartolomeo Scala, Ser Filippo Redditi, Bernardo Miniati and Giovanni Guidi whose family had been nominated in the scrutinies before 1434. But doubtless these were too many for some contemporaries, and patrician resentment against public officials probably had its source not so much in their admission to the ruling group as in the influence they wielded and in the shift in the fulcrum of power towards the Chancery.[125] The qualification of new families in the scrutinies obviously owed much to patronage, not only of the Medici but also of the other leading citizens of the regime and of those who were powerful in the *gonfaloni* where the first selection was made. But the choice was made from among families well established in Florence, on the edges of the ruling group for a long period. It does seem clear, however, that professional qualifications and expertise, both a reason for and a product of employment in the bureaucracy, did place citizens in a position to accelerate their own rise or that of their families. As suggested earlier, only twelve families in the *Consiglio Maggiore* had not been nominated in scrutinies for either the *arti maggiori* or *minori* before 1434. Of the twelve, three came from the magnate class. The remainder included the Bracciolini, Marsuppini, Buongirolami, and da San Miniato. Another three, the dell' Ancisa, Bellarno, and Vinacciesi, had notaries in their backgrounds as did six of the families nominated for the *arti minori* only before 1434.[126]

The families who were accepted into the *Consiglio Maggiore* after 1494 display much the same pattern as those admitted to the *reggimento* in the preceding sixty years. Of the twenty-two families in the *Consiglio Maggiore* in 1508 who had been readmitted in 1497 or admitted later, half had been nominated as major guildsmen before 1434 and another two for the *arti minori*.[127] Three had been among the highest taxpayers in 1427 and a fourth, Lorenzo Cantucci, was reputed wealthy and to have literally tried to buy his way into the *Consiglio Maggiore* by offering the Commune a gift of 1,000 florins and an interest-free loan of another 5,000 to help prosecute the campaigns against Pisa.[128] The *non-beneficiati* also included the First Chancellor, Marcello Adriani Berti, and the descendants of three immigrant lawyers, Maestro Mazzingo di Messer Paradiso Mazzinghi, Filippo Gaetani, and Messer Francesco di Messer Piero Ambrogini.[129] Seven had notaries in their backgrounds.[130]

III

The members of the *Consiglio Maggiore* could be and indeed were at times regarded as a class of *gentiluomini* or nobles comparable to that of Venice,[131] but contemporaries also made distinctions among them. The *Consiglio* was usually seen as divided into two groups, *case grandi* and *case basse; ottimati* or *nobili* and *popolani; primi cittadini* and *cittadini mezzani* or the *universale* or *moltitudine*.[132] Later historians have tended to emphasize the economic, social, and political differences among the members of the Council, to portray these differences as those of class and to argue that the *governo popolare* admitted or gave a greater share in government to the "middle classes."[133]

It is impossible to identify with any precision those families and individuals who were considered as *grandi* or *bassi*. There was no official register, nor could there be.[134] Contemporaries themselves were not always sure of the status of a family, and their individual perceptions differed. Historians are agreed that the main attributes of status in Florence were established wealth and a long and continuous record of political participation with more emphasis on the latter.[135] As a rough guide to the length of a family's political participation, the criterion of the election of the first member to the Signoria has been utilised.[136] There is little doubt that large old families continually at the centre of government from at least the first decades of the thirteenth century, families like the Rucellai, Strozzi, and Albizzi, were *case grandi* or that families who had their first member elected to the Signoria in the later fifteenth century and who had only one or two members in the *Consiglio Maggiore* were *case basse*. But there remain many families whose status presents problems for historians as it did for contemporaries.

There are problems too with the criterion of the date of a family's first entry into the Signoria, even as a rough guide to status. Not all old families enjoyed elevated status. Some families who dated their first prior back to the mid-fourteenth century were at that stage members of the *arti minori*.[137] Others had descended for long periods into the *minori* or moved back and forward between the *arti minori* and *arti maggiori*.[138] There were families too who while their first prior appeared in the early years of the Signoria had produced no more than a handful over two centuries or who were absent from the Signoria for long periods.[139] On the other hand, families whose status was not open to question like the magnate Buondelmonte and Nerli did not have their first prior until the mid-fifteenth century.

For the early sixteenth century, the problem remains too of how long a family's record of political participation had to be before it was accorded high status. Contemporaries had differing views on this. At times, Francesco Guicciardini — on whose not necessarily typical outlook historians have relied — appears to have regarded as lacking in reputation any family which did not trace its origins at least as far back as the early fourteenth century.[140] Yet his own father, Piero, writing twenty-five years earlier, had conceded that some of the families who had risen in the later fourteenth century, if not yet "nobili," were in the process of acquiring that status.[141] Giovanni Cambi placed a number of the later fourteenth century families like the Antinori, Bonsi, Carducci, and Vespucci on his list of "case grande."[142] Ugolino Verino, a humanist employed in the Florentine Chancery, included in the compilation of the great houses that he made in the 1480s not only families dating from the later fourteenth century but also others like the Pucci, Del Nerro, and Petrucci who had not sat in the Signoria as major guildsmen until the mid-fifteenth century.[143] Parenti in his *Storia fiorentina* described Bernardo del Nero as a man, "el quale di plebeo in principio al grado della nobilita passo."[144]

For contemporaries, the term "case grande" carried overtones of large *consorterie*. Cambi in the early sixteenth century defined the "case grande" as those "di più riputazione et huomini."[145] Numerous relatives were a crucial factor in establishing and maintaining political influence and power in Florence at all levels.[146] Conversely, large powerful families were viewed as potentially threatening and the application of the *divieto* regulations served to prevent such families monopolising political power.[147] One of the reasons given for Pier Soderini's election as *gonfaloniere a vita* in 1502 was that his family was not overly large, with the implication that there was less likelihood that he could make a successful bid for personal power.[148] For Francesco Guicciardini one of the characteristics of upstarts was that they were "spogliati di parenti." The size of a family's representation in the *Consiglio Maggiore* can give some rough indication at least of the political status of a family since the number of members was in part the result of the number who had been drawn for the *tre maggiori* in the past.[149] In the *Consiglio Maggiore* in 1508, there were 121 members who were the sole representatives of their families and another 73 families who had only two members. Thus over a third of the families had only minimal representation. Half of these small families had entered the ruling group after 1434. The remainder included old magnate families, like the Rossi, Pulci, and Cerchi, long in decline, families who had suffered proscriptions after 1434 and families who had not appeared in the Signoria for long periods or whose appearances were sporadic and rare. Although demographic factors certainly affected the size of a family's representation, it does seem likely that on the whole, regardless of the date of the first prior, the small families were not regarded as "case grande."[150]

If size and continuous political participation are taken as criteria for the identification of *case grande*, then families like the Bartoli, Del Benino, Busini, Carducci, Federighi, Ginori, Guidetti, Martelli, Morelli, Nasi, Niccolini, Nobili, Pandolfini, and Vespucci, all of whom had not established themselves in the ruling group until the mid or late fourteenth century, deserve to be considered as *case grandi* even if the more rarefied members of older families looked down on them. The role of members of these families at the centre of fifteenth-century government and their marriage patterns, another criterion of status, reinforce this classification. Fifteenth-century families present more of a problem, but at least the political status of the more successful of the parvenus like the Del Nero and Pucci is clear from the size of their representation in the *Consiglio Maggiore*.[151] The rise of the Pucci is graphically illustrated by their twenty-nine members in the Council, making the family the eleventh largest. Indicative of the very gradual nature of the normal rise of a family even under the Medici is the fact that apart from the Del Nero and Pucci, the Dazzi and Parenti were the only "new" families with nine or more members in the Council.[152]

The laws and electoral machinery in Florence assumed that the basic political unit was the *consorteria*, but it is by no means certain that all members of *case grandi* even within the *Consiglio Maggiore* enjoyed the same status.[153] While Parenti described the *popolani* as the "huomini di mediocre stirpe," Guicciardini included in his *universale* not only "gli uomini di case basse" but also "gli uomini di buone case, ma che avevano consorti di più autorità e qualita di loro."[154] For Guicciardini, it seems that the membership of the Council was divided between a large rank and file and a small elite of ability, experience and authority, the *primi cittadini* or *ottimati*.[155]

Regardless of the criteria for identifying the *case grandi* and *basse* or the *primi cittadini* and the *universale*, the establishment of the *governo popolare* did not alter the structure of the ruling group. At all stages it had included both old and new families, a central core of large established families and an outer fringe of families moving in and moving out, both temporarily and permanently. It had always contained relatively poor citizens as well as the wealthy.[156] To argue that the establishment of the *governo popolare* resulted in the entry into the ruling group of "la massa delle classi medie, piccoli commercianti ed artigiani" is misleading.[157] The small shopkeepers and artisans were predominantly in the *arti minori* which had always provided members for the councils and offices of government and the relative representation of the *arti minori* did not increase after 1494.[158] By the very criteria for membership, the citizens in the *Consiglio Maggiore* or their ancestors had belonged to the inner group of the *veduti* and *seduti*. But equally important and more striking is the fact that some seventy percent of the members of the *Consiglio Maggiore* were from 207 families who had been represented in the inner group of *uomini principali, arroti to Balìe* between 1438 and 1480.[159] The Medicean *Balìe* were very widely based in the ruling group except at its fringe and most *arriviste* levels.

IV

If the creation of the *Consiglio Maggiore* did not and could not by the very criteria for its membership change the composition of the political class in

Florence, it did confer a condition of equality among its component families, their branches and individual members.[160] Membership of the *reggimento* in the past had meant merely the opportunity to be selected for the *tre maggiori* and the other offices, although in fact most members did participate in major office.[161] To be *veduto* meant merely to have been drawn for office although, as was suggested earlier, the groups of the *veduti* and *seduti* appear to have been virtually the same. To be *beneficato* meant merely to be the descendant of a citizen *veduto* or *seduto*, and thus possibly to have little or no experience in government. Membership of the *Consiglio Maggiore* also meant in theory a permanent voice in all electoral proceedings and legislative proposals, including those relating to taxation and state finance. That legislative proposals be placed before a body as large as three-and-a-half thousand citizens, the assent of two-thirds of whom was required for their successful passage, was unprecedented in Florentine history. This is seen as the most fundamental and important change which took place with the establishment of the *governo popolare*.[162] The political class became the ruling group. However, as a ruling group as opposed to a political class, the *Consiglio Maggiore* was never as large as three-and-a-half-thousand citizens. Contemporaries made the distinction between "abili al consiglio" and "abili a ragunarsi al consiglio."[163] By no means did all citizens eligible for the *Consiglio Maggiore* attend its meetings. Absence from the city, voluntary abstention from what was a time-consuming activity, and above all indebtedness on the tax registers, reduced attendance at the meetings of the *Consiglio*.[164] Cardinal among Florentine political assumptions was the principle that political participation be confined to those who paid their taxes, and after 1494 the efforts to regain Pisa and the war situation in the peninsula necessitated very high levels of taxation. Non-attendance was a major problem from the inception of the Council, so much so that as early as May, 1496, it was decided to abandon its division into three six-month sessions. From February, 1497, the Council met as a permanent body with a quorum of one thousand for the passage of legislation. The voting records in the Council suggest that attendance at its meetings was rarely little more than the required quorum.[165] Thus, as an institution of government, the *Consiglio Maggiore* was much smaller than its eligible membership. While non-payment of taxes could be and was at times a gesture of protest against the new constitutional structure or current policies, it does seem plausible that the poorer or weaker members of the Council were those most likely to be absent.[166] The major officeholding group between 1495 and 1512 numbered some one thousand citizens, and it is likely that the active members of the *Consiglio Maggiore* more or less coincided with this inner group.[167] If the effective membership of the *Consiglio Maggiore* was little more than one thousand citizens, it was still double the combined size of the preceding Councils of the *Commune* and the *Popolo* and ten times larger than the Medicean *Consiglio dei Cento*, where in the later fifteenth century all important legislation finished. Regardless of its social composition, the very size of the *Consiglio Maggiore* was bound to make the passage of legislation and taxation proposals more difficult, the more so since a negative vote from one third of those present was sufficient to prevent enactment. At least some of the opposition to the *governo popolare* on the part of *primi cittadini* had its source in the sheer difficulty of securing the passage of legislation in such a large body, the more so in a period of profound external pressure and crisis.[168]

The *Consiglio degli Ottanta*—The Inner Oligarchy

I

Possessed of a legally defined, hereditary and virtually closed ruling class, the Florentine political and social structure was indeed comparable to that of Venice. Moreover, the ruling groups in Florence and Venice were much the same size. For some contemporary political commentators, Venice was an aristocracy.[169] If this were so, then as one of the speakers in Francesco Guicciardini's *Dialogo* pointed out, Florence was no less so.[170] Election, the method for filling offices adopted in 1494, was viewed by some Florentines as characteristic of aristocratic government.[171] But another image of Venice was that of a mixed government in which the *Consiglio Grande* represented the democratic element. Above the *Consiglio Grande* and the effective seat of power was the small *Consiglio dei Pregardi*. In 1494 alongside the *Consiglio Maggiore* the Florentines established their smaller council, the *Consiglio degli Ottanta*.[172] The assent of the *Ottanta* was required for legislative proposals before they were presented to the *Consiglio Maggiore*, and ambassadors and commissaries were elected there. The *Ottanta* also had some control over defence through its voice in the engagement of *condottieri* and troops. These were very limited powers.

While the formal power of the *Ottanto* was not great, it was intended that the Council should play an important role in the formulation of policy and that its members should form an inner circle of influence. In an attempt to curb the independence of the Signoria and to prevent the creation of an informal *de facto* inner group, the *Ottanto* was to be an institutionalized *practica:*[173] the Signoria was obliged to summon the Council at least once a week and lay before it all important issues and correspondence relating to both internal and external affairs. The membership of the *Ottanta* was to be elected every six months in the *Consiglio Maggiore* but special provisions were made to secure the election of worthy citizens. In addition to the candidates proposed by electioneers drawn from the *borse*, the *Sedici Gonfalonieri* were each to nominate six citizens and the *Dodici Buonuomini*, two. The total number of candidates nominated by members of the *Collegi* was three times greater than that nominated by the forty electioneers who could nominate only one citizen each. Reflecting the Florentine equation of wisdom with age, members of the *Ottanta* had to be over forty. In addition to the eighty elected members, the *Signoria, Collegi, Dieci de Libertà*, and *Accoppiatori* were to be *ex officio* members of the *Ottanta*. The *ex officio* component comprised over one third of the total membership. Nor were the *divieto* regulations which disallowed successive occupancy of the same office by a citizen to apply to the *Ottanta*. Parenti wrote that this was done in order to ensure the virtual continuous presence of the *huomini principali* in the *practica* of the *Signoria*.[174] In the suspension of this *divieto* regulation the Florentines were again following in the steps of Venice where the *contumacia* was not applied to the *Consiglio dei Pregadi*.[175] The special provisions for the election of the *Ottanta*, the suspension of the *divieto* and the presence of a large ex officio group suggests that the Council was much closer to an oligarchic institution than has hitherto been assumed.

As Nicolai Rubinstein has pointed out, at the time of its inception the new political structure was capable of both a democratic and an aristocratic interpretation.[176] Much depended on the outcome of the electoral procedures for the filling of the *Ottanta* and other offices. The subject of the second part of this paper is the inner circle of the participants in major office, described as the "inner oligarchy," and the problem of whether the more open procedures in the *Consiglio Maggiore* resulted in a wider distribution of office and a change in composition at this level of the ruling group.[177] Again discussion is confined to the *arte maggiore* component.

A survey of the more important offices suggests that some 1050 citizens from 287 families, that is just over a third of the members and fifty-five percent of the families in the *Consiglio Maggiore* participated at the higher levels of government and administration between 1495 and 1512.[178] Thus, while the size of the political class increased through the fifteenth century, that of the major officeholding group did not.[179] Nor did the establishment of the *governo popolare* lead to any enlargement. The inner oligarchy can, however, be identified with the membership of the *Consiglio degli Ottanta* because the families in the *Ottanta* were largely coincident with those who provided the occupants of major office.[180] Between 1495 and 1512, 736 citizens from 261 families sat in the *Ottanta*.[181] In the last eighteen years of the Medici regime, just over 800 citizens from 218 families had sat in the *Consiglio dei Cento*, which in this paper has been used to define the outer perimeter of the membership of the Medicean oligarchy.[182] Some 610 of the 736 members of the *Ottanta* were from families with members in the *Cento*, of whom the vast majority had themselves sat in the *Cento* or were *proximi consorti*, sons, brothers, paternal nephews and cousins, of citizens in the Medicean Council.[183] A further forty-six members of the *Ottanta* were from families among the *arroti to Balìe* in the second half of the fifteenth century.[184] Thus some ninety percent of those who sat in the *Ottanta* were from families who had participated in the inner circles of Medicean government. The degree of continuity between the Medici regime and the *governo popolare* is even more striking in the case of the Signoria. Of the priors who held office between 1495 and 1512, eighty-eight percent had either themselves sat in the Signoria, or were the sons or brothers of citizens selected as priors under the Medici.[185] Another seven percent had more distant relatives in the Signoria.

The individuals and families who appeared in the *Ottanta* were not of course equally present. The place of just under one-third of all the families in the *Ottanta* was marginal, and the members of the seventy-eight families whose representation in the *Consiglio* was confined to one or two positions, for the most part in the early years of the new regime, cannot really be regarded as forming part of an inner oligarchy of influence and status. The *Cento* also had its fringe membership of some forty-eight families. The occupation of eight or more positions in the Councils has been taken as a rough guide to identify the families who might be seen as forming their core memberships. In the *Ottanta*, they numbered 99, in the *Cento*, 97. In both Councils these families held 77% of the available places.[186] A brief glance at the families who formed the core of the two Councils brings into clearer perspective the real changes that had taken place in the composition of the inner oligarchy with the establishment of the *governo popolare*. Ten of the larger families in the *Ottanta* had not enjoyed membership of the *Cento*, and several more had made only rare appearances.[187] Prominent in this group were magnate families, those of the "vecchio stato" and other families with members who had compromised themselves in the eyes of the Medici.[188] Among the remainder were the Antinori, Guidetti, and Ugolini who had entered the political class in the middle of the fourteenth century and the Giraldi whose first prior held office in 1396. There were only four families whose first prior took office after 1434, the Boni, Dazzi, Gondi, and Parenti. Of the families with considerable presence in the *Cento*, apart from the Tornabuoni, only the Bonvanni, whose first prior in 1435 was a butcher, did not have members in the *Ottanta*.[189] Families whose rise dated from the period of Medicean predominance were also conspicuous among those with much less representation in the *Ottanta* than in the *Cento*. The Pucci, Giovanni, Rustichi (Lion Nero), and Salvetti fall into this group. Of the post-1434 families in the *Cento*, apart from the magnate Nerli and the older Zati, only the del Nero held their place in the inner group throughout the period of the *governo popolare.*.

The establishment of the *governo popolare* does not appear then to have led to any significant alteration in either the size of the composition of the group which occupied the main offices. This conclusion has relevance not only for *governo popolare* but also for the Medici regime. It suggests that the high degree of continuity at the level of the inner oligarchy was in large part the result of its wide base under the Medici. What the differences between the two regimes appear to amount to are a slightly lesser presence of fifteenth-century families after 1494, a higher representation of the old magnate families, and the return of a few of the families of the "vecchio stato."[190] These changes do not point to any "democratization" of the inner circles but rather to the reverse.

II

The preceding discussion of the size and the composition of the major office holding group relates to the period 1495–1512 and thus does not provide any perspective on changes which may have taken place over the life of the *governo popolare.* Neither does it furnish any evidence for contemporary perceptions of the composition of the inner group on which action and reaction was predicated. Francesco Guicciardini provides one contemporary viewpoint. The picture that emerges from his pages is of an overall trend towards an enlargement and "democratization" of the inner oligarchy.

In the first years of the new regime, according to Guicciardini, elections in the *Consiglio Maggiore* favoured "uomini popolari e buoni" rather than to "queqli che avevano più autorità e più esperienza."[191] Parenti also argued that in these years, "rimasono huomini popolari et bassi" and that many new men "in tal honore vennero."[192] A fifth of the members of the *Consiglio dei Ottanta* at the beginning of 1496, an election to which Parenti specifically referred, were from families who had entered the ruling group after 1434. *Non beneficiati* members of the *Consiglio Maggiore* also obtained some success in early elections. Salvo Borgherini sat in the *Ottanta* in 1496 and Pierantonio Bandini Banducci in 1498, and both were elected as *Ufficiali del Monte* in the same year.[193] At the end of 1496, Messer Francesco Ambrogini, who, according to Parenti, had launched an attack on the taxation policies of the government in the *Consiglio Maggiore* in the preceding August, was elected to the criminal court of the *Otto di Guardia*.[194] Parenti recorded his own amazement at this election and also the anger of the "nobiltà."[195] Ambrogini was an ardent follower of Savonarola and on the fall of the friar in 1498 was dismissed from the post he held in the territorial administration and banned from the *Consiglio Maggiore* for three years.[196]

Parenti attributed Ambrogini's punishment not only to his support for Savonarola but also to the fact that he stuck in the throats of many as a new man who had risen too high.[197] Ambrogini is listed as a member of the *Consiglio Maggiore* in 1508 but he does not appear again among the major officeholders. His rise was, however, exceptional. Indeed it was for this very reason that it attracted so much attention.

Thus it appears that the overthrow of the "tyranno" and the establishment of the "vivere libero" did open up the inner circles to "new men". But this was a temporary effect only and, according to Guicciardini, already by 1497 the results of elections were "più ragionevoli", and important offices were circulating among a small group of some 200 citizens.[198] In May 1499, however, there was a major change in the procedures for the filling of offices and lot replaced election as the last stage.[199] Whereas earlier in elections to major offices the candidates who obtained an absolute majority and the most votes were appointed, under the new system the names of all candidates who gained the absolute majority were placed in the *borse* and those whose names were drawn were appointed. The general shift from election to sortition between 1497 and 1499 had its source partly in the attempt to reduce the amount of time which the sessions of the *Consiglio Maggiore* consumed.[200] But there were also political motives. At the time of the introduction of the new electoral procedures, it had not been clear whom or what groups — *grandi* or *popolani, primi* or *mezzani* — election would favour. After the initial settling down period it became clear that the advantages lay with the traditional ruling families and leading citizens, and thus the rank and file members of the *Consiglio Maggiore* came to regard sortition as being more conducive to a wider distribution of office.[201] In April, 1498, the *Consiglio Maggiore* had also decided that the *divieto* regulations which prevented successive occupancy of the same office were henceforth to apply to the *Ottanta*. This was done according to the preamble to ensure "that the offices and dignities of the city, and especially those which are judged to be of some importance and status, should be as widely distributed as possible."[202] Guicciardini argued that the result of the shift from election to sortition was that the group of officeholders "cominciorono molto a piggioare ed a rallargarsi."[203] The change in electoral procedures also coincided with an increase in the expression of discontent with the *governo popolare* and moves to introduce reforms which would render it in some way *più stretto*.[204] According to Guicciardini, the distribution of office continued to widen and the quality of officeholders to deteriorate after the election of Pier Soderini as *gonfaloniere a vita* in 1502.[205]

If the shift to sortition did lead to an enlargement of the ruling group, it was again only a temporary effect. In the present study the end of the year 1502 has been taken as a dividing line. A comparison of the occupants of major offices from 1503 to 1512, with their predecessors, 1495–1502, suggests that rather than the inner oligarchy undergoing a process of enlargement and "democratization" over the life of the *governo popolare*, the trend was towards a contraction in size, a greater degree of continuity with the Medicean inner group and a lessening presence of more recently arrived families.

The moves between 1499 and 1502 to secure the creation of a more oligarchic council had failed, and the outcome of the attempts to secure some reform in the constitutional structure had been the election of a *gonfaloniere a vita*.[206] The law which provided for the election of a *gonfaloniere a vita*, however, also contained clauses relating to the *Consiglio degli Ottanta*. The Council had been included among the offices in the electoral reforms of 1499 where sortition replaced election as the final stage. The 1502 reform withdrew the *Ottanta* from this group. In future only the names of the 196 candidates, 112 for the *arti maggiori* and eighty-four for the *minori*, who had obtained the absolute majority and the most votes were to be placed in the *borse* for the final extraction. This was done so that "huomini più electi" would be present in the Council to advise the *Gonfaloniere* and Signoria.[207] The reform appears to have achieved some degree of success in that the number of families and citizens in the *Ottanta* dropped both absolutely and relatively after 1502. While between 1495 and 1502, 557 citizens from 241 families sat in the *Ottanta*, between 1503 and 1512 the number declined to 420 citizens from 190 families.[208] The crude average of places per family before January 1503 is 4 per family and 1.72 per man; after, it is 6 per family and 2.7 per man. Of the 78 families in the Council who occupied less than three positions, 60 had no representation after 1502. The proportion of members from families in the Medicean inner oligarchy rose after 1502 from 88% to 92% and the number of post-1434 families dropped. Between 1495 and 1502, 43 families who had entered the ruling group after 1434 had members in the *Ottanta* occupying 12% of the places, between 1503 and 1512, there were 24 occupying 8% of the places.

While in the case of the *Ottanta* the electoral procedures had been altered, for other offices sortition remained the last stage. But the trend observed in the membership of the *Ottanta* is also present in other major offices including the *Dieci*, responsible for foreign policy, war and defense,[209] the criminal court of the *Otto di Guardia*,[210] and the *Ufficiali del Monte*, the central financial institution.[211] Thus the view of Parenti, that the *Consiglio Maggiore* "never dishonoured the *primati*" and that in fact "they always occupied the first places even if occasionally a few *popolani* sat alongside them," appears as substantially accurate.[212]

III

The apparent discrepancy between the picture outlined above and that presented by Guicciardini calls for some consideration of his vocabulary of political and social classfication. The phrases which Guicciardini employed to describe those whose presence in high office he criticized were "di poca qualità," "di meno cervello e qualità" or "da pochi ed ignoranti."[213] While these words have been interpreted as denoting "middle classes," it is by no means certain that this was their intent if by "middle classes" is understood only the economically weaker or more recent members of the ruling group. Among those whom Guicciardini dismissed as unfit for high office were Tanai de'Nerli, "nobile, richissimo e potente pel numero de' figliuoli," but "nelle cose dello stato valeva poco," Piero Gualterotti, "uomo da poco nelle cose dello stato," Piero Carnesecchi, "uomo buonario ma di poca esperienza e giudicio nelle cose dello stato," Pandolfo Rucellai, brother of Bernardo, Andrea Giugni, Piero Corsini, Guglielmo de' Pazzi, Giovacchino Guasconi and Luigi della Stufa.[214] The social status of the families of these men was not open to question since they were either of magnate background or had participated at the centre of the public life of Florence from at least the end of the thirteenth century. For Guicciardini, family status and distinguished ancestors were not sufficient qualifications for leading positions. In his *Discorso di Logrogno*, written in 1512, he argued that debate should be permitted in the *Consiglio Maggiore*. This procedure would provide the opportunity for *opere* and *virtù* to be displayed so that reputation would derive from merit and not depend as was so often the case on nobility of family and deeds of ancestors. In this way, an excellent man of obscure lineage would not remain a nonentity nor a mediocrity of illustrious birth reach the highest levels.[215]

Those whom Guicciardini considered qualified for high office were the "cittadini savi e esperti", "nobili e prudenti," "uomini di qualità," "quegli che avevano più autorità e più esperienza."[216] It may be misleading to equate these terms with others such as "nobili" and "grandi," or "patrician," if by these latter is understood all and only members of the great houses. While the qualities Guicciardini demanded were more likely to be found among the scions of old families, less illustrious birth did not necessarily render a citizen unfit for high office. Among Guicciardini's citizens of authority and experience were Bernardo del Nero and Pierfilippo Pandolfini, described on another occasion as "spogliati di parenti e credito," and Messer Guidantonio Vespucci, whose family were winesellers and members of the *arti minori* in the fourteenth century.[217]

Guicciardini's primi *cittadini, uomini da bene, ottimati*, were, then, a small elite of status, ability, authority and experience, and his *universale*, the rank and file of the ruling group encompassing many citizens who bore illustrious names.[218] Thus, to show that the great majority of the occupants of major office under the *governo popolare* were from the same families or households as under the Medici, and that the proportion of citizens from newer families was if anything less after 1495 than before is not really relevant to Guicciardini's viewpoint. And the problem remains of who were the *primi cittadini*, the *uomini da bene*. Family name and tradition are not adequate for their identification.

In the second part of this paper, it has been suggested that the establishment of the *governo popolare* led to little change in the composition of the "inner oligarchy."[219] The pool of families who filled the *Ottanta* and other major institutions of government was slightly enlarged by the return of the enemies of the Medici, by an acceleration in the process of the full rehabilitation of the magnate families and by the arrival at the centre of one or two "newer" families who had been moving in that direction over the fifteenth century. The election and sortition processes by which offices were filled after 1494 no doubt created a more open and intense condition of competition than had been the case under the more controlled and manipulated Medicean system. This competition was an important factor in the political struggles of the period, but it took place among the families who were accustomed to be at the centre of Florentine political life. In the new circumstances, some families, their branches and individual members fared better, some worse; some were satisfied, others were not.

There was, however, one fundamental change at the level of the "inner oligarchy" and this was the creation of a condition of equality among its members and the removal of an institutional place for an inner group. Effective power in Florence lay in the hands of a small elite long before the Medici came on the scene.[220] But in 1480 with the creation of the *Consiglio dei Settanta*, the position of this inner group was institutionalised and its members were clearly visible.[221] The permanent and hereditary nature of the membership of the *Settanta* also served to separate its members and their families from the rest of the inner oligarchy.[222] With the abolition of the *Settanta*, an institutional place for a small inner elite was gone, and citizens and families who were in the process of acquiring a permanent and hereditary place at the centre of power lost their security of tenure. The third section of this paper will examine the changes that had taken place at the apex of the Florentine political structure.

The Elite

So far in this paper, the *Consiglio degli Ottanta* has been viewed as defining the inner oligarchy of the major officeholding group, and its membership has been compared with that of the *Consiglio dei Cento*. But some of the *primi cittadini* concerned in the establishment of the new regime had wanted the smaller council to be both a more powerful and a more exclusive institution, the equivalent of the Venetian *Consiglio dei Pregadi*, if not of the *Settanta*.[223] Although the battle for a powerful senate was lost with the establishment of the *Ottanta*, steps had been taken to try to ensure that its membership would be restricted.[224] Within a couple of years, however, measures were passed to secure the opposite effect and to prevent a small elite gaining a monopoly over power. Not only were the regulations disallowing successive occupancy of the same office applied to the *Ottanta* in 1498, but they were also introduced for the *Dieci*.[225] In these years, the *Dieci* had become the object of considerable suspicion and hostility, and there were difficulties in securing its election.[226] After the rebellion in Arezzo and the Val di Chiana, opinion swung back in favour of a more restricted membership for the *Ottanta* and, as we have seen, fewer citizens sat in the *Consiglio* in the last ten years of the life of the *governo popolare* than in the first eight. Even so, the membership of 420 between 1503 and 1512 was still much larger than that of the *Settanta* where between 1480 and 1494 just over 120 citizens from 73 families had sat as permanent members.

While there was no institutional place for an elite after 1494, the attempt can be made to identify the more influential and important citizens under the *governo popolare*. Whether these men enjoyed the same power, status and ego satisfaction as their predecessors in the *Settanta* and how they exercised their influence are different questions. Identification of those who were the leading citizens does, however, provide a perspective on the problem of the changes that took place at the inmost levels of government with the establishment of the *governo popolare*.

The identification of an informal elite is no easy task. For the earlier fifteenth century, historians have found the most useful criterion to be prominent participation in *pratiche*, the meetings where the Signoria and other executive institutions canvassed opinion, sought advice and established consensus.[227] As has been recognized, this criteria is not wholly satisfactory and leaves a considerable margin of error.[228] The problems are compounded for the period of the *governo popolare* when the records are very incomplete. In addition, the *Consiglio degli Ottanta* was intended to be institutionalized *practica* precisely to order to prevent the formation of *de facto* inner groups, and the majority of *pratiche* for which records survive were meetings where the *Ottanta* formed the nucleus, and the additional invited citizens sometimes numbered more than 200. These *pratiche larghe* were not the meeting place of an elite but rather of the inner oligarchy.[229] The more elitist *pratiche strette* attended by a small number of invited citizens did continue to meet,[230] but after 1502 they were summoned almost exclusively by the *Dieci*.[231]

In September, 1500, Parenti wrote that the Republic was being governed "per lo extraordinario et secondo l'uso di pochi sicome dal 1494 inanzi,"[232] and it is in the period, 1499–1502, that the most prominent and influential political figures stand out. They can be seen in the *pratiche strette*; in the special committees which, in the absence of the *Dieci*, were appointed by the Signoria or deputized from *pratiche* to deal with particular problems in foreign policy and defense, to manage and raise finance for the campaigns against Pisa, to pacify Pistoia; and among those citizens chosen as commissaries and envoys.[233] After 1502 more or less the same citizens were prominent in the *pratiche strette* summoned by the *Dieci*.[234] On the basis of appearances in special committees and legations between 1499 and 1502, and in *pratiche strette* in the central decade from 1499 to 1509, sixty-two citizens have been selected as forming an influential inner group. In addition, eleven citizens prominent in the earlier years but who had died by 1500 have been included as well as nine younger men who appear to have been moving into this group towards the end of the regime. Thus eighty-two citizens from sixty-one families have been isolated, of whom a third had died or dropped out before 1512.[235] It should be emphasized again that the method used to identify the elite is far from ideal and there may be a substantial margin of error. The *pratiche strette* of the *Dieci* were summoned to discuss issues in foreign policy and defence which may have influenced the invitations. In the *pratiche* between 1499 and 1502 which were concerned with the very pressing problems of state finance, a few citizens who never or rarely spoke at the *pratiche* of the *Dieci* were prominent. To offset error, a further group of forty citizens has been listed as occupying a place on the fringe of the elite.[236]

Although some families have more than one member on the present compilation of the elite, the number of members is not indicative of a family's status or influence but of the pattern of succession and division within it. Thus, for example, in the early years of *governo popolare*, Piero Corsini was at the centre of government. On Piero's death, his cousin, Amerigo, became prominent and on his death in 1502, Piero's son, Gherardo, appeared in the inner group. It was not until the death of his uncle, Bernardo, that the name of Alessandro Nasi appears with any frequency in the *pratiche* records. In other instances the older give way to the younger. The Salviati cousins, Giuliano di Francesco, Jacopo di Giovanni, and Alamanno di Averardo appear to have enjoyed a particularly close relationship. Alammano's father, Averardo, submitted a single *Catasto* return in 1480 for himself, Giuliano, and Jacopo, and in 1496 the cousins were engaged in the joint purchase of confiscated Medici lands.[237] Giuliano, who was thirteen years older than his cousins, was the leading member of the family in government until 1501 when both Jacopo and Alamanno turned forty and hence became eligible for the higher magistracies. Thereafter Giuliano does not figure in the inner circles. Both Alamanno and Jacopo Salviati were in the inner group at the same time but it should be noted that the number of their recorded appearances in *pratiche* is much less than that of citizens who like Piero Guicciardini or Antonio Canigiani were the only members of their families in the elite.[238] While at the level of the inmost circles of government, personal qualities and talents become important in securing a place, members of the elite were still viewed in the context of their families. Thus it was rare for two members of a family to be invited to *pratiche strette*, and some families were continually represented in the ranks of the elite and no doubt expected to be.[239]

If the membership of this projected inner group is compared with a list of the most prominent officeholders, there is a high degree of correlation but the coincidence is by no means total. Fifteen of the eighty-two made few appearances in office, and while nine of the fifteen had relatives who were conspicuous in office, the remaining six were from families who played little part in the official life of Florence during the period of the *governo popolare*.[240] The six included Medici partisans like Francesco Pucci and Filippo dall' Antella but also men like Guglielmo de'Pazzi and Lorenzo Dietisalvi Neroni whose families had challenged the Medici and suffered as a result of their defeat. That just under twenty percent of the projected elite did not enjoy even modest official careers indicates again that in Florence power and influence did not require or depend upon such careers. What in the context of the *governo popolare* is difficult to determine is whether these men sought high office but were unsuccessful, or whether they deliberately eschewed selection, and in the latter case whether avoidance of office was the means to show disapproval of or disassociate themselves from the *governo popolare*. As was mentioned earlier, in the late 1490s it was alleged that some citizens deliberately remained in arrears with their taxation payments (*a specchio*) in order to render themselves ineligible for office, and his hostility towards Pier Soderini led Bernardo Rucellai to withdraw from public life on Soderini's election as *gonfaloniere a vita*.[241]

If not all citizens in the elite were prominent as officeholders, there were also a number of citizens who had busy and prominent public

careers but whose names rarely if ever appear on the lists of special committees or among those speaking in *pratiche strette*.[242] While many in this group
had relatives in the elite, a few did not. Of the seventy families who on a
crude count occupied twenty or more important offices, two-thirds had
members in the elite and another ten were on its fringe. There are no obvious differences between the remaining nine families and those with
members in the elite.[243]

Biographical studies of the citizens who occupied a place at the
apex of the Florentine political structure or on its fringe might provide the
means to explore more fully some of the still unresolved problems about the
direction of political developments at the end of the fifteenth century, problems such as the extent to which public life had become a full time activity
for its practitioners who either *per forza* had to or else chose to divest themselves of mercantile and business interests.[244] The continued presence of
some citizens in offices and committees as well as at *pratiche* suggests that
their governmental and political activities were all consuming. The sons of
Tommaso Soderini were so frequently employed abroad on missions for the
Republic in the years of the *governo popolare* that they give the impression of
being career diplomats.[245] The Pandolfini and Acciaiuoli present a similar
if not quite so arresting image. Against this evidence and that of a different
kind presented by Niccolò Guasconi, who in his 1480 *Catasto* return stated
that he was "senza esercizio alcuno", should be set that provided by the lists
of guild consuls.[246] A cursory sampling of the records of two guilds, the *Arte
della Lana* and the *Arte del Cambio*, suggests that over forty percent of those
who have been included in the present compilation of the elite held office as
consuls in these two guilds alone.[247] Alongside the problem of the extent to
which politics and government were becoming the preserve of full time
careerists is the allied one of the extent to which they were also becoming an
area for professionals with trained expertise.[248] Lauro Martines has pointed
to the growing number of Florentines who took up the law in the late fifteenth and early sixteenth centuries and also to the increased presence of
lawyers in the Signoria and at the top levels of government.[249] The elite
under the *governo popolare* contained eight lawyers. A survey of the education
and background experience of others members of the elite might yield information on the extent to which and how Florentine families were prepar-
ing their sons for political life and the kind of training they believed to be
suitable.[250] The problem of whether families or their heads planned and
allocated a division of their manpower resources to protect and advance
their interests over a variety of areas also requires further investigation. A
biographical approach to the members of the elite along these lines might
also bring us closer to an understanding of the relative roles of the impulse

towards aristocratization and of the need for professional, efficient and effective government, in the development towards concentration of power at the apex of the political structure in Florence. Was Francesco Guicciardini calling for aristocracy or meritocracy?

The present study is, however, concerned with only one aspect of the inner circle of the political structure and that is the problem of what changes took place in its composition with the establishment of the *governo popolare*. Of the eighty-two citizens who have been viewed as belonging to this inner group, just under twenty-five percent had themselves sat in the *Settanta*, forty percent were *proximi consorti* of members and another ten percent had more distant relatives in the Medicean *Consiglio*. Thus just over one quarter of the republican elite were from families who did not belong to the inner group between 1480 and 1494. Once again it is members of the former magnate families who provided the biggest group of newcomers.[251] Of the remainder, all but three were from families whose first prior had held office before 1343, and Taddeo Gaddi was the only newcomer to elitist circles whose family had not been qualified for the *tre maggiori* before 1434. At the level of the elite, any change in social composition was if anything in the direction of greater conservatism. On the fairly crude but convenient criterion of a family's first prior as an indicator of political pedigree, two-thirds of the families with members in the elite were either magnates or had entered the Signoria before 1343, twenty percent, between 1343 and 1381, eight percent between 1382 and 1433 and only four had their first prior, or first prior for the *arti maggiori*, after 1434, the Pucci, del Nero, Zati and Gaddi. All four had a member in the Signoria by 1451. There was less "newer" blood in this elite than in any other that has been identified for the fifteenth century.[252] The "popular" elite also contained a greater number of citizens from magnate families both absolutely and relatively.

The factor which characterizes the families who entered the elite under the *governo popolare* was unacceptability or hostility to the Medici. Messer Antonio Strozzi, Messer Nicolò Altoviti, Giovacchino Guasconi, Giovanni Corsi and Messer Francesco Pepi all had ancestors punished by the *Balià* of 1434.[253] The Manelli although they did not suffer at the hands of the *Balià* had intimate connections with the anti-Medicean group and were described by Guicciardini in the *Storie fiorentine* as "inimici" of the Medici.[254] The father of Lorenzo Dietisalvi Neroni was one of the leaders of the 1465–1466 reaction against the Medici and the father of Antonio Giacomini was also exiled in 1466.[255] Antonio, himself, appears to have suffered the personal enmity of Piero di Lorenzo de' Medici.[256] It was only his marriage to the sister of Lorenzo de' Medici that saved the life of Guglielmo de' Pazzi in the vendetta against his family after the 1479 conspiracy.[257]

Although some members of the Bartolini family appear to have been strong Medici partisans — the sons of Lionardo di Bartolomeo bore the names of Cosimo and Damiano, and Lionardo di Zanobi came under suspicion in 1497 for pro-Medici activities — the father of Giovanbattista had been exiled for his part in the conspiracy of 1458 led by Girolamo Machiavelli.[258] And finally, Piero Alberti, whose family appears to have needed time to regain acceptability even after 1434, was regarded with some disfavour by Lorenzo de' Medici.[259] The remaining two families who provided members of the elite, the Carnesecchi and Da Ghiacceto, while not in the *Settanta* were very prominent in the *Cento* and appear to have been on the fringe of the Medicean inner group.

At the level of the elite, note should be taken not only of new families but also of families where the branch at the centre changed. Similar political allegiances and profiles cannot be assumed among all members of a family, even among *proximi consorti*.[260] In the case of the Nobili, Antonio di Lionardo was a member of the *Settanta* but it was his distant kinsman, Uberto di Francesco, who was prominent in the inner circles of the *governo popolare*. Antonio's son, Lionardo, was confined in the aftermath of the plot to restore Piero de' Medici in 1497, and played little role in the public life of Florence until 1513 when he was selected for the revived *Settanta*.[261] Cappone di Bartolomeo Capponi stands apart from the general pro Medici profile of his clan. He was implicated in the republican reaction of 1465–1466 and had no political career until the downfall of Piero de' Medici.[262] Other families which saw a shift in branch include the Acciaiuoli, Canigiani, Machiavelli, and, of course, the Medici. The sons of Pierfrancesco who had become estranged from Piero de' Medici played a prominent role in the early years of the new regime.[263]

If twenty-one new families entered or returned to the ranks of the elite after 1494, over a third of the families in the *Settanta* did not have members in the republican elite although eleven had members on its fringe and two more, the Alessandri and Sacchetii, were prominent in major offices. In the case of men like Bartolomeo Scala and Bernardo Buongirolami, it is not a case of families losing their place since they sat as individuals and Medicean dependants. It is difficult to find any pattern among the sixteen families who had little prominence in the public life of the Republic in the period of the *governo popolare*.[264] The group included large old families as well as smaller and more recent ones. Some of the smaller ones may not have had members of suitable age, interest, or aptitude for political life. Nevertheless, there is a strong impression that it is the lesser families in the *Settanta* who dropped out after 1494.[265]

* * *

The results of the exercise undertaken in the paper of a comparison of ruling groups under the *governo popolare* with that of the preceding regime suggest that the events of November-December 1494 were no more than a coup d'état. There was little change in the social composition of the political class. The "new" elements at the upper echelons of power can be accounted for by the return of some of the enemies of the Medici, by increased magnate representation and by the political arrival of one or two families who had been edging towards the centre during the fifteenth century. If anything, the proportion of old Florentine families in the inner circles was slightly higher during the popular regime than under the Medici. The removal of the *capo* had eliminated the most important avenue to political promotion, his sponsorship and patronage. The change that came with the establishment of the *governo popolare* — and this too can be exaggerated — was a wider distribution of power and a greater equality among the members of the ruling group. In theory, through their membership of the *Consiglio Maggiore*, all members of the ruling group, some 3,500 citizens, had an equal voice in legislation. In practice, the number of citizens who exercised this voice was much less, little more than 1,000 and thus a group that was equal in size to the annual membership of the Councils of the *Commune* and the *Popolo*. Certainly, even the effective membership of the *Consiglio Maggiore* was much larger than that of the *Consiglio dei Cento* where all important legislation reached its conclusion in the later years of the Medici regime. It was not much larger, however, than the group of citizens from which the membership for each session of the *Cento* was drawn.

Whether the change in the distribution of power was such that the political struggles of the period can be viewed primarily as conflict between socio-economic groups is open to question. It is indeed true that bitter battles were waged in the *Consiglio Maggiore* over taxation and financial policy and that successive Signorie found themselves paralyzed by their inability to raise revenue.[266] But these battles were also fought out in an abnormal situation when, in order to finance defense and the campaigns to recapture Pisa, the citizens of Florence were being called upon to contribute unprecedented sums. The failures before Pisa and the open contempt with which outside rulers treated Florence intensified the atmosphere of suspicion and recrimination.

Concentration on the political class in Florence has tended to distort our perspective on socio-economic distinctions and divisions. The inequalities among the 1,000 or so effective members of the *Consiglio Maggiore*, all of whom were guildsmen, taxpayers, political participants, tend to fade in importance when they are set beside the gulf between this tiny minority and those outside the ruling group in *città, contado,* and *distretto*.[267]

The introduction of the *governo popolare* also created a wider diffusion of power and a greater degree of equality among the citizens who formed the inner oligarchy. With the abolition of the Medicean system, the traditional offices of government headed by the Signoria regained their independence and initiative and the institutionalized power of a small inner group disappeared.

The efforts to regain an institutional place for an elite were one important aspect of the politics of the period. The pages of Parenti are full of bitter complaints about the "primati" and their machinations for "uno stato di pochi." From the time of the death of Savonarola, coinciding with the period of severe crisis in the external relations of the Republic, attempts were made and schemes were floated for the replacement of the *Ottanta* with a new more powerful council, the council that was finally but fleetingly realized in the brief moment between the flight of Pier Soderini and the summoning of the Medicean *Balià* in September, 1512.[268] But what was "uno stato di pochi"? *Governo largo* and *governo stretto* were not alternatives but the end points of a continuum. The size of the new council, the method of its election, the duration of the term of office of its members, the extent of its powers were all subject to debate and diversity of opinion. For Piero Capponi, effective government was only possible in Florence when power was in the hands of twenty or thirty *uomini da bene*.[269] At the other end of the continuum was the proposal made in the constitutional discussions which took place in 1502 for a council with a membership of three to four hundred.[270]

With the creation of the *Consiglio Maggiore* the Florentines had finally defined and fixed the boundaries of the political class. The constitutional and political struggles of the period of the popular regime reflect in part the efforts to define and fix the boundaries of the inner group. Thus political activity was not only directed towards regaining an institutional place for a small elite but also towards defining the size and the composition of this group.

The initiative in the expulsion of Piero de' Medici in 1494 had come from *primi cittadini* in the *Consiglio dei Settanta* who felt that their influence was waning.[271] The identification and description of an elite reveals nothing about the power its members held or the extent to which they felt that their ambitions for private interest and a voice in public policy were being met. Inner groups were composed of individuals, family and factional groupings competing for influence, prestige and private advantage. The *Consiglio dei Settanta* did not mark the final point in the articulation of circles of influence and power in Medicean Florence. This was to be found in the coterie around the head of the regime.[272] Nor were all members of the inner group after 1494 equally influential, equally able to meet their interest, equally satisfied. The faction which Guicciardini labelled as the "coda" of the party of Francesco Valori rallied around Pier Soderini and exerted considerable influence in the later years of the *governo popolare*.[273] Others were less able to secure their ambitions and interests as, for example, the Salviati cousins, Alamanno and Jacopo, discovered when their client was dismissed from his post as Chancellor of the *Mercanzia*, and when their advice on such policy issues as tactics against Pisa or the descent into Italy of the Emperor Maximilian was ignored. The Capponi found that their influence was weak when they failed in their efforts to secure the Archbishopric of Florence for Guglielmo after Rinaldo Orsini had resigned the see. Thus much of the political agitation of the period was no more than the traditional struggle among the leading citizens and families for place and power. As Nicolai Rubinstein has pointed out with specific reference to Cosimo, the role of the Medici in Florence was as much that of arbiters as of leaders and the source of their influence may have been their ability to bridge the differences among the *uomini principali* as well as their provision of effective leadership.[274] Even so, it should not be forgotten that the Medici faced challenges, plots, movements for reform from those who in their time felt neglected, dissatisfied, thwarted.

The restoration of the Medici to Florence in 1512 was the work of a very small group of malcontents.[275] The vast majority of Florentine citizens, *primi cittadini* as well as rank and file of the ruling group, had no desire to see the Medicean system re-erected. But they adapted in 1512 just as they had done in 1494 and once again chages in the composition of the inner oligarchy were limited.[276] If the majority adapted themselves to the new Medicean regime, the small group of families or their particular branches or individual citizens whose place in the inner circles was confined to the period of the popular regime should not be ignored. There was a core of republicans or at least anti-Mediceans in Florence who could not or would not be reconciled to Medicean leadership and who emerged into prominence again in 1527.[277]

Looking back from the viewpoint of the mid-sixteenth century when the Medici were securely entrenched in their Grand Duchy, it has been tempting to view the history of Florence from the mid-fifteenth century in terms of the rise of the principate. From this perspective the *governo popolare* is but an interlude, an anachronistic interruption. But few in Florence had regretted the departure of the Medici in 1494 and just as few welcomed their return in 1512 when their position in the city was far from solid and their future far from certain. The capture of the Papacy secured their situation and the period of the revived republican government, 1527–1530, made it permanent. Unlike the *governo popolare* of 1494–1527, that of 1527–1530 did witness a significant change in the composition of the ruling circles.[278]

NOTES

*A version of this paper in Italian was read at the *V Convegno di Studi sui Ceti Dirigenti nella Toscana dal Medioevo alla fine del Granducato*, Florence, December 1982.

1 Gene Brucker, *Florentine Politics and Society, 1343-1378* (Princeton, 1962); Nicolai Rubinstein, *The Government of Florence under the Medici, 1434-1494* (London, 1966); Anthony Molho, 'Politics and the Ruling Class in Early Renaissance Florence,' *Nuova Rivista Storica*, 59 (1968), 401-420; Dale Kent, 'The Florentine *Reggimento* in the Fifteenth Century,' *Renaissance Quarterly*, 28 (1975), 575-638; Ronald G. Witt, 'Florentine Politics and the Ruling Class, 1382-1407,' *Journal of Medieval and Renaissance Studies*, 6 (1976), 243-267; Gene Brucker, *The Civic World of Early Renaissance Florence* (Princeton, 1977); Nicolai Rubinstein, 'Oligarchy and Democracy in Fifteenth Century Florence,' *Florence and Venice: Comparisons and Relations*, 1, ed., Sergio Bertelli, Nicolai Rubinstein and Craig Hugh Smyth (Firenze, 1979), pp. 99-112. For overviews which place the results of these studies in the wider Italian context, v Sergio Bertelli, *Il Potere oligarchico nello stato-citta medievale* (Firenze, 1978); Philip Jones, 'Economia e societa nell' Italia medievale: la leggenda della borghesia,' *Storia di Italia. Annali, I, Dal Feudalismo al capitalismo* (Torino, 1978), 337-370.

2 On the continuity between the Medici regime and its predecessor, v Rubinstein, *The Government of Florence*, pp. 2-4, 8-9, 65-67, and 'Oligarchy and Democracy', p. 107; D. Kent, 'The Florentine *Reggimento*,' pp. 616-620.

3 Brucker, *The Civic World*, p. 81; D. Kent, 'The Florentine *Reggimento*,' pp. 615-616.

4 On the steady and continual expansion in the number of citizens qualified for the *tre maggiori* in the scrutinies between 1382 and 1449, ibid., pp. 613-615.

5 On elite groups before 1434, G. Brucker, *The Civic World*, pp. 250-252, 161-302; D. Kent, 'The Florentine *Reggimento*,' pp. 601-608; and after 1434, Rubinstein, *The Government of Florence*, p. 133, and 'Oligarchy and Democracy,' p. 107.

6 On the overthrow of the Medici and the establishment of the new regime, Nicolai Rubinstein, 'Politics and Constitution in Florence at the end of the Fifteenth Century,' *Italian Renaissance Studies*, ed. E. F. Jacob (London, 1960), pp. 148-166.

7 L. F. Marks 'La crisi finanziaria a Firenze dal 1494 al 1502.' *Archivio storico italiano*, 112 (1954), 45-46; Felix Gilbert, *Machiavelli and Guicciardini. Politics and History in Sixteenth Century Florence* (Princeton 1965) pp. 21-23; 49; Guido Pampaloni 'Fermenti di riforme democratiche nella Firenze medicea del Quattrocento,' *Archivio storico italiano*, 119 (1961), p. 37; Umberto Mazzone, *"El Buon Governo." Un progetto di riforma generale nella Firenze savonaroliana* (Firenze, 1978), pp. 8-9. For suggestions on the continuity between the *governo popolare* and the preceding regime, Rubinstein, 'Oligarchy and Democracy,' pp. 108-110; Roslyn L. Pesman, 'Comments,' ibid., pp. 113-115.

8 On the *Consiglio Maggiore*, Nicolai Rubinstein, 'I Primi anni del Consiglio Maggiore di Firenze (1494-99), *Archivio storico italiano*, 112 (1954), pp. 153-55, 163-165. Guicciardini argued that the *Consiglio Maggiore* "in effetto ha a tenere nella città el

luogo e la autorità del principe," 'Dialogo del Reggimento di Firenze,' Francesco Guicciardini, *Dialogo e Discorsi del Reggimento di Firenze*, ed. R. Palmarocchi [Bari, 1932], p. 103. On the problem of the locus of sovereignty in Florence, Lauro Martines, *Lawyers and Statecraft in Renaissance Florence* (Princeton, 1968), pp. 123–129.

[9] On the *Consiglio dei Cento*, Rubinstein, *The Government of Florence*, pp. 184–185, 194, 202–204.

[10] On the Medicean system of electoral controls, ibid., pp. 30–52.

[11] Rubinstein, 'Oligarchy and Democracy,' p. 109.

[12] Rubinstein, 'Politics and Constitution', pp. 152–159.

[13] Gilbert, *Machiavelli and Guicciardini*, pp. 23–28.

[14] The image of concentric circles was suggested by Martines, *Lawyers*, p. 388, and has been utilized by D. Kent, 'The Florentine *Reggimento*,' p. 578, and by Brucker, *The Civic World*, p. 252. Rubinstein's characterization of *uomini da reggimento*, *uomini principali* and *uomini più principali* is similar, *The Government of Florence*, p. 133.

[15] D. Kent, 'The Florentine *Reggimento*,' pp. 578–581, 583–585. Her definition makes possible comparative work between various regimes and has been accepted by Brucker, *The Civic World*, pp. 253–254, and Rubinstein, 'Oligarchy and Democracy,' p. 101.

[16] The members of the *arti minori* in the *Consiglio Maggiore* did not enjoy a position equal to that of the members of the *arti maggiori*. Dale Kent, in omitting the members of the *arti minori* who were qualified in the 1433 scrutiny from her analysis, argued that they lacked *prima facie* the attributes of the ruling class, and thus have no serious claim to be considered as part of it, 'The Florentine *Reggimento*,' p. 587.

[17] Rubinstein, 'I Primi Anni,' pp. 328–331.

[18] On the scrutinies, Rubinstein, 'Oligarchy and Democracy,' pp. 101–103.

[19] Ibid., p. 107.

[20] Ibid., pp. 103–108. In the past, since the results of the scrutiny were secret, it was not known — or it was assumed that it was not known — whether a citizen had been qualified unless and until his name was drawn from the *borse*.

[21] On Venice as a political model for Florence, Felix Gilbert, 'The Venetian Constitution in Florentine Political Thought,' *Florentine Studies* ed. Nicolai Rubinstein (London, 1968), p. 463–486; Renzo Pecchioli, 'Il *Mito* di Venezia e la crisi fiorentina intorno al 1500,' *Studi storici*, III (1962), 451–492; Pampaloni, 'Fermenti di riforme,' pp. 48–52.

[22] On the greater importance of Florentine traditions and experience in the reforms of 1494, Rubinstein, 'I Primi anni,' pp. 153–157.

[23] Ibid., p. 154.

[24] On the *divieto*, Nicolai Rubinstein, 'Florentine Constitutionalism and Medicean Ascendency in the Fifteenth Century,' *Florentine Studies*, p. 451.

[25] Rubinstein, *The Government of Florence*, pp. 56, 69, 115–117. *V* his distinction between those eligible for the *tre maggiori* as a legal class and the *seduti* and *veduti* as a political class, 'Oligarchy and Democracy,' p. 103.

[26] D. Kent, 'The Florentine *Reggimento*,' p. 588. For a brief summary of current opinion on the family in Florence, ibid., pp. 587-588. On the laws governing electoral processes and the *consorteria* as a political unit, Rubinstein, *The Government of Florence*, pp. 4, 8-10, 47, 63-65, 107; F. W. Kent, *Household and Lineage in Renaissance Florence* (Princeton, 1977), Ch. 4.

[27] Archivio di Stato Firenze, Provvisioni Registri (cit. Prov. Reg.), 185, c.10 All subsequent archival references are to the A.S.F. unless otherwise stated. *V* also Donato Giannotti, 'Discorso intorno alla forma della repubblica di Firenze,' *Opere politiche e letterarie*, ed. F. L. Polidori (Firenze, 1850), 1, p. 22 and F. W. Kent, *Household and Lineage*, p. 170.

[28] Prov. Reg., 185, c.12. In the registers of the results of elections for the *Ottanta* there are a number of instances where a third member of a *consorteria* was elected and subsequently disqualified, Tratte, 337, cc. 26-29, 141-189; 338, cc. 3-18v.

[29] Sergio Bertelli, 'Constitutional Reforms in Renaissance Florence,' *Journal of Medieval and Renaissance Studies*, 3 (1973), p. 164. In December 1494, the Signoria commissioned a number of magistracies to draw up drafts for constitutional reform. Some of the drafts have survived, Carte Storzziane, II, 95, insert, 12. Those of Domenico Bonsi and Piero Capponi have been published by Bertelli, pp. 156-164.

[30] Prov. Reg., 185, c. 10.

[31] This does not necessarily imply that a *consorteria* always acted in Florentine politics as a political unit or that all members of a *consorteria* enjoyed the same social and political status, *v* below, pp. 89, 96-97.

[32] Gilbert, *Machiavelli and Guicciardini*, p. 54.

[33] D. Kent, 'The Florentine *Reggimento*,' p. 614. For the period after 1433, no complete scrutiny lists survive. Her estimation is based on the results of the scrutiny of 1449 in three Quarters.

[34] Gilbert, *Machiavelli and Guicciardini, p. 53.*

[35] Ibid., pp. 53-54.

[36] This suggestion is based on a comparison of the 1508 list of the members of the *Consiglio Maggiore* for a sample of two *gonfaloni*, Carro and Vaio, with lists of their ancestors who sat in the Signoria or *Collegi*. For the members of the *Consiglio Maggiore*, Tratte, 1071; for presence in the Signoria, Priorista Mariani, Manoscritti, 248-253; for appearances in the *Collegi*, ibid., 256-266.

[37] On the Medicean practice of drawing *polizze* from the *borse* "solo per far vedere," Rubinstein, *The Government of Florence*, pp. 170, 189.

[38] *Reggimento, The Government of Florence*, p. 319; D. Kent, 'The Florentine *Reggimento*,' pp. 591-592; Brucker, *The Civic World*, pp. 67-68.

[39] For the results of the scrutinies of 1433 and 1453, D. Kent, 'The Florentine *Reggimento*,' Table 4, pp. 634-638.

[40] Francesco Guicciardini, *Storie fiorentine*, ed. R. Palmarocchi (Bari, 1931), pp. 101-107.

[41] The rehabilitation of the families of the "vecchio stato" had begun before 1494, Rubinstein, *The Government of Florence*, pp. 166, 216, 319; Dale Kent, *The Rise of the Medici. Faction in Florence, 1426-1434* (Oxford, 1978), pp. 344-345. But the

very sparse appearance of these families in the Signoria suggests that they were still subject to severe discrimination, *v* below, pp. 81–82.

[42] Rubinstein, 'I Primi Anni,' pp. 328–331.

[43] Prov. Reg., 185, cc. 10–10v.

[44] For suggestions that the establishment of the *Consiglio Maggiore* may have been a *serrata*, Bertelli, *Il Potere Oligarchico*, pp. 114–115, Roslyn Pesman Cooper, 'Comments,' *Florence and Venice*, I, p. 115. *V* also the argument given to Publio by Jacopo Pitti in his 'Apologia de' Cappucci,' ". . . se si considera il ristretto fatto da' nostri l'anno 1494, lo troverà più nobile che la chiusa de' Veneziani . . .," *Archivio storico italiano*, IV (1853), p. 277.

[45] For this legislation, Rubinstein, 'I Primi anni,' pp. 328–331.

[46] The *non-beneficiati* who had been successful in the 1484 scrutiny cannot be identified. Those in the Councils of the *Commune* and the *Popolo* and elected by the Signoria, together numbered 154, of whom all but c.16 were members of the *arti maggiori*, Tratte, 177, 60, cc. 398–398v. The lists in the Tratte do not distinguish the members of the *arti maggiori*. Their identification is based on the 1508 list of the members of the *Consiglio Maggiore* and on Giovanni Cambi, *Libro di tutti e' ciptadini, abili al chonsiglio d'anni XXIIII in su dal'anno 1495 al'anno 1510*, Biblioteca Nazionale Firenze (*cit.* B.N.F.), Manoscritti Passerini, 39.

[47] Piero Vaglienti, *Cronica*, B.N.F., Fondo Principale, II IV 42, c.20.

[48] The 20 were Giovanni da Ambra, Giovanni and Jacopo Biuzzi, Daniello Buini, Pierfrancesco Ciuffagni, Niccolò and Ottaviano Gherardini, Michele Gazetti, Jacopo Mormorai, Francesco Pollini, Lionardo Ringhiadori, Giovanni Tempi, Bendetto Tornaquinci, Piero Vaglienti, Valoriano Valoriani, Pierfrancesco Bandini Banducci, Francesco Pugi, Giovanni Simoni, Ser Niccolò and Ser Francesco da Romena. In February, 1497 the *non-beneficiati* who did not have the *beneficio* in their *consorteria* were dismissed from the *Consiglio Maggiore* with the right to apply for readmission, see below, pp. 77–78. All those listed above except the last five applied for readmission. The name of Pierfrancesco Bandini Banducci is struck out on the 1508 roll of the members of the *Consiglio Maggiore* as not having a legitimate *beneficio*. The names of the other four are not on the 1508 list, nor did they have relatives in the Council. Thus it is not clear whether they had the *beneficio* in the *consorteria* and had died before 1508 or whether they had been dismissed in 1497 and had not applied for readmission. Another of the *non-beneficiati*, Salvo Borgherini, had been elected to the Signoria in 1496 and acquired the *beneficio*.

[49] Rubinstein, 'I Primi anni,' pp. 158–159.

[50] Prov. Reg. 187, cc. 114–116; Rubinstein, 'I primi anni.' pp. 188–191. Also dismissed from the Council were those members who had acquired the *beneficio* after 1458 and whose fathers or grandfathers had been *famigliari* attached to the courts and other institutions of government.

[51] As Nicolai Rubinstein has argued, while the dismissal of those whose forebears had been *famigliari* and the *non-beneficiati* successful in the 1484 scrutiny and even those in the Councils of the *Commune* and of the *Popolo* can be viewed as moves against Medicean dependants, it is difficult to apply such an interpretation to

those admitted by the *Signorie* and *Collegi* at the beginning of 1495. He suggests that this move may have been directed against members of the old magnate families, but this seems unlikely since all those in this category, except two members of the Gherardini and one Tornaquinci, were not expelled, presumably because they had the *beneficio* in the family. Members of magnate families predominated among those subsequently elected to the *Consiglio Maggiore, v* below, p. 78.

[52] Prov. Reg., 187, c.116.

[53] Tratte Appendice, 5, cc.42, 42v, 43v, 44, 45, 48v, 50. Of the 20, 13 had been elected by the Signoria and the *Collegi* at the beginning of 1495, *v* above, n. 48. Another, Bastiano di Giovanni Albertinelli, had been a member of the Council of the *Comune* or of the *Popolo*. The other six were presumably qualified in the 1484 scrutiny, Messer Francesco di Piero Ambrogini, Francesco di Niccolò Calvanesi, Salvestro di Giovanni Buonguglielmi, Filippo do Piero Gaetani, Antonio di Tommaso Amidei, Piero di Andrea Mozzi. The dismissals from the *Consiglio Maggiore* may also have been an attempt by Francesco Valori and the *Frateschi* to purge the Council of some of their enemies. Just prior to the passing of the legislation, Savonarola had thundered from the pulpit on the need to cleanse the Council. Rubinstein, 'I Primi anni,' p. 188. Among the few dismissed from the Council and unsuccessful in the bid to return was the chronicler, Piero Vaglienti. In a letter which we wrote to Lorenzo de' Medici in April 1514, expressing his long held devotion to the Medici, the anti-Savonarolan Vaglienti clearly blamed Francesco Valori; ". . . mi fu dato lo stato quando Tanai de' Nerli fu ghonfaloniere di giustizia, e in quel tempo andai in tre luoghi in ufico. Dipoi quando Francesco Valori di nuovo fu ghonfaloniere per la legge se lo tolse a me e a molte altre persone, di che per questo e per altri suoi manchamenti n'acquistò la morte," Mediceo Avant il Principato, 26, 634.

[54] The section of the *provvisione* governing the processes for the readmission of the dismissed members of the Council states that "quegli e quelli saranno giudicati dal vostro Consiglio s'intendino essere habili al decto Consiglio, essendo così conveniente che nel senato fiorentino quelgli intervenghino che da decto senato saranno approvati et electi," c. 115. This is the only instance that I have come across where the *Consiglio Maggiore* is referred to in legislation as the "senato."

[55] Prov. Reg., 187, cc.114v, 115.

[56] Ibid., 189, c.48v.

[57] On the shift from sortition to election for the filling of offices, Rubinstein, 'I Primi anni,' pp. 323–347.

[58] Prov. Reg., 185, c.51v.

[59] Ibid., 187, c.114v.

[60] On citizenship, *v* below p. 83.

[61] Tratte Appendice, 6, cc; 72v, 166v; 7, cc.44v, 120v, 137v; 8, cc.27v–28, 11–11v; 9, cc.4v–6, 15v–16, 94v; 10c cc.49, 179–179v; 11, cc.3v–4v, 121–122. This record of elections appears to be complete. On the 1508 list of members of the *Consiglio Maggiore*, some 98 names are marked as being without the *beneficio*, 79 for the major guilds. Of the 79, 47 were *non-beneficiati* admitted at the beginning

of 1495 or subsequently elected, 17 were relatives of these men. There is no record of how the remainder entered the *Consiglio* but all except Cresci di Marchionne di Ser Marchionne Donati had relatives in the Council.

62 The six were members of the Da Gagliardo, Balducci, Boscoli, Fortini and Della Casa.

63 Magister Mazzingo di Messer Paradiso di Bartolomeo Mazzinghi, Messer Marcello di Messer Virgilio Adriani Berti, Lorenzo di Bartolomeo Cantucci, Magister Bernardo di Piero Bandini Banducci, Forese di Antonio di Forese Bizzeri, Niccolò di Ser Antonio de Giovanni Carsidoni, Francesco di Giovanni da Montealbergatore, Francesco di Niccolò di Zanobi Pollini who had been admitted by the Signoria at the beginning of 1495 and was re-elected in 1505 and his nephew, Girolamo di Cione di Niccolò Pollini, and Andrea di Lamberto di Luca Calvanesi whose cousin had apparently been qualified in the 1484 scrutiny and had successfully reapplied to the *Consiglio* for membership in 1497. The new members whose families had participated in the *reggimento* for the *minori* were Lorenzo Cantucci, Messer Marcello Adriani Berti and Francesco da Montealbergatore.

64 Jacopo Pitti, 'Istoria fiorentina,' ed. F.-L. Polidori, *Archivio storico italiano*, 1 (1842), p. 36.

65 *V* Lauro Martines, *The Social World of the Florentine Humanists* (Princeton, 1963), p. 47; D. Kent, 'The Florentine *Reggimento*,' pp. 580–581, 594.

66 Priorista Mariani, 253, cc. 1497–1501. The two for the *arti maggiori* were Urbano Cattani and Salvo Borgherini, both members of ancient families.

67 Ibid., cc. 1468–1496.

68 Ibid., cc. 1501–1516.

69 D. Kent, 'The Florentine *Reggimento*,' p. 612.

70 In her discussion of the *reggimento* in 1433, Dale Kent eliminated from her analysis fourteen members who did not have surnames, ibid., p. 587. Seven who have been identified have been added to her total of 325 families with successful nominees in the 1433 scrutiny, Benci-Guernieri, Cambi-Opportuni, di Chiarissimo, Giovanni (Santo Spirito), Pescioni, di Santi, Taddei. The Rustichi (Santa Maria Novella) have also been added and the Tosinghi have been separated from the della Tosa.

71 Tratte, 1071; for the families in the Council, Appendix 1. A figure of 3005 is suggested but there is a margin of error in the counting of names and the grouping of citizens into families. The names of the 1508 list are grouped alphabetically by first name under *gonfaloni* and according to whether a citizen had three, two or one *polizze*. The Priorista Mariani and Cambi's Libro have been used to establish families. Cambi's total for the *arti maggiori* membership of the *Consiglio*, 1495–1510, is 3618 citizens and 534 families. He in fact lists far more names under family headings than is indicated in his Indice and he appears to have included all male descendants of *beneficiati*. Citizens who died in 1495 and 1496 appear to have been omitted since some of those who held office in these years are not included on his list. Some citizens listed on the 1508 roll as *maggiori* who belonged to families whose members were predominately *minori* have been listed by Cambi as *minori*, e.g. Benintendi, da Ambra, di Baldo, del Rosselino. In the

notes to the manuscript, families who obtained the *beneficio* after 1510 have been added. Cases where Cambi has not been followed or where there are difficulties are discussed in the notes to Appendix I. The *arti minori* membership of the *Consiglio* in 1508 numbered 570, giving a total membership of c.3575.

[72] On the complexity of mobility in fifteenth century Florence, D. Kent, 'The Florentine *Reggimento*,' pp. 616–620. About 252 families in the *Consiglio Maggiore* did not have members qualified in the 1433 scrutiny. Of the 252, 87 had provided priors before 1433, and at least another eight had been qualified in earlier scrutinies. The eight are the da Barberino, Boni, Buondelmonte, Fedini, Ser Grifi, Libri, Nelli, di Stefano. The 1382 scrutiny list (14 *gonfaloni*) is published in *Delizie degli Eruditi Toscani*, XVI (Firenze, 1784), pp. 125–260. For the scrutiny of 1391, Tratte 397, and of 1411, Manoscritti, 555.

[73] About 157 families do not appear to have been qualified for the *tre maggiori* before 1434, of whom c.20 were *non beneficiati* specifically admitted to the Council. The five families without the *beneficio* who are assumed to have had members qualified in the 1484 scrutiny have been included in the 1434–1494 group, *v* above n. 53. There may be a margin of error in the assumption that families who had not provided priors before 1434 and who had not had success in scrutinies between 1382 and 1434 entered the political class for the first time under the Medici.

[74] Magnate families are identified in Appendix 1 and families with claims to antiquity are discussed in the notes to the Appendix.

[75] *V* D. Kent, 'The Florentine *Reggimento*,' p. 617, and Brucker, *The Civic World*, p. 257.

[76] Nicolai Rubinstein has shown that new families continued to enter the ruling group after 1434, *The Government of Florence*, Ch. 4. *V* also D. Kent, 'The Florentine *Reggimento*,' pp. 619–620.

[77] The fifteen were the Bartoli, Benvenuti, Betti, del Buono Ricco, Cambi, Canacci, Comi, Dazzi, Gondi, Della Lana, Particini, Petrucci, Riccardi, Salutati, Sassetti. This calculation is based on ibid., Table 4, pp. 634–638. The thirteen were the Ambrogini, Bartolelli, Bencini, di Buonaventura, da Castiglione, Cischi, Convenevoli, da Empoli, Giandonati, della Palla, Perini, Scarlattini, Squarcialupi. This calculation is based on the assumption that families who were not qualified in scrutinies between 1433 and 1453 and whose first prior postdates 1453 were qualified after 1453. There may be a margin of error in this assumption.

[78] Rubinstein, *The Government of Florence*, pp. 85–86; 'Oligarchy and Democracy', p. 107; D. Kent, 'The Florentine *Reggimento*,' p. 616.

[79] On the predominance of old established families in the ruling group in the fifteenth century, Rubinstein, *The Government of Florence*, pp. 56, 63–64; D. Kent, 'The Florentine *Reggimento*,' pp. 589–590; Brucker, *The Civic World*, pp. 254–255.

[80] The Pucci, del Nero, Parenti and Dazzi.

[81] Another nine families with members in the *Consiglio Maggiore* in 1495 had either temporarily or permanently dropped out of the Council by 1508. The nine are the Ammirati, Baldesi, Borsi (Drago, Santo Spirito), Compiobbesi, Guerrante, Lapozzi, Nerini, Salvini, Tigliamochi. Cambi's Libro has been used to identify families in the *Consiglio Maggiore* but absent in 1508.

[82] Forty six of the families qualified in the scrutiny of 1433 who did not have members in the *Consiglio Maggiore* had only one member qualified in 1433. Only six had more than five.

[83] On the party which constituted the opposition to the Medici, D. Kent, *The Rise of the Medici*, Ch. 2.

[84] Ibid., Appendix II, pp. 355–357.

[85] Rubinstein, *The Government of Florence*, pp. 18, 118.

[86] For the view that the families of the "vecchio state" were politically liquidated, Martines, *The Social World*, p. 49. Dale Kent regards this as exaggerated but the very limited presence of most of these families in the *Consiglio Maggiore* suggests that she may have underestimated their political ruin, *The Rise of the Medici*, pp. 344–345. The Aldobrandini and Bischeri (Vaio) had no members in the *Consiglio Maggiore* in 1508. The Anselmi with 14 members qualified for the *tre maggiori* in 1433, had one member in the *Consiglio Maggiore*, the Dello Scelto had dropped from 10 to 2, the Della Luna from 12 to 2, the Solosmei from 6 to 1, the Belfradelli from 7 to 1, the Barbadori from 10 to 4, the Castellani from 17 to 5, the Benizzi from 12 to 4.

[87] The Altoviti was one of the families where discrimination was applied only against particular branches. In the 1453 scrutiny, 29 members of the family were qualified for the *tre maggiori*.

[88] D. Kent, *The Rise of the Medici*, pp. 140–142.

[89] Copied out in the Priorista Ricci is the content of a letter which it is claimed Vaglienti sent to the Signoria around 1500 under the title of 'Apologia alla Signoria.' I have been unable to find the original of this letter but its tone and content is consistent with that of Vaglienti's Cronica, cc. 17v–19. The relevant part of the copy reads, ". . . Vorebbe che gli officii si dessino a chi li meriti. Dice che molti hanno paghato le gravezze in Firenze molti anni et non pervengono allo essere cittadini. Et per il contrario lo essere notaio haveva fatto scala, il che era mal fatto . . . Et vorebbe che fossino fatti cittadini solo quelli che per lo meno havessino habitato nella città anni cento et paghato le gravezze," Priorista Ricci, B.N.F. EB 14 1, Santo Spirito, cc.289v–290.

[90] Those qualified or nominated for the *arti minori* were the Bartolelli, Benci (Drago, San Giovanni), Benintendi, del Bianco, Bonvanni, Compagni, Corsellini, Formiconi, Del Giocondo, Guiducci (Lion Nero), Miniato di Dino, Da Pesciola, Redditi (Carro), Romoli, Del Zaccheria. The families who do not appear to have had members nominated in scrutinies before 1434 were the dell' Ancisa, Bellarno, Buongirolami, Bracciolini, Cattani, Cerchi, Convenevoli, Guidi, Marsuppini, Da San Miniato (Drago, San Giovanni), di Sandro Speziale, Vinacciesi.

[91] On the tightening requirements for citizenship and office holding, Julius Kirshner, 'Palo di Castro on *Cives Ex Privilegio*, A Controversy Over Legal Qualifications for Public Office in Early Fifteenth Century Florence,' *Renaissance Studies in Honour of Hans Baron*, ed. Anthony Molho and John A. Tedeschi (Firenze, 1970), pp. 229, 264.

[92] On the failure of historians to clearly distinguish these stages, Julius Kirshner, '"Ars Imitatur Naturam": A Consilium of Baldus on Naturalization in Florence,' *Viator*, 5 (1974), pp. 299–300.

[93] D. Herlihy and C. Klapisch, *Les Toscans et leur familles* (Paris, 1978), pp. 183, 310, 314.

[94] Ibid., p. 320.

[95] Kirshner, 'Paolo di Castro,' p. 231; '"Ars Imitatur Naturam,"' pp. 300–303. Entry into the *arti* appears to have been equally restricted as shown in the increasing proportion of matriculants from established families, *v* the figures on the *Arte della Lana* in Alfred Doren, *Le arti fiorentine* trans. G. B. Klein, 2 vols. (Firenze, 1940), 1:162. Only six families who entered the ruling group after 1434 had members elected as consuls of the *Lana* and *Cambio* in the last decades of the fifteenth and opening decade of the sixteenth century, the Dazzi, Gaddi, Giovanni, Del Nero, Pugliese, Zati, Arte della Lana, 32, cc. 56–67v; Arte del Cambio, 8, cc. 132v–209v.

[96] Kirshner, '"Ars Imitatur Naturam,"' p. 302. On the evidence of the lists in the eighteenth century Cittadinario, Manoscritti, 419, some 16 of the *arti maggiori* families in the *Consiglio Maggiore* were first granted citizenship after 1350. However, the list is incomplete. Kirshner's identification of the Del Nero as one family who first obtained Florentine citizenship after 1350 is open to question, Priorista Mariani, 252, c.1088.

[97] The five included Caterina Sforza of Imola, wife of Giovanni di Pierfrancesco de' Medici, Cittadinario, c.75.

[98] Anthony Molho, 'Politics and the Ruling Class in Early Renaissance Florence,' p. 414.

[99] In May, 1528 voting took place in the revived *Consiglio Maggiore* for the admission of new members. Of the 135 "cittadini mandati a partiti," 51 were successful. All came from families with members in the *Consiglio* between 1495 and 1512, Tratte 15, cc. 306–307.

[100] The 1415 statute which lists the magnates, identifies branches made *popolani* and when, *Statuti Populi Communis Florentiae*, 3 vols. (Friburgo, 1778), 1:444–448.

[101] D. Kent, *The Rise of the Medici*. pp. 346–347.

[102] Among the families who after 1434 had their first priors since the end of the thirteenth century were the Adimari, Agli, Bardi, Cerchi, Frescobaldi, Giachinotti, Pazzi and Tornabuoni. Since these families had priors in an earlier period, they have not been counted in the group of families who entered the ruling group for the first time after 1434. Clearly the distinction between the magnates who had priors in the late thirteenth century and those who did not is somewhat artificial.

[103] Two of the outlines for reform submitted to the Signoria in December, 1494 made a call for the integration of the magnates: ". . . tutti e'ciptadini seduti alchuno de' tre maggiori et tutti quelli che havessino vinto alchuno de'detti tre ufici et non fussino inborsati, et tutti quelli le famiglie et consorterie de'quali per alchuno tempo fussino stati seduti ad alchuni de'detti tre maggiori, et le famiglie antiche che si chiamorono le famiglie de'grandi o nobili. . . ." Carte Strozziane, 11, 95, 12, c.78. ". . . parendo dua cittadini per famiglia o tre o quattro della maggiore età perchè ancora le famiglie possino godere tale beneficio essendo cessato il sospetto della grandeza delle famiglie come è per essere quelle diminuite et moltiplicati è popolani," ibid., c. 71.

104 On wealth and mobility in Florence in general, Martines, *The Social World*, pp. 18–39.

105 'The Florentine *Reggimento*,' p. 597; Martines, *The Social World*, Tables V–VIII, pp. 365–378. As Kent points out, a number of the wealthy families with no representation in 1433 were only temporarily absent from the ruling group or were members of the *arti minori*.

106 It is difficult to be precise about the number given the existence of families with the same name and also the number of men on Martines' list without surnames or who were identified by place of origin. The attempt has been made to identify doubtful cases by comparison of first names. The economic activities of some of these families can be gauged from the list of Florentine firms which paid the 'Tassa dei Traffichi' in 1451, Anthony Molho, 'The Florentine "Tassa dei Traffichi" of 1451,' *Studies in the Renaissance*, 27 (1970), 73–118. On the foundations of the fortune and the economic activities of one of them, the Riccardi, see Paolo Malanima, *I Riccardi di Firenze. Una Famiglia e un patrimonio nella Toscana dei Medici* (Firenze, 1977), pp. 5–10.

107 The nine were the Dei, Salutati, Pucci, Cambi Mercatanti, Tanini, Del Giocondo, Da Pesciola, Balducci, Bernardi. The "setaiuoli grossi" were the Salvetti and Marsuppini; Bendettoi Dei, Cronica, Manoscritti 119, cc. 34–35. 56v–57.

108 On social mobility and the legal and notarial professions, Martines, *The Social World*, p. 75; *Lawyers*, pp. 68–71.

109 Ibid., p. 68.

110 On the Borromei, ibid., p. 497; on the Gaddi, ibid., p. 495, C. Bec, 'La Bibliothèque d'un grand bourgeois Florentin, Francesco d'Agnolo Gaddi (1496),' *Bibliothèque d'Humanisme et Renaissance*, 34 (1972), pp. 237–240.

111 Priorista Mariani, 253, c. 1435.

112 On the Buongirolami, Rubinstein, *The Government of Florence*, pp. 192–193; Martines, *Lawyers*, pp. 63–64; on the Da San Miniato, Priorista Mariani, 253, c. 1492.

113 Marvin B. Becker, *Florence in Transition*, 2 vols. (Baltimore, 1967–1968), II: 142–143; David Herlihy, 'The Tuscan Town in the Quattrocento. A Demographic Profile,' *Medievalia et Humanistica*, N.S. 1 (1970), p. 99. On notarial families among the "hew men" in the Medici party, D. Kent, *The Rise of the Medici*, pp. 119–120.

114 Kirshner, '"Ars Imitatur Naturam,"' p. 303.

115 Families with notaries in their backgrounds have been identified from the 1508 list of members of the *Consiglio Maggiore*, the Priorista Mariani, Arte dei Giudici e Notai, 26, and the Inventario, Notarile antecosimiana.

116 For notaries to the Signoria, D. Marzi, *La Cancelleria della Repubblica fiorentina* (Rocca S. Casciano, 1910), Appendice 1, pp. 483–513 and to other offices, Tratte, 78–81.

117 For the Chancellors and *Ufficiali delle Riformagioni*, Marzi, *La Cancelleria*, p. 514.

118 On Scala, Alison Brown, *Bartolomeo Scala, 1430–1497, Chancellor of Florence* (Oxford, 1979).

119 Rubinstein, *The Government of Florence*, pp. 215–216.

[120] Priorista Ricci, Santo Spirito, c. 289v. Vaglienti also complained of the rise of notaries and public officials in his Cronica, cc. 18v, 19v.

[121] Marzi, *La Cancelleria*, pp. 260-268. Most of those dismissed were subsequently reappointed.

[122] Prov. Reg. 186, cc. 12-12v; *Martines*, Lawyers, pp. 47-48.

[123] There was some doubt on this issue and the Signoria appointed a committee of lawyers to clarify the matter, Signori Deliberazioni, Ordinaria Authorità, 97, c. 32v.

[124] On the limited nature of Medicean favouritism in the interest of the members of the Chancery, Rubinstein, *The Government of Florence*, pp. 190-191. But the palace officials did have some privileges. In August 1473, they were allowed to add one name "per far vedere" to the *borse* for either the Signoria or its notariate, Alison Brown, *Bartolomeo Scala*, p. 152. It seems likely that it was their relatives whom they nominated.

[125] According to Parenti, the inner circle of Piero di Lorenzo de' Medici included a number of officials in the Chancery, Rubinstein, *The Government of Florence*, p. 231. On the influence of Ser Giovanni Guidi under Lorenzo, ibid., pp. 212, 213, 215-216. Francesco Guicciardini gave expression to patrician resentment of the influence of Chancery officials in his *Dialogo*, ". . . e che la authorità ed el pondo del governo è in cancellieri, personne villi e di pocca qualità ed el più delle volte sudditi nostri," *Dialogo e Discorsi*, p. 34.

[126] The two families who had not been nominated in scrutinies and who do not appear to have legal or bureaucratic backgrounds were the Convenevoli and di Sandro Speziale. The six families nominated for the *minori* before 1434 with notaries were the Compagni (Chiavi), Benci (Drago, San Giovanni), Giuducci (Lion Nero), Da Pesciola, Redditi (Carro), Romoli.

[127] These families are identified in Appendix 1. As well as the magnate families of Gherardini and Tornaquinci and the Mozzi who had been in the ruling group in the past, the 22 included the Ciuffagni, among the 'sbanditi e ribelli' in the Libro del Chiodo, S. Raveggi, M. Tarassi, D. Medici e P. Parenti, *Ghibellini, Guelfi e Popolo Grasso. I detentori del potere politico a Firenze nella seconda metà del Dugento* (Firenze, 1978), p. 72. Members of the Calvanesi and Tempi had participated in office in the late fourteenth and fifteenth centuries, Priorista Ricci, Santo Spirito, c. 320v, San Giovanni, c. 364. The Pollini were also well established in Florence. Cioni Pollini was a consul of the *Arte della Lana*, Priorista Ricci, Santa Maria Novella, c. 210v. There may be other families with similar records.

[128] The three were the Gaetani, Pollini and Tempi. On Cantucci, Cambi, Libro, c. 199v; Jacopo Nardi, *Istoria della Città di Firenze*, ed. Agenore Gelli, 2 vols. (Firenze, 1888), 1: 149-150.

[129] On the Adriani, Marzi, *La Cancelleria* pp. 281-282; on Mazzinghi, Armando F. Verde, *Lo Studio fiorentino 1473-1503, Ricerche e Documenti*, 3 vols. (Firenze, 1973-1977), 111: ii, 644-666; on Francesco Ambrogini and his father, Martines, *Lawyers*, p. 503 where the name is given as Ambrosini; on the Gaetani, ibid., pp. 415-416.

[130] da Ambra, Biuzzi, Buini, Bandini Banducci, Carsidoni, Mormorai, Tempi. The last four had provided notaries to the Signoria.

[131] ". . . chi non era d'esso chonsiglio non poteva avere alchuno ufito della terra quasi chome d'era gentiluomini alla veneziana," Piero Vaglienti, *Cronica* c.20. "Questi che possono avere magistrati, sono quelli che noi chiamiamo nobili; se come anco in Vinegia, soli quelli che possono avere magistrati sono gentiluomini cioè nobili," Donato Giannotti, 'Discorso,' *Opere* I, p. 17. See also the argument given to Bernardo del Nero in Francesco Guicciardini's *Dialogo, Dialogo e Discorsi*, p. 106.

[132] On the vocabulary of social and political classification, A. Anzilotti, *La crisi costituzionale della Republica fiorentina* (Firenze, 1912), pp. 1-2; Gilbert, *Machiavelli and Guicciardini*, pp. 23-28. This vocabulary and contemporary useage appear to require more precise investigation. It is by no means certain for example that terms such as *nobili, ricchi, principali, uomini savi* can be equated with each other.

[133] *V* above, n. 7.

[134] Rubinstein, 'Oligarchy and Democracy,' pp. 101-102.

[135] Martines, *The Social World*, pp. 18-84, G. Brucker, *Florentine Politics and Society 1343-1378* (Princeton, 1962), pp. 27-29.

[136] See Martines, *Lawyers*, pp. 62-65; D. Kent, 'The Florentine *Reggimento*,' pp. 594-595, 604-605; Brucker, *The Civic World*, p. 269.

[137] Families whose first priors sat in the Signoria as minor guildsmen included the Allegri (1348), Bellacci (1342), Ciari (1344), Gherucci (1343), Martelli (1343).

[138] e.g. Della Badessa and Cambi Opportuni.

[139] Long periods of absence from the Signoria have been noted in Appendix 1. In some cases of course the absence was due to political persecution and discrimination, e.g. the Alberti and del Bene. There are also a number of families who while they produced their first prior in the later fourteenth century had no more members in the Signoria until after 1434. The rise of these families might also be dated from the Medician period. The Alamanni and the Bonsi are two examples.

[140] *V* his characterization of Agnolo Niccolini and Pierfilippo Pandolfini as "spogliati di parenti e credito", *Storie fiorentine*, pp. 24-25.

[141] Rubinstein, *The Government of Florence*, pp. 214, 323. One of the families Piero Guicciardini placed in this category, the Taddei, did not have their first prior until 1424.

[142] *Istorie fiorentine*, ed. 1. di San Luigi, *Delizie degli Eruditi Toscani*, 20-32 (Firenze, 1785-1786), 20:28-31.

[143] *De Illustratione urbis Florentiae*, pp. 85, 105, 115.

[144] Piero Parenti, Storia fiorentina, in J. Schnitzer, *Quellen und Forschungen zur Geschichte Savonarolas* (Lipsia, 1902-1910), IV, p. 208.

[145] *Istorie fiorentine*, XX, p. 28.

[146] *V*, e.g., Guicciardini's description of Tanai de' Nerli as "potente pel numero de' figliuoli." *Storie fiorentine*, p. 115. On the importance of *parenti* in Florence, F. W. Kent, *Family and Lineage*, Ch. 4; D. Kent, *The Rise of the Medici*, pp. 37-49.

[147] Rubinstein, 'Florentine Constitutionalism,' p. 451.

[148] R. Pesman Cooper, 'L'elezione di Pier Soderini a gonfaloniere a vita,' *Archivio storico italiano*, 125 (1967): p. 177.

[149] On size of representation as a rough guide to status in a regime, *v* also Brucker, *The Civic World*, p. 255.

[150] The most obvious exception is the Valori, a family whose status was not open to question but who had only two members in the *Consiglio Maggiore* in 1508. It may be that it was his lack of family and numerous *parenti* which led Francesco Valori to build a political base among the *Frateschi* and become their leader.

[151] On the rise of the Pucci and the del Nero under the Medici, Rubinstein, *The Government of Florence*, pp. 9, 44, 86, 192.

[152] That is families who entered the Signoria after 1434 and do not appear to have claims to an ancient pedigree.

[153] Historians have noted the widely differing financial situations among members of families although they have diverged in their interpretations of its significance, Richard Goldthwaite, *Private Wealth in Renaissance Florence* (Princeton, 1968), pp. 258–259, F. W. Kent, *Household and Lineage*, pp. 149–163. Less attention has been paid to the problem of differing social and political status. Kent tends to view the weaker branches and lines as being outside political circles, p. 163.

[154] Parenti, *Storia fiorentina*, in Rubinstein, 'I Primi anni,' p. 324; Guicciardini, *Storie fiorentine*, p. 241.

[155] R. Pesman Cooper, 'Pier Soderini: Aspiring Prince or Civic Leader?' *Studies in Medieval and Renaissance History*, NS, 1 (1979), p. 82. This argument is discussed in greater detail in the second part of this study, below pp. 97–98.

[156] The variations in the economic positions of the members of the *Consiglio Maggiore* and the gulf between the wealthy minority and the much less prosperous majority has been emphasized by Gilbert who identified the "middle class" in the *Consiglio Maggiore* with its "economically weakest members," *Machiavelli and Guicciardini*, pp. 28–34. But concentration of wealth was a constant in fifteenth-century Florence (*v* Herlihy and Klapisch, *Les Toscans et leur familles*, p. 251 and Raymond de Roover, *The Rise and Fall of the Medici Bank, 1397–1494* [Cambridge, 1963], p. 29), and fifteenth-century ruling groups and their inner circles had contained old and influential families whose economic position was weak, D. Kent, 'The Florentine *Reggimento*,' pp. 599, Brucker, *The Civic World*, pp. 270–271.

[157] Marks, 'La crisi finanziaria,' pp. 45–46; *v* also Gilbert, *Machiavelli and Guicciardini*, pp. 22–24, 49–50.

[158] In 1411 the proportion of members of the *arti minori* in the *reggimento* was 17.3%; in 1433, 15.69%, D. Kent, 'The Florentine *Reggimento*,' pp. 615–616. In 1508 the proportion in the *Consiglio Maggiore* was 16%.

[159] For members of *Balìe*, Rubinstein, *The Government of Florence*, Appendices III–IX, pp. 254–315. All but 26 of the families who entered the ruling group before 1434 and who had six or more members in the *Consiglio Maggiore* were represented in one or more *Balìe* between 1438 and 1480. Of the 26, half came from the families subject to exile and discrimination, and four were magnate families. Only 26 of the families who entered the ruling group for the first time after 1434 had

members in *Balìe*, and a third of these were either magnates or old established families like the Gondi and Sassetti.

160 Guicciardini characterized the *governo popolare* as one "nel quale si faceva poca distinzione da uomo a uomo presente e da casa a casa," *Storie fiorentine*, p. 241.

161 Dale Kent suggests that most of those currently qualified to hold office between 1429 and 1434 actually did so, 'The Florentine *Reggimento*,' pp. 600–601.

162 Marks, 'La crisi finanziaria,' p. 44; Gilbert, *Machiavelli and Guicciardini*, p. 19.

163 Rubinstein, 'I Primi anni,' p. 161.

164 On the problems created by non attendance and the legislative measures to overcome them, ibid., pp. 161–194.

165 Libri Fabarum, 71, 72.

166 On arrears in taxation as political protest, Pesman Cooper, 'L'elezione di Pier Soderini,' p. 149–150.

167 *V* below, pp. 92–93.

168 Pesman Cooper, 'L'elezione di Pier Soderini,' p. 158.

169 *V* Gilbert, 'The Venetian Constitution,' p. 471.

170 *Dialogo e Discorsi*, p. 106.

171 Rubinstein, 'I Primi anni,' p. 324; Gilbert, 'The Venetian Constitution,' p. 473.

172 Prov. Reg. 185, c. 12.

173 The *pratiche* were informal meetings in which the government sought advice and established consensus. Since attendance was at the invitation of the Signoria, the *pratiche* provided the means by which citizens not in office at the time could exercise a voice in policy, *v* Felix Gilbert, 'Florentine Political Assumptions in the Period of Savonarola and Soderini,' *Journal of the Warburg and Courtauld Institutes* 20 (1957), pp. 187–214; Bertelli, *Il potere oligarchico*, pp. 111–112.

174 Storia fiorentina, B.N.F., Fondo Principales, 11 11 129 c. 93.

175 Bertelli, *Il Potere Oligarchico*, p. 108.

176 'Politics and Constitution,' pp. 178–179.

177 The term "inner oligarchy" is used by Martines, *Lawyers*, p. 5.

178 The offices in the sample are the Signoria, Consiglio degli Ottanta, Dieci di Libertà, Ufficiali del Monte, Otto di Guardia, Capitani della Parte Guelfa, Conservatori delle Leggi, Nove della Milizia (1507–1512), Capitano and Podestà of Pisa (1509–1512), Arezzo and Pistoia; Capitano of Volterra, Cortona, Livorno and Borgo San Sepolcro; Podestà of Prato, Castelfiorentino, and San Gimigniano, Tratte, 83, cc.3–3v, 18v–19v, 31–32, 115v, 123–126v, 128, 188–192, 221; 84, cc. 17–17v, 47–48, 69, 80–80v, 84–85, 112–113, 70, cc. 1–32v; 71, cc. 1–37v. The advisary *Collegi* to the Signoria, the *Sedici* and *Dodici*, were more widely shared. In the Quarter of Santo Spirito, there were twelve families with members in the *Collegi* who were not represented in the offices listed above; Amidei, Banchi, Barducci Cherichini, Benozzi, Brancacci, Data, Marsili, Palarcioni, Rinucci, Scolari, Stefani, Zampalochi, Tratte, 354, cc. 13–32v, 119v–137.

179 Dale Kent estimated that four-fifths of the 325 families in the *reggimento* in 1433 participated in major offices between 1427 and 1433, 'The Florentine *Reggimento*,' p. 602. Figures are not available for the size of the officeholding group under the

Medici but some 218 families had members in the *Consiglio Maggiore* between 1480 and 1494, *v* below pp. 93–94. The addition of families with members in the Signoria would increase the size of the Medicean officeholding group to about 280 families. In Santo Spirito over the period 1480–1494, fifteen families not in the *Cento* had members in the Signoria. These figures would not support the argument of Lauro Martines that a contraction in the size of the "inner oligarchy" took place in the course of the fifteenth century, *Lawyers*, pp. 389–390. Of course the identification of the size and the families in the major officeholding group does not tell us anything about the distribution of power nor invalidate the argument that power became more narrowly concentrated.

[180] All but 26 of the 287 officeholding families had members elected to the *Ottanta* and the share of the 26 in major office was minimal, confined for the most part to a single appearance in the Signoria. The 26 were the Alderotti, Amadori, Deti, Di Giachi, Lippi, Mozzi, Rossi, Bartoli Filippi, Da Magnale, Pieri, Da Rabatta (Ruote), Ambrogini, Beccanugi, Giandonati, Ricasoli, Sertini, Tornabuoni, Ubaldini, Agli, Bartolini Scodellari, Benivieni, Bonvanni, Bruni (Lion d'Oro), Scali, Solosemei, Sostegni. The only members of these families with more than a minimal appearance in office were Messer Ormanozzo Deti and Piergiovanni Ricasoli. Eleven families in the *Ottanta* did not have members in other major offices; the Bartollelli, Benizi, Biliotti (Bue) Del Guanto, Guiducci (Lion Nero), Martellini, Mini, Redditi (Carro), Riccardi, Del Rosso, Ughi.

[181] Tratte, 337, cc. 26–29, 141–189; 338, cc. 3–18v, *v* Appendix 2. This calculation is based on those who occupied positions. The inclusion of those who were elected but did not take up the office would not substantially change the picture of the composition of the *Ottanta* at the level of the family. The ex officio membership has also been ommitted for the same reason.

[182] For the membership of the *Cento*, Tratte 336; 337, cc. 1–25, *v* Appendix 3. In his discussion of the composition of the various levels of participation and power, Nicolai Rubinstein, has identified the *uomini principali* with the membership of the *Balìe*, and after 1480, with that of the *Consiglio del Settanta*, and the *uomini più principali* with the small group around the head of the regime, *The Government of Florence*, p. 133. In this paper for the period after 1480, the membership of the *Cento* has been viewed as a privileged circle within the ruling group and that of the *Settanta* as an inner elite. The members of the *Cento* as well as of the *Settanta* are viewed as "the prominent figures in the ruling group" by Felix Gilbert, *Machiavelli and Guicciardini*, p. 22, n. 20.

[183] On *proximi consorti*. F. W. Kent, *Household and Lineage*, p. 61. Since in many families, some first names are common, there is a margin of error in the identification of *proximi consorti*.

[184] For the membership of *Balìe*, 1452–1480, Rubinstein, *The Government of Florence*, Appendices V–IX, pp. 272–315.

[185] For the members of the Signoria, 1495–1512, Prov. Reg. 185–201; for their relatives in the Signoria under the Medici, Priorista Mariani, 248–253.

[186] In this count, members who sat ex officio through their election to the *Dieci* have been included, and thus there is some discrepancy with the figures in Table 3.

Since almost all families in the *Ottanta* had members elected to either the Signoria or *Collegi*, ex officio appearances in the *Ottanta* through these offices have not been included.

187 For the share of families in both the *Cento* and *Ottanta*, Appendix 3.

188 The ten without members in the *Cento* were the Guasconi, Gianni, Peruzzi, Serragli, Manelli, Risaliti, Giacomini, Scarlatti, Parenti and Dazzi. Members of the first four were punished by the *Balìa* of 1434 and the Manelli were closely associated with the exiled families. Priore di Jacopo Risaliti, according to Cavalcanti, was one of the two members of the *Otto di Guardia* who in 1433 had wanted Cosimo de' Medici strangled rather than merely confined. Piero di Tommaso Giacomini was deprived of right to hold office in 1466 and Daniello di Nofri Dazzi and his descendants were deprived of offices in perpetuity in 1458. For the Manelli and Priore Risaliti, D. Kent, *The Rise of the Medici* pp. 152, 184; for Dazzi, Libro di confinati e condennati dal 1434 al 1468, Manoscritti, 441. Among those with little representation were the magnates Adimari, Gualterotti, and Tosinghi, the "vecchio stato" families of Corsi, Gianfigliazzi and Strozzi, and the Manetti and Gondi, some of whose members fell foul of the Medici regime. On the Manetti and Gondi, Rubinstein, *The Government of Florence*, pp. 44, 165.

189 On the growing importance of the Tornabuoni in Florentine government after the marriage of Piero di Cosimo de' Medici and Lucrezia Tornabuoni, ibid., pp. 107, 126, 193, 231. On the Bonvanni, Priorista Mariani, 253, c. 1351.

190 Indicative of the permanent eclipse of most of the families of the "vecchio stato" is their limited presence in the *Ottanta*. Of the families who suffered almost total discrimination during the Medicean regime, seventeen had members in the *Ottanta* but only seven had more than minimal representation, the Corsi, Gianfigliazzi, Gianni, Guasconi, Peruzzi, Serragli, and Strozzi. Giovacchino Guasconi was the only member of the "vecchio stato" group of families to be elected as *gonfaloniere di giustizia* and he, Tommaso Gianni and Lionardo Strozzi, the only ones to be elected to the *Dieci*.

191 Guicciardini, *Storie fiorentine*, p. 135.

192 Storia fiorentina II II 129, c. 169 (January, 1496).

193 Tratte, 337, c. 28v; 83, c. 3v.

194 Ibid., 83, c. 188v; Parenti, Storia fiorentina, II II, 130, c. 37, in Marks, 'La crisi finanziaria,' p. 45 where Ambrogini is identified as Ambrogi.

195 Storia fiorentina, II II 130, c. 75v.

196 Martines, *Lawyers*, p. 504.

197 "Et parlardo ancora in favore del frate sendolui a stomaco a molti per essere nuovo huomo nell a città et fratesco, la Signoria medesimamente con uno bollettino alli octo privava dell 'ufficio et fece admonire per anni 3," Storia fiorentina, II II 131, c. 76v.

198 *Storie fiorentine*, p. 137.

199 For a full discussion of the shift from election to sortition which began in 1497, Rubinstein, 'I Primi Anni,' pp. 335-356.

200 Ibid., pp. 341-342.

[201] Rubinstein, 'Politics and Constitution', pp. 179–180.

[202] Prov. Reg., 189, c. 9v.

[203] *Storie fiorentine*, p. 137; *v* also his 'Discorso di Logrogno,' *Dialogo e Discorsi*, pp. 263–264.

[204] On the reform moves, Gilbert, *Machiavelli and Guicciardini*, pp. 58–73, and below, pp. 106–107.

[205] *Storie fiorentine*, p. 271.

[206] Gilbert, *Machiavelli and Guicciardini*, pp. 52–73; Pesman Cooper, 'L' elezione de Pier Soderini,' pp. 154–165.

[207] Prov. Reg., 193, cc. 51–51v. A similar explanation was given by Guicciardini, *Storie fiorentine*, p. 246.

[208] The *Ottanta* was elected nineteen times between the end of 1502 and the fall of the *governo popolare*. In July 1508 it was decided to change the months for the election of the *Ottanta* from July and January to May and November. The *Ottanta* elected in July, 1508 sat for nine months instead of the usual six, Prov. Reg., 199, cc. 23–23v.

[209] As the *Dieci* was elected only eleven times before December 1502 and 24 times after, the absolute number of citizens who held this office did not decline, 66 in the earlier period, 81 in the later, but the average number of places per man rose from 1.3 to just over 2. Before 1503, nineteen citizens sat in the *Dieci* on more than one occasion. Between 1503 and 1512, over half those in the *Dieci* sat at least twice and ten were present in the office on four or more occasions. Four citizens who were elected to the *Dieci* but did not take up their posts have not been included in this count. Tratte, 83, cc. 115–115v; 84, cc. 124v–125, 126–126v. On the failure to elect the *Dieci* for periods between 1495 and 1502, see Gilbert, *Machiavelli and Guicciardini*, pp. 61–63.

[210] The number of citizens who held office in the *Otto di Guardia* did not decline after 1502 as it was relatively rare for a citizen to be in the office more than once, as had also been the case under the Medici. (About 20 citizens sat in the *Otto* on two occasions between 1495 and 1512, and about 15 between 1480 and 1494). However, after 1502, as was the case with the *Ottanta*, the number of members of the *Otto* whose families had provided members of the office under the Medici rose and the number of post-1434 families declined. Between 1495 and 1502, 36.5% of those in the *Otto* were themselves or were *prosimi consorti* of citizens in this office between 1480 and 1494, and a total of 56% were from families in the *Otto*. Between 1503 and 1512, the relevant proportions are 49.5% and 69%. Before January 1503, 13 post-1434 families had members in the *Otto* who occupied 19 places, after, six who occupied 14, and six of the 14 places were held by members of the Gondi. Tratte 83, cc. 1–2v, 188–192; 84, cc. 84–85.

[211] Families with members among the *Ufficiali del Monte* numbered 39 before January 1503, and 31 after. In the former group, just under half were families who provided the *Ufficiali* and members of the *Consiglio dei Settanta* under the Medici, in the latter group, two thirds. Six post-1434 families had members among the *Monte* officials in the early years of the *governo popolare* but only one after 1502. The six were the Bandini Banducci, Borgherini, Dazzi, Gaddi, Del

Giocondo and Gondi: the one citizen after 1502 was Rinieri di Bernardo Dei. Tratte 83, cc. 3–3v, 32; 84, c. 69.

[212] Storia fiorentina, II IV 170, c. 185, in Gilbert, *Machiavelli and Guicciardini*, p. 27. Jacopo Pitti also argued that in the *Ottanta*, "risiedevano sempre li più riputati cittadini con autorità veramente più propria dello stato di pochi che della repubblica," 'Istoria fiorentina,' p. 74.

[213] *Storie fiorentine*, pp. 209, 225, 270.

[214] Ibid., pp. 115, 135, 203, 207, 240.

[215] *Dialogo e Discorsi*, p. 286.

[216] *Storie fiorentine*, pp. 135, 239, 272, 300.

[217] Ibid., pp. 24–25, 135, 143–144, 240.

[218] "Allo universale della città, che erano gli uomini di case basse e che conoscevano che negli stati stretti le case loro non arebbono condizione, erano gli uomini di buone case, ma che avevano consorti di più autorità e qualità di lore e però vedevano che in uno vivere stretto rimarrebbono adrieto," *Storie fiorentine*; p. 241. It seems plausible to assume that Parenti's *primati* and *cittadini principali* were also a small elite of leading citizens but Parenti's vocabulary of social and political classification requires further investigation.

[219] It should be stressed that this survey has been confined to the most important offices since the aim was to identify the inner oligarchy. Its extension to a wider sample of offices including the *utili* might have produced a different picture. The restriction of the sample to the most important offices may explain the discrepancy between my conclusion on the very limited nature of the changes in the composition of the officeholding group and Donald Weinstein's suggestion, based on a much wider survey of offices for the period 1495–1500, that Savonarola's objective of broadening participation in political life appeared to have been achieved, *Savonarola and Florence. Prophecy and Patriotism in the Renaissance* (Princeton, 1970), p. 265. The difference in viewpoints would also be influenced by the restriction of his sample to the early years of the *governo popolare* when, as mentioned above, some new men did appear in high office. There is also a difference in method. Whereas Weinstein traced the careers of Medicean officeholders after 1494, I have traced the careers of the republican officeholders before 1494.

[220] For analyses of the role and composition of inner elites in the earlier fifteenth century, D. Kent, 'The Florentine *Reggimento*,' pp. 601–608; Brucker, *The Civic World*, p. 251. A major theme of Brucker's study is the shift in Florence from communal to elitist politics. As Nicolai Rubinstein has pointed out, the stratification of the ruling group did not stop at the level of the *Settanta*. There were small and more powerful groups around the head of the regime, 'Oligarchy and Democracy,' pp. 105–106; *v* also below, p. 107.

[221] For the *Settanta*, Rubinstein, *The Government of Florence*, pp. 199–203.

[222] Vacancies in the *Settanta* were filled by co-option. Just over half of the 62 citizens who entered the *Settanta* after 1480 were the sons and brothers of former members. Eleven more were from families with members in the original *Settanta*. For a list of the members of the *Settanta* appointed in 1480, Rubinstein, *The*

Government of Florence, Appendices IX–X pp. 309–310, 316–317. For a list of citizens co-opted to the *Settanta* 1480–1494; *v* below, Appendix 4.

223 Rubinstein, 'Politics and Constitution,' p. 162.

224 *V* above, p. 91–92.

225 Prov. Reg., 189, c.9v.

226 On the struggles around the *Dieci* and the problems in filling the office, Gilbert, *Machiavelli and Guicciardini*, pp. 61–63; Martines, *Lawyers*, pp. 198–200.

227 Both Gilbert and Rubinstein have equated the leading citizens with the regular members of the *pratiche, Machiavelli and Guicciardini*, p. 65; *The Government of Florence*, p. 133. Dale Kent and Brucker have identified the citizens at the apex of the political structure for the periods 1429–1433 and 1403–1414 on the basis of participation in *pratiche*, 'The Florentine *Reggimento*,' pp. 601–602; *The Civic World*, pp. 264–265.

228 As Dale Kent has noted, identification of the prominent citizens with those who spoke most frequently in *pratiche* does not allow for absences of citizens from the city on private or government business, or for the quality or influence of contributions to the discussion, 'The Florentine *Reggimento*,' n. 119, p. 602.

229 On *pratiche larghe* and *pratiche strette* in the republican period, Gilbert, *Machiavelli and Guicciardini*, pp. 65–66; Bertelli, *Il Potere oligarchico*, pp. 111–112.

230 As early as 1495, Parenti noted the presence of extra constitutional influences. Commenting on the fall of the *accoppiatori*, he concluded, "imperochè loro sempre dalla Signoria quale faceano chiamati erano alla practica continua e sempre in continua amministrare del publico si trovavano," Storia fiorentina, II II, 129 c. 117v.

231 Pesman Cooper, 'Pier Soderini,' pp. 81–82.

232 Storia fiorentina, II II 132, c. 71.

233 For lists of members of various committees, Tratte Appendice, 5, cc. 87v, 88v, 103–103v, 109, 112, 121v–122, 127, 134; 6, 23v, 31, 40, 87v, 115v–116, 121v–122v, 141, 145–145v, 162v, 172v, 189v; *Consulte e Pratiche*, 65, cc. 94, 131, 148v, 197; 66, cc. 165v, 247v, 365; Parenti, Storia fiorentina, II II 132, cc. 4v, 121; II II 133, cc. 8–8v, 10v, 17; for commissioners and envoys Signoria Missive, Legazioni e Commissarie, 23, cc. 29–60v; Signoria Deliberazioni Speciale Autorità, 40, cc. 1–45.

234 *Consulte e Pratiche*, 68, 69.

235 For a list of the members of the projected élite group, *v* Appendix 5.

236 *V* Appendix 5. In a recent article, Humfrey Butters has identified the guests who were invited to the reception Pier Soderini gave on the eve of his entry into the office of *gonfaloniere a vita*, 'Piero Soderini and the Golden Age,' *Italian Studies*, 33 (1978), p. 71. Of the 47 guests, 33 are included in the present identification of the inner group and six in the fringe group. Five more were relatives of citizens in the inner group.

237 For the *Catasto* return, Verde, *Lo studio fiorentino*, III, i, p. 10; for the purchase of Medici lands, Signoria Deliberazioni Ordinaria Autorità, 97 cc. 103–103v.

238 Some care is needed in assessing the place of the Salviati in Florentine politics and government since Guicciardini in his *Storie fiorentine*, the source most relied

on by historians, may well exxagerate the role of his newly acquired father-in-law, Alamanno Salviati.

239 Nicolai Rubinstein views the first thirty members of the *Settanta* in 1480 as elected on the basis of individual qualifications, and the remainder on that of family, *The Government of Florence*, p. 203.

240 The nine were Messer Niccolò Altoviti, Messer Antonio Strozzi, Messer Matteo Niccolini, Giovanni Pitti, Francesco Pandolfini, Giuliano Mazzinghi, Guido Manelli, Tommaso and Cappone Capponi. The six were Messer Domenico Bonsi, Messer Antonio Malegonnelle, Filippo dall'Antella, Lorenzo Dietisalvi Neroni, Guglielmo Pazzi, Francesco Pucci.

241 On remaining *a specchio* as political protest, R. Pesman Cooper 'L'elezione di Pier Soderini,' pp. 149–150; on Bernardo Rucellai, Felix Gilbert, 'Bernardo Rucellai and the Orti Oricellari,' *Journal of the Warburg and Courtauld Institutes*, 12 (1949), 101–131.

242 Included in this group are Lorenzo di Antonio and Niccolò di Francesco Alessandri, both of whom served on the *Dieci*, Giovanbattista and Tommaso Giovanni, both of whom were elected as *gonfaloniere di giustizia*, the sons of Jacopo Mancini and the cousins, Andreuolo, Filippo and Nicol Sacchetti, and Tommaso Gianni who served in the *Ottanta* for thirteen terms.

243 The nine are the Alessandri, Cappelli, Galilei, Guidetti, Mancini, Manetti, Rinuccini, Sacchetti, Temperani.

244 On this problem, Martines, *Lawyers*, pp. 54–56; Bertelli, *Il Potere oligarchico*, pp. 128–135.

245 On the diplomatic activities of the Soderini, Pesman Cooper, 'L'Elezione di Piero Soderini,' pp. 173–175.

246 For Niccolò Guasconi, Verde, *Lo Studio fiorentino*, III, i, p. 530.

247 Thirty-four of the members of the elite were consuls in the *Lana* or *Cambio*, Arte della Lana, 32, cc. 56–67v; Arte del Cambio, 8, cc. 132v–209v. For guild consulship as an indication of continued mercantile activity, Brucker, *The Civic World*, p. 270.

248 Francesco Guicciardini was one Florentine who certainly believed that government should be the preserve of "cittadini savi ed esperti."

249 *Lawyers*, pp. 54–56, 75–76.

250 For information on the education and on the intellectual interests of some members of the elite, Verde, *Lo Studio fiorentino*, III, i–ii.

251 Seven of the 21 were in this group, Giacomini, Gualterotti, Manelli, Mazzinghi, Pazzi, Popoleschi, Tosinghi.

252 For pre-Medici elites, Brucker, *The Civic World*, p. 269 and D. Kent 'The Florentine *Reggimento*,' p. 605. Of the 73 families in the *Settanta*, 1480–1494, eleven had their first prior between 1382 and 1433, and seven between 1434 and 1494. Of the 61 families in the elite projected for the *governo popolare* the relevant figures are 7 and 4. In these calculations, magnate families have not been counted and the date of the first prior is that for the *arti maggiori*.

253 For those punished by the *Balìa* of 1434, D. Kent, *The Rise of the Medici*. Appendix II, pp. 355–357.

[254] Ibid., p. 148; *Storie fiorentine*, p. 288.

[255] On the republican reaction of 1465-1466, Rubinstein, *The Government of Florence*, pp. 136-166.

[256] Libro di Confinati, Manoscritti, 441, c.5; Jacopo Pitti, 'Vita di Antonio Giacomini,' ed. C. Monzani, *Archivio storico italiano*, iv (1853): 107-109.

[257] Guicciardini, *Storie fiorentine*, p. 37.

[258] Rubinstein, *The Government of Florence*, p. 109.

[259] *Dizionario Biografico degli Italiani*, I (Roma, 1960), pp. 716-717.

[260] As F. W. Kent has pointed out, more attention needs to be given to the whole subject of the nature of political allegiance in Florence. Richard Goldthwaite has viewed divided political allegiances within a family as indicative of the waning importance of the *consorteria* as a political until, *Private Wealth*, pp. 259-260. On the basis of the three families that he studied, Kent suggests that these divisions can be exaggerated, *Household and Lineage*, pp. 211-215.

[261] Cambi, *Istorie fiorentine*, xx, p. 109. For the members of the *Settanta*, Tratte 84, c. 66.

[262] F. W. Kent, *Household and Lineage*, pp. 89-90.

[263] On Pierfrancesco de' Medici and his sons, Alison Brown, 'Pierfrancesco de' Medici, 1430-1476: A Radical Alternative to Elder Medici Supremacy', *Journal of the Warburg and Courtauld Institutes*, 42 (1979), pp. 101-102.

[264] The sixteen were the Aldobrandini, Alamanni, Biliotti, Buongirolami, Cortigiani, Cresci, Dini, Lioni, Lorini, Masi, Mellini, Paganelli, Ridolfi di Borgo, Scala, Spinelli, Tornabuoni. The close ties of the Medici and the Tornabuoni have been discussed above.

[265] Of the sixteen families with little prominence under the *governo popolare*, only three were in the inner group which Dale Kent has identified for the early 1430s, 'The Florentine *Reggimento*,' pp. 604-605.

[266] On the struggles over taxation in the *Consiglio Maggiore*, Marks, 'La crisi finanziaria,' pp. 40-72.

[267] Felix Gilbert has drawn attention to the "basic enmity between those who were excluded from the Great Council and those who were members of it," *Machiavelli and Guicciardini*, pp. 19-21; F. W. Kent has voiced his suspicion that "the social and personal distance between a man taxed only a couple of florins and one who paid fifty was much less than between either of them and a consistent pauper," *Household and Lineage*, p. 150.

[268] On the moves for constitutional reform in this period, Gilbert, *Machiavelli and Guicciardini*, pp. 67-78; Pesman Cooper, 'L'elezione di Pier Soderini,' pp. 145-166; Sergio Bertelli, 'Petrus Soderini Patriae Parens,' *Bibliothèque d'Humanisme et Renaissance*, XXI (1969), pp. 93-98; 'La crisi del 1501: Firenze e Cesare Borgia,' *Essay Presented to Myron P. Gilmore*, ed. Sergio Bertelli and Gloria Remakus, I (Firenze, 1978), pp. 1-19.

[269] Rubinstein, 'Politics and Constitution,' p. 153.

[270] Gilbert, *Machiavelli and Guicciardini*, pp. 69-70.

[271] Rubinstein, *The Government of Florence*, pp. 228-230.

[272] Rubinstein, 'Oligarchy and Democracy,' pp. 105-106.

273 On factions in the later period of the *governo popolare*, Pesman Cooper, 'Pier Soderini,' pp. 105–110.

274 *The Government of Florence*, p. 133.

275 Pesman Cooper, 'Pier Soderini,' pp. 122–123.

126 Some idea of the changes in the inner oligarchy can be obtained from Appendix 3 where the families in the *Cento* and *Settanta*, 1514–1527, are listed. The identification of inner groups is even more difficult after 1512 when the separation between the constitutional forms and power and influence became even greater.

277 Families in this group include the Gualterotti, Giacomini, Guasconi, Manelli, Mazzinghi, Mancini, Rinuccini, Tosinghi, Del Bene. Pierfrancesco Tosinghi and Antonio Gualterotti were coopted to the *Settanta* in the 1520s but both families appear to have played little role in Medicean government. Particular branches of families who were prominent before 1572 and not after that year were the descendants of Simone Corsi, of Braccio di Niccolò Guicciardini and Bernardo di Simone del Nero.

278 A second part of this study will deal with the ruling group, 1527–1530.

The Consiglio Maggiore in 1508, Membership for the arti maggiori

	Gonfalone	Members	First[2] Prior	Long periods of absence from the Signoria
Acciaiuoli	Vipera	17	1282	
Adimari[3]	Vaio, Drago, S.G., Chiavi, Vipera, Scala	13	1286M	
Adriani Berti	Lion Nero	1	1394[+b]	
Agli	Drago S.G.	2	1285	1291/1508
Alamanneschi[4]	Vaio	4	1286M	1286/1439
Alamanni	Scala	9	1354	1354/1448
Alberti	Lion Nero	10	1289	1390/1438
Albertinelli	Bue	1	-[+]	
Albizzi	Chiavi	41	1282	
Ser Albizzo	Vaio	2	1464	
Alderotti	Ferza	1	1364	1378/1504
Aldobrandi	Ruote	3	1480	
Aldobrandini del Nero	Lion d'Oro	15	1320	
Alessandri[5]	Chiavi	4	1282	
Allegri	Lion Bianco	2	1348[d]	
Altoviti	Vipera	43	1282	
Amadori	Scala	3	1311	
Da Ambra	Chiavi	1	-[+c]	
Ambrogini	Unicorno	1	-[+]	
Amidei	Ferza	1	- M[+]	
Dell'Amorotta	Lion Rosso	4	1298	
Dell'Ancisa	Chiavi	6	1475	
Anselmi	Lion Bianco	1	1283	1434/-
Dall'Antella	Carro	11	1282	
Antinori	Drago S.S.	6	1351	1373/1431
Ardinghelli	Unicorno	8	1282	1417/1500
Arnoldi[6]	Bue	1	1491	
Arnolfi	Carro	2	1318	1446/1493
Arrighi	Chiavi	10	1373	
Arrighi da Empoli	Vaio	1	1382	
Arrigucci	Drago S.G., Vaio	8	1375M	

Degli Asini	Bue	3	1343	1343/1464
Del Badessa	Vipera	3	1287[c]	
Bagnesi	Lion Nero	5	1346	
Di Baldo	Ferza	1	1422[b]	
Baldovinetti	Vipera	8	1287	1433/1475
Baldovini[7]	Vaio	2	1440	
Balducci	Drago S.G.	1	1477	
Balducci Pegolotti	Drago S.S.,Nicchio	3	1346	
Banchi	Scala	5	1305	1449/-
Banchozzi	Lion Nero	3	1434	
Bandini Banducci	Lion Rosso	2	-[+]	
Barbadori	Nicchio	4	1295	1431/1513
Da Barberino	Bue	1	1490	
Bardi	Scala,Lion Nero	7	1282M	1290/1447 1448/1508
di Bardo lan.	Scala	3	-	
Barducci Cherichini	Scala,Ferza	7	1387	
Barducci Ottavanti	Chiavi	7	1372	
Baroncelli	Carro	7	1287	
Bartolelli	Drago S.G.	1	1395	
Bartolelli[8]	Unicorno	1	1387[b]	
Bartoli Filippi	Ruote	7	1361	1393/1510
Bartoli	Unicorno	22	1345	
Bartoli	Lion Bianco	2	1367[b]	1379/-
Bartoli	Lion d'Oro	1	1408	
Bartolini Salimbeni	Unicorno	8	1362	
Bartolini Scodellari	Drago S.G.	6	1299	
Barucci	Bue	2	1364	1379/-
Beccanugi	Lion Bianco	1	1284	1437/1495
Becchi Nettoli	Drago S.G.	1	1437	
Del Beccuto	Drago S.G.	5	1283	1355/1427
Belchari	Bue	1	1454	
Belfradelli	Nicchio	1	1321	1431/1501
Bellacci	Lion Nero,Carro	9	1342[d]	
Del Bellarno (?)[9]	Lion d'Oro	1	-	

Bellincioni [10]	Ferza	2	1442	
Benci Guernieri	Drago S.S.	4	1369	1369/1438
Benci	Drago S.G.	6	1407[a]	
Benci	Lion d'Oro	3	1380[a]	1380/1464
Benci	Vaio	2	1302	
Bencini	Unicorno	4	1345[a]	1345/1478
Del Bene	Vipera	11	1283	1379/1454
Del Bene di Spinello[11]	Unicorno	1	1420	
Benini	Carro	5	1321	1380/1446
Del Benino	Ferza	15	1345	
Benintendi	Carro	1	1435[ac]	
Benivieni	Vaio	7	1382	1382/1435
Benizi	Nicchio	4	1301	1427/-
Ser.Benozzo	Unicorno	1	1365	1365/-
Benvenuti	Bue	3	1365	
Benvenuti	Lion Rosso	3	1438	
Benvenuti	Lion d'Oro	2	1384	1384/1437
Berardi	Lion Rosso	4	1363	
Berlinghieri	Bue	3	1365	
Bernardi	Bue	1	1385[b]	
Berti della Scala	Scala	1	1441[bc]	
Berti[12]	Bue	1	1387[d]	
Betti	Unicorno	5	1441[a]	
Del Biada	Lion Bianco	4	1366	
Del Bianco	Vaio	2	1412[a]	
Biffoli	Bue	7	1356	1431/-
Biliotti	Nicchio, Ferza	19	1299	
Biliotti	Bue	2	1483	
Bindi Giunta	Vaio	3	1451	
Bini	Ferza	8	1352	
Bischeri	Bue	1	1396	
Biuzzi	Ferza	2	-[+·]	
Bizzeri	Bue	1	-[+]	
Boccacci	Unicorno	6	1342	1369/1447
Bonafe	Chiavi	1	1317	1330/1514

Bonciani	Vipera	8	1286	
Boni Meo	Ruote	1	1384[a]	1384/1463
Boni	Drago S.G.	15	1442	
Bonsi	Drago S.S.	11	1364	1380/1436
Bonvanni	Lion d'Oro	6	1435[a]	
Bordoni	Lion Bianco	2	1282	1423/-
Borgherini[13]	Vipera	1	1496[+?]	
Borghini	Bue	4	1340	1423/1472
Borgognoni	Ruote	7	1393	
Borromei	Vaio	2	1471	
Borsi	Chiavi	1	1345	
Boscoli[14]	Ruote,Chiavi	2	1484	
Boverelli	Ferza	3	1284	1448/-
Bracciolini	Carro	1	1455	
Brancacci	Drago S.S.	2	1317	1427/1491
Brandolini[15]	Bue	3	1393	
Brunelleschi	Drago S.G.	1	1468	
Bruni	Lion d'Oro	7	1375	1379/1439
Bruni	Bue	1	1443	
Bucelli	Bue	1	1284	1432/-
Del Bughaffa	Ferza	1	1387	
Buini	Carro	2	-[+]	
Buonaccorsi	Ferza	2	1302	1380/1435
Buonaccorsi di Vanni	Carro	5	1370	
di Buonaventura	Unicorno	1	-	
Buonagiusi[16]	Carro,Drago S.G.	3	1439	
Buonarotti-Simoni	Lion Nero	6	1343	
Buonavolti	Lion Rosso	3	1393[d]	
Buondelmonte	Vipera	17	1442M	
Buongirolami	Vaio	1	1467	
Buoninsegni	Lion Bianco	8	1393	
Del Buono Ricchi	Lion Bianco	2	1441	
Busini	Lion Nero	13	1345	
Del Caccia	Ruote	15	1381	
Caccini	Lion Nero	2	1350	
Cafferelli	Lion Nero	1	1324[c]	

Calandri	Chiavi	2	1386[c]	
Calvanesi	Ferza	2	- [+]	
Cambi di Napoleone	Nicchio	8	1439	
Cambi Opportuni	Unicorno	4	1302	
Cambi Mercatanti	Unicorno	2	1437	
Cambi	Drago S.G.	1	1312	
Cambini	Ferza	1	-	
Cambini	Lion d'Oro, Drago S.G.	7	1399[a]	
Di Cambio	Drago S.G.	1	1475	
Della Camera (di Ser Paolo)	Ruote	4	1383	1383/1475
Canacci	Vipera	3	1363[ac]	
Cancellieri [17]	Scala	1		
Canigiani	Scala	16	1282	
Cantucci	Drago S.G.	1	1396[+b]	1431/-
Capitani	Vaio	1	1308	1423/-
Cappelli	Drago S.G.	7	1326	
Capponi	Nicchio, Ferza, Scala, Drago, S.S.	30	1287	
Carcherelli [18]	Bue	2	1346	1346/1400/-
Carducci	Vipera	23	1380	
Carnesecchi	Drago S.G.	25	1297	
Carletti [19]	Chiavi	1	1351?	
Carsidoni	Bue	1	- [+]	
Della Casa	Drago S.G., Lion d'Oro, Lion Nero	9	1393	
Da Casavecchia	Ferza	5	1384	1384/1459
Cassella	Lion d'Oro	1	1344	1344/-
Castellani	Carro	5	1326	1439/-
Da Castiglione	Lion Bianco	5	1461M	
Da Castiglionchio	Lion Nero	1	1289	1387/-
Cattani	Lion d'Oro	1	1495M	
Cavalcanti	Carro, Ruote, Vipera, Lion Rosso	17	1450M	
Ceffi Masini	Ruote	5	1412	
Ceffini	Bue	7	1388	

Cei	Bue	5	1469	
Cennini	Carro	4	1426	
Cerchi	Carro	1	1285M	1292/1480
Cerretani	Drago S.G.	7	1282	
Di Chiarissimo	Chiavi	1	1300	1337/-
Ciacchi	Carro	10	1386	
Ciai	Lion d'Oro, Drago S.G.	6	1389	
Ciampelli	Carro	1	1385[d]	1432/-
Ciari	Ferza	2	1344[d]	
Cicciaporci	Ferza, Scala	6	1408	
Da Cignano	Vaio	1	1475	
Cini	Unicorno	5	1346	1360/1442
Cioni	Unicorno	2	1348	1363/1438/1526
Cischi[20]	Unicorno	4		
Cocchi Donati	Bue	5	1376	
Comi	Lion Rosso, Drago, S.S.	5	1397[ac]	
Compagni	Unicorno	5	1289	1301/1419
Compagni	Chiavi	1	-	
Convenevoli	Lion Bianco	1		
Corbinelli	Nicchio	24	1286	
Corsellini	Ferza	4	1404[a]	
Corsi	Bue, Lion Nero	12	1354	
Corsini	Ferza	21	1290	
Cortigiani	Vaio	13	1285M	1285/1402
Coverelli	Ferza	1	1385[c]	1427/1472
Covoni	Ruote	5	1303	1376/1436
Cresci	Vaio	6	1380	
Dati	Ferza	5	1380[d]	1428/1493
Davanzati	Unicorno	16	1320	
Dazzi	Lion Rosso	11	1437	
Dei[21]	Ferza	2	1473	
Deti	Scala, Nicchio	6	1335	
Dietifeci	Ferza	3	1381	

Dietisalvi Neroni	Lion Rosso	4	1291	1464/1495
Dini	Lion Nero	4	1370	
Doffi	Bue	8	1393	
Donati[22]	Vaio	2		
Doni	Vaio	1	1469[c]	
Da Empoli	Lion Rosso	3	1494	
Fabbrini	Drago S.G.	6	1457	
Fagiuoli	Unicorno	7	1313	
Fagni	Lion Nero	3	1295	1434/-
Falconi[23]	Scala	5	1327	
Falconi	Scala,Nicchio	7	1442	
Falconieri	Vaio	7	1282	1343/1462
Fatii	Lion Nero	5	1376	1379/1436
Del Fede[24]	Nicchio	1	1350?	
Federighi	Lion Rosso	16	1346	
Fedini	Unicorno	8	1397[cd]	
Ferucci	Drago S.S.	5	1299	
Da Filicaia	Ruote, Chiavi, Lion Nero	23	1284	
Della Fioraia	Carro	1	1371	
Fioravanti	Chiavi	1	1344	
Forese	Unicorno	1	1296	1453/-
Forese	Ruote	11	1389	
Formiconi	Ferza	4	1344[ac]	
Fortini	Chiavi	9	1386	1429/1473
Franceschi	Vipera	1	1380	
Franceschi della Mercanzia	Lion Rosso, Lion Bianco	7	1403	
Della Frasca	Drago S.G.	2	1417	
Frescobaldi	Nicchio, Ferza, Drago S.S.	14	1285M	1285/1434
Gaddi	Lion d'Oro	3	1437	
Gaetani	Unicorno	1	-[+]	
Da Gagliano	Drago S.G.	2	1487	
Galilei	Bue	11	1381	1381/1430

Gazetti	Ferza	3	- [+]	
Del Garbo	Bue, Carro	8	1358	
Gerini	Chiavi	4	1410	
Gherardi	Ruote	10	1352	
Gherardini	Carro	1	M? [‡]	
Gherardini della Rosa	Vaio	7	1303	
Gherucci	Chiavi	1	1343[d]	
Da Ghiacceto	Lion Nero	9	1294	
Di Ghiachi	Nicchio	5	1372	
Ghinetti	Vaio	1	1344	
Giachinotti[25]	Lion Bianco	3	1284M	1284/1443
Giacomini Tebalducci[26]	Lion Bianco	7	1414M	
Giandonati	Vipera	3	1477M	
Gianfigliazzi	Unicorno	9	1381M	
Gianni	Nicchio	6	1313	1431/1491
Ginori	Lion d'Oro	20	1344	1344/1390
Del Giocondo	Lion d'Oro	7	1375[ac]	1375/1446
Giovanni[27]	Nicchio, Ruote	7	1435	
Giovanni	Lion d'Oro	1	-	
Giraldi	Chiavi	5	1396	
Girolami	Lion Bianco	2	1282	1318/1385
Girolami	Carro	6	1296	1301/1467
Giugni	Ruote	16	1291	
Giuntini	Unicorno	6	1432	
Gondi[28]	Lion Bianco, Bue	10	1438	
Gori [29]	Carro	1	1450	
Gori	Lion d'Oro	1	1357?	
Grassi	Chiavi	6	1482	
Ser Grifi	Lion Nero	4	-	
Guadagni	Chiavi	2	1289	1433/1499
Gualterotti[30]	Scala	14	1282M	1282/1437
Del Guanto	Scala	1	1488	
Guardi	Ruote	2	1443[ac]	

Guasconi	Lion d'Oro	10	1314	1432/1478/1496
Gucci	Unicorno	4	1357	1424/1477
Guicciardini	Nicchio	15	1302	
Guidacci	Carro	3	1470	
Guidetti	Nicchio, Scala	20	1346	
Guidi [31]	Drago S.G.	3	-M?	
Guidi da Prato vecchio	Drago S.G.	2	1471	
Guidotti	Drago S.G.	7	1400^d	
Guiducci	Lion Nero	2	1461^{ac}	
Guiducci	Unicorno	10	1344	
Iacopi	Lion Nero	7	1373	1373/1420
Infanghati	Chiavi	1	1518M	
Inghirami	Lion d'Oro	2	1387	
Lamberteschi [32]	Carro	1	-	
Della Lana	Lion Rosso	2	1453	
Lanfredini	Drago S.S.	6	1334	
Lapaccini del Toso	Lion Bianco	12	1389^d	
Lapi	Chiavi	4	1374	
Lapi	Vaio	8	1394^d	
Lapi Vaiai	Lion d'Oro	2	1376	
Larioni [33]	Scala, Ferza	3	1282M	1282/1460
Lenzi	Unicorno	4	1386	
Libri	Bue	5	1531	
Lioni	Ruote	3	1326	
Lippi	Ferza	6	1350	
Lorini	Drago S.G.	6	1327	
Lottieri	Vaio	1	-	
Lotti	Nicchio	16	1301	
Lottini	Ruote	4	1360	1360/1479
Lucalberti	Lion Bianco	4	1345	
Della Luna	Lion Bianco	2	1372	1431/1501
Da Lutiano	Lion d'Oro	2	1393	1393/1440
Machiavelli	Nicchio	11	1283	

Maciagnini	Lion d'Oro	1	1395[a]	1395/1451
Macinghi	Vaio	9	1392	1392/1436
Magaldi	Bue	3	1305	1359/1417
Magalotti	Bue	3	1283	1430/1491
Da Magnale	Bue	6	1302	1431/1509
Malefici	Nicchio	3	1371	
Malegonnelle	Lion Bianco	9	1304	
Mancini	Bue, Lion Nero	7	1284	
Manelli	Scala, Nicchio	8	1343M	1343/1461
Manetti	Drago S.S.	7	1337	1374/1439
Mangioni	Lion Bianco	1	1289	1426/-
Mannini	Lion Nero	1	1369	1419/-
Mannucci	Carro	2	1379[cd]	1457/-
Manovelli (ozzi)	Drago S.G.	1	1283	1433/-
Marchi 34	Vaio	2	1389	1429/-
Marignolli	Lion d'Oro	3	1287	
Marsili	Nicchio	3	1307	
Marsuppini	Bue	7	-	
Martelli	Lion d'Oro, Drago S.G.	13	1343[d]	
Martellini 35	Drago S.S.	4	1474	
Martellini	Drago S.S.	2	1520	
Martini	Lion Nero	1	1349[d]	
Martini	Drago S.G., Lion d'Oro	14	1428	
Martini di Guccio	Chiavi	4	1373	
Masi	Lion d'Oro, Vaio	16	1416	
Masini	Drago S.S.	5	1394	
Mazzei	Vaio	1	1404[bc]	
Mazzinghi	Vipera	10	1377M	
Mazzinghi	Unicorno	1	1523[+]	
Medici	Lion d'Oro, Drago, S.G., Vaio	34	1291	
Mei	Ferza	3	-	
Da Meleto	Bue	1	-	
Mellini	Lion Nero	3	1380	

Da Mezzola	Ferza	2	1361	
Michi	Lion Rosso	1	1329	1431/-
Migliori	Drago S.G.	4	1394	1440/-
Milanesi	Drago S.G.	3	1484	
Minerbetti	Lion Rosso	8	1283	
Mini	Chiavi, Vaio	6	1479	
Miniati di Dino	Ruote	4	1357[ac]	
Da San Miniato [36]	Drago S.G.	4	1492	
Da San Miniato	Vaio	1	1493	
Monaci	Lion Nero	1	1366	1373/-
Monaldi	Unicorno	1	1283	1287/1487
da Monterinaldi	Lion d'Oro	1	-	
Morelli	Lion Nero	21	1387	
Mori	Unicorno, Lion Bianco	4	1300	
Mormorai	Lion Nero	3	1518[+]	
Mozzi	Scala	1	1326[+]	1373/1510
Naldini	Chiavi	2	1389	1419/1525
Nardi	Carro	11	1350	
Nasi	Scala	10	1375	
Nelli	Lion d'Oro	13	1445	
Nerli	Nicchio, Scala	7	1437M	
Del Nero	Scala	11	1382[a]	
Nesi	Bue	1	1372[a]	1381/1465
Di Niccolai	Lion d'Oro	3	1344[a]	
Niccoli	Drago S.G.	4	1342	1369/1454
Niccolini della Scala	Scala	3	1347[b]	
Niccolini	Ruote	17	1356	
Nobili	Vipera	16	1355	
Orlandi	Ruote	1	1345	
Orlandini	Lion Nero	4	1286	
Orlandini	Drago S.G.	11	1420	
Ottavanti	Lion Bianco, Lion Rosso	8	1409	
Del Pace	Nicchio, Carro	4	1397	
Pacholi	Bue	1	1475	

Paganelli[37]	Scala	6	1282	
Pagnini	Bue	2	1477	
Del Palagio	Vaio	2	1328	1431/1485
Palarcioni	Ferza	3	1473	
Della Palla Spez.	Lion Rosso	1	1478	
Del Pancia	Scala	1	1354[d]	1430/-
Panciatichi[38]	Drago S.G.	3	1483	
Pandolfini	Chiavi	17	1381	
Da Panzano	Bue	19	1312	
Da Panzano	Lion d'Oro	2	1440	
Del Papa	Ruote	2	1324	1447/-
Parenti	Drago S.G.	9	1351[a]	1351/1450
Particini	Lion Rosso	5	1400[a]	1400/1443
Pazzi	Chiavi, Vaio	12	1288M	1290/1439
Peccori	Drago S.G.	9	1284	
Pepi	Lion Nero	10	1301	
Peri	Lion Nero	5	1359	
Perini	Lion Rosso	1	1474	
Peruzzi	Lion Nero	14	1283	1432/1495
Da Pesciola	Lion d'Oro	1	1402[a]	1402/1488
Pescioni[39]	Lion Bianco	7	1368	
Petrucci	Lion Rosso	5	1425[a]	
Maestro Piero (Toscanelli)	Nicchio	3	-	
Pieri	Scala	4	1407[b]	
Pilli	Carro	6	1288M	1288/1358 1365/1459
Pitti	Ferza, Nicchio	41	1283	
Pollini	Lion Bianco	2	-[+]	
Popoleschi[40]	Lion Rosso Lion Bianco	10	1284M	1284/1396
Portinari	Vaio	9	1282	1287/1446
Pucci	Vaio	29	1396[a]	
Pucci del Chiassolino	Lion d'Oro	2	1408[a]	
Pulci	Carro	1	1282M	1290/-
Del Pugliese[41]	Drago S.S.	5	1463	

Quaratesi	Scala	13	1317	
Da Rabatta	Drago S.G.	6	1321	1388/1438
Da Rabatta	Ruote	1	1409	
Raffacani	Lion Rosso	2	1285	1433/-
Raugi	Carro	4	1304	1417/-
Redditi	Carro	1	1463[a]	
Redditi	Vipera	2	1397[d]	
Della Rena	Chiavi	2	1305	
Ricasoli	Vipera, Unicorno, Lion Nero	14	1468M	
Riccardi	Lion Rosso	3	1451	
Ricci	Ruote, Vaio, Drago S.S.	12	1298	
Riccialbani	Bue	6	1294	
Ridolfi di Borgo	Nicchio	13	1290	
Ridolfi di Piazza	Ferza	32	1321	
Rimbaldesi	Scala	1	1311	1375/-
Rinaldi	Drago S.G., Lion d'Oro	5	1282	
Rinieri	Vaio	7	1284	1380/1435
Rinucci	Ferza	1	1367	1383/1450
Rinuccini	Bue	9	1347	1381/1437
Risaliti	Bue	13	1302	
Ristori	Drago S.G.	2	1357	
Romoli	Drago S.G.	2	1430[a]	
Rondinelli	Lion d'Oro, Vaio	18	1296	1432/1484
Del Rosselino	Ruote	1	1448[bc]	
Rossi	Nicchio	1	1285M	1285/1496
Del Rosso	Chiavi	5	1384	1384/1437
Rucellai	Lion Rosso	49	1302	
Del Ruota	Scala	2	-	
Rustichi	Unicorno	6	1398	
Rustichi [42]	Lion Nero	6	1475	
Sacchetti	Bue	8	1335	
Del Saggina	Lion Bianco	1	1299	1346/-

Salterelli	Carro	1	1291	1300/-
Salutati	Vipera	2	1439	
Salvetti	Bue	6	1436	
Salviati	Ruote, Chiavi	13	1297	
di Sandro Spez.	Drago S.G.	1	-	
Sannini	Ferza	1	1387	1433/-
Di Santi	Bue	3	1344	1344/1395
Sapiti	Nicchio	6	1351	
Sassetti[43]	Lion Bianco	6	1453	
Sassolini	Scala	4	1302	
Scali	Vipera	3	1374M	1378/1480
Dello Scarfa	Lion Rosso	7	1363	
Scarlatti [44]	Drago S.S.	11	1428	
Scarlattini[45]	Lion Bianco	8	1477	
Dalla Scarperia	Lion d'Oro	2	1441	
Dello Scelto	Drago S.S.	2	1353	1433/-
Schiattesi	Bue	2	1379[d]	
Scolari	Scala, Nicchio	2	-M	
Segni	Nicchio	8	1347	
Serchelli	Ferza	1	1436	
Sermini	Bue	1	1457[c]	
Sernigi	Unicorno	6	1390	
Serragli	Drago S.S. Lion Nero	19	1325	1433/1453 1468/-
Serristori	Lion Nero	5	1392	
Sertini	Lion Bianco	3	1376	
Serzelli	Bue	4	1376	
Signorini	Unicorno	7	1387	
Sinibaldi Dei	Bue	5	1487[bc]	
Soderini	Drago S.S.	13	1283	
Del Soldato	Drago S.S.	2	1388	
Soldani	Lion Nero	7	1343	1375/1435
Soldi	Lion d'Oro	3	1330	1375/-
Solosmei	Lion d'Oro	1	1364	1429/-

Da Sommaia	Unicorno, Lion Bianco	2	1350	
Sostegni	Drago S. Giovanni	7	1333	1382/1448
Spina Falcone	Carro	1	1289	1289/1374/1443
Spinelli	Lion Nero	10	1327	
Spini	Unicorno, Carro	9	1284	
Squarcialupi	Vipera	3	1494M	
dello Steccuto	Lion Bianco	1	1391	1391/1438/1498
Stefani Bettoni	Ferza	4	1330	1330/1400/1429
Di Stefano	Chiavi	1	-	
Stradi	Ferza	11	1332	
Strinati	Drago S.G.	2	1438[a]	
Strozzi	Lion Rosso	44	1283	
Della Stufa	Lion d'Oro	16	1328	
Taddei	Lion d'Oro	4	1424	
Talani	Lion Nero	2	-	
Tanagli[46]	Chiavi	10	1452	
Tanini	Lion d'Oro	1	1478	
Tedaldi	Vaio	8	1283	1300/1399/1437
Temperani	Lion Rosso	8	1307	
Tempi	Drago S.G.	1	- [+]	
Tieri	Ferza	1	1474	
Tolosini	Bue	1	1318	1375/-
Tornabuoni	Lion Bianco	6	1284M	1284/1445
Tornaquinci	Lion Bianco	4	1284M[+]	1284/-
Torrigiani	Ruote	2	1303	1389/1438
Della Tosa	Drago S.G.	8	1285M	1285/1397
Tosinghi	Drago S.G.	9	1285M	1285/1395
Del Toso da Fortuna	Lion d'Oro	1	1383[a]	1383/1442
Ubaldini [47]	Chiavi	2	-	
Ubertini	Ferza	2	1382	
Ughi [48]	Drago S.G.	4	1475	
Ugolini	Ferza	7	1350	1360/1437

Uguccioni Lippi	Scala, Carro	15	1434	
Ulivieri	Lion Bianco	1	1349	1386/-
Valori	Chiavi	2	1322	
Vechietti	Lion Bianco	5	1371M	
Velluti	Nicchio, Ferza	5	1283	
Ventura	Lion Bianco	15	1382	
Vernacci	Lion Bianco	9	1290	1303/1436
Da Verrazzano	Ruote, Scala	12	1319	
Vespucci	Unicorno	11	1350^{d}	
Vettori	Nicchio	11	1320	
Di Vieri	Ferza, Drago S.S.	9	1349	1364/1473
Del Vigna	Lion Rosso	5	1291	1325/1401
Villani	Drago S.G.	9	1300	1328/1443
Vinacciesi	Carro	1	1470	
Dal Vivaio	Drago S.S.	2	1388	
Viviani	Vipera	6	1393	
Viviani	Drago S.G.	3	1306	1416/-
Del Zaccheria di Jacopo	Bue	3	1417^{ac}	
Zampalochi	Drago S.S.	1	1382	1382/1436
Zati [49]	Ruote	9	1438	

NOTES TO APPENDIX 1

a. Families whose priors were for the *arti minori* before 1434.
b. Families whose appearances in the Signoria were for the *arti minori* only.
c. Families with members in the Council for the *arti minori* as well as the *maggiori*.
d. Families whose first priors were for the *arti minori* but who had priors for the *maggiori* before 1434.
+. Families without *beneficiati* in the *Consiglio*.
M. Magnate families.

[1] Tratte 1071.
[2] The Priorista Mariani has been used to establish the date of a family's first prior. Where families have not been traced or identified in Mariani, other Prioristi have been consulted. These cases are indicated in the footnotes.
[3] Large former magnate families tended to be dispersed over a number of *gonfaloni, v* also the Cavalcanti and Ricasoli.

⁴   Branch of the Adimari made *popolani* in 1396 with their first prior in 1439,
    Mariani, 248, c. 158. In cases where families are branches of older families, the
    year of the first prior of the original family is given in the Table and that of the
    branch in the footnotes.

⁵   A branch of the Albizzi which separated in 1372 with their first prior in 1376,
    ibid., c. 53.

⁶   According to Mariani, an old family mentioned in the Libro del Chiodo, ibid.,
    253, c. 1389.

⁷   Mariani describes the Baldovini as an ancient family mentioned in the Libro
    del Chiodo, 253, c. 1389. The Priorista Ricci lists Baldovini as priors between
    1283 and 1380, B.N.F. EB 14 7, San Giovanni, c. 22. Chello Baldovini was a
    notary from the Romagna who was a notary to the Signoria and then Chancellor
    of the Commune in the late thirteenth and early fourteenth centuries, Marzi,
    La Cancelleria, pp. 55–60.

⁸   For the first prior, Priorista Ricci, Manoscritti, 242, c. 301; Priorista del Palazzo
    (no pagination).

⁹   This name is not clear.

¹⁰ According to Mariani, this family is not the same as the magnate Bellincioni,
    253, c.1400.

¹¹ For the first prior, Priorista Ricci, Manoscritti 242; Priorista del Palazzo.

¹² This is the same family as the Berti in Vipera, Priorista Bischeri, Manoscritti
    265, c.120.

¹³ According to Mariani, an ancient family of Ghibellines who came to Florence
    around 1400, 253, c.1499.

¹⁴ According to Mariani, an ancient family mentioned in the Libro del Chiodo
    and the Peace of Cardinal Latino, ibid., c. 1480. Boscoli are included in the list
    of consular families in *Delizie degli eruditi toscani*, VII, p. 159.

¹⁵ Known earlier as di Giorgio and listed as such in the 1433 scrutiny.

¹⁶ According to Mariani, an ancient family, 253, c.1386. Buonaguisi are among
    the consular families listed in *Delizie*, VII, p. 159.

¹⁷ A noble family in Pistoia, see Robert Davidsohn, *Storia di Firenze*, trans., G. B.
    Klein, 6 vols. (Firenze, 1972), III, p. 698–699.

¹⁸ Also written as Carchelli.

¹⁹ This appears to be the same family as that in Lion Rosso, in the Signoria,
    1351–1379, Priorista Mariani, 251, c.772; Priorista Ricci, Santa Maria
    Novella, c.104.

²⁰ Also written as Cisti.

²¹ Mariani gives the *gonfalone* of Milano di Domenico Dei who sat in the Signoria
    in 1473 as Vipera. Dei's *Catasto* return in 1480 declared that he resided in Fer-
    za, in Verde, *Lo Studio fiorentino*, III, i, p. 138.

²² This Donati does not appear to be the same as the ancient family of Donati.

²³ Cambi lists all the Falconi together but Mariani distinguishes two families,
    250, c.572; 253, c.1394.

²⁴ The Priorista Ricci, 241, has Del Fede in San Giovanni with the first prior in
    1350. Members of the family were nominated in Chiavi in the scrutiny of 1391,

Tratte, 397, c.160. It is not certain that the Del Fede in the *Consiglio Maggiore* in Nicchio is the same family.

25 A branch of the Tornaquinci made *popolani* in 1379 with the first prior in 1443, Mariani, 248, c.117.

26 A branch of the Malespini, Martines, *The Social World*, pp. 214–237.

27 I would like to thank Mrs. Elaine Rosenthal, who is writing a dissertation on the Giovanni, for the information that the descendants of Messer Rosso Giovanni in Ruote are the same family as the Giovanni in Nicchio.

28 An old family, *v* Goldthwaite, *Private Wealth*, pp. 157–158.

29 Mariani has only one Gori, in Lion d'Oro, 253, c.1412, but the Priorista Ricci has a Gori in Santa Croce with the first prior in 1357, 242, c.236.

30 A branch of the Bardi made *popolani* in 1395 with the first prior in 1437, Priorista Mariani, 248, c.4. Cambi gives the Bardi, Larioni and Gualterotti as a single *consorteria*.

31 It is not certain whether this is the old magnate family of Guidi.

32 An ancient consular family, *v* D. Kent, *The Rise of the Medici*, p. 160.

33 Consorti of the Bardi with the first prior in 1460, Mariani, 248, c. 5, *v* also above, n. 30.

34 In the late fourteenth and early fifteenth century this family was in Drago, Santo Spirito, Mariani, 252, c.1182.

35 Mariani distinguishes two families of Martellini in Drago, Santo Spirito, the first, a family of wealthy doctors from Casetino, the second from Cervia, 253, cc.1459, 1504.

36 Mariani distinguishes two families, one descended from a doctor, the other from a lawyer, and both containing notaries, 253, c.1492.

37 A Branch of the Canigiani with the first prior in 1372, Mariani, 249, c.12.

38 A noble family from Pistoia, Martines, *The Social World*, pp. 63–65.

39 Also known as di Ser Michele.

40 Branch of the Tornaquinci made *popolani* in 1364 with the first prior in 1396, Mariani, 248, c.115.

41 According to Mariani, an ancient family with members among the Anziani, ibid., 253, c.1434; Martines, *The Social World*, p. 236.

42 According to Mariani, the same family as the Berti Rinieri who had their first prior in 1344, 253, c.1465.

43 An old family, *v* Philip Jones, "Florentine Families and Florentine Diaries in the Fourteenth Century," *Papers of the British School at Rome*, 24 (1956) pp. 184–185.

44 According to Mariani, an ancient family of Ghibellines described in the Libro del Chiodo, 253, c. 1339.

45 Mariani gives Scarlatti only. Cambi in the *Libro* of members of the *Consiglio Maggiore* distinguishes the Scarlatti from the Scarlattini but in his *Istorie* lists the Scarlatti with the Scarlattini as a "case grande," *Delizie*, XX, p. 29. The Priorista Ricci distinguishes the two with the first prior of the Scarlattini in 1477, Santa Maria Novella, c. 294v. The Priorista del Palazzo has a Scarlattini in the Signoria in 1477 but also uses the names Scarlatti and Scarlattini as alternatives for the same citizens.

46   According to Mariani, an ancient family, possibly a branch of the Rinaldi, 253, c.1417; v also Martines, *The Social World*, pp. 331–332.

47   Ubaldini are mentioned among the consular families in *Delizie*, VII, p. 159. It is uncertain whether the Ubaldini in the *Consiglio Maggiore* are the same family.

48   According to Mariani, an ancient family of the first circle, 253, c.1463.

49   According to Mariani, the name is a diminuitive of Davanzati, and the family were established in Florence as rich merchants by the early fourteenth century, 253, c.1377.

APPENDIX 2

Membership of the Consiglio degli Ottanta
for the arti maggiori, 1495-1512[1]

	1495-1501	1502-1512
ACCIAIUOLI		
Neri Piero Neri	96,98,99	07,09
Giovanni Piero Neri		06
Pandolfo Piero Neri		12
Alessandro Donato Neri		06,07,08,09,11,11
Ruberto Donato Neri		10
Agnolo Lodovico Adovardo	00	
Lodovico Angolo Lodovido		11,12
ADIMARI		
Bernardo Pacho Bernardo	01	04,05,06.08
Guglielmo Bernardo Guglielmo	92	
Piero Bernardo Guglielmo	01	03,05,06,06
ALAMANNI		
Alessandro Francesco Piero	99	03,05,05,08,09,12,12
Domenico Andrea Francesco		06,08,09
ALBERTI		
Benedetto Francesco Gianozzo	95,96,00	
Daniello Francesco Gianozzo	01	
Piero Daniello Piero	95,96,01,02	04,05,06,07,08,08,12
Niccolò Antonio Niccolò	98,99,02	03,04,05,06,06,07,10,11
Charoccio Bernardo Antonio	99	
ALBIZZI		
Alessandro Rinaldo Maso	02	
Francesco Luca Maso	95,96,97,98	
Luca Maso Luca Maso	97,98,02	03,03,04
Luca Antonio Luca Maso	00,01	
Piero Lucantonio Niccolò	95	
Zanobi Lucantonio Niccolò	02	11
Niccolò Tedice Antonio	96,01,02	03,05,06,07,07,08,09,10,11,12,12
Giovanni Tedice Antonio	96	
Piero Paolo Piero	00	
Giovanbattista Paolo Piero	00	05
Matteo Andrea Matteo	01	09,11,12
Bancho Andrea		11
ALDOBRANDI		
Domenico Carlo Tommaso	98,01,02	
ALDOBRANDINI del Nero		
Napoleone Jacopo Giorgio	97	
Giorgio Jacopo Giorgio	99	
Francesco Jacopo Giorgio	99	
M. Piero Salvestro Aldobrandino		04,05,06,06,08,10,10,11,12,12
Francesco Giorgio Jacopo		06
ALESSANDRI		
Alessandro Jacopo M. Alessandro	95,96,98,99,00	
Lorenzo Antonio M. Alessandro	99,00	04,05,06,09
Guglielmo Antonio M. Alessandro		07,10
Francesco Nicolaio Ugo	96,97	
Nicolaio Francesco Nicolaio		11

1. Tratte 337, c.c. 26-29, 141-189; 338, cc. 3-18v. This list is of those who occupied
    positions in the Councils.

ALTOVITI

Guglielmo Bardo Guglielmo	97,00,01	04
Giovanni Bardo Guglielmo	01,02	04
M.Niccolò Simone Giovanni	98,99	10,
Giovanni Simone Giovanni	99,00,02	05,07,10,11
Lionardo Tommaso Giovanni	01	
Stoldo Bindo Antonio		05

DELL'AMORETTA

Mariotto Piero Mariotto	95,98	

DALL'ANTELLA

Filippo Giovanni Taddei	99,00,01	12

ANTINORI

Tommaso Bernardo Tommaso	95,96,98,99,02	
Niccolò Tommaso Bernardo	98,99	03,10
Raffaello Gregorio Matteo	99,02	04,06
Lionardo Gregorio Matteo		03,07,10,11

ARDINGHELLI

Tommaso Neri Tommaso	99,01	09
Piero Niccolò Piero		10,10,11

ARNOLDI

Luigi Giovanni Francesco	01	

ARRIGHI

Giovanni Alessandro Jacopo	95,97,97,98,99	
Francesco Alessandro Jacopo	00	

ARRIGUCCI

Francesco Giovanni Filippo	96	

DEGLI ASINI

Mariotto Niccolò Francesco	96,98	
Bernardo Bernardo Mariotto		04,06,08,10,11

BAGNESI

Schiatta Francesco Gueriante	02	

BALDESI

Antonio Turino Antonio	00	

BALDOVINETTI

Giovanni Guido Francesco	95,98,01	03,05
Bartolomeo Mariotto M. Niccolò	02	

BALDUCCI PEGOLOTTI

Pegolotto Bernardo Pegolotto	95,96	

BANDINI   BANDUCCI

Pierantonio Guaspare	98	

BARDI

Bernardo Giovanni Tommaso		05
Agnolo Bernardo Agnolo		04

BARDUCCI   OTTAVANTI

Giovanni Stagio Lorenzo	01,02	07

BARONCELLI

Tommaso Lorenzo Agnolo	97,02	
Agnolo Lorenzo Agnolo	00	
Giovanni Agnolo Cionaccio	96	

BARTOLELLI (S.G.)

Francesco Bartoletto Francesco	00	

BARTOLI

Lionardo Giovanni Domenico	96	
Domenico Giovanni Domenico	95,96	
Lorenzo Giovanni Domenico	97,97	
Giovanbattista Lionardo Giovanni		08,10
Marco Lionardo Marco	97	
Girolamo Marco Lionardo		04
Giovanni Luigi Marco	96	08
Giovanbattista Bernardo Carlo		06,07,07,11
Francesco Bernardo Matteo		07
Bartolomeo Bartolomeo Tommaso	02	

BARTOLINI SALIMBENI

Cosimo Lionardo Bartolomeo	02	
Damiano Lionardo Bartolomeo	97,98	
Piero Bernardo Lionardo		10,12
Giovanbattista Niccolò Bartolomeo	96,98,99,02	03,04,05,06,08,11

DEL BECCUTO

Felice Deo Deo	96	

BELFRADELLI

Matteo Agnolo Agnolo	99,01	

BELLACCI

Tinoro Marco Bello	99,00	03,04,11,11
Matteo Alessandro Matteo	02	
Marco Tinoro Marco		11

BENCI (Vaio)

Niccolò Giovanni Amerigo	95	
Bartolomeo Giovanni Amerigo		06,08,12
Giovanni Amerigo Giovanni		12

BENCI (Drago, S.G.)

Paolo Benci Niccolò	99	10

BENCI GUENIERI

Francesco Antonio Giovanni	96,98	
Antonio Francesco Antonio		09,11

DEL BENE

Tommaso Antonio M. Riccardo	96,97,98,01	05

BENINI

Paolo Giovanni Stefano	95,01	

DEL BENINO

Piero Niccolò Andrea	95,96	
Gregorio Piero Niccolò	96,97,98	05,08
Andrea Piero Niccolò	00,01	03
Alessandro Piero Niccolò	02	
Carlo Lionardo Pietro		07,11
Pietro Lionardo Pietro	97,00	09,10,11
Jacopo Neri Niccolò		07,10,12,12
Niccolò Neri Niccolò	99	

BENIZI
Giovanni Matteo Piero   01

BENVENUTI (S.M.N.)
Benedetto Benvenuto Giovanni   01
Francesco Bartolomeo Luigi   00   05

BENVENUTI (S.C.)
Lorenzo Mariotto Lorenzo   96

BENVENUTI (S.G.)
Domenico Benvenuto Piero   99,02

BERARDI
Giovanni Corrado Berardo   95,96   03,05,07,08,08,09,11,12
Matteo Niccolo Gianno   00

BERLINGHIERI
Francesco Niccolò Giorgio   95,96
Antonio Jacopo Giorgio   00   05,08
Giovanni Berlinghieri Francesco   98   04,05,05,

DEL BIANCO
Benvenuto Bartolomeo Salvestro   97

BILIOTTI (S.S.)
Niccolò Sandro Giovanni   96
Giuliano Agostino Sandro   02   05
Matteo Bernardo Matteo   05

BILIOTTI (S.C.)
Biliotto Jacopo Francesco   97

BINI
Niccolò Piero Giovanni   08

BOCCACCI
Jacopo Bartolomeo Federigo   01,02   03,10

BONCIANI
Simone Gagliardo Carlo   99,00   03,05

BONI MEO
Bernardo Bernardo Ambrogio   97,00

BONI
Andrea Bono Giovanni   95,96,97
Lionello Giuliano Lionardo   96,97,98
Stefano Piero Jacopo   99   08
Matteo Giovanni Matteo   00

BONSI
Donato Ugolino Donato   00

BORGHERINI
Salvo Francesco Salvo   96

BORGHINI
Zanobi Giovanni Tommaso   10,10

BUONAGIUSI
Domenico Stagio Matteo   99,02

BUONDELMONTE

Filippo Lorenzo M. Andrea	96,01	04
Bartolomeo Rosso M. Andrea	95,99,02	
Giovanni Lorenzo M. Gherardo	99,01	08,11
Antonio Lorenzo M. Andrea	95	

BUONGIROLAMI

M. Giovanni M. Bernardo M.Giovanni   12,12

BUONINSEGNI

Giovanbattista Ruberto Domenico	98	03,04,07,08,08
Giovanni Niccolò Domenico	00,02	10
Ridolfo Francesco Domenico	95	

BUSINI

Lionardo Tommaso Niccolò	96	
Piero Antonio Niccolò	96	
Ridolfo Antonio Niccolò	96,98	
Miniato Francesco Tommaso	96	05,12
Agnolo Nofri Domenico	00	

DELLA CACCIA

Matteo Nofri Giovanni	95,96,96,97,97,99	04
Girolamo Nofri Giovanni	98,00	06,10
Agnolo Giovanni Nofri	99,00,01	03,04,05,05,08.09,09,11
Nofri Giovanni Nofri	99,01	
Michele Galeotto Michele	01	

CAMBI OPPORTUNI

Nero Stefano Alessandro	95,96,97,98	
Giovanni Nero Stefano	01,02	

CAMBI MERCATANTI

Giovanni Niccolò Giovanni	98	04,07
Piero Niccolò Giovanni	01,02	04,09

CAMBI di Napoleone

Napoleone Filippo Francesco   98,02   07,08

CAMBI (S.G.)

Guido Niccolò Luca   97,01

CAMBINI

Lionardo Antonio Cambio   01

CANACCI

Giovanni Antonio Dino   96

CANIGIANI

Adovardo Simone Antonio	00	03,05,06,08
Antonio Simone Antonio	95,96,97,98	07,08
Matteo M. Giovanni Antonio	95	
Carlo Daniello Luigi	99,01	03,05,07,07,11,12
Francesco Daniello Luigi		07,11

CAPPELLI

Filippo Giovanni Filippo	95,96,97,98,99,00	03
Luigi Barone Giovanni		10,11
Piero Lorenzo Filippo	96	

CAPPONI

Piero Gino Neri	96	
Cappone Gino Neri		07,12
Bernardo Niccolò Piero	95,96	
Piero Giovanni Piero	95,96,97,97	
Girolamo Gino Piero		07,07,09,11
Cappone Bartolomeo Piero	95,98,02	
Lorenzo Recco Uguccione	98,99,01	03,03,04,05
Galeotto Luca Agostino		06,08
Francesco Luca Agostino		07,12

CARDUCCI

Filippo Andrea Niccolò	97,99	05,06,08
Benedetto Andrea Niccolò		03,04
Baldassare Baldassare Niccolò		04,05,12
Niccolò Jacopo Giovanni	00	
Agnolo Lorenzo Agnolo	02	05,06,06

CARNESECCHI

Piero Simone Paolo	96,96,98	03
Paolo Simone Paolo	95,96,99	
Lionardo Giovanni Paolo	01	
Giovanni Lionardo Giovanni		10
Mariotto Antonio Paolo	01	05
Pierantonio Francesco Berto	01,02	04,05
Matteo Manetto Zabobo	95,00,01	03,07,09,10,12
Antonio Manetto Zanobi		03,05,06,08,11
Bernardo Francesco Berto		03,07,10,11
Zanobi Francesco Berto		12

DELLA CASA

Ottaviano Ghezzo Agnolo	00
Alfonso Giovanni Ghezzo	95

DA CASAVECCHIA

Francesco Banco Francesco	02
Chiaro Francesco Banco	96,98
Pellegrino Francesco Banco	98

DA CASTIGLIONE

Bernardo Dante Bernardo	98	11
Taddeo Dante Bernardo	02	

CAVALCANTI

Giovanni Niccolò Giovanni	95	
Francesco Tommaso Niccolò	96	
Lodovico Papero Lodovico	02	
Mainardo Bartolomeo Mainardo		12,12

CEFFI

Andrea Lorenzo Ceffo	95,97

CEFFINI

Filippo Marco Salvestro	96
Giuliano Marco Salvestro	00
Salvestro Giuliano Salvestro	95

CERRETANI

Matteo Niccolò Matteo	99	
Paolo Niccolò Matteo	96,98,99,01	05
M. Giovanni Niccolò Matteo	95	08

CERCHI

Bindaccio Michele Consiglio	01	08,10

CIAI

M. Bartolomeo Ridolfo Jacopo   03,07

CIACCHI

Alessandro Bernardo Jacopo	96,99	
Jacopo Bernardo Jacopo	01	
Francesco Bernardo Jacopo	01	03
Tommaso Bernardo Jacopo	02	12
Jacopo Scolaio Tommaso	98	04,10
Tommaso Scolaio Tommaso	01	

CICCIAPORCI

Giovanni Benedetto Giovanni	99	04,06,07,12
Bernardo Benedetto Giovanni	95,00,01	05,08
Niccolò Giovanni Pazzino		10

CINI

Niccolò Bernabo Piero   02

COMPAGNI

Piero Giovanni Cante	97,98,00	05,08
Neri Dino Neri		07

CORBINELLI

Pandolfo Bernardo Tommaso		09,10
Girolamo Bernardo Tommaso	02	05,09,10
Niccolò Bernardo Tommaso	99,02	03,05,08,11
Andrea Lorenzo Parigi	95	
Simone Lorenzo Parigi	00	
Maffeo Lorenzo Parigi	01	04,06
Giovanbattista Antonio Bartolomeo	96,97,98,99,01	04,05
Piero Tommaso Giovanni	00,01	05
Giovanni Tommaso Giovanni	00,02	

CORBIZZI

Filippo Giovanni Filippo   95

CORSELLINI

Piero Francesco Buonaccorso	95	
Giovanni Piero Francesco	01	

CORSI

Giovanni Jacopo Simone	95,98,02	05,05,06,07,10
Simone Jacopo Simone	98,02	03,04,07,08,10
Bardo Bartolo Domenico	96,97	
Lorenzo Bartolo Domenico	01	

CORSINI

Filippo Bartolomeo Bertoldo	95	
Amerigo Bartolomeo Bertoldo	95,97,98,99,00	
Antonio Bartolomeo Bertoldo		04,06,10,11
Piero Bertoldo Gherardo	96,97	
Gherardo Bertoldo Gherardo	02	12
M. Luca Bertoldo Gherardo		05
Castello Tommaso Bartolomeo		10
Niccolò Piero Corsino		09
Corsino Piero Corsino		04
Luigi Giovanni Stefano	96	
Ruberto Giovanni Stefano	98,00	
Albertaccio Andrea Giovanni	02	06,07,07,12

CORTIGIANI

Gherardo Andrea Gherardo	99	
Antonfrancesco Andrea Gentile		04,04
Carlo Francesco Gentile		07,10,11,11

COVONI

Piero Giovanni Niccolò	95,96,97,97	
Giovanni Benedetto Giovanni		12

DAVANZATI

Francesco Lorenzo Piero		05,06,07,10,12
Piero Lorenzo Piero		08,10,12
Francesco Francesco Lottieri		03

DAZZI

Marchione Daniello Nofri	97	06,08
Paolo Daniello Nofri	00,01	
Piero Daniello Nofri		05,10

DEI

Domenico Bernardo Domenico	99	

DIETISALVI NERONI

Lorenzo Dietisalvi		05,07,07
Girolamo Antonio Nerone		05,08,10

DINI

Jacopo Francesco Piero		09,11

FAGIUOLI

Piero Tommaso Domenico	98	04,07,07,09,10
Domenico Tommaso Domenico	95	
Taddeo Tommaso Domenico		06

FALCONI [1327]

Ridolfo Giovanni S. Falcone	95,98	

FALCONIERI

Paolo Francesco Paolo	95,98	

FEDERIGHI

Girolamo Paolo Jacopo	01	04
Salvestro Domenico Jacopo	95,97,97,98	
Benozzo Domenico Jacopo	96,99	
Domenico Domenico Jacopo	01,02	06,10
Giovanni M. Carlo Francesco	97,98	03,04,06,10
Piero Giovanni M. Carlo		06,07,07

FERUCCI

Niccolo Antonio Lionardo	00	

DA FILICAIA

Antonio Nicolaio Antonio	98	03,07,08,10,11
Antonio Piero Nicolaio	97,97	
Berto Francesco Berto	95,96,99,02	04,06,07,08,09,10,11,12
Alessandro Antonio Luca	99	
Ivomaria Alessandro Antonio		05,06,07,09,10,12
Antonio Tommaso Azerello		11

FORESE (S.C.)

Nofri Niccolò Nofri	97,98	08

FORMICONI

Giovanni Simone Giorgio	96,97,98,00	04,06,08

FORTINI

Tommaso Bartolomeo Benedetto	95	
Benedetto Bartolomeo Benedetto	95,98,99	06,10,11
Girolamo Bartolomeo Benedetto		03,06

FRANCESCHI

Giovanni Filippo S. Francesco	98	

FRESCOBALDI

Bartolomeo Lionardo Filippo	99,01	
Piero Lionardo Filippo		07,10,11
Francesco Stoldo Lionardo	01	

GADDI

Taddeo Agnolo Zanobi	96,97,97,99	04

GALILEI

Alessandro Bernardo Galileo	95,99	03,09
Galileo Bernardo Galileo	97,02	04,05,11
Lorenzo Bernardo Galileo	01,02	
Girolamo Bernardo Galileo		12
Francesco Bernardo Galileo	02	11

GERINI

Girolamo Attaviano Piero	98,02	10

GHERARDI

Francesco Orlando Bartolomeo	95	
Tommaso Orlando Bartolomeo	98,00	03,04,07,07,11

DA GHIACCETO

Antonio Carlo Zanobi	98,99,01	04
Bernardo Carlo Zanobi	95,99,02	04,05,07
Gaspare Lapo Gaspare	00,02	09,11,12
Francesco Bernardo Carlo		06,10,11
Francesco Zanobi Paolo		09
Lorenzo Bernardo Carlo		**09**

GIACHINOTTI

Girolamo Adouardo Cipriano	96,96	

GIACOMINI TEBALDUCCI

Tommaso Piero Tommaso	96,97,97,00,02	05,06,08,10,11,12
Francesco Piero Tommaso	99	05,10,11,12
Antonio Jacopo Tommaso	98	

GIANFIGLIAZZI

Bertoldo Bertoldo Antonio	96,97,99,02	04
Gherardo M.Buongianni Buongianni		04,05,06,08,09
Jacopo M.Buongianni Buongianni		10,11
Gianozzo Giovanni Gianozzo	99	

GIANNI

Tommaso Jacopo Luigi	98,00,01	03,04,05,06,07,07,08,10,11,12

GINORI

Gino Giuliano Francesco	95,96,97	
Alessandro Gino Giuliano	98	05
Girolamo Gino Giuliano		07,09
Simone Giuliano Simone	02	
Tommaso Zanobi Tommaso	95,96,98	06,08,09
Bartolomeo Lionardo Francesco		10,12

DEL GIOCONDO

Antonio Zanobi Antonio	95,98	
Amadeo Zmadeo Zanobi	01	
Paolo Zanobi Antonio	02	

GIOVANNI

Tommaso Niccolò Tommaso	97	
Giovanbattista Francesco Tommaso	96,99,01	06
Tommaso Francesco Tommaso	95,97	

GIRALDI

Antonio Francesco Antonio	02	03,04,06,08,10,12
Giraldo Francesco Antonio	96,01	03,04,04,06
Niccolò Giovanni Niccolò	02	03

GIROLAMI (S.C.)

Francesco Zanobi Bernardo	96,97,99	07,08,10
Raffaello Francesco Zanobi		12

GIROLAMI (S.M.N.)

Geri Zanobi Testa		03,04,05,12

GIUGNI

Andrea Niccolò Andrea	97	04,06,06,07,09,10,11
Bartolomeo Domenico Giovanni	96,01	03,05,06,07,07,10,11
Luigi Bernardo Domenico	97,98,99	03
Antonio Giovanni Filippo	95,97,00	03,03,04,05,06,12
Raffaello Rinieri Niccolo		11

GIUNTINI

Niccolò Giuntino Guido	95	
Giuntino Guido Giuntino		12

GONDI

Giuliano Lionardo Lionardo	95,97	
Lionardo Giuliano Lionardo	98	04,06
Belichozzo Giuliano Lionardo	01	
Giovanbattista Giuliano Lionardo	02	03
Federigo Giuliano Lionardo		10
Alessandro Antonio Lionardo		12
Bernardo Carlo Salvestro		03,03,04,06,07.08,11,12

GRASSI

Chimente Amerigo Bartolo	97,02	

GUCCI

Giovanni Jacopo Dino	95,96,98	03,09,10,12

GUALTEROTTI

Filipozzo Lorenzo Bartolomeo	00,02	03,09,10,11,12,12
M.Francesco Lorenzo Bartolomeo	98	03,04,06
Piero Bartolomeo Lorenzo	95,96,97,98,01	
Antonio Piero Bartolomeo		04,10,12

DEL GUANTO

Girolamo Piero Simone	01	

GUARDAGNI

Uliviere Simone Vieri		06,11

GUARDI

Gherardo Andrea Lapo	97,99,01	

GUASCONI

Niccolò M. Zanobi Jacopo	95,97,98,00	
Francesco Francesco Jacopo	96,01	03
Giovacchino Biagio Jacopo		05,08,11
Giovanbattista Carlo Jacopo		05,07,09,11
Albertaccio Beltrame Bernardo		12

LOTTI		
Giovanpaolo Paolo Ridolfo	98	
Bastiano Lotto Piero	00	
Benedetto Bernardo Paolo		08 11

LOTTINI		
Francesco Appardo Nicolaio	00	

LUCALBERTI		
Pazzino Bernardo Pazzino	98,99,01	05
Spinello Bernardo Pazzino	00	12

DELLA LUNA		
Domenico Pierozzo Francesco	96	
Francesco Antonio Giovanni		07,08,11,12

MACHIAVELLI		
Niccolò Alessandro Filippo	96,99,00,02	03,04,04,08,10,11,11,12
Filippo Alessandro Filippo		03
Piero M.Francesco	95,96,97	
Francesco Piero M.Francesco		11
Giovanni Gherardo Giovanni		11,12,12

MACINGHI		
Giovacchino Filippo Giovacchino		08
Francesco Bernardo Domenico	99	

MAGALDI		
Domenico Niccolò Domenico	95	03,11

MAGALOTTI		
Francesco Bese Guido		11

MALEGONNELLE		
Antonio Piero Niccolò		06

MANCINI		
Bartolomeo Jacopo Duccino	98,00	05,09,10,10,11,12
Duccino Jacopo Duccino	96,98,99,01,02	03,04,06,07,07,11,11,12
Antonio Jacopo Duccino	98,00	06,12
Giovanni Jacopo Duccino		03,03,12
Albizzo Andrea Taddeo	95,98	
Girolamo Andrea Taddeo	02	03,05,08,08

MANELLI		
Alessandro Lionardo Niccolò	95,97	04,04
Francesco Lionardo Niccolò		03,05,12
Guido Francesco Guido	01	
Luigi Giovanni Niccolò	02	

MANETTI		
Bernardo M. Gianozzo Bernardo	95	
Giovanni M. Gianozzo Bernardo	98	
Gianozzo Bernardo M. Gianozzo	00,02	05
Filippo Bernardo M. Gianozzo		05,07,11,11
Bernardo Filippo Bernardo	02	04,08
Antonio Tuccio Marabottino	95	

MARIGNOLLI		
Piero Zanobi Piero	97,98,99	

MARTELLI		
Braccio M.Domenico Niccolò	97,99	
Gismondo Francesco Niccolò	99,01	04,04,05
Galeotto Francesco Niccolò	99	
Ilarione Bartolomeo Niccolò	00	03
Francesco Bartolomeo Niccolò		12
Lorenzo Niccolò Ugolino		04,08,09,11,12
Niccolò Antonio Niccolò	95	

MARTELLINI,
Baldinaccio Giovanni   98

MARTINI di Guccio
Giuliano Tommaso Antonio   02
Antonio Tommaso Antonio   07,08

MARTINI (Drago S.G.)
Bernardo S. Giovanni Luca   05

MASI
Lodovico Antonio Tommaso   95
Antonio Duti Antonio   00,02
Bernardo Duti Antonio   01   04

MAZZINGHI
Domenico Bernardo Domenico   95   04,05,08,10
Girolamo Bernardo Domenico   95
Francesco Bernardo Domenico   99
Giuliano Jacopo Ugolino   05,08,09

MEDICI
Bernardo Alamanno Bernardo   01   04,04,06,07,09,11,12
Francesco Giuliano Giovenco   98   03,07,09,11
Vieri Cambio M.Vieri   95,96,01,02 12
Gianozzo Cambio M.Vieri   96

MINERBETTI
Giovanni Antonio Tommaso   96,97   03,03,05
Andrea M.Tommaso Andrea   05,07,10,11,12

MINI
Bernardo Giovanni Paolo   02

MORELLI
Lorenzo Matteo Morello   95   06,08,12
Tommaso Paolo Morello   96,98,99   05,06,07
Bernardo Girolamo Matteo   05,10
Giovanni Jacopo Giovanni   95,97,98
Lodovico Jacopo Giovanni   02   03,06,08,11,12

MORI
Bartolo Bartolo Giovanni   95
Giovanni Bartolo Bartolo   97,00   04,06,07,08,09,11
Filippo Niccolò Giovanni   00

NARDI
Niccolò Piero Salvestro   00   04
Salvestro Piero Salvestro   96   05,09

NASI
Dionigi Piero Lutozzo   96
Filippo Lutozzo Jacopo   97
Bernardo Lutozzo Jacope   95,97,99   03,04,04,07
Lutozzo Piero Lutozzo   03,06,08,12
Alessandro Francesco Lutozzo   07
Agostino Giovanni Jacopo   95
Battista Giovanni Jacopo   95,96
Lutozzo Battista Giovanni   03,06,08,10,11

NELLI
Antonio Bartolomeo Antonio   01
Francesco Bartolomeo Antonio   02
Giovanni Matteo Giovanni   02

NERLI

Tanai Francesco Filippo	97	
Benedetto Tanai Francesco	95	03,07,11
Jacopo Tanai Francesco	01	
Neri Tanai Francesco	02	03,10
Francesco Tanai Francesco	98	
Piero Tanai Francesco		05,07,07,11,11

DEL NERO

Bernardo Nero Filippo	96,97	
Nerozzo Piero Filippo	99,01	
Nero Francesco Nero	96,97	07,08,10
Piero Francesco Nero		08
Lorenzo Francesco Nero	00	
Simone Bernardo Simone	95,96,99,02	03,04,04,05,06,10,11,12
Niccolò Bernardo Simone	96	

NESI

Giovanni Francesco Giovanni	02	04,05

NICCOLINI

Michele Bernardo Lapo	96,97,99	
Marco Lorenzo Lapo	00,02	
Antonio Lorenzo Lapo	02	
Jacopo Paolo Lapo	01	
Andrea Paolo Lapo		10,12
Andreuolo M.Otto Lapo		07,10,11

NOBILI

Antonio Francesco Bartolomeo	97	
Simone Francesco Bartolomeo		04
Niccolò Ruberto Antonio	95,97,97	
Uberto Francesco Uberto	96,99,01	05,10,12
Giovanbattista Francesco Uberto		10
Carlo Niccolò M.Guccio	98,99	
Alessandro Carlo Niccolo		11
Niccolo Carlò Niccolò		11,12

ORLANDINI (S.C.)

Giuliano Piero Simone	96,01	05,09,10,11
Piero Giovanni Simone		07,11

ORLANDINI (S.G.)

Bartolomeo Giovanni M.Bartolomeo		08,11

PAGANELLI

Antonio Bernardo Antonio	97,98	04

PANCIATICHI

Giuliano Piero Cosimo	96	

PANDOLFINI

Pierfilippo M.Gianozzo Agnolo	96	
Jacopo M.Gianozzo Agnolo	00,01	
Agnolo Pandolfo M.Gianozzo	98	08
Battista Pandolfo M.Gianozzo	99	
Bartolomeo Pandolfo M.Gianozzo	99,02	03,04,06,06,07,08,12
Giovanni Pandolfo M.Gianozzo		08
Domenico Pandolfo M.Gianozzo		11
Domenico M.Carlo Agnolo	98,00,02	
Agnolo Domenico M.Carlo	01	
Francesco Bartolomeo M.Carlo		10,12

PARENTI

Marco Parente Giovanni	95	
Piero Marco Parente	98,00,02	04,04,05,10,11,12,12
Stefano Giovanni Bernardo	00	03

PAZZI

Guglielmo Antonio M. Andrea	96	10
Giovanfrancesco Luigi Ghinozzo	01	

PECCORI

Guidaccio Giovanni Guidaccio	99,01	03,07,08
Alessandro Piero Bartolomeo	95	

PEPI

Francesco Chirico Giovanni	95	06,08,09
Ruberto Chirico Giovanni	98	

PERI

Lodovico Bernardo Niccolò	00,02	03

PERUZZI

Bindaccio Bernardo Bindaccio	95,97,99	
Piero Donato Bonifazio	95	
Filippo Giovanni Rinieri		10,12
Francesco Niccolò Cante		11,12

PESCIONI

Michele Lionardo Michele		10

PETRUCCI

Annibale Domenico	96	
Alamanno Cesare Domenico	00,02	06,08,10
Ottaviano Cesare Domenico	01	

PILLI

Latino Giovanni Latino	97	

PITTI

Giovanni Buonaccorso M.Luca	95,00	04,08
Lorenzo Buonaccorso M.Luca	97,98	
Amerigo M.Luca Buonaccorso		10,12
Piero M.Luca Buonaccorso		10,11
Raffaello Alfonso M.Giovanozzo		07
Bartolomeo Salvestro Ruberto	00	
Giovanni Salvestro Ruberto	02	
Piero Francesco Neri	01	

POPOLESCHI

Niccolò Giovanni Salvestro	96	05
Salvestro Giovanni Salvestro	95,97	
Girolamo Giovanni Salvestro	00	09,11
Lorenzo Giovanni Salvestro	96,99	03,03,06,06,09,10
Bartolomeo Giovanni Salvestro	95,98	
Giovanni Bartolomeo Giovanni		10,12
Piero Bartolomeo Giovanni		12

PORTINARI

Giovanni Adovardo Giovanni	99	
Bernardo Adovardo Giovanni	01	06,10,10
Tommaso Folco Adovardo	96,97,98,99	

PUCCI

Tommaso Puccio Antonio	97,98	
Francesco Giovanni Antonio	98	07,08,11
Lodovico Benintendo Antonio	01	

DEL PUGLIESE

Francesco Filippo Francesco	97	

QUARATESI

Girolamo Luigi Giovanni	98,01	06
Riniere Giovanni Giovanni	02	04,05
Simone Benedetto Simone	99,02	
Piero Bernardo Donato	01	

REDDITI (S.M.N.)

Antonio Tommaso Antonio	00,02	

REDDITI (S.C.)

M. Bartolomeo Andrea Antonio	02	

RICCARDI (SMN)

Luca Taddeo Luca	00	

RICCI

Federigo Giovanni Federigo	97	11
Ruberto Giovanni Federigo	99	03
Giovanni Ruggiero Ruggiero	96	

RIDOLFI di Borgo

Bernardo Inghilese Schiatta	95,97,99	

RIDOLFI di Piazza

Francesco Giovanni M.Lorenzo	00	
Giovanbattista Luigi M.Lorenzo	96	03,07,12
Giovanni Tommaso Luigi		04,05
Lionardo Bernardo M.Lorenzo		09,10
Ridolfo Pagnozzo Bartolomeo	97,98	03
Girolamo Pagnozzo Bartolomeo	98	
Bartolomeo Pagnozzo Pagnozzo	00	06,06,08,08,09,12
Ruberto Pagnozzo Pagnozzo	04	04
Piero Jacopo Pagnozzo	01	
Zanobi Girolamo Pagnozzo		06,09
Pierfrancesco Giorgio Niccolò	02	
Piero Giuliano Niccolò		04,06,08
Piero Girolamo Pagnozzo		06

RINALDI

Rinaldo Borgo Borgo		03

RINIERI

Bernardo Stoldo Luca	95	
Stoldo Filippo Stoldo		12

RINUCCINI

Neri Filippo Cino	95,99	03,05,06,06,07,07
Francesco Filippo Cino	01	
Giulianmaria Jacopo Cino	01	05,07
Giovanni Simone Giovanni		06
Buonaccorso Simone Giovanni		03,04,04,08,10,11,12
Giovanmaria Jacopo Cino	95	

RISALITI

Geri Gherardo Geri	95,97	06,07,08,09,10,11
Ubertino Geri Ubertino	00	

RONDINELLI

Nofri Giovanni Simone	95	
Benintendo Lorenzo Giovanni	00	06

DEL ROSSO

Rosso Pierozzo Domenico	00	

RUCELLAI

Girolamo Filippo Vanni	95,98	
Cardinale Guglielmo Cardinale	99	03,05
Tommeso Filippo Brancazio	99	
M.Niccolo Brancazio Niccolo		07,08,11
Antonio Giovanni Antonio	00	03,06,07,07,08,11,12,12
Adovardo Carlo Antonio	02	
Lorenzo Antonio Sandro	00	
Piero Mariotto Piero	01	04,05
Paolo Pandolfo Giovanni		06,09

RUSTICHI (S.M.N.)

Bartolomeo Giovanni Betto	97	

RUSTICHI (S.C.)

Antonio Marabottino Antonio	00	03,05

SACCHETTI

Andreuolo Andreuolo Nicol	98,99,00	03,07,07,09,09,11
Filippo Niccolò Andreuolo		03,06
Nicol Matteo Nicol	98,01	05,06,07,11,12

SALVETTI

Salvetto M. Tommaso	95	
Niccolò Tommaso M. Tommaso	96	
Niccolò Salvetto M.Tommaso		12

SALVIATI

Giuliano Francesco Alamanno	96,98	09
Alamanno Averardo Alamanno		07,07
Jacopo Giovanni Alamanno		04,06,11
Giovanni Vieri Giovanni	95,97,98,99,00	03,07,08,11,12,12
Lorenzo Lotto Giovanni	95,99,00	04,05,05,06,08,10,11,12
Gherardo Marco Giovanni	00	
Gianozzo Bernardo Marco	01	07,08,08,09,09,12

SAPITI

Otto Francesco Filippo	02	

SASSETTI

Cosimo Francesco Tommaso		03,04,04,08,10

SCALI

Antonfrancesco Bartolomeo Luigi	95,97,97	03,07

DELLO SCARFA

Francesco Martino Francesco	96,00	

SCARLATTI

Luigi Antonio Scarlatto	00	
Scarlatto Antonio Scarlatto	96	
Francesco Antonio Scarlatto	99	
Riniere Bernardo Antonio	00,02	
Alessandro Bernardo Antonio	99,00	03,06,09,11
Niccolò Tommaso Antonio		09

SEGNI

Francesco Stefano Francesco	97	
Mariotto Piero Mariotto		03,05,06
Alessandro Piero Mariotto		11

SERNIGI

Andrea Cipriano Chimente	98,00	06,11,12
Chimente Cipriano Chimente	95,98	07,10,11,11,12

SERRAGLI

Niccolò Piero Paolo	00	05,09
Agnolo Piero Paolo	00,01	06
Agnolo Buonaiuto Niccolò	02	08

SERRISTORI

Ristoro Antonio Salvestro	96,97	
Battista Giovanni Antonio	96,97,98	
Antonio Averardo Antonio		04,07,10,10,12

SIGNORINI

Piero Antonio Signorino	99	06,12
Tommaso Andrea Signorino	02	

SINIBALDI

Sinibaldo Francesco	99,01

SODERINI

Paolantonio M. Tommaso Lorenzo	96,98	
Piero M.Tommaso Lorenzo	02	
Giovannvettorio M. Tommaso Lorenzo		04,06,07,08,10
Bernardo Niccolò Lorenzo	95,98	
Girolamo Luigi Giovanni		05

DA SOMMAIA

Francesco Guglielmo Ridolfo	99	03,04,06,07,09

SPINELLI

Giovanni Francesco Lorenzo	02	07
Giovanni Cristofano Bartolomeo	98,99,00,	04,05,06,07,10,11
Fruosino Francesco Fruosino	00,01	04

SPINI

Antonio Giovanni Antonio	99	
Scolaio Agnolo Scolaio	00,02	04,08,11

DELLO STECCUTO

Mariotto Lorenzo Giovanni	97	03,03,08

DI STEFANO

Chimente Andrea Andrea	95,00

STRADI

Bartolomeo Giovanni Bartolomeo	99

STROZZI

Lionardo Benedetto Francesco	96,97,98	04,07
Lodovico Francesco Benedetto	99	
Andrea Carlo Piero	97,98	03,04,07,08
Michele Carlo Piero	00	03
Palla Carlo Francesco		07
Cosimo Vanni Francesco		06
M.Antonio Vanni Francesco	95,99,01	08
Marco Giovanni Jacopo	01	

DELLA STUFA

Girolamo Giovenco Lorenzo	97,00,02	03,04,04,05,05,07,07,08,10
M. Enea Giovenco Lorenzo	98,00	05
Luigi M.Agnolo Lorenzo	98	04,04,06,08
Pandolfo M.Agnolo Lorenzo	97	
Niccolò Giovanni Lorenzo	95	
Ugo Niccolò Giovanni	02	12,12

TADDEI

Piero Antonio Taddeo	98	03,07,09,10
Francesco Antonio Taddeo		06,09
Taddeo Francesco Antonio		12

TANAGLI

Jacopo Francesco Guglielmo	99,00	
Filippo Giovanni Filippo	01	03,03,11
Marco Amerigo M.Guglielmo	93	

TEDALDI

Lattantonio Francesco Papa	97	04,05,07,08,08,10
Bartolo Lionardo Papa		03,04,05,08
Jacopo Piero Maffeo	95,96,97,00	

TEMPERANI

| Francesco M.Manno Giovanni | 95,96,97,99,00 | 07,08,09,10,11,12 |
| Temperano M.Manno Giovanni | 00 | 03,04,05 |

TORNAQUINCI

Giovanni Francesco Tieri	00,01,02	
Tieri Francesco Tieri	02	
Niccolò Piero Tieri	02	

DELLA TOSA

Francesco Bernardo M.Baldo	96,97,98,99	
Carlo Niccolò M.Baldo	01	
Carlo Bernardo M.Baldo		03,05

TOSINGHI

| Pierfrancesco Francesco Rinieri | 96,99,00 | 03,03,06,09,10,12 |
| Tommaso Francesco Rinieri | | 05,05,06,07,10,10,11,11 |

UBERTINI

| Bartolomeo Bartolomeo Gregorio | 95 | |

UGHI

| Giorgio Mariano Giorgio | 00 | |

UGOLINI

| Niccolo Giorgio Niccolò | | 03,04,06,06,07,08,08,10,11 |
| Luca Giorgio Niccolò | 01,02 | 04,12 |

UGUCCIONI

Giovanni Francesco Bernardo	98	03
M.Simone Bernardo Simone	00	
Bernardo M.Simone Bernardo	00	

VALORI

| Francesco Filippo Bartolomeo | 97,97 | |
| Niccolo Bartolomeo Filippo | | 05,07,10,11,12 |

VECHIETTI

| Antonio Marsiglio Bernardo | 99 | 03 |

VELLUTI

| Biagio Buonaccorso M.Donato | 97 | |

VENTURA

Neri Jacopo Jacopo	95,98,02	05,06,08,11,12
Luigi Francesco Jacopo	98	03,07,12
Ruberto Giovanni Francesco	00,02	
Jacopo Francesco Jacopo		11

DA VERRAZZANO,

Antonio Cecco Fruosino	02	
Fruosino Lodovico Cecco	99	
Lodovico Fruosino Lodovico		06
Alessandro Bartolomeo Lodovico	00,01	03
Bertoldo Bartolomeo Lodovico	02	
Pierandrea Bernardo Bernardo	00	

VERNACCI,

Luigi Giovanni Agnolo	01	

VESPUCCI,

Piero Bernardo Piero	95,98,00	07
M.Guidantonio Giovanni Simone	01	

VETTORI,

Bernardo Francesco Paolo	96,97,97,99	03,05,10,11,11
Piero Francesco Paolo	95	
Jacopo Luigi Neri	01	
Giovanni Luigi Neri	01	
Giovanni Gianozzo Giovanni	01	

DEL VIGNA

Antonio Bartolomeo Antonio	95,98	
Niccolò Filippo Antonio	99	

VILLANI

Jacopo Giovanni Jacopo	∪2	
Piero Giovanni Jacopo	02	

DAL VIVAIO

Fatino Alberto Pierozzo	95	
Niccolò Pierozzo Bartolomeo		06,11

VIVIANI,

Giuliano Francesco	95	
Raffaello Giuliano Francesco	01	03,11,12

ZATI,

Bartolo Piero Bartolo	98,99,02	03,04,05,08,10,11,12
Niccolò Simone Amerigo	95,97,97,00	03,05,10,12
Ruberto Simone Amerigo	99,01,02	
Francesco Andrea Francesco	95,96,02	04,06,07,08,09

APPENDIX 3

	Consiglio dei Settanta 1480-1494[1]	Consiglio dei Cento 1480-1494[2]	Consiglio degli Ottanta			Consiglio dei Cento 1514-1527[3]	Consiglio dei Settanta 1514-1527[4]
			1495-1512	[1495-1502	1503-1512]		
ACCIAUIOLI	X	6-10[5]	7-17	(2-4	6-13)	6-28	X
ADIMARI		1-4	3-11	(3-3	2-8)	3-8	
AGLI		-	-			2-6	
ALAMANNESCHI		1-6	-			1-6	
ALAMANNI	X	4-10	2-11	(1-1	2-10)	5-18	X
ALBERTI		3-14	5-27	(5-12	2-15)	4-20	X
ALBIZZI	X	9-25	12-39	(11-19	6-20)	10-32	X
ALDOBRANDI		-	1-3	(1-3	-)	-	
ALDOBRANDINI del Nero	X	3-10	5-14	(3-3	2-11)	1-2	
ALESSANDRI	X	3-6	5-16	(3-9	3-7)	3-9	X
ALTOVITI		9-28	6-19	(5-11	5-8)	6-29	X
AMADORI		-	-			2-5	
DELL'AMOROTTA		1-5	1-2	(1-2	-)	-	
DALL'ANTELLA	X	4-16	1-4	(1-3	1-1)	4-15	X
ANTINORI		1-6	4-17	(3-9)	3-8)	1-4	
ARDINGHELLI		-	2-6	(1-2	2-4)	1-3	X
ARNOLDI		-	1-1	(1-1	-)	2-13	
ARNOLFI		-	-	-	-	1-1	
ARRIGHI		1-1	2-6	(2-6	-)	-	X
ARRIGUCCI		1-6	1-1	(1-1	-)	2-10	
DEGLI ASINI		-	2-7	(1-2	1-5)	-	
BAGNESI		1-4	1-1	(1-1	-)	1-1	
BALDESI		-	1-1	(1-1	-)	-	
BALDOVINETTI		-	2-6	(2-4	1-2)	1-3	
BALDOVINI		1-1	-	-	-	-	
BALDUCCI PEGOLOTTI		-	1-2	(1-2	-)	-	
BANDINI BANDUCCI		-	1-1	(1-1	-)	-	
BARBADORI		-	-	-	-	1-8	X
BARDI		-	2-2	(-	2-2)	-	
BARDUCCI OTTAVANTI		1-7	1-3	(1-2	1-1)	1-5	

BARONCELLI		3-13	3-4	(3-4	-)	2-2	
BARTOLELLI (S.G.)		-	1-1	(1-1	-)	-	
BARTOLI (Unicorno)	X	13-39	10-17	(6-8	5-9)	3-11	X
BARTOLINI SALIMBENI		7-27	4-15	(3-7	2-8)	8-24	X
DEL BECCUTO		-	1-1	(1-1	-)	1-4	
BELCHARI		2-5	-			-	
BELFRADELLI		-	1-2	(1-2	-)	-	
BELLACCI		1-9	2-8	(2-3	2-5)	2-9	
BENCI (Vaio)		-	3-5	(1-1	2-4)	1-1	
BENCI (Dr.S.G.)		-	1-2	(1-1	1-1)	1-2	
BENCI GUERNIERI		1-1	2-4	(1-2	1-2)	1-2	
DEL BENE		-	1-5	(1-4	1-1)	-	
BENINI		-	1-2	(1-2	-)	-	
Del BENINO	X	6-21	8-23	(6-11	5-12)	4-19	X
BENIZI		-	1-1	(1-1	-)	-	
BENVENUTI (S.M.N.)		1-1	2-3	(2-2	1-1)	-	
BENVENUTI (S.C.)		2-6	1-1	(1-1	-)	2-3	
BENVENUTI (S.G.)		1-1	1-2	(1-2	-)	1-1	
BERARDI	X	4-12	2-11	(2-3	1-8)	3-6	X
BERLINGHIERI	X	5-20	3-9	(3-4	2-5)	2-15	
DEL BIANCO		1-1	1-1	(1-1	-)	-	
BILIOTTI (S.S.)	X	7-22	3-4	(2-2	2-2)	6-24	
BILIOTTI (S.C.)		-	1-1	(1-1	-)	1-4	
BINI		1-2	1-1	(-	1-1)	4-7	X
BOCCACCI		-	1-4	(1-2	1-2)	-	
BONCIANI		2-11	1-4	(1-2	1-2)	3-13	
BONI MEO		1-1	1-2	(1-2	-)	-	
BONI		1-1	4-9	(4-8	1-1)	-	
BONSI	X	7-28	1-1	(1-1	-)	4-20	
BONVANNI		4-16	-	-	-	-	
BORGHERINI		-	1-1	(1-1	-)	1-2	
BORGHINI		3-21	1-2	(	1-2)	1-1	
BORGOGNONI		1-4	-	-	-	-	
BOSCOLI		1-1	-	-	-	-	

BRUNI		1-1	-	-	-	-
BUONAGIUSI		1-4	1-2	(1-2	-)	-
BUONDELMONTE	X	3-16	4-11	(4-8 | 2-3)	4-13	X
BUONGIROLAMI	X	1-2	1-2	(- | 1-2)	1-8	X
BUONINSEGNI		5-15	3-10	(3-4	2-6)	1-3
BUSINI		3-5	5-8	(5-6	1-2)	5-12
DELLA CACCIA	X	9-39	5-25	(5-14 | 3-11)	2-12	X
CACCINI		2-2	-	-	-	-
CAMBI OPPORTUNI		1-5	2-6	(2-6	-)	-
CAMBI MERCATANTI		1-1	2-7	(2-3	2-4)	1-5
CAMBI di Napoleone		-	1-4	(1-2	1-2)	-
CAMBI (S.G.)		-	1-2	(1-2	-)	-
CAMBINI		3-8	1-1	(1-1	-)	1-3
CANACCI		-	1-1	(1-1	-)
CANIGIANI	X	7-20	5-22	(4-8 | 4-14)	3-17	X
CAPPELLI		3-17	3-10	(2-7	2-3)	2-5
CAPPONI	X	16-44	9-27	(5-13 | 5-14)	13-46	X
CARDUCCI	X	4-11	5-15	(3-4 | 4-11)	4-19	X
CARNESECCHI		10-46	10-33	(6-13 | 8-20)	8-28	X
DELLA CASA		-	2-2	(2-2	-)	-
DA CASAVECCHIA		1-2	3-4	(3-4	-)	-
CASTELLANI		-	-	-	-	2-12
DA CASTIGLIONE		-	2-3	(2-2	1-1)	-
CAVALCANTI		1-6	4-5	(3-3	1-2)	3-11
CEFFI		1-1	1-2	(1-2	-)	-
CEFFINI		3-5	3-3	(3-3	-)	1-3
CENNINI		1-5	-	-	-	1-4
CERCHI		2-5	1-3	(1-1	1-2)	-
CERRETANI		4-14	3-8	(3-6 | 1-2)	2-17	X
CIACCHI		5-19	6-11	(6-7 | 3-4)	2-10	X
CIAI		2-8	1-2	(-	1-2)	1-7
CIARI		1-3	-
CICCIAPORCI		4-17	3-11	(2-4	3-7)	2-5

DA CIGNANO		1-7	-	-	-	-	
CINI		-	1-1	(1-1 | -)	-	
COCCHI DONATI		1-2	-	-	-	4-17	
COMPAGNI		3-21	2-6	(1-3 | 2-3)	3-16	
CORBINELLI	X	11-36	9-29	(8-15 | 6-14)	9-34	X
CORBIZZI.		1-3	1-1	(1-1 | -)	-	
CORSELLINI		3-6	2-2	(2-2 | -)	-	
CORSI		1-4	4-18	(4-8 | 2-10)	2-5	X
CORSINI	X	9-27	12-26	(7-13 | 7-13)	5-23	X
CORTIGIANI	X	2-3	3-7	(1-1 | 2-6)	-	
COVONI		1-10	2-5	(1-4 | 1-1)	1-2	
CRESCI	X	2-5	-	-	-	1-1	
DATI		-	-	-	-	1-1	
DAVANZATI	X	4-12	3-9	(- | 3-9)	7-21	X
DAZZI		-	3-7	(2-3 | 2-4)	-	
DEI		-	1-1	(1-1 | -)	-	
DETI		1-6	-	-	-	1-3	X
DIETISALVI NERONI		-	2-6	(- | 2-6)	3-6	X
DINI	X	3-12	1-2	(- | 1-2)	2-12	X
FAGIUOLI		3-16	3-8	(2-2 | 2-6)	-	
FALCONI (1327)		1-5	1-2	(1-2 | -)	-	
FALCONI (1442)		-	-	-	-	1-6	
FALCONIERI		1-9	1-2	(1-2 | -)	-	
FEDERIGHI	X	8-38	6-21	(5-11 | 4-10)	5-17	X
FERUCCI		3-3	1-1	(1-1 | -)	2-5	
FIGIOVANNI		-	-	-	-	1-2	
DA FILICAIA	X	6-20	6-28	(4-8 | 4-20)	7-31	X
FOLCHI		1-1	-	-	-	1-1	
FORESE (S.C.)		-	1-3	(1-2 | 1-1)	-	
FORMICONI		1-1	1-7	(1-4 | 1-3)	-	
FORTINI		2-13	3-9	(2-4 | 2-5)	1-1	
FRANCESCHI		3-7	1-1	(1-1 | -)	1-10	
DELLA FRASCA		1-3	-	-	-	2-8	
FRESCOBALDI		-	3-6	(2-3 | 1-3)	1-3	
GADDI		1-1	1-5	(1-4 | 1-1)	-	

GALILEI		3-9	5-14	(4-7	4-7)	-	
GERINI		-	1-3	(1-2	1-1)	-	
GHERARDI	X	4-13	2-8	(2-3	1-5)	5-21	X
DA GHIACCETO		5-24	6-20	(3-8	6-12)	5-21	
GIACHINOTTI		3-7	1-2	(1-2	-)	-	
GIACOMINI TEBALDUCCI		-	3-17	(3-7	2-10)	-	
GIANDONATI		-	-	-	-	1-3	
GIANFIGLIAZZI	X	2-4	4-13	(2-5	3-8	3-12	X
GIANNI		-	1-13	(1-3	1-10)	1-6	
GINORI	X	5-28	6-16	(4-8	4-8)	4-20	X
DEL GIOCONDO		1-1	3-4	(3-4	-)	-	
GIOVANNI		3-19	3-7	(3-6	1-1)	-	
GIRALDI		1-3	3-15	(3-4	3-11)	1-2	
GIROLAMI (S.C.)		1-7	2-7	(1-3	2-4)	3-11	X
GIROLAMI (S.M.N.)		1-1	1-4	(-	1-4)	-	
GIUGNI	X	11-39	5-31	(4-9	5-22	7-32	X
GIUNTINI		3-5	2-2	(1-1	1-1)	1-5	
GONDI		1-1	7-18	(4-5	5-13)	1-6	X
GRASSI		1-1	1-2	(1-2	-)	-	
GUCCI		-	1-7	(1-8	1-4)	-	
GUALTEROTTI		3-6	4-20	(3-8	3-12)	1-1	X
DEL GUANTO		-	1-1	(1-1	-)	-	
GUARDAGNI		-	1-2	(-	1-2)	-	
GUARDI		1-2	1-3	(1-3	-)	-	
GUASCONI		-	4-15	(2-6	4-9)	-	
GUICCIARDINI	X	5-10	5-15	(2-3	5-12	3-18	X
GUIDACCI		1-3	2-3	(1-2	1-1)	-	
GUIDETTI		3-6	3-17	(3-6	3-11)	2-3	
GUIDI		2-4	-	-	-	1-3	
GUIDOTTI		5-19	2-6	(1-1	1-5)	3-9	X
GUIDUCCI (S.M.N.)	X	6-19	2-4	(2-4	-)	4-19	X
GUIDUCCI (S.C.)		-	1-1	(-	1-1)	-	
INGHIRAMI		-	1-1	(-	1-1)	-	
JACOPI		2-6	1-6	(1-2	1-4)	2-9	

LANFREDINI	X	3-5	2-7	(2-3	2-4)	3-9	X
LAPACCINI		-	3-7	(3-5	1-2)	1-4	
LAPI (Vaio)		2-9	2-8	(1-2	2-6)	1-3	
LAPI (Chiavi)		1-4	2-7	(1-4	2-3)	1-5	
LAPOZZI		1-5	-	-	-	-	
LARIONI		-	-	-	-	2-2	
LENZI	X	2-16	2-9	(2-4	1-5)	-	
LIONI	X	2-2	1-2	(-	1-2)	5-18	X
LIPPI		2-11	-	-	-	2-13	
LORINI	X	3-16	3-11	(2-3	2-8)	-	
LOTTI		2-8	3-4	(2-2	2-2)	2-10	
LOTTINI		-	1-1	(1-1	-)	-	
LUCALBERTI		3-8	2-6	(2-4	2-2)	-	
DELLA LUNA		1-1	2-5	(1-1	1-4)	-	
MACHIAVELLI	X	3-14	5-20	(2-7	4-13)	5-23	X
MACINGHI		-	2-2	(1-1	1-1)	-	
MAGALDI		2-9	1-3	(1-1	1-2)	-	
MAGALOTTI		1-1	1-1	(-	1-1)	1-5	
MAGLI		1-1	-	-	-	-	
MALEGONNELLE	X	3-9	1-1	(-	1-1)	6-26	X
MANCINI		3-8	6-35	(5-12	5-23)	3-6	
MANELLI		-	4-9	(3-4	2-5)	-	
MANETTI		3-6	6-13	(5-6	3-7)	-	
MARIGNOLLI		1-3	1-3	(1-3	-)	1-4	
MARTELLI	X	9-35	7-17	(5-7	4-10)	7-28	X
MARTELLINI		-	1-1	(1-1	-)	1-2	
MARTINI di Guccio		1-3	2-3	(1-1	1-2)	-	
MARTINI (Drago, SG)		-	1-1	(-	1-1)	-	
MASI	X	5-19	3-5	(3-4	1-1)	-	
MAZZINGHI		6-12	4-10	(3-3	2-7)	1-1	
MEDICI	X	10-39	4-19	(4-7	3-12)	20-48	X
MELLINI	X	1-4	-	-	-	-	
MILANESI		1-1	-			-	
MINERBETTI	X	6-19	2-10	(1-2	2-8)	2-6	X
MINI		1-1	1-1	(1-1	-)	-	
MINIATI		-	-	-	-	2-10	

MONTEGONZI		-	-	-	-	1-4	
MORELLI	X	5-22	5-21	(4-8	4-13)	10-42	X
MORI		1-3	3-10	(3-4	1-6)	-	
MORMORAI		-	-	-	-	1-1	
MOZZI		-	-	-	-	1-8	
NARDI		4-11	2-5	(2-2	2-3)	1-3	
NASI	X	10-36	8-22	(5-8	4-14)	5-14	X
NELLI		-	3-3	(3-3	-)	1-2	
NERLI	X	3-8	6-14	(5-5	3-9)	6-12	X
DEL NERO	X	9-38	7-24	(6-12	3-12)	3-8	
NESI		1-5	1-3	(1-1	1-2)	1-4	
NICCOLINI	X	9-40	6-12	(4-7	2-5)	9-39	X
NOBILI	X	5-11	8-17	(4-9	5-8)	2-11	X
NORI		-	-	-	-	-	X
ORLANDINI (SC)	X	3-6	2-8	(1-2	2-6)	2-5	
ORLANDINI (SG)		3-6	1-2	(-	1-2)	1-4	
PAGANELLI	X	3-11	1-3	(1-2	1-1)	1-2	X
PALARCIONI		1-1	-	-	-	-	
DELLA PALLA		1-1	-	-	-	-	
PANCIATICHI		-	1-1	(1-1	-)	-	
PANDOLFINI	X	10-28	10-23	(7-11	5-12)	12-41	X
PARENTI		-	3-13	(3-5	2-8)	-	
PARTICINI		1-3	-	-	-	1-1	
PAZZI		-	2-3	(1-2	1-1)	2-5	X
PECCORI		2-11	2-6	(2-3	1-3)	4-16	
PEPI		2-2	2-5	(2-2	1-3)	-	
PERI		-	1-3	(1-2	1-1)	-	
PERUZZI		-	4-8	(2-4	2-4)	1-6	
PESCIONI		1-1	1-1	(-	1-1)	-	
PETRUCCI		1-1	3-7	(3-4	1-3)	1-1	
PILLI		2-4	1-1	(1-1	-)	-	
PITTI	X	6-23	8-14	(5-7	4-7)	8-22	X
POPOLESCHI		7-24	7-20	(5-8	5-12)	3-10	
PORTINARI		2-5	3-9	(3-6	1-3)	3-10	
PUCCI	X	15-42	3-7	(3-4	1-3)	8-28	X
DEL PUGLIESE		-	1-1	(1-1	-)	2-3	

QUARATESI		-	4-9	(4-6	2-3)	-	
DA RABATTA (S.C.)		1-1	-	-	-	1-2	
REDDITI (S.M.N.)		-	1-2	(1-2	-)	1-2	
REDDITI (S.C.)		-	1-1	(1-1	-)	-	
DELLA RENA		-	-	-	-	1-5	
RICASOLI		1-1	-	-	-	3-6	X
RICCARDI		-	1-1	(1-1	-)	-	
RICCI		2-7	3-5	(3-3	2-2)	2-9	X
RICCIALBANI		3-7	-	-	~	1-2	
RIDOLFI di Borgo	X	3-12	1-3	(1-3	-)	-	
RIDOLFI di Piazza	X	14-45	13-30	(8-9	9-21)	12-45	X
RINALDI		-	1-1	(	1-1)	-	
RINIERI		1-1	1-2	(1-1	1-1)	1-6	
RINUCCI		1-2	-	-	-	-	
RINUCCINI		3-11	6-21	(4-5	4-16)	-	
RISALITI		-	2-9	(2-3	1-6)	1-1	
RONDINELLI		-	2-3	(2-2	1-1)	1-3	
DEL ROSSO		-	1-1	(1-1	-)	-	
RUCELLAI	X	9-23	9-25	(7-8	5-17)	9-33	X
RUSTICHI (S.M.N.)		2-15	1-1	(1-1	-)	3-8	
RUSTICHI (S.C.)		-	1-3	(1-1	1-2)	1-4	
SACCHETTI	X	3-13	4-18	(2-5	3-13)	2-15	X
SALVETTI		3-20	3-3	(2-2	1-1)	2-14	
SALVIATI	X	5-15	7-38	(5-12	6-26)	5-28	X
SAPITI		2-3	1-1	(1-1	-)	-	
SASSETTI		1-2	1-5	(-	1-5)	5-11	X
SCALA	X	1-1	-				
SCALI		1-1	1-5	(1-3	1-2)	-	
DELLO SCARFA		2-11	1-2	(1-2	-)	-	
SCARLATTI		-	6-12	(5-7	2-5)	1-4	
SCOLARI		-	-	-	-	1-1	
SEGNI		4-12	3-5	(1-1	2-4)	3-13	
SERNIGI	X	3-8	2-12	(2-4	2-8)	4-7	X
SERRAGLI		-	3-8	(3-4	3-4)	1-5	

SERRISTORI	X	7-25	3-10	(2-5 | 1-5)	4-12	X
SERZELLI		2-4	-	-	-	-
SIGNORINI		-	2-4	(2-2	1-2)	-
SINIBALDI		-	1-2	(1-2	-)	-
SODERINI	X	2-8	5-11	(3-5	2-6)	-
SOLDANI		1-1	-	-	-	1-4
DA SOMMAIA		1-1	1-6	(1-1	1-5)	2-4
SOSTEGNI		2-7	-	-	-	-
SPINELLI	X	3-13	3-14	(2-6 | 3-8)	1-7	X
SPINI	X	4-13	2-6	(2-3 | 1-3)	4-13	X
DELLO STECCUTO		-	1-4	(1-1	1-3)	-
DI STEFANO		-	1-2	(1-2	-)	-
STRADI		-	1-1	(1-1	-)	-
STRINATI		-	-	-	-	1-2
STROZZI		1-2	8-21	(6-11 | 6-10)	5-21	X
DELLA STUFA	X	8-20	6-25	(6-9 | 4-16)	8-33	X
TADDEI	X	5-22	3-8	(1-1 | 3-7)	4-18	X
TANAGLI		-	3-7	(3-4	1-3)	-
TEDALDI		3-6	3-15	(2-5 | 2-10)	1-9	X
TEMPERANI		3-6	2-15	(2-6	2-9)	2-11
TORNABUONI	X	11-25	-	-	-	6-28	X
TORNAQUINCI		1-1	3-5	(3-5	-)	-
DELLA TOSA		2-2	3-7	(2-5	1-2)	-
TOSINGHI		1-4	2-17	(1-3 | 2-14)	2-2	X
UBERTINI		4-10	1-1	(1-1	-)	-
UGHI		-	1-1	(1-1	-)	1-5
UGOLINI		2-7	2-13	(1-2	2-11)	5-23
UGUCCIONI		1-1	3-4	(3-3	1-1)	2-4
VALORI	X	2-7	2-7	(1-2 | 1-5)	1-1	X
VECHIETTI		-	1-2	(1-1	1-1)	-
VELLUTI		-	1-1	(1-1	-)	-
VENTURA	X	3-17	4-15	(3-6 | 3-9)	4-22	X
DA VERRAZZANO		3-7	6-8	(5-6	2-2)	3-20
VERNACCI		-	1-1	(1-1	-)	-
VESPUCCI	X	2-5	2-5	(2-4 | 1-1)	3-14	X

VETTORI	X	4-9	5-13	(5-8	1-5)	2-7	X
DEL VIGNA		3-4	2-3	(2-3	-)	1-3	
VILLANI		-	2-2	(2-2	-)	1-2	
DAL VIVAIO		-	2-3	(1-1	1-2)	-	
VIVIANI		-	2-5	(2-2	1-3)	1-1	
ZATI	X	4-18	4-29	(4-13	3-16)	6-17	X

NOTES TO APPENDIX 3

²   For the members of the *Settanta* in 1480, Rubinstein, *The Government of Florence*, Appendix IX, X pp. 309–310, 316–317. For those who entered the *Settanta* after 1480, *v* above, n. 222 and below Appendix 4.

²   Tratte 336, 337, cc. 3–18v.

³   Tratte 338, cc. 22v–74.

⁴   Tratte 84, c. 66.

⁵   The first figure is the number of members of the family who occupied a position in the Council, the second, the number of positions occupied by the family.

APPENDIX 4

<u>Citizens co-opted to the Consiglio dei Settanta 1480-1494</u>[1]

Acciaiuoli, Nofri di Zanobi
Alamanni, Messer Piero di Francesco
Alessandri, Maso di Niccolò
Albizzi, Luca di Maso
Dall'Antella, Filippo di Giovanni
Biliotti, Agostino di Sandro
Bonsi, Messer Domenico di Baldassare
Buondelmonte, Giovanni di Gherardo
Della Caccia, Nofri di Zanobi
Della Caccia, Galeotto di Salvadore
Canigiani, Messer Antonio di Giovanni
Capponi, Giovanni di Niccolò
Capponi, Piero di Gino
Corbinelli, Antonio di Bernardo
Corbinelli, Girolamo di Bernardo
Corbinelli, Ruggiero di Niccolò
Corsini, Piero di Bertoldo
Cortigiani, Francesco di Gentile
Davanzati, Lorenzo di Piero
Federigli, Niccolò di Messer Carlo
Da Filicaia, Alessandro di Antonio
Gherardi, Francesco di Orlando
Giugni, Andrea di Niccolò
Guicciardini, Piero di Jacopo
Guiducci, Tommaso di Simone
Lenzi, Lorenzo di Nofri
Lorini, Antonio di Giovanni
Lorini, Filippo di Giovanni
Machiavelli, Paolo di Giovanni
Malegonnelle, Messer Antonio di Piero
Martelli, Niccolò di Ugolino
Masi, Cosimo di Antonio
Medici, Piero di Lorenzo
Medici, Attilio di Niccolò
Minerbetti, Tommaso di Andrea
Morelli, Lorenzo di Matteo
Nasi, Francesco di Lutozzo
Nasi, Lorenzo di Lutozzo
Nerli, Tanai di Francesco
Niccolini, Messer Agnolo di Messer Otto
Orlandini, Bartolomeo di Giovanni
Paganelli, Antonio di Bernardo
Pandolfini, Domenico di Messer Carlo
Pucci, Dionigi di Puccio
Pucci, Messer Puccio di Antonio
Ridolfi (di Piazza), Niccolò di Luigi
Ridolfi (di Piazza), Ridolfo di Pagnozzo
Ridolfi (di Borgo), Bernardo di Inghilese
Rucellai, Bernardo di Giovanni
Rucellai, Bernardo di Piero
Salviati, Giuliano di Francesco
Scala, Messer Bartolomeo di Giovanni
Soderini, Paolantonio di Messer Tommaso
Spini, Antonio di Giovanni
Della Stufa, Gismondo di Messer Agnolo
Taddei, Francesco di Antonio
Tornabuoni, Giovanni di Francesco
Tornabuoni, Giovanfrancesco di Filippo
Ventura, Jacopo di Francesco
Vespucci, Messer Guidantonio di Giovanni
Vettori, Piero di Francesco
Zati, Simone di Amerigo

1. Tratte 20, c.5; 337; (no pagination) Tratte Appendice, 2, cc. 19, 32, 83, 87v,
   117v, 126, 133, 136v, 145v, 173, 185, 198, 218v; 4, c.36v.

APPENDIX 5

Projected Leadership Elite

Membership of leadership élite, 1499-1509

Alberti, Piero di Daniello di Piero
Albizzi, Luca di Maso di Luca
Altoviti, Messer Niccolò di Simone di Giovanni
Dall'Antella, Filippo di Giovanni di Taddei
Bartolini, Giovanbattista di Niccolò di Bartolomeo
Bonsi, Messer Domenico di Baldassare di Bernardo
Canigiani, Antonio di Simone di Antonio
Capponi, Tommaso di Gino di Neri
Capponi, Cappone di Bartolomeo di Piero
Carducci, Filippo di Andrea di Niccolò
Carnesecchi, Piero di Simone di Paolo
Carnesecchi, Pierantonio di Francesco di Berto
Corsi, Giovanni di Jacopo di Simone
Corsini, Amerigo di Bartolomeo di Bertoldo
Corsini, Gherardo di Bertoldo di Gherardo
Davanzati, Francesco di Lorenzo di Piero
Dietisalvi Neroni, Lorenzo di Dietisalvi di Nerone
Da Filicaia, Alessandro di Antonio di Luca
Gaddi, Taddeo di Agnolo di Zanobi
Da Ghiacceto, Bernardo di Carlo di Zanobi
Giacomini, Antonio di Jacopo di Tommaso
Ginori, Tommaso di Zanobi di Tommaso
Giugni, Bartolomeo di Domenico di Giovanni
Gualterotti, Messer Francesco di Lorenzo di Bartolomeo
Guasconi, Niccolò di Messer Zanobi di Jacopo
Guasconi, Giovacchino di Biagio di Jacopo
Guicciardini, Piero di Jacopo di Piero
Lanfredini, Lanfredino di Jacopo di Orsino
Lenzi, Lorenzo di Nofri di Lorenzo
Lenzi, Piero di Nofri di Lorenzo
Machiavelli, Niccolò di Alessandro di Filippo
Malegonnelle, Messer Antonio di Piero di Niccolò
Manelli, Guido di Francesco di Guido
Martelli, Gismondo di Francesco di Niccolò
Mazzinghi, Giuliano di Jacopo di Ugolino
Medici, Lorenzo di Pierfrancesco di Lorenzo
Morelli, Lorenzo di Matteo di Morello
Nasi, Bernardo di Lutozzo di Jacopo
Nerli, Benedetto di Tanai di Francesco
Del Nero, Piero di Francesco di Nero
Nobili, Uberto di Francesco di Uberto
Pazzi, Guglielmo di Antonio di Messer Andrea
Pepi, Messer Francesco di Chirico di Giovanni
Pitti, Giovanni di Buonaccorso di Messer Luca
Popoleschi, Piero di Niccolò di Bartolomeo
Pucci, Francesco di Giovanni di Antonio
Ridolfi, Giovanbattista di Luigi di Messer Lorenzo
Rucellai, Bernardo di Giovanni di Paolo
Salviati, Giuliano di Francesco di Alamanno
Salviati, Alamanno di Averardo di Alamanno
Salviati, Jacopo di Giovanni di Alamanno
Sernigi, Chimente di Cipriano di Chimente
Soderini, Piero di Messer Tommaso di Lorenzo
Soderini, Messer Giovanvettorio di Messer Tommaso di Lorenzo
Della Stufa, Luigi di Messer Agnolo di Lorenzo
Strozzi, Messer Antonio di Vanni di Francesco
Tedaldi, Jacopo di Piero di Maffeo
Tosinghi, Pierfrancesco di Francesco di Rinieri
Valori, Niccolò di Bartolomeo di Filippo
Vespucci, Messer Guidantonio di Giovanni di Simone
Zati, Niccolò di Simone di Amerigo

<u>Citizens prominent in early years</u>

```
Capponi, Piero di Gino di Neri
Corsini, Piero di Bertoldo di Gherardo
Ginori, Gino di Giuliano di Francesco
Martelli, Braccio di Messer Domenico di Niccolò
Nerli, Tanai di Francesco di Filippo
Del Nero, Bernardo di Nero di Filippo
Niccolini, Messer Agnolo di Messer Otto di Lapo
Pandolfini, Pierfilippo di Messer Gianozzo
Serristori, Battista di Giovanni di Antonio
Soderini, Paolantonio di Messer Tommaso di Lorenzo
Valori, Francesco di Filippo di Bartolomeo
```

<u>Citizens moving into prominence towards the end of the regime</u>

```
Acciaiuoli, Alessandro di Donato di Neri
Federighi, Giovanni di Messer Carlo di Francesco
Giangfigliazzi, Gherardo di Messer Buongianni di Buongianni
Ginori, Bartolomeo di Lionardo di Francesco
Nasi, Alessandro di Francesco di Lutozzo
Niccolini, Messer Matteo di Messer Agnolo di Messer Otto
Pandolfini, Francesco di Pierfilippo di Messer Gianozzo
Serristori, Antonio di Averardo di Antonio
Vettori, Francesco di Piero di Francesco
```

<u>Citizens on fringe of élite group</u>

```
Acciaiuoli, Giovanni di Piero di Neri
Albizzi, Francesco di Luca di Maso
Antinori, Tommaso di Bernardo di Tommaso
Antinori, Niccolò di Tommaso di Bernardo
Bartoli, Domenico di Giovanni di Domenico
Del Bene, Tommaso di Antonio di Messer Riccardo
Del Benino, Pietro di Lionardo di Pietro
Berardi, Giovanni di Currado di Berardo
Berlinghieri, Giovanni di Berlinghieri di Francesco
Buondelmonte, Filippo di Lorenzo di Messer Andrea
Della Caccia, Matteo di Nofri di Giovanni
Carducci, Niccolò di Jacopo di Giovanni
Carducci, Messer Baldassare di Baldassare di Niccolò
Ciacchi, Jacopo di Scolaio di Tommaso
Corbinelli, Giovanbattista di Antonio di Bartolomeo
Corsi, Simone di Jacopo di Simone
Corsini, Messer Luca di Bertoldo di Gherardo
Da Filicaia, Antonio di Nicolaio di Antonio
Da Filicaia, Berto di Francesco di Berto
Gherardi, Francesco di Orlando di Bartolomeo
Da Ghiacceto, Paolo di Zanobi di Paolo
Giraldi, Giraldo di Francesco di Antonio
Girolami, Francesco di Zanobi di Bernardo
Giugni, Andrea di Niccolò di Andrea
Gondi, Bernardo di Carlo di Salvestro
Guiducci, Francesco di Simone di Francesco
Machiavelli, Piero di Messer Francesco di Lorenzo
Mazzinghi, Domenico di Bernardo di Domenico
Medici, Vieri di Cambio di Messer Vieri
Del Nero, Niccolò di Simone di Bernardo
Orlandini, Giuliano di Piero di Simone
Pandolfini, Jacopo di Messer Gianozzo
Pucci, Tommaso di Puccio di Antonio
Ridolfi, Ridolfo di Pagnozzo di Bartolomeo
Spini, Scolaio di Agnolo di Scolaio
Tedaldi, Bartolo di Lionardo di Papa
Tedaldi, Lattantonio di Francesco di Papa
Uguccioni, Messer Simone di Bernardo di Simone
Ventura, Jacopo di Francesco di Jacopo
Vettori, Bernardo di Francesco di Paolo
```

THE DOUBLE MARTYRDOM
OF THOMAS BECKET:
HAGIOGRAPHY OR HISTORY

Jennifer L. O'Reilly
University College, Cork, Ireland

THE DOUBLE MARTYRDOM
OF THOMAS BECKET:
HAGIOGRAPHY OR HISTORY

Introduction

Twelfth-century theologians debated whether Thomas Becket's cause sufficed to make him a martyr, and modern historians have acknowledged that it was not his personality but the circumstances of his death in December 1170 and the rapid popular acclaim of the posthumous miracles which secured formal canonization in February 1173.[1] Political as much as religious considerations have been cited to explain the cult of a saint who in life had been "vain, overbearing . . . not a likeable type of feudal prelate."[2] Reappraisals occasioned by the eighth centenary of the murder in the cathedral rescued Becket both from earlier excessive denigrations of his character and from the vogue for psychoanalyzing him as an actor playing a part or series of roles,[3] but the accusation contained in the royal proclamation suppressing his cult in 1538 was not challenged: "there appereth nothynge in his lyfe and exteriour conversation whereby he shuld be callyd a sainct."[4]

Even Becket's contemporary biographers, it has recently been argued, "were encouraged to concentrate on the historical, non-hagiographical elements because Becket's only claim to sanctity was his martyrdom."[5] Although Dom David Knowles, one of Becket's most sympathetic modern commentators, felt that the earliest biographers were "in every way, and above all in their analysis of character, committed to the ultimate sanctity of their subject," he conceded that on their evidence "Thomas Becket does not display fully the characteristics of a saint;" because the biographers were writing when the canonization was already assured or formalised, they had no need to overplay their hand and "the purely laudatory or pious paragraphs can be separated fairly easily from the rest."[6]

The earliest biographers were writing c.1171–77 and faced the difficult task of producing the *Vita et Passio Sancti Thomae* in the first spectacular wave of the cult following the martyrdom and miracles, yet within

185

immediate memory of Archbishop Becket's often provocative and still controversial behaviour. No contemporary account of the archbishop of Canterbury, 1162–70, could confine itself to the conventional model of commemorative biography, remarking on the subject's exemplary piety, spirituality and service to his monastic house or see, even if these had been striking attributes; some reference to events and issues of national and indeed international importance was unavoidable. Furthermore, the continuance in office of some of Becket's ecclesiastical opponents and the continuing reign of Henry II would counsel a certain caution in reporting the conflicts within the Church and between *regnum* and *sacerdotium* which characterized Becket's archiepiscopate.

Yet, in the tradition of saints' *Lives*, the celebration of a saint involved demonstrating his sanctity. Death alone does not constitute martyrdom, however heroically borne or sacrilegious the circumstances, as Lanfranc was aware when he questioned the claim to sanctity of Elphege, an earlier murdered archbishop of Canterbury.[7] Such apparently contradictory demands on Thomas Becket's biographers raise a number of basic questions to be considered here: Did they concentrate on vindicating the just cause for which St. Thomas allegedly died, (as Anselm had done when successfully resolving Lanfranc's doubts about the sanctity of St. Elphege), rather than attempt to create an image of personal holiness for their problematic subject? Or did they simply depend on the evidence of St. Thomas's abundant miracles, a proof of sanctity eloquently convincing to contemporaries? Either way might have enabled the biographers to confine their use of hagiographical conventions to garnishing at predictable moments (such as the archbishop's birth, consecration and death) an otherwise admirably historical account. Does a close study of the biographies confirm this assumption of a clear-cut distinction between hagiography and history?

Recent research has not been centrally concerned with what image of Thomas Becket his earliest biographers tried to project or with their techniques but has concentrated on the antecedents, the political and ecclesiastical context and the technical legal issues of the Becket Controversy and on the phenomenon of the martyr's cult. However, specialist work on twelfth-century letter collections, canon law, and the theology of the schools which has, in the last two decades or so, greatly illumined the intellectual milieu in which the Becket Controversy occurred in the 1160s, also casts new light on the way it was reported in the 1170s. It has made possible a re-examination of the long-published biographical materials. It has prompted the reformulation of questions concerning how the writers understood and executed their task, their relationship to the conventional modes and objectives of sacred biography and to the vigorous contemporary revival in historical and epistolary writing and the growth of written records.

The best of the independent narratives do not fit neatly into any existing literary genre, though the problem facing St. Thomas's biographers, and some of their solutions, were not without precedent. St. Wilfrid of Hexham, for example, had also been a provocative personality at odds with episcopal colleagues and the king, who appealed his case to Rome amid royal protests. Though without the advantage of a violent death to commemorate and embellish, Wilfrid's biographer Eddius Stephanus was aided by the hagiographer's repertoire of scriptural parallelism, the prophetic nature of the prelate's birth, his miracles and posthumous signs of his sanctity, in order to praise a saint whom to know was a sure road to virtue.[8] He clearly accommodated some events to this interpretation, particularly when defending the saint from his critics. But he also used eyewitness accounts, quoted documentary evidence and set his subject in a wider historical context, partly as a means of proving the veracity of his testimony. St. Anselm offered a more recent example of an archbishop at variance with crown and bishops, whose biography involved a detailed commentary on contemporary church-state relations, informed by oral and archival evidence. Sacred biography's traditional concern with exalting the monastic house associated with the saint (and his biographer) had long stimulated interest in local and occasionally national history: "Thus hagiography resulted in historical research and the historical interpretation of evidence."[9] It was difficult to identify Anselm with his monastic house; like Thomas Becket he incurred censure from the Christ Church community for his prolonged exile from Canterbury. Criticism did not abate with his death and necessitated the later supplementation of his biography with stories which modern readers would classify as hagiographical. Like Bede, however, Eadmer authenticated his sources for miracle stories; he did not present them as a different kind of truth from other events he reported.[10] Furthermore, he urged the interdependence of his intimate account of Anselm's spirituality and private conversation contained in the *Vita Sancti Anselmi*, and his record of the public relations between the archbishop of Canterbury and kings of England in the *Historia Novorum in Anglia*, both being necessary for a full understanding of St. Anselm.[11]

The best of the early Latin accounts of St. Thomas of Canterbury[12] are vividly narrated, substantially eyewitness reports of national events immediately within the public memory. "The exceptional quality of the biographies . . . in contrast with other contemporary hagiographical literature, stems in part from their subject, but mainly from their direct reliance on the surviving records of the dispute"; in particular, the use of the archives of Gilbert Foliot and of Becket by William of Canterbury and William FitzStephen respectively "made possible an approach to true historical writing."[13] Dr. Anne Duggan has shown how the huge collection of nearly six hundred relevant letters made by Alan of Tewkesbury, c.1174–76, and used by all the other biographers to varying degrees, was probably drawn from archetypal collections of Becket's two-way correspondence compiled before the canonization, or even before the murder, as "an authentic record of the controversy and not a monument to the literary skill of the martyr."[14]

The *Lives* include vehement criticism of the archbishop voiced by fellow churchmen. Yet, like the biographers of St. Wilfrid and St. Anselm, St. Thomas's biographers were not impartial reporters. Benedict of Peterborough, William of Canterbury and Alan of Tewkesbury were all members of the Christ Church community in the 1170s and hence concerned with promoting the cult of St. Thomas by producing accounts of the martyr's life and passion and collections of his miracles for pilgrims.[15] "Anonymous IV" had a paraliturgical function of providing a memorial of the saint to be read during his feast. William FitzStephen had known Becket from the days of his chancellorship, stood by him at his trial and witnessed his death. Herbert of Bosham and John of Salisbury were members of the group of learned clerical companions who variously attended the archbishop at his trial, exile and the events leading up to his death and not only shared, but prompted his ideology on relations with secular authority.[16] Herbert of Bosham dedicated his reminiscences to a later archbishop of Canterbury in the specific hope that Baldwin and his successors would be inspired to emulate St. Thomas in defending the Church (3:155–6). Two important writers, though outside these groups, had formative personal experience of their subject: "Roger of Pontigny" probably served him in exile and Edward Grim witnessed his death. While some are deservedly famed as examples of the contemporary renaissance in historical writing, the accounts of Thomas Becket's death do form a partisan interpretation to which some circumstantial details were accommodated, by the humanist scholar John of Salisbury and the sometime royal official William FitzStephen as readily as by the monastic custodians of the Canterbury shrine.

The present work suggests that the extent of the biographers' use of "hagiographical" techniques has been obscured in the general modern approval of their historicity. Purple passages might, of course, be anticipated in descriptions of the martyr's death; in considering whether the biographers' accounts of the archbishop's private and public life represent a different kind of writing and intention from their presentation of the *passio*, Part I examines the degree to which literary devices conventional in the genre of sacred biography were employed to demonstrate the sanctity of Becket in life as in death. It questions whether such conventions can be uniformly regarded as pious flourishes detachable from an essentially historicaly narrative. The writers' spiritual interpretation of events sometimes accurately reflects a polemical interpretation of current affairs and of history actually made in the 1160s by the archbishop and his circle, but viewed as historically authenticated prophecy by his champions in the light of his martyrdom. The context of the biographers' liturgical allusions in particular often suggests they are not simply hagiographic asides or dating devices but reflect a historical situation in which both king and archbishop were able to use the symbolism and ceremony of liturgy to powerful propagandist effect. The importance of the epistolary evidence of the Controversy and of modern research in other contemporary uses of rhetoric, in canon law and the schools, for understanding the relationship between hagiography and history and their supposedly distinctive concerns and language, is further illustrated through a detailed example in Part II. A reconsideration of the biographers' familiar accounts of an extraordinary liturgical event on the crucial last day of Becket's trial at the Council of Northampton on 1164 may suggest new insights, not only into the biographers' attitudes and techniques, but into the conduct of events precipitating Becket's flight and the formulation of his defense during the exile.

PART I

Red Martyrdom

It has been observed that Thomas Becket "worked no miracles when alive and, apart from a reputed vision experienced by his mother before his birth, the biographers had a hard time finding parallels from other saints' lives for events in Becket's."[17] This need not necessarily demonstrate the historical, "non-hagiographical" character of their narratives. In the elastic genre of saints' *Lives* there were important precedents for the omission of miracle stories and their role is restrained in the *Lives* of Anselm, Ailred and Hugh of Lincoln.[18] While it is true that few parallels are made with other named saints, the Becket biographers do use other means of modelling their subject on an acknowledged norm of sanctity, most obviously but not solely in their accounts of his death.

St. Thomas is shown to have been extraordinary from the beginning, even before his suffering distanced him so markedly from others. Although some of his champions tried to claim that his life alone offered a model for imitation, it was his death and miracles which revealed his exceptional nature and argued that he must, therefore, have been set apart throughout life. The hagiographer's premise finds conventional expression in the birth and infancy stories and in the comparison of Thomas's parents with Elizabeth and Zachariah, the parents of John the Baptist (2:356). Jeremiah 1:5 had been quoted by St. Wilfrid's biographer in relating his birth and William FitzStephen alluded to it too: "And the Lord knew and predestined the blessed Thomas before ever he issued from the womb" (3:13). Similarly, Eddius Stephanus had cited the usual text from Romans 8:30 in his opening chapter to show that God foreknew, predestined, called, justified and glorified his confessor Wilfrid, as was signified by the extraordinary circumstances of his birth. Both saints' births were heralded by a remarkable theophany in the form of a house-fire, in both cases likened to a light being set up on a candlestick, a prophetic allusion to the text from Luke 11:33 used in the ceremony of translating saints' relics and setting them up so that they could be properly venerated (2:358).

However, the biographers' methods of demonstrating Thomas's predestination to sainthood become more complex when they deal with his adult life. Intimation of approaching death, a standard feature of saints' *Lives*, punctuate their narratives, but the hagiographic stock device of dreams and visions is used very sparingly, even by Herbert of Bosham. Instead, with the insight of the archbishop's intimate companion in exile and the hindsight of a partisan writing from exile perhaps fifteen years after the canonization, he pondered the past to disclose, as Eadmer did, the prophetic nature of apparently coincidental details and to report insights vouchsafed to the discerning at the time. Thomas's ill-fated reconciliation with the king at Fréteval, for example, took place "as we learnt long afterwards" in a meadow locally known as the Traitor's Field (3:466). In 1169 Henry II had come as a pilgrim to the shrine at Mont Martre, traditional site of St. Denis's martyrdom, where he sought terms with Thomas Becket. One of the archbishop's household there and then noticed the ominous portent of Thomas waiting in the Chapel of the Martyrdom when he received news of the king's refusal of the requested kiss of peace. The prophecy was fulfilled a year later in Thomas's dying invocation of the martyred bishop St. Denis and in the manner of his death (3:445-9, 499).

The readiness to see signs and symbols was not the prerogative of the hagiographer, but reflects the practice in *lectio divina* of ruminating on the literal word of scripture to discern spiritual meaning. Contemporary events were seen as a continuation of this process of revelation. Nor was the practice confined to the scholarly exegete, but familiar to all who made constant liturgical use of scripture. As Thomas's envoys quipped to the French king Louis (when he cited an improving text from Ephesians which Henry II should have recalled and applied in his dealings with his archbishop):

"My lord, perchance he would have remembered it, if he had heard it as often as we do in the canonical hours" (3:333). This helps explain why Herbert of Bosham, recalling his master's return to Canterbury in early December, 1170, to the popular acclamation "Blessed is he that cometh in the name of the Lord," could confidently address his reader: "And you would certainly have said, had you seen it, that the Lord was a second time approaching his Passion" (3:478).

Thomas Becket entered Canterbury during the first week in Advent, the liturgical season celebrating the coming of Christ not only at his Incarnation, but at his Passion and the end of time. The Gospel for Advent Sunday was the same as for Palm Sunday, Matt. 21.1–9, recounting Christ's Entry into Jerusalem and ending with the acclamation "Blessed is he that cometh in the name of the Lord." The Gospel is echoed in the antiphon and anthems accompanying the Palm Sunday procession about the church and its precincts which is evoked in Herbert's description of St. Thomas's triumphal procession into his cathedral. In all probability, Herbert is here describing an *Adventus*, namely the liturgical ceremony for the reception of a king or bishop to his city or church, which directly used the Messianic and eschatological associations of Christ's Entry into Jerusalem and actually incorporated the acclamation "Blessed is he that cometh in the name of the Lord." The coincidence of the opening of the Advent season with the archbishop's *Adventus* into Canterbury would have made such a ceremony particularly evocative. His return to Canterbury was later kept as a liturgical feast (the *Regressio*) and the emotive parallel with Christ's entry into Jerusalem was preserved among the popular vernacular texts of the *Early South English Legendary*.[19] Of course, St. Thomas's martyrdom at the end of the Advent season powerfully completed Herbert of Bosham's allusion to Palm Sunday and the Passion narrative, but his report cannot be dismissed as merely a pious gospel parallel retrospectively introduced long after the martyrdom and canonization.

William FitzStephen had early described Becket's homecoming journey through his diocese to tumultuous popular acclaim, his ceremonial reception by the bishop and clergy of Rochester and especially by the canons of Southwark who met him in procession at the door of the church (as in the *Adventus* ceremony), singing the anthem "Blessed be the Lord God of Israel." Royal messengers insisted Becket end his triumphal progress and confine himself to Canterbury, and various prophetic signs warned him of the evil awaiting him (3:121–3). This is substantiated in a letter written in early December 1170 by an eyewitness, John of Salisbury. His description of the archbishop's return is heavy with the menace of the royal officials who might there and then have used force "but they were afraid of a riot and were restrained by the great crowds which were as excited in receiving back their bishop as if Christ himself had come down from heaven among men" (Ep. 304, p. 721). Becket's return to Canterbury in Advent, 1170, greatly stirred friend and foe and caused the day to be enshrined among the other "memorable Tuesdays" of his life, ranging from the day of his birth to the last day of his trial and flight into exile and the day of his martyrdom.[20] Thus the calendar itself attested to the predestined nature of the saint's career.

St. Thomas's death recalls not earlier medieval saints, but the primitive age of persecution. In the *acta martyrum* prophecies and dreams point to the inevitability of the sufferings to be endured by Christ's champions, as apparitions and miracles posthumously confirm their virtue. Similarly, Thomas prophesied that he would suffer martyrdom and be slain in a church, which one biographer actually likens to Polycarp's prediction of his immolation (3:406), and was martyred on the very spot "where long ago in a dream he had seen himself crucified" (1:132). William of Canterbury and Benedict of Peterborough made bulky collections of Thomas's posthumous appearances and miracles, which the other biographers cite in varying detail.[21]

A second point of similarity with the *acta martyrum* is that, as the early martyrs (mindful of Eleazer and the seven sons in 2 Maccabees 6:7) refused counsel and means of escape, sometimes provoking their tormentors for fear of delaying or losing martyrdom, so St. Thomas's biographers insist that "had he wished, the archbishop might easily have turned aside and saved himself by flight" (3:140), but that he could not be persuaded by entreaty or argument. He dreaded that the opportunity for martyrdom "might be deferred or lost if he took refuge in the church" (2:434), refused to take the elementary precaution of bolting the transept door and, in the opinion of John of Salisbury, who was present, imprudently and needlessly provoked his pursuers (2:9). In the *acta martyrum* the essentially voluntary nature of martyrdom is often conveyed by the joy with which the martyrs eagerly sought their grace-given reward, rejoicing "as though invited to a bridal banquet instead of being a victim of the beasts."[22] The eschatological image was also suggested by St. Thomas's longing for martyrdom as he prepared to meet his murderers: "It seemed to us who were present, he sat there waiting as unperturbed . . . as if they had come to invite him to a wedding," recalled Edward Grim (2:433). Like the early martyred bishop Felix, he is described as deliberately extending his neck to the sword and dying in an attitude of prayer.[23]

Thirdly, the language in which even eyewitnesses recount Becket's death in the cathedral further invites comparison with the heroes of the arena: he appears as God's athlete, his ordeal as a contest, his murderers as gladiators, torturers, even lictors. All the biographers, including Herbert of Bosham who generally portrays a vigorous, combative saint, admire Thomas's personal bravery specifically for its exemplification of the virtues of patience and fortitude which had distinguished the early martyrs in their dying agonies, borne without flinching or complaint, as the *acta* repeatedly testify. And so with St. Thomas. "In all his sufferings the illustrious martyr displayed an incredible steadfastness. Neither with hand nor robe, in the manner of human frailty, did he oppose the fatal stroke. Nor when smitten did he utter a single word, neither cry nor groan" (2:438). John of Salisbury exclaimed, "With all reverence for the martyrs I venture to say that in my judgment none surpassed him in constancy" (2:319). Several writers comment to the effect that the pains he endured were even sharper than those of earlier martyrs, for they at least were slain by non-believers, but the archbishop was slaughtered by his spiritual sons; the sacrilege was greater than all the persecutions of Nero and Diocletian (3:143,509; 2:438).

Having established St. Thomas's glorious credentials in the manner of meeting his death, the biographers cite St. Augustine's dictum that "it is the cause that makes for martyrdom, not the sufferings" and emphasise that to die for the statutes of the Church is even finer than to die for the faith (2:440; 4:135). They quote the archbishop's dying intention that in his blood the Church might have liberty and peace and observe that his offering on behalf of the universal Church distinguished him from earlier martyrs (2:436,438,14). Thus, in the steadfastness of his endurance, the bitterness of his pain and above all, in the justice of his cause, the biographers show that Thomas's claims to sanctity did not merely parallel but surpassed those of earlier saints.

This helps explain the absence of a particular saintly model even in the narratives of Becket's death. It was not for want of an appropriate prototype of clerical martyrdom. Although all the early biographers quote Archbishop Becket's dying invocation of St. Denis, none elaborates this apparently promising parallel with the martyred bishop of Paris, Herbert of Bosham alone noting later, and obscurely, the similarity of the two saints' headwounds.[24] St. Stephen's death had provided a classic model for early accounts of martyrdom and informed the general iconographic type of saints kneeling in prayer before their executioners, as St. Thomas does in many medieval representations. In 1164 Becket had said the mass of St. Stephen in memorable circumstances during his own trial at the Council of Northampton (3:56) and the liturgy for the protomartyr, celebrated by Becket in Canterbury cathedral in 1170 only three days before his own martyrdom there, must have taken on a new significance for his household, including future biographers, which the subsequent celebration of St.

Thomas's feast on 29 December, the anniversary of his death, not of his Translation, can only have perpetuated. In 1186 Baldwin, Archbishop of Canterbury, was to propose founding a collegiate church in Canterbury dedicated to St. Thomas and St. Stephen, and their proximity in the liturgical calendar was reflected in several works of art which pictured the two saints together.[25]

    While the omission of any reference to St. Stephen in the narratives of Becket's death may be partly explained by the biographers' prudent reluctance to cast Henry II in the role of stone-thrower, it does not necessarily point to their 'historical' rather than 'hagiographical' character. Other portents in the cluster of liturgical feasts preceeding St. Thomas's are duly noted. In dating Becket's murder, Edward Grim observes that on the morrow of the Feast of the Holy Innocents, the murderers came out against the innocent (2:430). Becket was born on the feast of St. Thomas, 21 December. William FitzStephen adds that by his death, Thomas of Canterbury lit up the West as his apostolic namesake, Thomas of India, lit up the East, their December feastdays balanced either side of the feast of the Incarnation (3:154). The absence of the more immediately obvious parallel of St. Stephen receives a gloss in Benedict of Peterborough's account of a vision in which the glorified Becket is revealed among the Apostles themselves, of greater dignity than Stephen and other saints from the age of persecution (2:31–2).

    An anonymous *passio* says that Thomas Becket prayed for his murderers (4:198). Abbott suggested this unsubstantiated story was an attempt to show that Christ's most recent martyr had very properly echoed the dying words of the protomartyr.[26] But St. Stephen's prayer in Acts 7.60 itself imitates Christ's prayer of forgiveness from the Cross. Similarly, Thomas's dying prayer in William FitzStephen's account, "Into thy hands O Lord, I commend my spirit" directly evokes Christ's last words in Luke 23.46 (recalling PS.30.6), also repeated by Stephen and often accredited to dying saints (including those who, like Ailred, did not suffer a violent death). By dispensing with the hagiographical device of modelling their subject on named saints, the biographers strengthened the effect of another hallowed convention which derived from the notion succinctly expressed in Romans 8.29: "Whom he did foreknow, he also did predestinate to be conformed to the image of his Son." The circumstances of Thomas's death enabled his biographers to recall and surpass the earliest heroic age of persecution which had regarded violent martyrdom as the most complete expression of the imitation of Christ. All the biographers, including the earliest, the most scholarly and those who had been eye-witnesses of the murder, make remarkably sustained use of the device of Gospel parallelism for this purpose. It need only be briefly illustrated.

The archbishop's entry into the cathedral preceded by his cross-bearer is likened to Christ's approach to Calvary (3:491): Gethsemane is recalled in Becket's reproach to the knights, "And came you to me in arms?" He imitated his Saviour in forbidding them to harm his followers, some of whom fled, even as the disciples deserted Christ. The four knights were joined in the murder by Hugh 'Mauclerc,' "that a fifth blow might not be wanting to the martyr who in other things had imitated Christ" (2:438); Becket's head was pierced as Christ's side was by Longinus (3:506). Pillagers meanwhile ransacked the archbishop's palace "even as those who crucified Christ parted his garments among them"; the very sun was veiled in darkness at that hour (3:142-4). As an early biographer observed, "It would be hard, we believe, to find any other martyr whose passion so closely follows the Lord's" (2:18-19). It was an argument which rendered particular saintly models superfluous.

This hagiographical technique derives from a particular view of history. One of the functions of the hagiographer, shared to varying degrees by St. Thomas's biographers, was to show how God is glorious in his saints because they reveal his continuing work of salvation. Martyrs of the age of persecution were revered as worthy successors of the age of the Apostles, "for these new manifestations of virtue will bear witness to one and the same Spirit who still operates."[27] In the very different context of the post-persecution era, the confessor St. Wilfrid served as a reminder of the longer-term continuity of the divine purpose stretching from creation to the present day. Eddius Stephanus presents Wilfrid as one of the successors of the Old Testament prophets, as well as of the Apostles, all united in making known to the sons of men God's mighty acts.[28] The allusion to the psalmist is preserved by John of Salisbury in praising the miracles of St. Thomas (2:322). Other biographers conventionally compare him to Old Testament figures like Joseph, Moses, David, and Job who in medieval exegesis were regarded as "types" of Christ.

Alongside the notion of salvation gradually being revealed through the linear unfolding of time, with pre-Incarnation figures foreshadowing Christ as subsequent saints were living reminders of him, the contemporary interpretation of history was also profoundly shaped by the concept that the redeeming Cross is eternally present. This view of history underlies medieval exegesis, iconography, and the complex ordering of biblical texts which comprise the liturgy; from it stems the hagiographer's technique of identifying a saint with an Old Testament type of Christ. Like the device of Gospel parallelism, it could be used to show that not only do the saints imitate Christ, but that Christ is crucified in his saints. For example, Thomas Becket's biographers likened him to Abel, interpreted as the first of Christ's martyrs in Matt. 23.34–5, but also an utterly familiar type of Christ's own sacrifice in exegesis, cited in the Roman canon of the Mass and early represented in art at the eucharistic altar. Thomas was frequently depicted receiving his death blows either standing or kneeling at an altar, wearing a chasuble, with a chalice to denote the sacrificial as well as the sacrilegious nature of his martyrdom.[29]

This "non-historical" representation of the death scene was entirely in accordance with the biographers' interpretation. The most learned of them, John of Salisbury and Herbert of Bosham, actually relocated Thomas's martyrdom, setting it before the altar in order to stress the archbishop's Christ-like combination of the roles of priest and victim in offering up his own blood (2:318; 3:498,501). The reliquary which thirty years later depicted St. Thomas's death and Christ's crucifixion directly juxtaposed[30] was no more extreme than the observation by William FitzStephen, an eyewitness of the murder, that "as Christ once suffered in his own body, so now he was suffering in Thomas'" (3:142). The biographers' narration of the martyrdom was affected by the posthumous proof of how precious was the death of his saint in the sight of the Lord. Benedict of Peterborough, referring to the miracle-working diluted relics of the saint's blood, even noted that the blood of the lamb of Canterbury is drunk as the blood of the Lamb of Bethlehem is drunk — and of no other holy person could that be said (2:43). William of Canterbury reported an early (pre-canonization) apparition in which Thomas was celebrated in English with an antiphon including the lines "A rare thing did our Lord/That He thy water changed to wine" (1:151). Allusion to the miracle at the Marriage of Cana, the first of Christ's "signs," was part of the hagiographer's repertoire, but the most detailed Gospel parallelism of all, and the extravagant claim that Thomas's murder was even more unjust than Christ's Passion, occurs already in the earliest account of the martyrdom, a letter written by John of Salisbury in early 1171 and incorporated, unchanged, in his biography.[31]

Accounts of the death thus used hagiographical techniques which were not simply pious surface embellishments of an otherwise "historical" narrative, but reflect in a more fundamental way the biographers' understanding of the past, even when reporting an event some of them had recently witnessed. To what extent, however, is their image of the martyr's death consistent with their view of his life? It has been argued, for example, that Thomas's change of life at his consecration "merely entitles him to be regarded as a good churchman, not a saint . . . (The biographers) only tried to prove that he was personally a good man, frugal and chaste."[32] Does their account of the martyrdom then represent a radical break in either the intentions or the techniques of their work? How, in short, do they reconcile the image of one who was simply a good man of conventional piety with one who "trod the winepress alone" (3:523)?

White Martydrom

In their description of the carnage at Thomas's death is an important indication of the biographers' attitude to his life. Edward Grim wrote: "The blood, whitening from the brain, and the brain no less reddening from the blood, empurpled the face with the colours of the lily and the rose . . . the colours of the life and death of a confessor and martyr" (2:437). He is followed by Anonymous X; two early biographies, by William FitzStephen and the French poet Garnier of Pont-Ste-Maxence, as well as the early Anonymous IV and the late compilatory Icelandic *Thomas Saga*, based on twelfth-century accounts, all use variations of the image.[33] It draws on a complex and recently revivified tradition of exegesis on Canticles 5.10 and related texts, using *candet* and *rubet* both to comment on Christ's wounded body and to denote his spotless life and bloody death, and also to describe the confessors and martyrs who shared in his suffering. The particular contrast of lilies, to signify the inner tribulation and asceticism of white martyrdom, and roses to designate the red martyrdom of public persecution to death was an established convention, summarised in a sermon by Gregory the Great, who was echoing Jerome and Cyprian before him:

> There are two types of martyrdom: one in the soul and another in deed as well as soul . . . one hidden and the other public. . . . Holy Church is full of flowers of the elect, that in times of peace she has lilies and, in times of persecution, roses.[34]

St. Thomas's distiction was, Christlike, to combine both, as William Fitz-Stephen explained:

> Verily in the garlands of the Church neither lilies nor roses are lacking and in the passion of the blessed Thomas both the gleaming white of the brain and the crimson red of the blood . . . were sure and certain signs that he was a good shepherd of Christ's sheep, inasmuch as he laid down his life for them; archbishop and champion, confessor and martyr, destined to receive from the Lord a stole of two-fold colour — white in token of his faithful governance of his archiepiscopal see, and purple (crimson) in token of the happy consumation of his martyrdom.[35]

Despite the sacrilege of his murder, the personal sanctity of the archbishop had not been immediately evident to the monks of Canterbury, however. Edward Grim, an outsider, recalls one of them saying that the archbishop ought not to be regarded as a martyr having been slain as the reward of his own obstinacy (2:440). Critical in changing their response was the discovery when they stripped the body that Thomas had secretly worn not only a hairshirt, but sackcloth from thighs to knees, a spectacular proof of chastity and "a circumstance of which we have neither read nor heard of an example in the case of any other saint" (2:17). All was so vermin-ridden that "anyone might have thought that the martyrdom of that day was less grievous than that which these small enemies continually inflicted" (2:442). William FitzStephen also stresses the importance of the disclosure:

> Having seen with their own eyes his two-fold martyrdom, the voluntary one of his life and the violent one of his death, they prostrated themselves on the ground, they kissed his hands and feet, they invoked him as a saint and proclaimed him God's holy martyr (3:148).

Although the personality of Archbishop Anselm more readily suggested sanctity, earlier monks of Christ Church had entertained doubts about Anselm's claims to sainthood long after his death, so Eadmer appended miracle stories to his biography. Despite the important precedents for the omission of miracles from saints' *Lives*, by the twelfth century "the question of sanctity was one that only a generous supply of miracles could settle decisively."[36] Such proof was not wanting in the case of Thomas. All his biographers, including those who wrote before the canonization, were writing in the context of immense popular acclaim for the posthumous miracles. Certainly they form an important part of their testimony; John of Salisbury classified them rather as Christ listed his miracles in answer to John the Baptist's question, "Art thou he that should come?" (2:322). Miracles were regarded as grace-given signs of a saint's virtue. Caesarius of Haisterbach, reporting debates on Becket's sanctity occasioned by the lack of miracles in his lifetime, vindicated his reputation by citing the many and great *posthumous* proofs of his sainthood (2:291). But however crucial such proofs may have been in securing popular and canonical recognition for Becket, (indeed, because of this), the biographers insist that St. Thomas's claim to sanctity was not *based* on his miracles.

Walter Daniel, while supplementing and defending the miracle stories in his *Vita Ailredi*, felt the need to explain, "The miracles wrought by Ailred . . . were grounded in his merits"[37] and the contemporary monastic and particularly Cistercian insistence on virtue as the basis for sanctity was acknowledged by Becket's biographers. The evidence of John of Salisbury is revealing:

Many folk in diverse places strove at the devil's prompting to hide by false interpretation the virtues and good works of the most blessed Thomas, while yet he laboured for God's law and the Church's liberty. So now, since God has made manifest (i.e. through the posthumous miracles) what manner of man, how great the archbishop was, they are compelled even if unwillingly to proclaim his glory.[38]

This letter dates from as late as 1177–79. It suggests that there had been, and continued to be a real need for Becket's biographers to explain how "false interpretation" of his life had arisen and been credible and to demonstrate, in the light of the martyrdom and the continuing miraculous proof of his sanctity, the true nature of St. Thomas's virtues and good works in the cause of the Church's liberty. In 1186–87, Herbert of Bosham still needed to demote the posthumous miracles as signs for unbelievers and asserted, "I have set forth this man, not to be wondered at for his signs, but to be imitated for his works"; to Baldwin, a successor to the saint's see, he commended St. Thomas as "an example of purity whereby you should regulate your own life" (3:156). As early as 1171–72 Edward Grim had urged his readers to consider not the martyrdom or the miracles of the saint but "the life that was full of martyrdom" (2:354).

Yet clearly there were problems involved in substantiating the claim of "white martyrdom" as a vital part of the biographers' larger claims for Thomas's sanctity. Confronted with the hairshirt, the Canterbury monks had been frankly "astounded at this proof of a hidden piety greater than would have been credited the archbishop." In resolving, it also voiced misgivings about his life: "Could he ever have set his thoughts upon an earthly kingdom, who had thus preferred sackcloth to all worldly pleasures?" (2:17). His magnificence as Chancellor was well-known. Even after his alleged conversion, he remained a connoisseur and patron of the arts. He travelled to Tours in state and even in exile with a large entourage. The pope commended him to the Cistercians "in order that you, who have hitherto lived in affluence and luxury, may learn in future . . . a lesson which can only be learnt from poverty" (2:34).

The biographers dealt with the problem in a variety of ways. Their description of Becket's *conversio* on his election to Canterbury in 1162 — putting off the secular man and utterly abandoning the world — has tended to be regarded as rhetoric on their part or theatricality on Becket's. But despite rhapsodic epithets, they do not describe a total revolution in Becket's personal life; after all, even as Chancellor, he had not exceeded the bounds of chastity and honour. The real revolution lay in his attitude to the Church. On an unknown date, but probably immediately after his consecration

on 3 June 1162, he resigned the chancellorship in which office he had pro-
fited from the Canterbury vacancy since the death of Archbishop Theobald
in 1161 and had been privy to the king's alleged design against the Church
(3:180; 4:14). The biographers do not dwell on the disappointment Becket
must have caused his mentor, Archbishop Theobald, who had recommended him, while Becket was Archdeacon of Canterbury, for the chancellorship probably in late 1154. Theobald had presumably hoped thereby to
give some safeguard to the interests of the Church in the new reign, but
Becket had put off the deacon and put on the Chancellor.[39] The biographers insist, however, that on his promotion to the archiepiscopal office,
Becket "opposed the king's design by every means in his power." Henry II's
disappointment and rage against the archbishop, even before their formal
confrontation at Westminster in October, 1163, concerning the judicial
treatment of criminous clerks, could therefore be related by the biographers
to "the king's design against the clergy of England as a body," which
originated, they claimed, from "sometime before, in the episcopate of Archbishop Theobald" (3:43). This partly deflects attention from Becket's personal responsibility in alienating royal favor, so vital to the security of the
Church, through his early peremptory actions such as the attempts to
recover alienated Canterbury possessions, to excommunicate a royal
tenant-in-chief, and to contest a royal taxation measure. John of Salisbury
bitterly lamented from exile in 1165 that the archbishop had "seemed from
the start to have roused the resentment of the king and his associates by his
zeal — somewhat inadvisedly" (Ep. 150, p. 49).

Becket's reluctance to accept the archiepiscopal office because, as
Chancellor, "he had destroyed holy Church and despised her laws," was
reportedly overcome by Henry of Winchester's injunction: "You must and
shall change from Saul the persecutor to Paul."[40] The archbishop and his
supporters certainly made some attempt to promote the Pauline image but
it was rendered exceedingly difficult by the post-conversion behaviour of
Becket's "who yielded in the Church's cause at Clarendon [January 1164]
and who, when summoned legally for a financial offence [at the Council of
Northampton, October 1164], conscious of wrongdoing, lost confidence in
his pretexts, and by a secret flight both unwise and impudent, professed his
own guilt."[41]

In trying to create an image of personal sanctity for their provocative subject therefore, the biographers chiefly relied on showing that although "his outward visage was like that of ordinary man," his death had
revealed that "within, all was different" (3:37). The very paradox was part
of the martyr's appeal: "All ran to view clad in sackcloth, him whom as
Chancellor they had beheld vestured in purple and satin" (3:148). The same

writer noted that at his consecration, the archbishop took as his pattern St. Sebastian and St. Cecilia, public figures who had also concealed their asceticism "mortifying the flesh with sackcloth" while appearing "outwardly adorned with vesture of gold." Likewise, St. Thomas endeavoured to be more devout than he appeared. His dietary austerities were hidden from general view by his virtues as a host; the hairshirt adopted at his consecration was worn throughout exile "unknown even to his nearest friends" (2:346); the daily scourgings were only revealed after death by his confessor, when it became evident at last that "this saintly man had in his secret life all the tokens of sanctity and religion" (4:79; 3:147).

Another contrast noted between public image and private life, appearance and reality, was that, although a secular clerk ordained only the day before his consecration, inwardly the archbishop was a monk. To some extent this reflects the anxiety of the Christ Church monks that the archbishop of Canterbury, and therefore their abbot, should be a regular (2:368; 4:15–16). An anonymous account has Prior Odo discoursing on the qualities desirable in the archbishop, most notably that he should be a monk. He cites at length Thomas Becket's predecessors who had fulfilled this requirement (4:181–5). Alan of Tewkesbury, who became a monk of Christ Church c.1174 and its prior in 1179, explains that Thomas in exile felt unworthy to receive back his pastoral charge from the Pope unless he also received the monastic habit because "he had learnt that from the first foundation of the Church of Canterbury the archbishops had nearly all been monks, nor according to the histories of olden times had there ever been a schism in the kingdoms . . . save when the archbishop had been a secular priest" (2:345). Clearly, Thomas and his biographers tried to make good this deficiency. But the most authoritative biographers — William FitzStephen, Edward Grim, Herbert of Bosham — were themselves secular clerks. Other considerations may have prompted their insistence on Becket's quasi-monastic status.

White martyrdom, or the willingly undertaken living death to self for love of God, had been exemplified in the asceticism and isolation of the Desert Fathers in the post-persecution era when the red martyrdom of physical death for Christ no longer marked out his saints. The tradition was made available to the West through Evagrius' translation of Athanasius' *Life of St. Anthony*, Rufinus of Aquilea's translation of the rules of St. Basil, and Cassian's *Collations*. It was given authoritative expression in the works of Jerome, Augustine, Caesarius of Arles, and Gregory the Great. It was popularised through the influence on hagiography of Sulpicius Severus, who acclaimed St. Martin's willing endurance of watchings and fasting, the scorn of the envious and the persecutions of the wicked as a living bloodless martyrdom.[42] For many early saints, notably St. Columba, *peregrinatio* — wandering like a fugitive, deprived of the consolation of friends and kin — formed an important part of their practice of this bloodless martyrdom.[43] Pilgrimage, either imposed as a penance or voluntarily undertaken as an ascetic and devotional exercise, was a characteristic feature of medieval spirituality. Thomas's exemplar Archbishop Anselm had been harrassed like a common fugitive in 1097, but nothing could efface the memory of how he had dignified his journey by publicly taking the pilgrim's scrip and staff from the altar at Canterbury before setting off into exile.[44] Herbert of Bosham's prolonged description of Thomas' flight as a fugitive, his arrival, like Anselm, at St. Bertin, his continental wanderings, his dispossession, the lamented banishment of his friends, makes a virtue of necessity and evokes something of the *peregrinatio pro Christi* (3:318–22, 357–62, 373–5).

However, by the twelfth century the concept of white martyrdom had become particularly identified with the strict observance of the eremitcal and coenobitic life, which provided a penitential pilgrimage of the spirit and had undergone profound renewal in the practice of the Camaldonese and early Cistercians: obedience to monastic vows amounted to the daily crucifixion of the monk. In his spiritual counsels Anselm vigorously upheld the superiority of the pilgrimage provided by the monastic life.[45] Herbert of Bosham asserts that Thomas personally chose to retreat to the Cistercian house of Pontigny (3:357) which John of Salisbury referred to as "the land of your pilgrimage" and Garnier has the archbishop call to mind the example of Abraham leaving his country and kin (Gen.12.1), which was a classic model of peregrination in hagiography.[46] Through the good offices of John aux Bellesmains, Bishop of Poitiers (a banished member of Becket's circle who was closely connected with the Cistercians), the Pontigny community had already been praying for Thomas before the exile and remained faithful to him throughout.[47] Accounts of his retirement to a life of monastic poverty there "as befits an exile and athlete of Christ" (2:34), detail observation of the canonical hours, *lectio divina* and such austerities of fasting and flagellation as to endanger his health (3:376). After his enforced withdrawal from Pontigny, his exile at the Benedictine abbey near Sens "where the body of the glorious virgin and martry St. Colomba lies," from November, 1166, until the month before his death (half of his archiepiscopate), was marked by asceticism, compunction, and the fervent interior life of the contemplative (2:415,417). Over his hairshirt Thomas continued to wear the coarse, ill-fitting habit with which he had been vested by the abbot of Pontigny (2:345) and to administer daily the discipline which had become a common feature of contemporary monastic penitential practice, offering the flagellant a particular share in the sufferings of Christ. He died near the altar in Canterbury cathedral dedicated to St. Benedict, "under whose protection and by whose example he was crucified to the world," and this monastic asceticism is identified with his endurance of "every penalty inflicted by the executioners of the flesh" at his murder (2:436). The Canterbury monks who discovered the evidence of their abbot's white martyrdom exclaimed: "See, see, he was a monk and we knew it not" (2:442); "Behold, one who was indeed a monk and indeed a hermit, who endured torments not only in death but also in life" (4:79).

The next question which needs to be considered is whether the biographers' claims for Thomas's personal sanctity were confined to such descriptions of his private asceticism and spirituality, whose very secrecy conveniently defied refutation by his critics. How does this image accord with the treatment of his memorable public life? The biographies give a remarkably vivid account of the passionate denunciations of the archbishop by his fellow-bishops, which is corroborated by the contemporary correspondence. While this may win modern approval for the biographers as historians, it is not necessarily incompatible with their demonstration of the saint's sanctity, though at times it exercises their ingenuity and affirms that public doubts on this score had not been entirely allayed by the martyrdom. The Anonymous of Lambeth in particular felt the need to meet criticisms of St. Thomas — for his lapse at Clarendon, his flight, the uncounselled excommunication of his episcopal colleagues from Vézelay, his vainglory. All pass swiftly over the archbishop's inglorious behaviour at the Council of Clarendon. He had there been required to give formal assent to a written version of the customs concerning relations between royal and ecclesiastical authority, which allegedly represented the practice of Henry I's time, and which Becket had, with reluctance, verbally undertaken to observe, "saving his order." FitzStephen alone says that at length, in fear of his life and anxious to placate the king, Becket appended his seal, though even Herbert of Bosham admits that "with some caution he did not utterly refuse" to do so, but sought a delay and took away a copy of the Constitutions (3:288). William of Canterbury made the best of the capitulation before the king by piously observing that the failings of a saint are sent as a warning to the faithful, rather as St. Wilfrid's biographer had loyally, if unoriginally, commented that lightning strikes the peaks first (1:17). Few *acta* have survived from Thomas's archiepiscopate and it seems likely that "he was unable to exercise much jurisdiction in England during exile."[48] His somewhat shadowy pastoral image receives some reflected light from allusions to St. Martin, exemplary bishop and friend of monks.[49] Benedict of Peterborough contrasts the archbishop with the bishops who were "hirelings rather than pastors in God's church" (2:14) and their criticism is accordingly defused to some extent. Thomas's frequent consultations with his *eruditi* offset the bishops' complaints that he acted without counsel. The defection of some bishops after the Council of Westminster is interpreted as a demonstration of how God constantly tries those whom he calls to be his saints (3:275).

Thomas's vulnerability on the serious charge of deserting his flock for six of the eight years of his office by flight into exile is met partly by insistence that he had been in grave danger, and also by editorial vindications citing scriptural precedents for justified flight. It is tempting to skip such passages in order to get on to the next "historical" part of the narrative — Herbert of Bosham apologizes for his own prolixity and tediousness on these occasions — but they can often reveal clues about the biographers' techniques and historicity. Herbert defends Becket's flight by twice citing Christ's exhortation in Matt. 10.23: "And when they shall persecute you in this city flee into another" (3:319). Herbert later ponders on the theme of spiritual flight to the Cross. His apparently haphazard patchworking of scriptural allusions however, and inversion of John 10.11–16 (he has the Good Shepherd fleeing, not the hireling!) is not simply a tortuous attempt to manufacture a line of defence for Becket's behaviour. It draws on the standard paradox posed in patristic exegesis: If the Apostles were good shepherds and not hirelings, why did they flee in time of persecution? John 10.11–16 presented a formidable challenge to the fugitive prelate. Its strictures could only be countered by expounding another question: And why did our Lord say, "When they persecute you in this city, flee ye to another"? Even so, the extenuating circumstances justifying the flight of a priest were considered to be very limited.[50] Matt. 10.23 was cited not only in exegesis but in hagiography too, for instance, to explain the flight of the Salonika martyrs in the early *acta martyrum*.[51] Just such a historical example, invoking the same Gospel precept, was actually read by Becket and his intimates (including Herbert himself) at supper after the dramatic end of the trial at Northampton and apparently helped in the very formulation of the plan for Becket's "evangelical flight" that night (3:312). In short, the case for the defence was ready made once the initial identification of Becket's cause with that of Christ's Apostles and martyrs had been established. And clearly, that identification was being claimed, long before the martyrdom.

From exile another of the *eruditi* had fully listed, in order to refute, the damning charges then being levelled against Becket — his vacillation at the Council of Clarendon, exposure of the Church to danger and especially the secret flight which professed his guilt. John of Salisbury's main line of defence in his tireless correspondence rallying faltering sympathizers in 1166–67 was to accuse the bishops of perfidy and to justify Becket's behaviour with lengthy citations of scriptural precedents: "It is the right

course and based on the examples of the prophets and apostles"; in particular, the archbishop had St. Paul and, supremely, Christ himself "as
authority for his flight."[52] This alludes to Matt. 10.23 and the foregoing
gospel passage describing Christ's predictions of the persecution and
betrayal by false brethren awaiting his Apostles, a passage traditionally applied to Christian martyrdom, both physical death and the living martyrdom of those who endure temptation and persecution for Christ's sake.
From this perspective, Herbert of Bosham's use of scriptural allusion no
longer seems simply a hagiographical excursus written with the rose-tinted
hindsight of the martyrdom: it elaborates the rhetoric with which the archbishop's circle is known from the epistolary evidence to have constructed his
defence already in the 1160s.

To a modern reader it would seem that they protest too much.
Recent study of the opposition's argument may help to suggest why. The
archbishop's flight into exile was seen by his enemies as the indictment of
his career and produced particularly dangerous criticism. E. M. Peters has
shown how Gilbert Foliot, Bishop of London, did not limit himself to traditional allegorical techniques in applying to Becket's flight an alternative
scriptural maxim from Prov. 28.1, "The wicked flee and no man pursueth"
(4:337). His letter to Becket in 1166, *Multiplicem nobis*, skillfully uses canon
law to build up a charge of Becket's "canonical culpability for having
deserted his flock." The crucial text from Matt. 10.23, used by Becket's supporters to justify his exile, had also been cited in Gratian's discussion of the
episcopal office, but so had John 10.12 and, in the interests of pastoral
stabilitas, the *Decretum* envisaged very few circumstances which could justify
episcopal flight; indeed, it could constitute "one of the technical grounds for
removing a bishop."[53] Foliot's version of Becket's and particularly the king's
behaviour at Clarendon and Northampton claimed that the archbishop's
flight was not provoked by any such extenuating circumstances and was
therefore illegal. Becket's supporters could only counter this in the
mid-1160s with scriptural typology and emotive images of the forced exile
of the persecuted.

But this confrontation between Foliot's use of 'modern' legal
language and the "old-fashioned" rhetoric of Becket and his supporters can
be misleading. Foliot's letter gives little support to the view that precise
technical language is necessarily any more truthful or historical than the
allegorical mode. Foliot did not oppose Becket on ideological grounds but
largely because he judged the archbishop's alienation of the king had been
unnecessary and highly dangerous to the Church. He used the arguments
of very recently formulated canon law to show that Becket was personally
unworthy of his office. At Northampton, Hilary of Chichester had voiced

the longing that Becket cease to be archbishop, and other bishops urged him to resign as a way out of the impasse. His reinstatement by Alexander III in November, 1164, was not enough to vindicate him, either to silence Foliot or to reassure some of Becket's own supporters who had been uneasily aware that he had already tried to flee the country after Clarendon, where his weakness before the king had in itself constituted a flight (1:29). After Clarendon, one of his own household had already reproached him through allusion to John 10.12: "When the Shepherd has fled the sheep lie scattered before the wolf" (2:324–5). This strengthened the need of the *eruditi* to identify the exiled archbishop with the cause of the Church and to promote as far as possible an image of sanctity. Of urgent necessity there was a hagiographic element in their discussion of current affairs. Herbert of Bosham supplied the learned footnotes to the discussion of the flight in his biography some twenty years or so later, when the reproach of John 10.12 evidently still caused him some trouble. Paradoxically, after martyrdom, the biographers were best able to strengthen Becket's case not by exegetical ingenuity, but by citing the authenticated testimony of recent history. William FitzStephen's eyewitness report of the Council of Northampton partly refutes the premiss and counters the language of Foliot's accusation by demonstrating the extenuating circumstances in which the archbishop had fled from his trial.

Accounts of the archbishop's public life are dominated by courtroom confrontations with accusations and defence continuing throughout the exile. The bishops, especially Gilbert Foliot, are revealed as false witnesses in this prolonged trial and Thomas's endurance of their betrayal as part of his white martyrdom. Even his prophetic dreams of red martyrdom are staged in a courtroom where his prosecutors, Hilary of Chichester and Foliot, are struck dumb and putrefied.[54] For the biographers, the justice of the respective causes of the real-life courtroom protagonists is manifested in the contrast between their rhetorical performances. *Thomas Saga* recalls that the young Thomas Becket had a slight stutter and the partisan Stephen of Rouen jibed that Becket had remained silent at the Council of Tours in 1163 because of his inadequate command of spoken Latin.[55] Nevertheless, William FitzStephen specifically portrays Archbishop Becket delivering his inspired defence at Northampton in 1164 without stammering (3:63), and Garnier depicts him later at the papal court in Sens arguing his case in fair Latin as if he were Solomon. Garnier labours the point. The archbishop was constantly interrupted and his every argument exhaustively contested by one favourable to the king, William of Pavia, because, remarks Garnier, he suspected Becket of having learned his speech off by heart! The biographer insists that Becket was undaunted by this interrogation, which lasted half a day, and his language sounds to have been businesslike: "He completed his excellent chain of reasoning; he demolished the laws (i.e. the Constitutions of Clarendon) by well-supported argument, by consistent logic and clearly-demonstrated proof."[56] This might just mean that the archbishop had done his homework, but that is not what chiefly strikes the biographers in reporting the courtroom exchanges.

The learned and usually eloquent Gilbert Foliot is shown at a loss for words, and the other rhetorically accomplished royal envoy, Hilary of Chichester, (who "trusted in his own eloquence rather than in truth and justice," remarked Alan of Tewkesbury), is left floundering in grammatical error and mispronunciation when attempting to accuse his spiritual superior (2:338). Eadmer's skill in presenting his account of the Council of Rockingham in 1095 as a piece of on-the-spot reporting has perhaps obscured his rather different use of this traditional device of contrasting the rhetoric of courtroom protagonists. The chief instigator of discord between Anselm and the king (and, like Foliot, allegedly desirous of the archiepiscopal office) was the Bishop of Durham. He was "quick-witted and of ready tongue, rather than endowed with true wisdom" and marvelled at the artless simplicity of Anselm's unanswerable defence.[57]

Such courtroom "proofs" of the true or false wisdom of the speaker, demonstrated through a particular quality of language and delivery, need not have been entirely unhistorical. Indeed, the fact that most of Becket's biographers report Hilary of Chichester's grammatical slip and that Herbert of Bosham, an eyewitness, also mentioned it in a private letter soon afterwards, strongly suggests that something extraordinary did happen (5:341-2). But what made such incidents *noteworthy* to the medieval author of sacred biography was the resonance they carried of the famous gospel passage immediately preceeding Matt. 10.23 already discussed. In Matt. 10.16-22 Christ warns that, for his sake, his followers will be betrayed by false brethren, scourged in synagogues, delivered up in councils and brought before kings and governors. His true disciples are exhorted and promised: "Be wise (prudent) as serpents and simple (foolish) as doves. . . . When they shall deliver you up take no thought how or what to speak, for it shall be given you in that hour what to speak. For it is not you who speak but the spirit of your Father." Thus Garnier notes that Becket in delivering his defence speech was prudent, filled with the Holy Ghost and intelligible to all. Christ's promise as recorded in Luke 21.15 ("I will give you a mouth and wisdom, which all your adversaries shall not be able to gainsay nor resist") had been early fulfilled in the protomartyr's disputation with his opponents in the synagogue: "And they were not able to resist the wisdom and the spirit that spoke" (Acts 6.10). The spirit prompted subsequent martyrs on trial to fluency or eloquent silence, or struck their wrongful accusers dumb or incoherent. The liturgy for martyrs uses references from the Old Testament Wisdom literature to this concept of trial by rhetoric: "Blessed is he that hath not slipped with his tongue." Herbert of Bosham actually cites one such text (Eccles. 20:20) to show how the falsity of the bishops' case is revealed in their uncharacteristic slips of the tongue when accusing Becket at the papal court (3:336).

The martyr's trial, sometimes featuring such manifestations of divine judgment while based in some sense on court records related by an eyewitness sympathizer, had formed an important part of many of the *acta martyrum*. Thomas's clerk William FitzStephen, who witnessed and reported the trial of Northampton, reflected "O how great was the martyrdom he bore in spirit that day" (3:68). At the papal court in Sens, Herbert of Bosham floridly described that trial as a spiritual gladiatorial combat and the tribulations of the archbishop's subsequent flight in terms reminiscent of St. Paul's account of his heroic sufferings. Alexander III was moved to tears and proclaimed that the archbishop "while still living, could claim the privilege of martyrdom" (3:335).

If the biographers' account of Becket's death constitute a *passio* of the martyr, it may be asked how far their descriptions of his life resemble that other main hagiographic type, the *vita* of the confessor? A life story characterised by secret asceticism and endurance of public opposition as has so far been described, would, in itself, scarcely qualify: the confessor's *vita* is generally structured on the gradual progress of the saint's spiritual ascent.[58] In explaining why the Becket biographers concentrated on the "historical non-hagiographical elements in their subject," Dr. Gransden has observed that Becket "underwent neither sudden religious conversion . . . nor perceptible slow improvement in his spiritual life."[59] The problems involved in depicting the archbishop on the road to Damascus in June 1162 have already been indicated. Yet a remarkably full historical account of contemporary criticism of Becket after this "conversion" and of his own admissions of error, is not entirely incompatible with the image of the *confessor Christi, futurus martyr*. Answering criticisms of the archbishop in 1165–66, John of Salisbury conceded that Becket had done wrong both before and after his consecration but that he had repented, confessed and been absolved, and that both his learning and character had improved during the early months of exile. His urgent entreaty that Becket show patience, humility, and moderation in his dealings with the king and bishops ("above all be cautious that you show no sign of arrogance") makes its own comment on the archbishop's demeanour, but in the same letter John commends his cause and identifies those who persecute Becket with those who persecute Christ.[60]

It is possible to discern a story of spiritual progress in the biographers' revelation that growing opposition sharpened the archbishop's sense of his own vocation, leading him to confess past weakness and renew his dedication. They recount not only Gilbert Foliot's denunciation of Becket's lack of courage, prudence and humility, but the taunting accusation of a member of his own household after his vacillation at Clarendon: "What virtue is left to him who has betrayed his conscience and his reputation? . . . having left posterity an example hateful to God, thou hast joined with the wicked servants of Satan to the confusion of the Church's freedom." All the biographers present this as a major crisis for the saint: "I repent and am so aghast at my transgression that I judge myself unworthy as a priest to approach him whose Church I have thus basely sold."[61] He did penance, and abstained from celebrating Mass until ordered to do so again by the pope (1:24; 5:88). He attempted to take a stand at Northampton but again faltered. After fleeing the country he dramatically resigned his archbishopric to the pope, confessing that his appointment had been uncanonical and that his strength was unequal to the task. While this is open to interpretation as an astute diplomatic move,[62] Alan of Tewkesbury's informed and detailed narrative reports Alexander reinstating Thomas with the acclamation "Now at last it is plain to us . . . how pure a confession you have witnessed from the time you were first made archbishop . . . we know you to be a man tried and proved in manifold temptations" (2:344). Such outbursts of compunction, accompanied by the charismatic gift of tears abundantly evident from his consecration till the eve of his death, mark the saint's spiritual pilgrimage in the biographies and form part of his white martyrdom. Remorse culminated in his final confession and resolution before his murderers: "Once I fled like a timorous priest. Now I have returned to my Church. . . . Nevermore will I desert her" (3:134–5).

The extensive use of the idiom of early persecutions in the accounts of Becket's *passio* has already been remarked but may now be seen to have had a significance greater than that of illustrating his courage or attempting to supplement the deficiency of saintly models in his life by the provisions of a classic martyr's death. Martyrdom had been the essential context of the intense discussion of flight in early exegesis. As has been seen, this attempted to reconcile the precepts of John 10.11–13 and Matt. 10.23, on which both the *Decretum* (and therefore Gilbert Foliot) and Becket's supporters drew. The *apologia* for his flight could only be completed in his return from exile to face his murderers without flinching. Attention has already been drawn to the concerted testimony of the biographers, including eyewitnesses of the events immediately leading up to Becket's murder, emphatically declaring that "had he wished, the archbishop might

easily have turned aside and saved himself by flight" (3:140), that he refused such counsel, dreaded the opportunity for martyrdom might be lost if
he took refuge in the church, and refused even to take the precaution of
bolting the door against his murderers. The similarity with Nehemias in 2
Esdras 6.10–11 was noted by a subsequent archbishop of Canterbury,
Stephen Langton, when he extolled St. Thomas as a model of the steadfast
good prelate.[63] Edward Grim's eyewitness and pre-canonization description of the martyrdom not only repeatedly uses the image of the Good
Shepherd from John 10.12, but specifically links it with the crucial passage
from Matt. 10.23 (italicized below): Becket's followers were scattered
before the murderers "like sheep before wolves"; he was urged to flee to the
church "but he, mindful of his former promise that he would not through
fear of death flee from those who kill the body, rejected flight. For in such
case it were not meet *to flee from city to city*". He chose "to die by the sword
rather than see the divine law and sacred canons subverted." In defending
the cause of his flock that good shepherd "would not delay the hour of his
death, when it was in his power to do so . . . that the fury of the wolves,
satiated by the blood of the shepherd, might spare the sheep."[64] Such
passages, which may easily be dismissed as purely laudatory, pious set-
pieces, detachable from an essentially historical narrative, may now appear
to reflect a vital and continuing contemporary debate. The biographers'
triumphal reply to the taunts of Foliot and the suspicions of others that
Becket had been a "fugitive prelate" was to be annually exalted in the liturgy
for St. Thomas's feast, which enshrines John 10.11–16 as the Gospel
reading for his mass and as a lection for his Office.[65]

Alongside the attempt to demonstrate the archbishop's personal
sanctity in life, and especially to vindicate his flight into exile, his supporters argued that his cause was that of the Church, despite the king's and
eventually most of the bishops' opinion to the contrary. The formulation of
the argument, associating Becket's case with that of former archbishops of
Canterbury, will be examined more closely in Part II, but its essential features may be sketched here. Thomas Becket's veneration of St. Anselm is
well known and the similarities between their two archiepiscopates is
evident — their alienation from episcopal colleagues in the conflict with the
crown over royal customs and divine law; the qualification to their promises to uphold such customs "according to the will of God" or "saving their
order"; their citation of the Petrine claims; their appeals to Rome, long exile from the Christ Church community and vigorous concern with the possessions and privileges of Canterbury, especially its primacy over York.

The manner in which Becket had fled the royal court and the
country markedly distinguished him from saintly Anselm however. At the

papal court after the Council of Northampton, Gilbert Foliot claimed that the dissension there had arisen over "a minor and unimportant matter, which might easily have been resolved if a discreet moderation had been shown"; Becket, acting on his own opinion had pushed matters to extremes and fled simply to escape blame for his own rashness. Similarly, Roger of York argued that Becket's inveterate obstinacy and vanity were at fault (2:332-9). The limitations of a defence depending on Matt. 10.23 during the exile have been indicated. John of Salisbury countered the charge in his correspondence: "Those who persecute the archbishop of Canterbury in this case do not persecute him because he is Thomas" but because, like the prophets and apostles of old he performed the unpopular but holy task of summoning "the princes of Sodom and the people of Gomorrah to hear and obey the law of God".[66] By setting the archbishops of Canterbury in the biblical tradition of seers persecuted for witnessing to Christ, and by emphasising Becket's role as one of the custodians of Canterbury, Becket's defenders and Becket himself sanctified his flight with the aura of exile and cast his critics in the role of persecuting his sacred office, not his provocative personality. The privileges and possessions of Canterbury, Becket reminded the English clergy in 1166, were "the patrimony of our crucified Saviour, not given for our use but entrusted to our stewardship. Although the divine mercy has sometimes allowed the archbishop of Canterbury to be exiled unjustly, yet whoever heard of his being tried and condemned, compelled to give bail in the king's court, above all by his own suffragans?"[67]

The propaganda potential of liturgy and the cult of saints in medieval society was considerable. Anselm offered an instructive model in emphasizing the unique vocation of Canterbury and the role of the archbishop as steward of its patrons. He had revived the liturgical honour accorded St. Gregory and the Canterbury saints, notably Dunstan and Elphege, before the Conquest. Professor Southern has ascribed to Anselm a sermon for a revived feast of St. Gregory, possibly preached before a meeting of the Curia Regis in 1101, where its plea for a renewal of the bond established between Rome and England by Pope Gregory I would have had a particularly topical application.[68] Before delivering the controversial sentences of excommunication of his enemies, originally intended to include the king, from Vézelay in 1166, Becket journeyed to Soissons and spent three nights in vigil before the shrine not only of its patron bishop "the refuge of those about to fight," but of the Canterbury patron St. Gregory "the founder of the English Church who lies buried in the same city."[69] In 1166 Becket reminded the king of his promise made to the previous archbishop of Canterbury, to preserve the liberty of the Church and particularly enjoined him to restore to the church of Canterbury "from which you received your promotion and consecration, the rank it held in the time of your predecessors and mine, together with all its possessions."[70] Writing to the Bishop of Exeter in 1169, John of Salisbury reported King Henry's astute demand at Montmirail that the archbishop simply preserve the customs observed by his predecessors at Canterbury. It stole Becket's own argument. Some clerics there, deceived by the apparent moderation of the royal demands, cited scripture to exhort Becket to defer and follow the customs of his fathers! Becket retorted: "In evil deeds it is not right to imitate our fathers" and anyway, he argued, "none of his predecessors had been compelled . . . to make profession of customs, save only St. Anselm who went into exile for seven years for the same cause."[71] He again cited the example of Anselm in asserting the rights of Canterbury at Fréteval in 1170 (3:110), and interpreted the coronation of the young king by the Archbishop of York on 14 June that year as a calculated insult to Canterbury.[72]

The authoritative example of predecessors at Canterbury was thus enunciated during Thomas's exile as an important part of his case. His opponents did not question the sanctity of his pattern, but denied he was cast in the same mould. Dismissing as a deception the archbishop's claim to be suffering for justice and the Church, King Henry asserted at Montmirail in 1169, "I have always been willing and I am willing still, to allow him to possess and govern the Church, over which he presides, in the same freedom as any of his holy predecessors" (3:424). But Becket was, in return, required to preserve for the king the customs observed by his five predecessors at Canterbury, "some of whom are saints and shine brightly with their miracles," Henry added pointedly. Similarly, Foliot counselled Becket to emulate his Canterbury predecessor St. Augustine, whose concern for the interests of the Church had been manifest in his moderation towards the king. Foliot scorned Becket's stance as the exiled martyr in a venerable tradition: he had abandoned the Church and fled to escape the death with which no one threatened him.[73] John of Salisbury found it necessary to write to Christ Church in 1170, spelling out Thomas's parallel with the exiled Anselm and exhorting the monks to welcome his return accordingly.[74] Even Herbert of Bosham was uneasy that the saint did not from the outset measure up to the founding fathers of his cause and had him confessing this shortcoming after Clarendon: "It is through me, and because of my sins, that the English Church is reduced to bondage, that Church which my predecessors . . . led through so many and great dangers," withstanding the enemy even to the shedding of blood (a clear reference to St. Elphege) (3:289).

However, Herbert also shows Becket a year before his martyrdom still apologetic about the flight from Northampton, and aware that "there have been archbishops before me, holier and greater than I," but equally aware that their historic task of extirpating abuses of the Church was incomplete. With a composure that exasperated those trying to mediate peace and end the exile, Becket declared he was ready to resume the charge of his church with all its liberties, such as the holy men his predecessors had enjoyed, but would condemn as contrary to their institutes any fresh customs detrimental to the Church. He therefore declined to submit unconditionally to the king's demands. Herbert of Bosham did no harm to his later image of St. Thomas in reporting after the martyrdom what was in all probability historically true: those present at Montmirail imputed the failure of the negotiations to Becket's arrogance. But in commenting that they lacked the discernment to see that the archbishop was standing firm and resolute in the tradition of his saintly predecessors, Herbert was accurately reporting what Becket and his circle claimed at the time. As has been observed of St. Wilfrid, another image-conscious archbishop, there is no reason to doubt that the biographer cast his subject in the same general mould as St. Thomas would have cast himself.[75]

PART II

The first part of this study has discussed the biographers' use both of conventional rhetorical devices and of documented, eyewitness accounts and has made some comparisons of their language and interpretation of events with that of the contemporary epistolary evidence. It has suggested that, despite the problematic nature of their subject, St. Thomas's biographers were concerned in their accounts of his death and hidden life and even of his controversial public life to promote an image of personal sanctity and a just cause, and were not content to rely upon the circumstances of his martyrdom or the posthumous miracles. Their image of Thomas Becket's combination of red and white martyrdom, whatever modern readers may personally feel about its plausibility, questions the notion that the biographers simply laid a hagiographic veneer over parts of their essentially historical narrative.

The second part of this work will try to explore more fully some of the themes outlined in the introductory survey. It begins by looking at examples of the language used, or allegedly used, in the debates at the Councils of Clarendon and Northampton. Finally, it examines in some detail aspects of the biographers' accounts of the crucial last day of Becket's trial at Northampton in October 1164, on the eve of his flight into exile. This may throw new light, not only on the biographers' techniques but again on the events they record.

The Language of the Debate

The accounts of St. Thomas's living martyrdom are free from the extended gospel parallelism which glorifies his death, yet incorporate biblical and liturgical allusions. It has been suggested above that such allusions do not necessarily denote a change from the historical to the hagiographical mode. Further discussion of the biographers' use of such language had been made possible by recent scholarship in three important areas of twelfth-century activity which has greatly illumined the intellectual context in which the Becket controversy occurred in the 1160s and in which it was reported in the 1170s. First, the correspondence of the controversy, the largest of all twelfth-century letter collections, has received a detailed textual history and the letters of Gilbert Foliot and John of Salisbury monumental critical editions.[76] Secondly, the study of canon law has transformed understanding of the problems arising from the rapid development of two overlapping and conflicting systems of law in which the position of criminous clerks in particular was still unclear. Charles Duggan showed that Becket's arguments against the Constitutions of Clarendon were not of his own devising but grounded in canon law. Notably, his case against chapter three's apparent proposal that unfrocked criminous clerks be handed over to the royal courts for sentence is, as reported by his biographer William of Canterbury, a patchwork of quotations from Gratian's *Decretum* linked by phrases from Rufinus.[77] Professor Duggan has argued for a direct canonical source, even of biblical and patristic *dicat* "wherever we find a precise record of the controversy as allegedly argued by the principal contestants." In citing John of Salisbury's *Policraticus* as a precedent for Becket's use of the Septuagint text of Nahum 1.9 ("God will not punish twice for the same offence"), he observes that "the canonical source of John's phrases is not hard to find."[78]

Thirdly, attention has been drawn to the relevance of contemporary theological debate to the Becket dispute. Beryl Smalley has shown how the *eruditi sancti Thomae*, particularly his future biographers John of Salisbury and Herbert of Bosham, encouraged Thomas to defy the king and briefed him in the teaching of the schools on relations between *regnum* and *sacerdotium*. While agreeing that canon law provided an arsenal of texts from which William of Canterbury and, to a lesser extent, Herbert of Bosham and William FitzStephen could retrospectively draw up a dossier of suitable arguments in their presentation of Becket's case, Dr. Smalley has also pointed out that in his prophetic *Policraticus*, John of Salisbury "cites no canon law authority to support his application of the scriptural maxim" from Nahum 1.9: "it is just as likely therefore that Becket drew his text from a theological as from a canon law context."[79] Richard Fraher has since used illustrations of the ambiguous and inconsistent state of canon law on *privilegium fori* in the 1160s and even the 1170s as additional arguments for locating "the actual source of Becket's contention among the theologians rather than the canon lawyers."[80] Recently, Professor Duggan has warned against any false polarization: "the canonical and theological arguments are complementary, not contradictory; there were experts in both disciplines in Becket's household, and some key texts are found in canonical and theological sources"; similarly, the editor of John of Salisbury's letters had acknowledged the theologian's legal expertise.[81]

The technical details about textual sources remain open to scholarly discussion; what is clear is that contemporary letter collections, canon law and the schools provided the best of Becket's biographers not only with their documentary material and their intellectual training, but with a common language. The allegorical interpretation of scripture was not the only language of the second half of the twelfth century, but it was a fundamental tool of exposition and polemic in canon law and in political debate conducted through the rhetorical art of letter writing, as well as in theology. The Becket correspondence shows that well before the martyrdom and canonization, the allegorical interpretation of scripture was being applied to the general jurisdictional issues raised by the Constitutions of Clarendon and specifically to Becket's own case. Moreover, it was used not only by Becket and his *eruditi* but by his opponents, as one instance may illustrate. In the course of the famous denunciation of Becket in the letter *Multiplicem* in 1166, Gilbert Foliot commented "Thus Israel went down into Egypt."[82] The standard exegetical interpretation of Israel as referring to Christ or his body, the Church, is here applied to the circumstances of the Council of Clarendon in 1164 when, Foliot maintained, Christ's Church was delivered into bondage by Becket's fainthearted submission to the king's demands for an unconditional promise to observe "the ancient customs of the realm." Repudiating Foliot's taunts and vindicating the archbishop in a letter later the same year, however, John of Salisbury rhetorically asked: "Was not Egypt afflicted with plagues because it kept the Church in slavery by an ancient grandfatherly custom of nigh on three hundred years standing?"[83] Age, he suggests, does not make wrongful customs lawful; Henry II's claim at Clarendon to be upholding the customs of his grandfather's day is seen as the cause of the Church's present bondage in this alternative application of the same scriptural allusion to the same contemporary event.

The letters of the controversy, and others of the period, also show that the practice of presenting a range of arguments, including biblical allusions, which the writer considered would have been suitable to a particular occasion, rather than reporting the actual discussion verbatim, was by no means peculiar to hagiographers. Herbert of Bosham reports that Becket's criticism of chapter three of the Constitutions of Clarendon was on the grounds that Christ is once again judged before the seat of Pilate when clerics in criminal and civil causes are handed over to secular justice (3:281).

Whether or not the biographer was quoting the argument precisely as for-mulated in January, 1164, Becket himself was discussing the issue in similar, indeed, more radical terms in his letter to the English Church in 1166 when he claimed that at his own trial at Northampton in October 1164 "Christ was judged in my person before the tribunal of the prince" (5:494). Caution is necessary before dismissing the biographers' biblical allusions as pious passages overlaying the essentially "historical" core of their narrative.

The point may be illustrated in more detail by a passage in William FitzStephen's account of that Council of Northampton. FitzStephen's biog-raphy, probably completed 1173–74 in its first version, is generally re-garded as the most informed and authoritative on events before and after the exile. The writer's personal knowledge of Becket and his familiarity with legal matters are evident, and he had "epistolary evidence for nearly every statement which was not derived from his own personal knowledge or ex-perience."[84] It is therefore perhaps surprising at first to read in his masterly eyewitness report of Becket's trial that the archbishop's refusal to be judged on the secular charge laid against him and his appeal to Rome was greeted by some present with the words, "Behold, we have heard the blasphemy proceeding out of his mouth" (3:64). It is highly improbable that in 1164 Becket's critics did him the honour of condemning him with the words in which Christ had been condemned by the High Priest in Matt. 26.65. But the biographer's quotation of the gospel passage here need not necessarily be dismissed as a momentary lapse into the hagiographic vein, an inter-polation of a gospel parallel made appropriate only by Thomas's subse-quent martyrdom.

Already in the *Policraticus* of 1159, dedicated to Chancellor Becket, John of Salisbury had specifically cited the High Priest's condemna-tion of Christ as an ironic illustration of the method by which contemporary royal tyranny condemned clerks who invoked their clerical privilege in resisting the demands of Caesar.[85] The context of William FitzStephen's quotation of the same gospel text as a hostile response to the archbishop's insistence on his privilege is instructive. First, Becket's speech outlining his respective duties to God and the king was in reply to King Henry's angry reminder, delivered through his barons, of Becket's duties as the king's liege man and of his promises at Clarendon to preserve the royal privileges. Secondly, the archbishop's insistence on his overriding obedience to God, condemned at Northampton in the words of the High Priest, is followed in the very next sentence of FitzStephen's narrative by magnates near the king threateningly citing Henry's father and grandfather as examples of strong rulers who had successfully crushed disruptive clerics. By implication they counsel Henry to do likewise, a tableau which contrasts with the ideal presented in *Policraticus* 4:6 of the wise prince advised on God's law by priestly *litterati*.

Although the king was surrounded not only by bellicose barons but by most of his bishops, Becket and his circle denounced these priestly *litterati* as false interpreters of the law, familiar with the mechanics of allegorical interpretation but misguided and perverse in its application. Commenting on the bishops' censorious letter to Becket in 1166 "dictated by Achitophel" (Foliot), John of Salisbury declaimed: "Judas the betrayer, whom Achitophel prefigured, left in Christ's death an example of treachery and treasonable murder not only to the Jews but to our scribes and pharisees too." Again alluding to Henry II's "grandfatherly customs" of Clarendon, John shows that the scribes and pharisees falsely charge Christ/Becket with attacking the laws of Caesar, and betray their own prophetic calling so that passing through clouds of foggy reasoning and destroying the law by abuse of correct language they finally conclude that: 'He is worthy of death: Crucify him. . . .'"[86] Later in the exile John denounced those who said "We have no king but Caesar. Crucify him, crucify our bishop . . . who asserts that God's law is to be preferred to human custom."[87]

The problem of correctly interpreting the divine law on relations between *regnum* and *sacerdotium* was not confined to England. The contemporary papal schism presented the unedifying spectacle of the pharisaical Archbishop of Cologne assisting the tyrant Emperor to blaspheme the holy one of Israel (in this case Alexander III) by falsely citing scripture to support the imperial cause: "We know no king but Caesar."[88] Nor was the problem confined to the 1160s. Sacred biography and history written over half a century before the *Policraticus* provided the improving example of an appropriate application of scripture to the issue in a courtroom situation which in some ways foreshadows Becket's trial. At the Council of Rockingham in 1095, Archbishop Anselm was opposed by his own bishops who "wishing to be on the king's side and having no regard for justice," tried to prove to Anselm that recognition of Urban as pope entailed breaking the faith he owed to the king. But Anselm confounded them with the words of Christ to the pharisees who had tried to ensnare him: "Render unto Caesar the things that are Caesar's and unto God the things that are God's." The bishops were reduced to clamouring that Anselm was "blaspheming against the king."[89] Eadmer noted that Anselm inspired popular sympathy: "If you had been there you would have heard this or that bishop dubbed now by one man, then by another with some nickname . . . such as 'traitor Judas,' 'Pilate,' or 'Herod.'" The application of such names to those who persecuted the martyrs was an early hagiographical commonplace yet used by John of Salisbury in a letter commenting on Becket's death.[90] William FitzStephen's account of Becket saying in exile, "And he among my brethren occupied the place of the traitor Judas," with reference to Hilary of Chichester who had betrayed him at Northampton, has the appearance of an anecdote (3:55). Such parallels came readily to lips and pen and were not confined to an exclusively hagiographic genre.

The charges of blasphemy against God and Caesar made against Christ before the High Priest and Pilate and his condemnation on the evidence of his own mouth, were echoed in the trials of the early martyrs.[91] But Becket's biographers were hampered in casting him in this heroic mould in 1164, not only by his subsequent flight, but by the fact that his stance at Northampton, attended by *eruditi* alone, appealing to divine law and treating his bishops as friends of Caesar, was in marked contrast to his inglorious behaviour at Clarendon only nine months earlier. There it was Becket who had been the friend of Caesar, Gilbert Foliot claimed in 1166: "The archbishop himself acquiesced in the king's royal prerogative and the ancient customs of the realm," abruptly betraying the united episcopal stand against the "threats of princes." Foliot denounced Becket's subsequent Christ-like posturings and cast *him* in the role of Judas.[92] Time and the martyrdom vindicated the *eruditi*'s interpretation of events. The martyr's biographers could appropriately draw parallels with the sufferings of Christ. Read with hindsight, the condemnation of St. Thomas at Northampton in the same words by which Christ had been condemned was, of course, a splendid piece of irony. But this does not reduce it to a "non-historical" hagiographic commonplace. William FitzStephen's statement that some at Northampton had judged Becket's refusal to render the king his apparent due as "a blasphemy proceeding out of his own mouth," if not reporting a historical incident, uses the very language in which the debate is known to have been conducted long before the martyrdom.

13 October 1164

An incident took place earlier the same day, the seventh of the Northampton trial, which affords further insight into the archbishop's line of defence and its reception. It may also serve to illustrate in more detail some of the foregoing general observations about the biographers' techniques and language and the degree to which they were able to reconcile their image of the saint's martyrdom and personal sanctity with the vivid memory of the archbishop's controversial public behavior. Examination of this incident may also sharpen the focus on the biographers' attitudes to related issues already outlined in Part I, particularly the relevance of the opening year of Becket's archiepiscopate to the crisis with the king in 1163–64 which culminated at Northampton; the contribution of the last day of that Council to the role of Becket's Canterbury predecessors in the development of his claims to be representing the interests of the Church; the importance of his flight from that Council, both immediately and in the subsequent debate about his sanctity.

W. L. Warren noted, when commenting on Thomas's famous entrance at the final session of the Council of Northampton, bearing his own cross, "It was St. Stephen's day, 12 October, and the archbishop first celebrated mass, with its significant *Introit*, 'Princes also did sit and speak against me; but thy servant is occupied in thy statutes'. So would Becket behave, and being Becket he could not omit the melodramatic gesture."[93] The feast of Stephen is on 26 December, however, and the biographies, particularly the detailed chronology of William FitzStephen's account which modern historians have found convincing, place the mass on the liturgically curious date of Tuesday, 13 October. It was, therefore, not the regular liturgy of the day which prompted Becket's "melodramatic gesture" of taking up his cross: that liturgy had been chosen.

The lesson for the feast (Acts 6.8–10, 7.54–60) describes the martyrdom of the deacon Stephen after his trial by the Sanhedrin, the Gospel in Christ's prophecy of the persecution of his true disciples and the opening of the introit or office, repeated in the gradual, is "Princes also did sit and speak against me, wicked men have persecuted me. . . ." Some present straightway interpreted it "that the archbishop had said the mass for himself, like another Stephen, against the king and his wicked persecutors" (3:56). Besides the polemical pertinence of the clerical protomartyr's liturgy to the archbishop's own situation at a critical moment of his trial, the actual date on which he chose to celebrate it may have been a further cause of provocation.

The formal canonization of Edward the Confessor had been procured only three years earlier at the instigation of the abbot of Westminster and with the active cooperation of the king. By honouring his Anglo-Saxon ancestor, Henry II emphasised the continuity of the royal house and the unity of its peoples and presumably hoped to acquire prestige for the Angevin monarchy after the style of the Capetian cult of sacred kingship and the canonization in 1146 of Edward's older contemporary, Henry II of Germany. In supporting the cult of Edward the Confessor the king demonstrated his piety and may also have been attempting to capture a potentially subversive popular appeal to the past.[94] By the third quarter of the twelfth century canonization was clearly regarded as a papal prerogative and official recognition of royal saints in the post-Gregorian period had been limited to the 1146 precedent.[95] Despite interest shown in their royal ancestor by William the Conqueror, Henry I and Stephen and the devotion to Edward at Westminster fostered by prior Osbert of Clare, a petition for his canonization had been refused by Innocent II in 1139. Eventual official sanction for such royal propaganda in 1161, even if granted as a diplomatic expedient by Alexander III seeking support in the papal schism, must have been particularly gratifying to the crown.

Gilbert Foliot, Roger of York and Hilary of Chichester were among those who sent letters testimonial in Edward's cause.[96] Probably during the Canterbury vacancy after the death of Theobald, Foliot further petitioned the pope for the translation of the new saint's relics, though the privilege of officiating at the ceremony eventually went to his successful rival to the archiepiscopal see, Thomas Becket (5:19; 3:261). St. Edward's relics were translated at Westminster in 1163 on 13 October. Becket's neglect of the first anniversary of such an important royal event in favour of the mass of St. Stephen must have seemed studied in the context of the Northampton trial. The royal envoys, Gilbert Foliot and Hilary of Chichester, subsequently denounced his celebration of that mass to the pope,[97] though modern commentators have not explored its implications.

Roger of Pontigny, who probably received his information directly from Thomas Becket during his exile, recounts a heated exchange on temporal and ecclesiastical authority between the king and the archbishop, not long after their dissension at the Council of Westminster in October 1163. Answering Henry's jibes about his lowly origins, Thomas had retorted, "I am not 'sprung from royal ancestors'; neither was St. Peter, prince of the Apostles, on whom the Lord deigned to confer the keys of the kingdom" (4:28). Thomas's Gregorian secularizing view of monarchy could have carried the additional sting of alluding to Henry's very recent attempt to demonstrate his lawful inheritance to the sanctity of the royal office by ceremonially shouldering his kinsman's sainted royal remains to the high altar at Westminster. Edward the Confessor's biographer had stressed his exemplification of sacramental kingship. At his consecration the king, probably through the unction of chrism, "became *christus dei.*"[98] In spite of the post-Gregorian papacy's attempts to prevent the royal use of chrism (because of its association with the ordination of priests and consecration of bishops), Gilbert Foliot testified that chrism had been used at Henry II's own anointing in 1154.[99] That consecration had been received at the hands of Becket's predecessor at the church of Canterbury however, as the archbishop was to remind the king in a letter of 1166: "Kings receive their power from the Church" (5:281, Ep. CLIV). Like other twelfth-century rulers, Henry doubtless recognized the propaganda value of a canonized king as an argument in the debate between *regnum* and *sacerdotium*,[100] a contest which the biographers suggest was planned by Henry even before Becket's consecration in 1162: the king "believed his design against the Church could be most effectively carried out through Thomas" (4:14, 3:43-4).

The "design against the Church" can no longer be regarded as a hagiographer's bogey. Work on the first eight years of Henry's reign shows that "far from biding his time until Theobald died, he had at once began to pursue a vigorous and comprehensive policy of asserting royal authority against the Church," anticipating several of the Constitutions of Clarendon.[101] The design, however, was thwarted by the new archbishop's unexpected resignation of the royal office of chancellor and the rapid deterioration of his relations with the king.[102] In letters from exile in 1166, John of Salisbury was to admit that Chancellor Becket had been "the servant of wicked men, putting the king before God" but that since his consecration he had preferred "to use God's word as master."[103] John's further admission that, as archbishop, Becket had provoked the king from the start, and the biographers' terse accounts of the opening year of the archiepiscopate, point to their unease at the rapidity of the breakdown in relations with the king, even before the overlapping jurisdictional claims of royal and ecclesiastical authority were hotly debated at the series of councils beginning with Woodstock in July, 1163. The spring of 1163 would seem to have been a critical period.

Becket's modelling of himself on Anselm has long been recognized as probably "the most important of all the clues for understanding the transformation of the archbishop after his election."[104] Anselm's formidable performance in the early rounds of the conflict between *regnum* and *sacerdotium* has recently been stressed, particularly his responsibility for "the first decisive check to the English sacerdotal monarchy"; furthermore, "in compensation for the loss of ecclesiastical character which Henry [I] suffered in 1107, there arose a new cult of sacramental kingship," demonstrated in the development of Edward the Confessor's cult at Westminster.[105] It has often been suggested that Becket's request at the Council of Tours, in May 1163, for the canonization of Anselm was an attempt to counterbalance the canonization of Edward the Confessor, and an indication of already strained relations with the king.[106] On 9 June, Alexander III remitted Anselm's case to Becket, promising to uphold the decision of the archbishop's provincial council. No record of such a council has survived and it has generally been assumed that proceedings were abandoned or interrupted by Becket's exile. R. W. Southern, however, discovered that the Feast of Anselm's Translation was already being observed on 7 April at Canterbury before Becket's death, and deduced it was "just possible that a Translation may in 1163 or earlier have preceded the process of canonization."[107] Ursula Nilgen has since argued strongly for the 1163 date and has further suggested that on 7 April that year Anselm was very probably translated, at Becket's behest, to the chapel in Christ Church cathedral then dedicated to the Princes of the Apostles, SS. Peter and Paul. In honour of the occasion, it is suggested,

Becket commissioned the decoration of the chapel with scenes of the lives and persecution of Peter and Paul "who stood for the Church and her freedom which Anselm had defended."[108] Archbishop Becket's implicit identification with their cause through the iconography of his commission and its occasion would, in the contemporary conflict between *regnum* and *sacerdotium*, have amounted to a political statement.[109] The ideas of various scholars outlined in this paragraph were evolved over a long period and in pursuit of rather different questions. They have not so far been used as a standpoint from which to view the biographers' accounts of the last day of Becket's trial.

The Translation of St. Edward the Confessor had been deferred after his canonization in 1161 because of the king's prolonged absence abroad. Although Henry returned in January 1163, the Translation was not arranged for the anniversary of the Confessor's canonization (7 February). It seems possible it was planned during a royal council held in March that year.[110] If so, Becket's presumed translation of Anselm on 7 April, and his certain and well-prepared application on 19–21 May for Anselm's formal canonization (thereby pre-empting the eventual Translation of Edward the Confessor on 13 October 1163), looks more pointed still. October 13 became St. Edward's feast day (not the anniversary of his death or canonization). At Northampton on 13 October 1164, Becket's neglect of the feast of the king's holy royal predecessor in favour of a votive mass would have been conspicuous. His alternative celebration of St. Stephen (a martyr for the Church, like SS. Peter and Paul) with the introit "Princes also sat against me," might seem of a piece with his promotion of his own priestly ancestor at Canterbury, Archbishop Anselm, "the hammer of tyrants" (5:35, Ep.XXIII; 3:210). It was not a cause with which Henry II would have sympathized.

The king had gone to considerable lengths to prevent the archbishop from posturing in the guise of the persecuted Church at Northampton. Becket had been summoned there on the entirely secular charge of John the Marshal (3:49). After his full submission, he had been faced with a further secular charge for which he had not been summoned, and then arraigned on financial matters arising from his conduct of the chancellorship, despite the fact that he had been relieved of all such accountability at his consecration. On the fourth day of the trial, when it was evident that the king could not be pacified with money, the archbisop's advisers felt his only hope was to throw himself entirely on the king's mercy. The Council did not formally meet for the next two days, during which there were intensive consultations and rumoured plots against Becket's life. It was before appearing at the seventh session of the Council that Becket offered the mass of St. Stephen. Clearly, it was open to the interpretation that the archbishop was dramatically insisting that he was being tried, not on the ostensible secular charges, but as a representative of the Church. The biographers' brief description of the consternation caused by Becket's celebration of a votive mass on 13 October, 1164 becomes more intelligible in this wider context.

It does, however, again raise the question here being investigated of whether the biographers were able to reconcile the archbishop's provocative, apparently politically motivated behaviour with their image of the blameless martyr, persecuted in life as in death for the cause of the Church. Their omissions concerning Anselm and Edward the Confessor are of interest here. The cult of St. Anselm was eclipsed after 1170 by that of his martyred and miracle-working successor at Canterbury. Any reminder that the latter had advanced Anselm's cause would not have lent much lustre to St. Thomas's reputation and may, indeed, have recalled an aspect of his relations with the king best forgotten. This could explain why Herbert of Bosham, writing in the mid-1180s, omits mentioning Thomas's request for Anselm's canonization at the Council of Tours, although he describes Thomas's journey and honorable reception there, and elsewhere shows reverence for Anselm's memory (3:254-5, 210). None of the other biographers mentions the canonization either, not even John of Salisbury who was commissioned to rewrite Eadmer's *Life* of Anselm, probably the work presented to the pope at Tours in 1163. The biographers describe the king later that year, enraged with Becket's attitude over criminous clerks, storming out of the Council of Westminster, whose members had arrived in London on 1 October, according to the *Summa causae inter regem et Thomam* (4:201). There are difficulties in imagining that the splendid ceremony of the Translation of Edward the Confessor on 13 October, conducted by the archbishop in the presence of the king, took place after their dramatic dissension at the council. Professor Barlow commented that if the thinly-attested date for the opening of the council on 1 October be discounted and the two Westminster ceremonies conflated so that "the council described by Becket's biographers opened with Edward's translation, we have to accept that most contemporary writers either forgot the ceremony or considered it irrelevant to their story."[111] As reference to the liturgical calendar was so commonplace a dating device, it is perhaps unlikely that every early biographer save one simply forgot such a feast, but there are some grounds for supposing they did consider it "irrelevant" to their story.

The evidence of Herbert of Bosham who alone refers to the ceremony is, perhaps, revealing. First, he emphatically insists that the translation of the royal saint was a harmonious occasion when king and archbishop were still of one heart and mind (3:261). He does not, however, date the event or associate it with the Council of Westminster but places it in an unchronological list of examples of Becket's sacramental and liturgical duties as archbishop, in the chapter *before* his material on the outbreak of dissension culminating in the summoning of the Council of Westminster (3:264–6). Secondly, although all the biographers mention Becket's celebration of the Mass of St. Stephen during the Council of Northampton in October 1164, none says that it occurred on the feast of St. Edward the Confessor. Only Herbert of Bosham makes any reference at all to the liturgical calendar in commenting on Becket's timing of the Mass. His wording is ambiguous: "Et hancquidem missam, die qui festus non erat, cum pallio celebravit, nisi quia beati Calixti papae et martyris natalitium fuit" (3:304). Dom D. Knowles felt that Herbert based his chronology "on the assumption that the feast of St. Calixtus (14 October) fell on the critical Tuesday of the council;" Herbert simply made a mistake when trying to date the event twenty years later and the problematic wording may be due to a scribe subsequently tampering with Herbert's text "in order to eliminate a difficult date."[112] However, the ambiguity of wording does not preclude the possibility that Herbert, a cleric and an eyewitness of the event, was aware that Tuesday 13 October 1164 was only the eve of St. Calixtus' feast. It is possible that by alluding to the martyred pope and omitting any mention of the feast of the royal saint Edward the Confessor, Herbert hoped to suggest a reason for Becket's choice of that particular date for celebrating a special mass in pontificals which would underline the identification of his cause with that of the persecuted Church (so effectively made in the mass of the protomartyr), yet would be less open to censure.

Herbert tried to present Thomas of Canterbury as *the* English saint, a potential counterpart to the martyred bishop Denis of France, whose flourishing contemporary cult had been promoted by Capetian royal patronage.[113] There may have been some embarrassment, acknowledged by the silence of all the other biographers, in recalling that the would-be patron of England had slighted so prestigious a royal saint as Edward the Confessor, whose veneration was by no means confined to royal partisans. Henry's petition for the canonization of his kinsman claimed the support of the whole English Church.[114] Becket had sought the spiritual support of Cistercian houses, including Rievaulx, soon after his consecration; the order assisted him in exile as long as possible and promoted his cult, yet the most revered English Cistercian, Ailred of Rievaulx (d.1167), had himself composed, if not actually delivered, the homily for St. Edward's Translation at the request of his kinsman the Abbot of Westminster. Ailred also rewrote Osbern of Clare's *Life of St. Edward* which became the basis of the royal saint's liturgical commemoration. The revised *Life* was dedicated as a spiritual model to Henry II whom Ailred hailed as the cornerstone binding together the two walls of the English and the Norman race.[115] In the reign of such a monarch, the Church might prosper, combining the best of its hallowed Anglo-Saxon past with the post-Conquest reforms of a wider Christendom. This was strikingly exemplified in Ailred, the foremost English abbot of the international Cistercian reform, yet loyal to the memory of the local Anglo-Saxon saints of Hexham, Wilfred, and Cuthbert, from the custodians of whose shrines Ailred was himself descended.[116] Henry II's espousal of Edward the Confessor's cause astutely appropriated such sentiments; the saintly Ailred's active support of this piece of royal piety offered a marked contrast to Becket's behaviour on St. Edward's feast in 1164.

Furthermore, the subversive implications of Becket's conduct were only too clear: "In the person of Becket resistance to the king had been canonized,"[117] hence Henry's penance at the martyr's tomb, rewarded by his victory at Alnwick. Though Herbert of Bosham mused on this striking example of cause and effect (3:544–8), the biographers writing during the reign of Henry II, unlike the later royal suppressor of the cult of St. Thomas, had no wish to present Archbishop Becket as "a rebell and traytour to his prince." After the immediate memory of Henry's reign, the fine reliquary châsse of c. 1200, possibly ordered by the monks of Christ Church and intended for the Translation of St. Thomas's relics, was able to provide him with a much more seemly setting.[118] Its decoration features Christ flanked by the early martyrs, Peter and Paul, and the martyred Thomas Becket amongst his holy predecessors at Canterbury — Augustine, Elphege, Dunstan, and Anselm — but, significantly, it also reveres two canonized Anglo-Saxon kings, St. Edmund and St. Edward the Confessor. Herbert of Bosham in the 1180s could not go so far but it is worth noting that Herbert, the sole biographer to mention the Translation of Edward the Confessor,[119] not only separates it in his narrative from any suggestion of involvement in the controversy between Becket and Henry, but directly couples it with another splendid liturgical ceremony conducted by the archbishop in the presence of the king and illustrating their concord (3:260–261). That ceremony, the consecration of the abbatial church at Reading, would also, like the Confessor's Translation, have served to glorify the piety of the royal house because the Cluniac foundation at Reading had been lavishly patronised by the king's grandfather, Henry I, whose great tomb was exalted to a place of honour before the High Altar in the newly completed church.

Other features of the Becket biographies remain unexplained by any account of the purely political motivation of his behaviour. All agree that the mass of St. Stephen marked a turning point in his trial. From then on the archbishop insisted on his clerical privilege. It was directly from celebrating this votive mass that he planned to re-enter the council, bare-foot, vested (presumably in the red of martyrs), carrying the viaticum and his processional cross. Gilbert Foliot regarded the last detail as a declaration of war and, for different reasons, St. Thomas's champions later prized the image: Herbert of Bosham saw it as a battle standard, a literal response to the injunction "Take up thy cross" (3:305–6) and the *Early South English Legendary* was to describe the saint's cross as a banner "for holi churche to fighte," his St. Stephen's mass vestments, worn into the council, as armour befitting such a knight of Christ.[120] However, Roger of Pontigny and William FitzStephen specifically state that Thomas's clerks successfully dis-suaded him from going into the council in full pontificals; he retained only the stole (4:45, 3:56). Furthermore, it was *courtiers* present at the mass of St. Stephen who had considered it to portend something special: "informers, spying on him for the king, told him how this mass had been sung, maliciously interpreting it (*maligne interpretantes*) that the archbishop had said the mass for himself, like another Stephen, against the king and his wicked persecutors."[121]

In the great psalm of the Law from which the introit for the mass is taken, the Lord's persecuted servant meditates on the divine statutes in order to understand them aright (Ps. 118.17–24). St. Stephen's exposition of the Old Covenant in Acts 7 forms his defence speech at his trial where he is charged before the High Priest and scribes and martyred for blasphe-mously asserting that Christ will change the customs of Moses (Acts 6.11–14). The opposition of custom and the truth of Christ's law, and the identifica-tion of the accusers with those who should have understood the divine law yet persecuted the prophets (Acts 7.51–3) has obvious relevance to the earlier conduct of the Becket debate and to the polemical defence of the archbishop's case by his *eruditi* after Northampton. But if in saying the mass of St. Stephen that day Becket had been deliberately presenting himself as a second Stephen undergoing persecution in the royal council before false scribes and pharisees, then it would seem that his *eruditi* did not directly take up this emotive battlecry when promoting his case from exile, though they did not hesitate to use more extravagant parallels.

Reviewing Becket's continued vulnerability to criticism in 1166, especially concerning his behaviour at Northampton and flight, John of Salisbury relied heavily on scriptural parallels to show that (whatever the archbishop's personal errors of judgment) his cause set him firmly in the hallowed tradition of prophets and apostles persecuted as Christ's martyrs for witnessing to truth and justice. John's omission of St. Stephen from his examples of early martyrs is all the more surprising as he refers to the familiar martyrdom text in Matt. 23 (discussed above) which immediately precedes the passage used in the Gospel reading for St. Stephen's day. Furthermore, v.32, cited by John in asserting that those who persecuted Becket "fulfill the measure of their fathers," was quoted in one of the nocturn lections for St. Stephen's feast and directly applied to his persecution.[122]

Alan of Tewkesbury, supplementing John of Salisbury's conventionally pious biography of Becket, says that the archbishop's cross-bearer had bitterly accused him of having failed to withstand the civil power at Clarendon in defence of the Church's freedom, and applied to that council the words of the psalmist: "Princes did sit and gather themselves together against the Lord's Anointed" (2:324). In a letter of 1167, still trying to justify Becket's flight, John of Salisbury adapted this text to the circumstances of the Council of Northampton: "The archbishop saw that kings and princes were conspiring together against the Lord and his anointed. So he fled to the Pope."[123] The last sentence was something of a let-down. John had already admitted that, as Chancellor, Becket had himself been "the servant of wicked men" and even that "with Saul he attacked the Church." (Saul had consented to the stoning of Stephen.) John of Salisbury was anxious to assure the Bishop of Exeter in June, 1166 that his exiled archbishop was now "prepared with Paul to lay down his life" for the Church,[124] which represented a change of attitude, some might have wryly observed, dating not from Becket's consecration, as John tried to suggest, but from some time *after* 13 October 1164.

If in saying the mass of the protomartyr Becket had publicly presented himself as a second Stephen at Northampton, and if his supporters could have sympathized with such a gesture, then his subsequent martyrdom and its annual victorious liturgical commemoration within three days of the regular feast of St. Stephen, would have rendered the Northampton mass extraordinarily prophetic. As has already been shown however, the narratives of Becket's death stress his *imitatio Christi* but nowhere mention St. Stephen. Thomas' devotees did exploit the reverberations of St. Stephen's liturgy but indirectly. The gospel for the feast mentions Abel and Zacharias (generally identified in exegesis with the High Priest's son who, like Stephen, was inspired by the Spirit of the Lord to denounce the transgressions of his people and was accordingly stoned to death in the Temple by order of the king). The Gospel reading, expounded in the lections, presents Stephen's martyrdom as one fulfillment of Christ's prediction of the persecution of his true disciples at the hands of scribes and pharisees; future saints are here united with earlier witnesses of the redemption:

And some you will put to death and crucify, and some you will scourge in your synagogues and persecute from city to city: that upon you may come all the just blood that hath been shed upon earth, from the blood of Abel the just, even unto the blood of Zacharias the son of Barachias, whom you slew between the temple and the altar (Matt. 23.34–5)

In 1172 before Becket's canonization was secured, supporters appealed to the Archbishop of Sens, claiming that the blood of the Lord's anointed (Becket) "calls forth from the earth to the Lord more than the blood of Abel the righteous."[125] In a letter probably the following year, John of Salisbury described Becket as "the son of Barach" who had shed his blood in a holier place than between the temple and the altar.[126] In 1173, on the first celebration of St. Thomas's feast (and therefore only three days after the feast of St. Stephen on 26 December), Gervase of Chichester preached that St. Thomas was "our new Abel, the righteous man," offering his blood that one might die for the many."[127] Both the Anonymous of Lambeth and the anonymous *passio* which was to form a lection for St. Thomas's feast use the reference to Abel specifically made in the gospel reading for the feast of Stephen.[128] Abel and Zacharias, the first and last innocent victims recorded in the Old Covenant, are not only prefigurings of the persecutions of Christians in general or of laity and clergy or of individual martyrs (of whom Stephen and Thomas are the first and latest examples). They, and most notably Abel, prefigure Christ. St. Thomas's supporters depicted him as a new Abel, but not as a second Stephen.

Instead, the biographers attribute the identification of Thomas and Stephen only to hostile critics. Whether or not Becket intended that the informers, spying on him for the king, should deliver his political ultimatum, the timing of the Northampton mass must have been provocative in effect. Open to the obvious interpretation that Becket was presenting himself as the sole upholder of the divine law amidst the pharisees, it would further alienate him from his fellow bishops as well as from the king, making compromise impossible. It was not that the *eruditi* disapproved of his cause, but their disquiet at Becket's conduct of the case, in such a way as to precipitate crisis and flight, is evident. John of Salisbury's attitude has already been noted. Herbert of Bosham recalls in his biography the frequent occasions when he personally gave the archbishop advice and William FitzStephen reports in detail the counsel he himself offered Becket during the last day of the Northampton trial. Neither claims responsibility for urging Becket to say the St. Stephen mass that morning and FitzStephen goes to some lengths to minimize any militant implications.

The biographers suggest that the mass was not a calculated act of political provocation but an anguished plea for protection, reached after Becket had been taken ill and retired trembling to his monastic lodging at a critical moment of his trial. Omitting all reference to the feast of St. Edward the Confessor, they severally explain the timing of the mass of St. Stephen by testifying that the previous day the archbishop had been secretly warned by sympathetic nobles that if he attended the council next day, he would undoubtedly be arrested or gaoled, some said maimed or even killed "by a conspiracy of wicked men against him, as though without the king's knowledge" (3:58, 305, 4:44). He consequently spent a troubled night in vigil and on the advice not of his *eruditi* but of a certain religious, perhaps his confessor Robert of Merton, in the morning before returning to his trial he said the entire office and then the mass of St. Stephen at his altar with such fervent devotion and abundant tears of compunction that he frequently had to stop and start the collect again (2:330, 393; 3:304, 4:44-5). He offered the mass "with the intention that on that day he would not be harmed by the malice of his foes" (2:393); the central petition of the introit was repeated in the psalm: "Help me, O Lord my God."

If the biographers give reasons why Thomas Becket offered a special votive mass that particular day, do they give any additional hints concerning the choice of the saint to whom it was dedicated, or the connection between this mass and the archbishop's behavior on returning to his trial? St. Stephen had early become a particularly popular intercessor. Because he had prayed for his enemies, it was presumed in the *acta martyrum* he would be even more ready to act on behalf of his friends; he had a privileged position in the Litany and, of all the martyrs, the reading of his life story was alone allowed to remain within the mass. During the eleventh century Stephen was included among the small group of saints to whom special prayers, stemming from the collects and expanded Litany, were framed and to whom St. Anselm had addressed his famous prayers.[129] In the quite separate context of describing Thomas's piety after his consecration and conversion, Herbert of Bosham stressed his customary fervour and tears of compunction when saying mass and his practice of using Anselm's prayers, especially when saying mass, but also elsewhere. They were practically his *enchiridion*, particularly conducive to promoting true contrition (3:210).[130] One can, of course, only speculate on the contribution they might have made to the context of devotion and compunction in which the biographers set Thomas's decision to invoke St. Stephen at his time of peril, when he recalled past weakness and tried to take fresh courage; they reveal him in the small hours of 13 October 1164 as a tearful suppliant beseeching divine aid through the merits of the holy martyr. The account of Stephen's trial in Acts 7 which forms the epistle for his feast, evokes in Anselm's long prayer to St. Stephen a meditation on compunction. The sinner stands before the tremendous Judge. "He is accused of many and great offences.

He is convicted by the witness of his conscience." He fears sentence of imprisonment and stands continually in danger. He begs St. Stephen make haste before he is condemned: Stephen's merits are so great they suffice for the sinner too. The prayer closes with a meditation on Stephen's martyrdom. His prayer of forgiveness for his enemies becomes a moving refrain and the sinner adopts it to invoke Stephen's aid that God "lay not his sins to his charge." Finally, the sinner describes his own discord, "the soul cannot follow the flesh without fear, and longs to be at rest."[131]

In this light several features in William FitzStephen's account of Becket's return to his trial from the votive mass, generally obscured by the more dramatic and durable image of the militant defender of holy Church, are thrown into relief. After a hostile reception, Thomas was left in silence with his clerks while the bishops were summoned into the king's presence. The biographer here recalls the rumours of Thomas' arrest and death threatened for that day: "No wonder that grief and groaning and contrition of heart beset the archbishop' (3:58). Countering Herbert of Bosham's advice that he lay excommunication on any who impiously threatened him, FitzStephen reminded Thomas "not so did God's holy apostles and martyrs when they were seized and lifted up on high; rather, should this occur, let him pray for them and forgive them. . . ." The point is argued in a letter to Thomas in his tribulation from one of his friends in 1164. Referring to the example of *Stephanus noster* in a context which clearly means Becket's martyred predecessor St. Elphege, the writer considers the dilemma of the pure and innocent when violently threatened by the impious: he is to imitate his Lord and offer himself up for immolation, uncomplaining — and praying for his enemies (5: 107–8 Ep. LIX). After the trial, Thomas privately exhorted his followers "let no word of bitterness proceed out of your mouth. Make no response to them that speak evil of you. . . ." (3:68). At FitzStephen's suggestion he fixed his attention on the uplifted Crucifix for consolation while delivering his final defence, imputing the blasts of adversity "not to the lord my king or any other man, but chiefly to my own sins" (3:64). In resolving anew to stand fast, he acknowledged his earlier lapse; "If we fell at Clarendon (for the flesh is weak) we ought to take fresh courage." However his appeal to Rome caused uproar; he sought a safe conduct but feared that the king's delay in answering "boded some future ill" and fled that night.

FitzStephen's account of Northampton,[132] now much admired for its historicity, is generally supposed to have been based on notes taken at the time. It is without obvious hagiographical stylization yet for contemporaries it must have carried echoes of the classic format of martyrs' trials. St. Stephen had been brought before a council of scribes and pharisees

descended from those who had persecuted the prophets (and Becket's episcopal colleagues were regularly identified with such in the correspondence
of the exile). The justice of Stephen's cause was evident from the inspired
manner of his speech and delivery and FitzStephen likewise commends
Becket's delivery. As Stephen was sustained by a vision of Christ, so Becket
gazed at an image of the Crucified. He began his address with the opening
salutation of Stephen's famous courtroom oration: "Viri, fratres . . ." and
was similarly denounced for blasphemy. This may reveal that Becket's
cause was that of the martyr's but the biographers tacitly admit that in 1164
Becket personally fell short of the ideal presented by Stephen "the perfect
martyr" who, without prompting, prayed for those who used him cruelly
and steadfastly continued his exposition of the true law before his accusers
until silenced by death. Becket's image on the last day of his trial is augmented in FitzStephen's account by the maxims on true sanctity which the
biographer alleges he offered the archbishop at the time, or which he
possibly considered on reflection would have been appropriate to the occasion. Either way, his picture is not of a triumphant second Stephen, but of a
still fearful penitent emerging from the votive mass, heroically striving but,
by the end of the day, failing to emulate his holy intercessor. Six years later
he was to surpass him.

It has been suggested above that the biographers present examples of Thomas's faltering courage, injudicious behavior and confessions
of weakness as steps by which he painfully came to comprehend and accept
his predestined vocation to martyrdom. Accordingly, they show that fear,
piety, and contrition were essential elements in his decision to offer up the
mass of the great intercessor St. Stephen to secure divine protection at his
trial. Although they indicate that it was open to hostile interpretation as a
polemical act of defiance, they make no attempt to show why its actual timing would have been particularly provocative. Instead, their emphasis is on
showing that (whatever his personal short-comings) Thomas's cause was
that of the Church, in life as in death. In this they were not simply project-
ing back an image forged in the liturgy and bloodshed of 26 and 29
December 1170, but reporting and reflecting an interpretation of current
events and of history made at the time by Thomas and his circle. Thomas's
viewpoint was not novel, his plight was not peculiar to him personally. It
was part of the sufferings traditionally endured by archbishops of Canterbury in defending the Church in England. The argument involved a veri-
table cult of spiritual ancestors.

John of Salisbury wrote to Thomas early in the exile, commend-
ing the memory of the holy patrons of Canterbury in the midst of the present storm and bidding him recall how zealous his immediate predecessor

Theobald had been until the day of his death.[133] Thomas also extolled his mentor Theobald, whom he had accompanied in defying the royal prohibition to attend the papal council of Rheims in 1148. Such fidelity to Rome, Thomas argued in a letter to Cardinal Boso in 1166, served as an example of the lesson of history. Alone among English bishops, the archbishops of Canterbury had been prepared to resist princes in order to defend the liberty of the Church, even though some of them suffered persecution, exile and death. And so it continues, observed Thomas, writing from his own exile (6:57–8 Ep. CCL). His letter echoes the advice he had received three days before celebrating the mass of St. Stephen and making his defence at Northampton. He had sought counsel from his ecclesiastical colleagues and although some had recommended he appease the king or resign his office, one had urged him "Far be it from the archbishop to consider the safety of his person and dishonour the church of Canterbury. . . . Not so did any of his predecessors, although they in their days suffered persecution" (3:55–6). The argument was to be amplified early in Thomas's exile in a letter by Herbert of Bosham. He praises his master's illustrious predecessors SS. Dunstan, Elphege, and Anselm, strongly emphasising their zeal for Canterbury and continued protection of its interests from beyond the grave. "In our present troubles they are our consolation. . . . We are protected by their merits, informed by their example" (5:340, Ep. CLXXVI). He recalls that Dunstan and Anselm suffered exile and persecution, while Elphege drank the full chalice of martyrdom, praying for his executors on bended knee as they stoned him "that in this too he might show himself to us another Stephen" (5:338).

This manifesto declaring that the Canterbury patrons offered protection for one who succeeded to their inheritance, illumines the testimony of Roger of Pontigny, probably received from Becket at Pontigny which he entered a few weeks after his flight from Northampton.[134] Describing Thomas's fear and contrition on hearing rumours during the trial of his threatened arrest and even death, the biographer quotes the counsel Thomas received from a certain religious "with whom, for a long while, he discussed the issue." The religious reminded him it was still possible to extricate himself from danger and escape the king's wrath. Nevertheless, "it is not your undertaking but God's." He counselled the archbishop to celebrate the mass of St. Stephen first thing in the morning before returning to the council. Thomas was to commend the cause of the Church before the Eucharist not only to Christ, the Virgin, and St. Stephen, but also "to our blessed apostle Gregory as well as to St. Elphege and to the other patrons of Canterbury" (4:45).

Invocation of sainted *antecessores* stressed the continuity and sancitity of the Canterbury office not only from the Norman Conquest but from the very foundation of the Roman Church in England. Understandably, there is no suggestion it was intended to trump Henry II's championing of his own predecessor Edward the Confessor whose feastday it was. But Thomas's commendation of the Church's cause to Gregory, the papal patron of his see, to its saints his predecessors and specifically to St. Elphege, whose manner of death had emulated that of the first martyr of the universal Church, succinctly summarised the archbishop's identification of his plight with that of Canterbury and therefore of the whole Chuch in England. He returned to his trial with a programme: "now I know what I do, for it is to preserve the peace of God for my person and the Church of the English" (3:57). His first encounter was with his own episcopal colleagues, not the king; his defense was based not simply on sacerdotalism but on his Canterbury office. When the bishop of London criticized him for taking up his cross, he replied: "If you were here in my place, you would feel otherwise."

William FitzStephen next censures the archbishop of York for infringing the privileges of Canterbury by appearing outside his province with his own processional cross. Thomas's conduct of his argument was highly controversial among his bishops, and doubts about his eligibility for sanctity probably lingered for some of FitzStephen's early readers. At this point he refers at length to a discussion between Robert of Melun, whom Thomas had consecrated bishop of Hereford, and other ecclesiastics, on whether the archbishop should be regarded as a martyr if killed in the cause of the freedom of the Church. Whether the debate took place then (or indeed at all) its position in the narrative is of interest. It serves to emphasise that the prospect of Becket's death was in the air (and implicitly makes his invocation of SS. Stephen and Elphege — and his flight — seem less extreme). And it is an occasion for arguing the case that martyrdom can have many causes other than the classic one of death for the faith. Significantly, the most detailed example cited in the discussion is Anselm's justification of Elphege's disputed claim to sanctity (3:60–1).

While it was customary in a saint's *Life* to glorify the relics and history of his monastic house (usually the hagiographer's own) by likening the saint to the established luminary of the place, the several references to St. Elphege in the *Lives* of St. Thomas cannot be so readily explained. Only one comes from a Christ Church monk. It was emphatically not as abbot that Thomas was celebrated and Elphege's reputation must, if anything, have been augmented by association with St. Thomas rather than vice versa. Although salvaged from neglect by Anselm and Christ Church hagiography, honoured by an altar next to the High Altar at Canterbury and an increasing number of feasts there, Elphege was not a national figure.[135] Almost nothing was known about him. Yet the biographers' testimony that Elphege figured in the formulation of Thomas's large claims is confirmed by letters such as those already cited. Elphege's murder was obviously crucial here. But perhaps it was Elphege's relative obscurity as well, his safe distance from the time and circumstances of Thomas's situation, which made him a more telling authority to cite than Anselm, with whom Thomas felt affinity but who had alienated king, bishops, and the community of Christ Church before peacefully expiring on a bed of sackcloth and ashes.

Thomas's claim that his sufferings were those of a great tradition culminated in the "splendid sermon" he preached in the presence of his predecessors' tombs and altars at Canterbury on Christmas Day 1170: "and when he made mention of the holy fathers of the church of Canterbury who were therein confessors, he said that they already had one archbishop who was a martyr, St. Elphege, and it was possible that in a short time they would have yet another" (3:130). William of Canterbury, a monk of Christ Church and guardian of St. Thomas's tomb, who had been ordained deacon by the Archbishop shortly before that Christmas sermon, pointed to the saint's combination of the two traditions of sanctity exemplified by the martyr and confessors who were his predecessors. Even in life, notably his endurance of admonitions at the Council of Clarendon, Thomas had recalled St. Elphege's endurance of martyrdom (1:16). Thomas's commendation of the Church's cause to St. Elphege and the Canterbury patrons in 1164, and the citation of them in exile as precedents for his own actions, though derided by opponents, was shown by the biographers to have been prophetic. He stood fast at the approach of his murderers "that under the wonderful providence of God he might receive death in front of the sepulchres of his dead co-archbishops" (4:131, 1:133). He invoked the Canterbury patrons at the moment of death; two writers specify that he actually named St. Elphege.[136] A third, Edward Grim, reserves until his description of Thomas's yearning for martyrdom and refusal to escape, an account of what the archbishop is reported to have said in the hearing of many since his return from exile: "You have here a martyr, Elphege, beloved of God and a true saint. The divine compassion will provide you with yet another; he will not tarry" (2:434).

Becket's ominous reception by royal officials and the young king on his return from exile to Canterbury is attested in a contemporary letter by John of Salisbury: "We await God's salvation in great danger"; the archbishop and his attendants are threatened by "the snares of those who thirst for the church's blood."[137] In the atmosphere of impending doom at Canterbury when the archbishop celebrated High Mass on the feast of Stephen, 26 December 1170, members of his household, including three future biographers, must have recalled his extraordinary celebration of that feast on 13 October 1164, allegedly in fear of his life. Herbert of Bosham later described Thomas's martyrdom in terms of the Priest of the Most High sacrificing himself to the Most High "in the temple and before the altar" (3:498). In a narrative larded with scriptural allusions by a master in spiritual interpretation, this apparently non-historical detail may well allude to the Gospel for St. Stephen's day. As has been seen, it was evoked in a nocturn lection for St. Thomas's own feast. Later that St. Stephen's day, Herbert of Bosham was ordered to Sens on a final mission for the archbishop, so was not present on the twenty-ninth to offer his customary radical counsel. But Thomas had absorbed previous lessons. The Anonymous of Lambeth notes the actual location of the murder, but comments that the saint had intended to take up his stand before the High Altar "to pour forth his blood for Christ in the very spot where he had been wont to offer up Christ." The words of the St. Stephen's day liturgy may still have been ringing in Thomas's ears, as they patently were for his biographer when he described the sacrilege: "If the blood of Abel . . . and the blood of Zacharias who fell between the temple and the altar call out to the Lord from the earth, how much more terribly doth intone the blood in front of the altar by which the Holy of Holies was profaned?" (4:133). On hearing of the outrage, the archbishop of Sens immediately informed the pope in a letter which already accords with the general interpretation expressed by Herbert of Bosham in his biography of c.1186–87. Herbert may have been on hand in Sens to help interpret the news from Canterbury; one manuscript attributes the letter to him.[139] It describes Thomas standing before the altar embracing the cross, offering himself up—and praying for his persecutors. This powerful myth was not created by the biographies but was already present in the news reports.

In Conclusion

This closing, liturgical image of St. Thomas is appropriate. The role of liturgical events, language and allusions in his life and biographies has here been stressed as a body of material which is often undervalued as a historical source. The liturgy itself embodies an allegorical interpretation of Scripture which not only celebrates and interprets past historical events and anticipates their future consumation, but refers directly to the present celebrant and congregation. While this would usually have a spiritual application, in certain circumstances and times, liturgy could continue to make a very dramatic, public and ritualised exegetical commentary on current events.

A canonization, translation, episcopal *Adventus* or votive mass could make a powerful political statement. Liturgy could both influence and express contemporary attitudes and, it has been suggested here, even behavior. The sheer number and quality of the early Becket biographies and the quantity of relevant correspondence, as illumined by the scholarship of the last twenty years or so, provides an unrivalled illustration of the role of allegorical language, alongside the developing languages of law, disputation and reporting, in the writing of history in the twelfth century. Certain historical events automatically evoked for eyewitnesses the universal and poetic language of liturgy, nothing more so than Thomas Becket's death, which was perceived by his supporters, and then revealed to others, as a sacramental sacrifice, effecting what it symbolised.

It has been seen that the biographers used, with restraint, the conventional devices of dreams and apparitions, together with the spiritual interpretation of historical events, to show that Thomas's death was predestined and prophesied in the time-honored manner of saints. But the epistolary evidence shows that, in their depiction of Archbishop Thomas himself using the techniques of spiritual interpretation to promote his cause, the biographers were reporting a view of events taken at the time in his household and intelligible to others, though doubtless regarded by opponents simply as the misguided and presumptuous polemic of contemporary political debate. Thomas's uncompromising identification of his cause with that of Christ's Church exasperated contemporaries as much as it has done some modern critics. Gilbert Foliot thought Thomas rashly and lightly invoked martyrdom. Even the normally sympathetic King Louis was provoked into saying to him at Montmirail in 1169, rather sarcastically, "My lord archbishop, do you seek to be more than a saint?" Herbert of Bosham could report the incident ironically, however, for ten years later the same king had come as a pilgrim to the shrine at Canterbury (3:425,538). Thomas's increasingly frequent, explicit and public predictions of his death during the last months could therefore be revealed not simply as conforming to a hagiographical stereotype, or as eyewitness accounts of his use of inflamatory propagandist formulae. His predictions are interpreted as well-attested historical proofs of his predestined and lonely vocation to martyrdom, culminating in the willing acceptance of death which was implicit in his decision to return from exile. (3:113) Herbert of Bosham implied that he understood this aspect of his master's white martyrdom all along, but William FitzStephen hints that until the archbishop's death, even those most intimate with the formulation of his defence of the *sacerdotium* did not fully appreciate that he meant what he said. On his return from exile Thomas explained to his clerks that the cause of the Church could not be concluded without the shedding of blood. He made spiritual preparation for the end. They "did not understand, attending only to the words. But later, those who saw the deeds, remembered the words" (3:126–7).

The biographers' claims for Thomas's sanctity did not rest with their elaboration of the circumstances of his death, the continuing testimony of the posthumous miracles or even the cause for which he died, crucial though these were in securing canonization and perpetuating his cult. As the Evangelists, particularly St. Matthew, had used scriptural allusions to show that the life and passion of Christ had fulfilled the requirements of the Messianic prophecies of the Old Covenant, so the twelfth-century writers used Old Testament typology and Gospel parallels to show that in his life and passion, Thomas of Canterbury fulfilled the requirements of sanctity more completely than other saints, exemplifying both white and red martyrdom in his imitation of Christ.

But the biographers also inherited a longstanding tradition of using the medium of a saint's *Life* for the history of the monastic house or see, privileges and relics associated with him, or for events of more than local significance, this historical material in turn helping to demonstrate the truth of the testimony about the saint. Hagiographical techniques and the historical evidence of eyewitness reports and archival records were not mutually exclusive, neither did their use distinguish the monastic from the secular writer, the ignorant from the educated. Hagiographic conventions are most obvious at predictable moments such as the saint's birth, conversion, and death. However, it has been suggested above that their use was, perhaps, more extensive than is sometimes acknowledged and that it did not invariably take the form of pious purple passages detachable from an otherwise historical narrative. Still less can "hagiographical" and "historical" elements be readily distinguished to denote the fanciful and the true, or to represent a hierarchy of truths. Rather, the biographers' interpretation of history and therefore their reporting of the past, was affected more profoundly by the notion of sanctity traditionally expressed through venerated conventions. Like the Gospel writers—and Herbert of Bosham actually referred to himself, frequently, as "the disciple who wrote these things"— the biographers wrote from their experience of an event which transformed and made sense of the past and whose significance was still being miraculously confirmed. Seen from this vantage point the conventions were renewed, spiritual and historical truths were one.

NOTES

I am most grateful to Dr. Bernard Hamilton and Professor C. N. L. Brooke for their encouragement and helpful comments on earlier versions of this paper. Any remaining errors are my own.

[1] Beryl Smalley, *The Becket Conflict and the Schools,* (Oxford, 1973), p. 201; David Knowles, "Archbishop Thomas Becket. A Character Study," Raleigh Lecture, (London, 1949), p. 5.

[2] J. C. Russell, "The Canonization of Opposition to the King in Angevin Englnd," *Anniversary Essays in Medieval History Presented to C. H. Haskins,* ed. C. H. Taylor (Boston, 1922), p. 280. D. W. Rollason, "The Cults of Murdered Royal Saints in Anglo-Saxon England;" *Anglo-Saxon England,* 11, ed. P. Clemoes, (Cambridge,1983), p. 22.

[3] Charles Duggan, "The Significance of the Becket Dispute in the History of the English Church," *The Ampleforth Journal,* 75.3 (1970), p. 367; D. Knowles, "Archbishop Thomas Becket—The Saint," *The Canterbury Chronicle,* 65 (1970), p. 10 and *Thomas Becket* (London, 1970), pp. 53-4; J. W. Alexander, "The Becket Controversy in Recent Historiography," *Journal of British Studies,* 9 (1970), pp. 4-7.

[4] Proclamation of Henry VIII, 16 November 1538 quoted by Tancred Borenius, *Thomas Becket in Art,* (London, 1932), App. I.

[5] Antonia Gransden, *Historical Writing in England c. 550-c. 1307,* (London, 1974), p. 297.

[6] "Becket. A Character Study," p. 4; "Becket—The Saint," pp. 17, 7.

[7] *Vita Sancti Anselmi. The Life of St. Anselm, Archbishop of Canterbury by Eadmer,* ed. Richard W. Southern (London, 1962), pp. 50-4.

[8] *The Life of Bishop Wilfrid by Eddius Stephanus,* ed. Bertram Colgrave (Cambridge, 1927).

[9] A. Gransden, *Historical Writing,* p. 106.

[10] *Vita Sancti Anselmi,* pp. 149, 152; Benedicta Ward, 'Miracles and History. A Reconsideration of the Miracle Stories used by Bede' in *Famulus Christi. Essays in Commemoration of the 13th Centenary of the Venerable Bede,* ed. Gerald Bonner, (London, 1976), pp. 70-6.

[11] *Vita S. Anselmi,* p. 2.

[12] *Materials for the History of Thomas Becket,* ed. James C. Robertson *(Rolls Series,* 1875-79), vols. 1-4. References will be made in parenthesis in the text to the volume and page numbers of this work.

Vol. 1:   William of Canterbury, *Vita, Passio et Miracula*

Vol. 2:   Benedict of Peterborough, *Passio* pp. 1-19, *Miracula* pp. 21-281; John of Salisbury, *Vita,* pp. 301-22, supplement of Alan of Tewkesbury pp. 299-352; Edward Grim, *Vita* pp. 353-450.

Vol. 3:   William FitzStephen, *Vita* pp. 1-154; Herbert of Bosham, *Vita,* pp. 155-534.

Vol. 4:   Roger of Pontigny ("Anon. I"), *Vita,* pp. 1-79; The Anonymous of Lambeth ("Anon. II"), *Vita* pp. 80-144; "Anon. IV," *Passio* pp. 186-95.

13 Anne Duggan, *Thomas Becket: A Textual History of his Letters*, (Oxford, 1980), Preface: p. 226; cf. pp. 175-203 for the use made of the Becket correspondence by Edward Grim, William of Canterbury, William FitzStephen, Herbert of Bosham.

14 "The French Mss. of the Becket Correspondence," *Thomas Becket. Actes du Colloque International de Sédières 1973*, ed. Raymonde Foreville, (Paris, 1975), pp. 2, 33. The Becket correspondence is printed in *Materials for the History of Thomas Becket, Rolls Series, 1881-85* vols. 5-7; critical modern editions of parts of the correspondence in *The Letters and Charters of Gilbert Foliot* ed. Adrian Morey and C. N. L. Brooke (Cambridge, 1967) and *The Letters of John of Salisbury*, vol. 2 (1163-80) ed. W. J. Millor and C. N. L. Brooke (Oxford, 1979). References to John of Salisbury's letters will cite the Epistle number and the page number of this edition.

15 For the dating, interrelationship and the authors of the biographies *v* Emmanuel Walberg, *La tradition hagiographique de Thomas Becket avant la fin de XIIᵉ siècle* (Paris, 1929); A. Gransden, *Historical Writing*, pp. 296-301; A. Duggan, *Becket. A Textual History of his Letters*, pp. 175-204.

16 For recent work on individual biographers *v* Margaret A. Harris "Alan of Tewkesbury and his Letters," *Studia Monastica* 18 (1976), pp. 77-108; Mary Cheney, "William FitzStephen and his Life of Archbishop Thomas," *Church and Government in the Middle Ages. Essays presented to C. R. Cheney* ed. C. N. L. Brooke, G. Martin, D. Owen (Cambridge, 1976), pp. 139-156; B. Smalley, *The Becket Conflict and the Schools*, pp. 59-86 for Herbert of Bosham, pp. 87-108 for John of Salisbury.

17 A Gransden, *Historical Writing*, p. 297.

18 James Harper, "John Cassian and Sulpicius Severus," *Church History* 34 (1965), pp. 371-3 and Patrick Wormald, "Bede and Benedict Biscop," *Familus Christi*, pp. 151, 167 n. 86 for early examples; R. W. Southern, *St. Anselm and his Biographer*, (Cambridge, 1963), pp. 323-4 for the tradition of commemorative monastic biography in the tenth and eleventh centuries; Benedicta Ward, *Miracles and the Medieval Mind*, (London, 1982), pp. 171-177, for the restrained role of miracles in the *Lives* of SS. Anselm, Ailred and Hugh of Lincoln.

19 Ed. C. Horstmann, *Early English Text Society* 87, (London, 1887), pp. 159-160. For full liturgical references to the *Adventus* ceremony and its connection with Palm Sunday and Advent, *v* Ernst Kantorowicz, "The King's Advent and the enigmatic panels in the doors of Santa Sabina," *Art Bulletin*, 26 (1944), pp. 207-231. The last recorded time Henry II visited Canterbury before coming as a penitent to St. Thomas's tomb, had been in the company of the archbishop at the Palm Sunday procession of 1163. R. W. Eyton, *Court, Household and Itinerary of King Henry II*, (London, 1878), p. 60.

20 These five "holy Tuesdays" in Becket's life clearly impressed contemporaries. The coincidence is remarked in the Latin biographies, (Herbert of Bosham, 3:326) and in the vernacular work of the French biographer, Garnier of Pont-Ste-Maxence: J. Shirley, *Garnier's Becket*, (London, 1975), p. 156. It is perpetuated in the *Early South English Legendary*, p. 177 and in the fifth lection at Matins in the Office for the feast of St. Thomas's Translation, *Breviarium Ad*

Usum Insignis Ecclesiae Sarum, fasc. III, ed. F. Procter and C. Wordsworth, (Cambridge, 1886), p. 447.

[21] For the miracle collections *v* Raymonde Foreville, 'Les Miracula S. Thomae Cantuariensis', *Actes du 97e Congrès National des Sociétés Savantes, Nantes, 1972*, (Paris, 1979), pp. 443–468, reprinted in *Thomas Becket dans la tradition historique et hagiographique*, (London, 1981), and Benedicta Ward, *Miracles and the Medieval Mind*, pp. 89–109.

[22] *Acts of the Christian Martyrs* ed. J. Musurillo, (Oxford, 1972), p. 797.

[23] Ibid., pp. 271, 129; *Materials for the History of Thomas Becket*, 2:320, 437; 3:498, 506; 4:77.

[24] 3:499; G. M. Spiegel, "The Cult of St. Denis and Capetian Kingship," *Journal of Medieval History*, I (1975), p. 50, n.8.

[25] D. Knowles, *The Monastic Order*, (Cambridge, 1940), p. 319; T. Borenius, *Thomas Becket in Art*, pp. 49, 83–4 and plates; P. A. Newton, "Some New Materials for the Study of the Iconography of Thomas Becket," *Actes . . . de Sédières*, p. 256.

[26] Edwin Abbott, *St. Thomas of Canterbury. His Death and Miracles*, 2 vols., (London, 1898), 1, pp. 108–9. The various biographers' accounts of the martyrdom may be conveniently compared in Abbott's parallel texts.

[27] From the influential account of the martyrdom of Perpetua and Felicitas, *Acts of the Christian Martyrs*, pp. 131, 107.

[28] *Life of Bishop Wilfrid*, p. 39; pp. 15, 19, 29 for examples of such parallelism. Gregory the Great's *Dialogues*, Bk. II, a most authoritative influence on hagiography, had stressed that St. Benedict's miracles in imitation of biblical saints were performed by the power of the single "Spirit of all the just," manifesting the grace of Christ.

[29] This iconography is already established in the earliest extant illustration of the scene, c. 1180, prefacing a copy of John of Salisbury's letter describing the martyrdom (B. L. MS Cotton, Claudius B.II) and also on the earliest example, c.1190, of the 45 surviving Limoges reliquary châsse. *V* catalogue of the Arts Council of Gt. Britain exhibition, *English Romanesque Art, 1066–1200*, (London, 1984), nos. 72, 292. For other examples, *v* T. Borenius, *Thomas Becket in Art*, pl. XXVII, XXVIII, XXX–XXXIX; Marie-Madeleine Gauthier, "Le meurtre dans la cathédrale, thème iconographique médiéval," *Acts . . . de Sédières;* Raymonde Foreville, "La diffusion du culte de Thomas Becket dans la France avant la fin du XIIᵉ siècle," *Cahiers de civilisation médiévale, XIX* (Poitiers, 1976), pp. 360–65, and plates.

[30] Op. cit., pl. 18, reliquary from Guelph Treasure, Cleveland Museum of Art, c. 1200.

[31] Ep. 305, pp. 725–39,

[32] A. Gransden, *Historical Writing*, p. 297.

[33] Edward Grim 2:437–8; William FitzStephen 3:143; Anon. IV 4:194; Anon. X 4:436. *La vie de saint Thomas le martyr*, ed. E. Wallberg (Lund, 1922), p. 190 for Garnier's metrical *Life* of 1172–4; *Thomas Saga Erkibyskups*, ed. Eirikr Magnusson (*Rolls Series*, London, 1875), vol. 1, pp. 552–9 for the Icelandic compilation.

[34] *PL* 76:1263-4; 22:905; 4:249-50. The exegetical tradition behind this imagery is discussed in J. O'Reilly, *"Candidus et Rubicundus* in the *Lives* of Thomas Becket," *Analecta Bollandiana,* 99 (1981), pp. 303-314; *v* also Peter Brown, *The Cult of the Saints,* (Chicago and London, 1981), p. 77 for non-exegetical examples of the antique *topos.*

[35] Translations of William FitzStephen are from George Greenaway, *The Life and Death of Thomas Becket,* (London, 1961), pp. 157-8.

[36] R. W. Southern, *St. Anselm and his Biographer,* p. 330.

[37] *The Life of Ailred of Rievaulx by Walter Daniel,* ed. M. Powicke, (London, 1950), p. 81, also p. 78: "I marvel at the charity of Ailred more than I should if he had raised four men from the dead." *V* B. Ward, *Miracles and the Medieval Mind,* pp. 98, 191 on the importance of the papal canonization process in sanctioning this trend in twelfth century biography, which regarded virtue as the basis of sanctity, "to be established beyond all possible doubt by an account of the life of the saint" and an authenticated and improving account of miracles as evidence of divine approval.

[38] Ep. 325, p. 803. John here testifies to one of the many examples of punishment miraculously administered to those who doubted the power or sanctity of St. Thomas or showed him insufficient honour.

[39] 3:168, 173. For Becket's career as Chancellor, *v* L. B. Radford, *Thomas of London before his Consecration,* (Canterbury, 1894), pp. 153-184.

[40] *La vie de saint Thomas le martyr,* 1.490; J. Shirley, *Garnier's Becket,* p. 14.

[41] This is John of Salisbury, ruefully putting the case for the opposition, Ep. 187, p. 237.

[42] Louis Gougaud, *Devotional and Ascetic Practices in the Middle Ages,* (London, 1927), pp. 205-210; Augustine McGregor, "Martyrdom and the Monastic Life," *Hallel, Review of Monastic Spirituality and Liturgy,* 9 (1981), pp. 57-72; Clare Stancliffe, "Red, white and blue martyrdom," *Ireland in Early Medieval Europe. Studies in Memory of Kathleen Hughes,* ed. D. Whitelock, R. McKitterick, D. Dumville, (Cambridge, 1982), pp. 29-32.

[43] K. Hughes, "The Changing Theory and Practice of Irish Pilgrimage," *Journal of Ecclesiastical History,* 11 (1960), 143-151; Arnold Angenendt, *Monachi Peregrini. Studien zu Pirmin und den Monastischen Vorstellungen des frühen Mittelalters,* (Munich, 1972), pp. 137-8, 146-7, 151-2.

[44] Eadmer, *Historia Novorum in Anglia,* ed. M. Rule (*Rolls Series.* London, 1884), pp. 87-8.

[45] Giles Constable, 'Monachisme et pèlerinage au Moyen Age,' *Revue Historique,* 258 (1977), pp. 3-27; Jean Leclercq, 'Monachisme et pérégrination du IXe au XIIe siècle,' *Studia Monastica,* 3 (1961), pp. 33-52.

[46] Ep. 179, p. 191; *La vie de s. Thomas Becket,* 1. 2616, pp. 80-1.

[47] "The Place of the Cistercian Order in the Early Years of the Becket Controversy," Bernard McGinn, *The Golden Chain. A Study in the Theological Anthropology of Isaac of Stella,* (Washington, 1972), pp. 34-50. I am indebted to Fr. Hugh McCaffery of Mt. Melleray Abbey for this reference.

[48] Anne Duggan, *Actes . . . de Sédières,* p. 35.

[49] 3:197, 202, 404. For the influence of Sulpicius Severus' *Vita S. Martini* "as the paradigm of the life of a monk who also held episcopal or abbatial authority," particularly in the *Lives* of St. Ailred and St. Hugh, *v* B. Ward, *Miracles and the Medieval Mind*, pp. 173, 268, n.21.

[50] E.g. Augustine, *In Iohannis evangelium*, xlvi, 7 in *Corpus Christianorum*, Series Latina, t. xxxvi, pars viii (Turnhoult, 1954), p. 402. Tertullian's *De fuga in persecutione* is extreme in its recommendation of martyrdom, but its insistence that Matt. 10.23 was applicable only to the apostles was an argument which could readily be used to undermine any citation of the Gospel passage as a justification of flight. It may help explain the attempts to represent Becket as a latter-day apostle. *V* T. D. Barnes, *Tertullian, A Historical and Literary Study*, (Oxford, 1971), pp. 176–196 for the early Christian debate about flight.

[51] *Acts of the Christian Martyrs*, p. 281.

[52] Ep. 187, p. 237; Ep. 225, pp. 391–3. William of Canterbury recounts, c. 1173, a vision at the time of Becket's flight, in which a hedgehog with the book of the Acts of the Apostles on its back was driven into the sea by the royal hunt (1:40–42). Beryl Smalley notes it "signified that St. Paul had set the example of fleeing from his persecutors, as Becket did," *The Becket Conflict and the Schools*, p. 108. The vision would seem an accurate reflection of the contemporary debate described here.

[53] "The Archbishop and the Hedgehog," *Law, Church and Society; Essays in honour of Stephen Kuttner*, ed. K. Pennington and R. Somerville, (Pennsylvania, 1977), pp. 167–184 (p. 173). *The Letters and Charters Gilbert Foliot*, no. 170, pp. 229–243 for the text of *Multiplicem nobis*.

[54] *La vie de saint Thomas le martyr*, 11.3636,3861; *Garnier's Becket*, pp. 97, 102.

[55] *Thomas Saga*, I, p. 28; R. Somerville, *Pope Alexander III and the Council of Tours*, (Los Angeles, 1977), p. 14.

[56] *La vie de saint Thomas le martyr*, 11.2360–72; *Garnier's Becket*, p. 63.

[57] *Historia Novorum in Anglia*, pp. 60–1. I am indebted to Dr. J.-M. Picard for the observation that the contrast between eloquence and true wisdom is a classical topos too.

[58] C. F. Altman, "Two Types of Opposition and the Structure of Latin Saints' Lives," *Medievalia et Humanistica*, 6 (1975), pp. 1–4.

[59] *Historical Writing in England c.550–c.1307*, p. 297.

[60] Ep. 175, pp. 163, 165. Also Ep. 150, p. 49; Ep. 167, p. 99; Ep. 168, p. 107; Ep. 187, p. 237.

[61] 2:324–5, translation from *English Historical Documents*, 2, ed. D. C. Douglas and G. W. Greenaway, (London, 1953), p. 723.

[62] W. L. Warren, *Henry II*, (London, 1973), p. 491.

[63] Beryl Smalley, *The Study of the Bible in the Middle Ages*, (2nd ed. Oxford, 1952; repr. Notre Dame, 1978), p. 252, n.2.

[64] 2:433–4; Herbert of Bosham also alludes to John 10.12, 3:483.

[65] *Breviarium Ad Usum Insignis Ecclesiae Sarum*, fasc. I, ed. F. Procter and C. Wordsworth, (Cambridge, 1882), third nocturn, p. cclv.

[67] 5:490–512, Ep. ccxxiii. As early as January 1165, John of Salisbury was warning Becket to seek papal protection against encroachments on the possessions of Canterbury during his exile, Ep. 144, p. 35.

68 *St. Anselm and his Biographer*, pp. 364–6.

69 John of Salisbury, Ep. 168, p. 111. Becket's vigil ended on Ascension Day, June 2nd, which in 1166 "concurred with that of St. Drausius," J. C. Robertson, *Becket, Archbishop of Canterbury*, (London, 1859), p. 184.

70 5:282, Ep. CLIV.

71 John of Salisbury, Ep. 288, p. 643.

72 Anne Heslin, "The Coronation of the Young King in 1170," *Studies in Church History* 2, ed. G. J. Cuming, (London, 1965), p. 166.

73 *Letters and Charters of Gilbert Foliot*, no. 170, p. 239–40.

74 Ep. 303, p. 713.

75 H. Mayr-Harting, *The Coming of Christianity to Anglo-Saxon England*, (London, 1972), p. 141.

76 *V* above, nn. 13 and 14.

77 "The Becket Dispute and the Criminous Clerks," *Bulletin of the Institute of Historical Research* 35 (1962), pp. 1–28; "The Reception of Canon Law in England in the later Twelfth Century," *Proceedings of the Second International Congress of Medieval Canon Law*,(Vatican City, 1965) pp. 360–5. For the text of the Constitutions of Clarendon and a detailed commentary, particularly on ch. 3, *v Councils and Synods with Other Documents Relating to the English Church*, vol. 1, Part II 1066–1204 ed. D. Whitelock, M. Brett, C. N. L. Brooke (Oxford, 1981), pp. 855–83.

78 *Actes . . . de Sédières*, pp. 130–1; "The Becket Dispute and the Criminous Clerk," pp. 17–18.

79 *The Becket Conflict and the Schools*, pp. 127–128; 124ff.

80 "The Becket Dispute and Two Decretist Traditions: the Bolognese Masters revisited and some new Anglo-Norman Texts," *Journal of Medieval History* 4 (1978), pp. 348, 353–4. Fraher notes that William of Canterbury used the *Summa Rufini* extremely selectively in his account of Becket's argument at Clarendon quoting out of context and omitting passages favourable to the king's case.

81 *Addenda et Corrigenda* p. 6 to the Variorum reprint of Charles Duggan's articles on the Becket Dispute and decretal collections *Canon Law in Medieval England*, (London, 1982); C. N. L. Brooke in *The Letters of John of Salisbury* 2, p. xii.

82 *The Letters and Charters of Gilbert Foliot*, no. 170, p. 234.

83 Ep. 187, p. 233.

84 A. Duggan, *Thomas Becket. A Textual History of his Letters*, p. 200.

85 *Policraticus*, ed. C. C. J. Webb (Oxford, 1909) vol. 2, pp. 6–7, conflating Christ's trials before the High Priest and Pilate (Matt. 26.65 and John 19.12 and the charges of blasphemy against God and Caesar. Dr. Smalley discusses the relevance of the text to the Becket dispute but without reference to the biographies, *The Becket Dispute and the Schools*, pp. 100–101. R. Foreville discussed the general relationship between Becket and *Policraticus* in *L'église et la royauté en Angleterre sous Henri II Plantagenet* (Paris, 1943), pp. 260–3.

86 Ep. 175, pp. 155, 159.

87 Ep. 244, pp. 487–9; also Ep. 295, p. 681.

88 Ep. 186, pp. 227–9.

89 *Historia Novorum in Anglia*, pp. 64–5, 104; *Vita Anselmi*, p. 86.

90 Ep. 305, p. 729; Musurillo, *Acts of the Christian Martyrs*, p. 7.

[91] Ibid., pp. 287, 307.

[92] *Letters and Charters of Gilbert Foliot*, no. 170, p. 240.

[93] *Henry II*, p. 487.

[94] In late twelfth century England "national sentiment developed in opposition to the policies of the Crown . . . a strong sentimental attachment to the past became one of the chief instruments of opposition to the Crown"; the canonization of Edward the Confessor was part of the magnates' appropriation of the Anglo-Saxon past, R. W. Southern, *Medieval Humanism and Other Essays*, (London, 1970), pp. 147, 155. C. N. L. Brooke designated the Westminster movement for the canonization as "the religious counterpart to the growing opinion that King Edward represented the tradition of Old England, that good law must be related to the 'law of King Edward' and good kings to his family," *The Saxon and Norman Kings*, (London, 1963), p. 208.

[95] E. W. Kemp, *Canonization and Authority in the Western Church*, (Oxford, 1948), p. 89.

[96] Printed in Frank Barlow, *Edward the Confessor*, (London, 1970), pp. 312–315; *The Letters and Charters of Gilbert Foliot*, no. 133, pp. 175–7.

[97] Herbert of Bosham, 3:335–6; Garnier of Ponte-Sainte Maxence adds that Foliot accused Becket of having sung the Mass 'pur sorcerie . . . E el despit le rei', *La Vie de Thomas Becket*, p. 54, 11, 1559–1560.

[98] *Vita Aedwardi Regis*, ed. F. Barlow, (London, 1962), pp. 9–10; *Edward the Confessor*, pp. 61–4, 119, n. 2.

[99] A. Morey and C. N. L. Brooke, *Gilbert Foliot and his Letters*, (Cambridge, 1965), pp. 176–7. For the probable use of chrism at the coronation of the young Henry, v P. E. Schramm, *A History of the English Coronation*, (London, 1939), pp. 126–127.

[100] Bernard Scholz, "The Canonization of Edward the Confessor," *Speculum*, 36 (1961), pp. 50–60. "Henry's support of the canonization had thus a purpose similar to the designation of his devoted chancellor to the highest office of the English Church," p. 57.

[101] Henry Mayr-Harting, "Hilary Bishop of Chichester (1147–69) and Henry II," *English Historical Review* 78 (1963), p. 224; A. Saltman, *Theobald Archbishop of Canterbury*, (London, 1956), pp. 44–5.

[102] C. Duggan notes that Ralph de Diceto "makes explicit comparison with the archbishops of Mainz and Cologne as imperial chancellors, and records Henry's anger at Becket's resignation of the chancellorship on election to Canterbury," "Bishop John and Archdeacon Richard of Poitiers. Their Roles in the Becket Dispute and its Aftermath," *Actes . . . de Sédières*, p. 74, n. 20 and 'Ralph de Diceto, Henry II and Becket with an Appendix on Decretal Letters', *Authority and Power: Studies on Medieval Law and Government in Honour of Walter Ullmann*, ed. B. Tierney and P. Linehan, (Cambridge, 1980), p. 66.

[103] Ep. 168, p. 106; Ep. 187, p. 245.

[104] R. W. Southern, *St. Anselm and his Biographer*, p. 338; Raymonde de Foreville, *L'église et la royauté en Angleterre sous Henri II Plantagenet*, pp. 270–4.

[105] F. Barlow, *The English Church, 1066–1154* (London, 1979), p. 302.

[106] B. W. Scholz, "The Canonization of Edward the Confessor," p. 57; F. Barlow, *Edward the Confessor*, p. 284; R. Somerville, *Pope Alexander III and the Council of Tours*, pp. 59-60.

[107] *St. Anselm and his Biographer*, p. 340. The only years in Becket's archiepiscopate when 7 April fell on a Sunday liturgically appropriate for such a ceremony were 1163 and 1168; the latter seems improbable.

[108] "Thomas Becket as Patron of the Arts. The Wall Painting of St. Anselm's Chapel at Canterbury Cathedral," *Art History*, 3 (1980), p. 363, 370 n. 13. Professor Nilgen does not discuss the image of of SS. Peter and Paul in Anselm's own *Prayers and Meditations*, a book Becket is known to have used constantly; *v* Part II below, and nn. 129-131.

[108] Art. cit., p. 362. It is suggested (pp. 363-6) that traditional exegesis on the subject of the surviving painting (showing St. Paul, newly saved from shipwreck but attacked by a viper) would have had a topical application to the attacks on Becket following his recent salvation from the spiritual shipwreck of earthly vanities at his conversion. Professor Nilgen set this commission in its artistic context in a paper, "Intellectuality and Splendour: Thomas Becket as Patron of the Arts," delivered to the *Symposium on Patronage of the Arts in England, 1066-1200* (Victoria and Albert Museum, London, 1984). In another paper there on "Prior Wibert's Wall-Paintings" (i.e. in the crypt of Christ Church), Dr. Deborah Kahn gave further stylistic and archaeological support for assigning the painting of St. Paul and the viper in the chapel of St. Anselm above to the early 1160s. Neither speaker referred to John of Salisbury's letter to the subprior of Christ Church, 1167, chastising him and the community for failure to support their abbot and archbishop in exile while thoughtlessly squandering money on pictures and delighting the eyes of the ignorant multitude with vain paintings (Ep. 243, p. 480). This may refer, not to the Pauline scheme in the chapel of St. Anselm (as suggested in p. 480, n. 2), but to the decoration of the chapels of St. Gabriel and the Holy Innocents immediately below, following extensive rebuilding of the crypt to strengthen the lateral towers, c. 1160.

[110] F. Barlow, *Edward the Confessor*, p. 282, notes the presence of both Ailred and Prior Laurence at a council held at Westminster in March 1163.

[111] F. Barlow, *The English Church, 1066-1154*, (London, 1979), p. 302.

[112] *The Episcopal Colleagues of Archbishop Thomas Becket*, (Cambridge, 1951), Appendix IV, pp. 164-5.

[113] G. M. Spiegel, "The Cult of Saint Denis and Capetian Kingship," pp. 43-69.

[114] F. Barlow, *Edward the Confessor*, App. D, pp. 309-24 for texts of surviving letters of petition.

[115] In the letter prefixed to the *Life* of Edward; *v Life of Ailred*, pp. xlvii–li forAilred's sympathies with Henry II and his friendship with Gilbert Foliot. *Vita Aedwardi Regis*, ed. F. Barlow, (London, 1962), pp. 130-2.

[116] M. Powicke, *Life of Ailred*, pp. xxxvii ff. cites evidence (omitted from Walter Daniel's *Life*) for Ailred's patriotic spirituality and for his role in powerfully reconciling the old and new orders in Church and kingdom. Particularly interesting in

the present context is Ailred's work on the *Saint of Hexham*, part of which he probably read as the homily at the translation of their relics there in 1154–5 after their "adoption" by the new Austin canons who had actually displaced Ailred's own forebearers from the custodianship of the shrine.

[117] J. C. Russell, "The Canonization of Opposition to the King in Angevin England," p. 280. The *Thomas Saga* says "the highest lords of the land forbid, under peril of life and limbs, any one to call archbishop Thomas a holy man or even a martyr. But . . . threaten the people with all its might as the king's power would, the pilgrimages to the archbishop's grave multiply all the more," vol. 2, p. 91.

[118] W. D. Wixom, "A Reliquary Châsse attributed to Canterbury, c. 1200," paper read at the *Symposium on Patronage of the Arts in England, 1066–1200*, (London, 1984). The Châsse is in the Cloisters Museum, New York.

[119] *V* B. Scholz, "The Canonization of Edward the Confessor," p. 53, n. 73 for later medieval references to the Translation of Edward the Confessor, including the *Thomas Saga* 1, pp. 136–7.

[120] Ed. Horstmann, pp. 133–4.

[121] 2:330; 3:56. The *Thomas Saga*, 1, pp. 207–9 has much the same story. Thomas said all the Hours of the blessed martyr Stephen before singing the Mass himself; it was "certain king's folk and clerks" who happened to be near the church, "thinking in their mind with some wonder, what this song (*Etenim sederunt*) might import, or why it should happen to be sung at this time." The *Thomas Saga* drew on the *Quadrilogus*, (*Materials for the History of Thomas Becket*, 4:266–430), a composite of the accounts by Benedict of Peterborough, William of Canterbury, Herbert of Bosham and Alan of Tewkesbury, but also names another twelfth century source, now lost, a *Life* of St. Thomas by Robert of Cricklade, prior of St. Frideswide's, Oxford, 1141–c. 1174.

[122] Ep. 187, p. 247.

[123] Ep. 225, p. 393, (Ps. 2.2).

[124] Ep. 168, p. 107.

[125] Attributed to John of Salisbury in Alan of Tewkesbury's letter collection. *V The Letters of John of Salisbury* 2, Ep. 307, pp. 745, xliv.

[126] Ep. 310, p. 757.

[127] Unpublished. Quoted by B. Smalley, *The Becket Conflict and the Schools*, p. 224; *v* pp. 202–3 for Peter the Chanter's citation of Becket as a sound Abel.

[128] 4:133, 194; *Breviarium Ad Usum Sarum*, fasc. 1, p. cclvi. Herbert of Bosham also alludes to Abel in describing Becket's betrayal by his brother bishops, 3:275.

[129] Benedicta Ward, *The Prayers and Meditations of St. Anselm*, (Harmondsworth, 1973), pp. 38, 42.

[130] Similarly, St. Ailred habitually carried one particularly edifying book, wont to produce tears, the *Confessions* of St. Augustine, "which had been his guide from when he was converted from the world," *Life of Ailred*, p. 50. Becket is the first named instance of someone outside Anselm's own circle using these fervent, affective *Prayers*, but they were frequently copied, with an early tradition of illustration. *V* Otto Pacht, "The Illustrations of St. Anselm's Prayers and Meditations,"

Journal of the Warburg and Courtauld Institutes 19 (1956) pp. 68–83. Becket, a biblio-phile and art patron, may well have possessed an illustrated copy.

131 *The Prayers and Meditations of St. Anselm*, pp. 175–7, 179, 182. Anselm's *Prayers* also show that SS. Peter and Paul, like St. Stephen, could be fervently invoked in a context of compunction and longing for true conversion, and not only as trium-phalist examples of the Church's defence against her persecutors. Becket's known and frequent use of Anselm's affective *Prayers* may suggest at least an ambiguity in the meaning of the wall paintings of SS. Peter and Paul which Becket may have commissioned for Anselm's translation, (*v* above and n. 108).

132 For text and commentary *v Councils and Synods with other Documents relating to the English Church* I, pt. II, pp. 895–914.

133 Ep. 152, p. 57; Ep. 315, p. 775.

134 Joseph van der Straeten, "Les vieux latines de Saint Thomas Becket et son exil en France," *Actes . . . de Sédières*, pp. 30, 32 for the date usually given for Becket's arrival in Pontigny, 30 November or early December 1164. However, Martin Preiss, *Die politische Tatigkeit und Stellung der Cisterzienser in Schism 1159–77,* (Berlin, 1934), p. 81 and n. 71 argued that Becket's arrival was not before the first half of January 1165.

135 R. W. Southern, *St. Anselm and his Biographer*, pp. 265–7.

136 Interestingly enough, they are Roger of Pontigny and William of FitzStephen (4:77; 3:141), who also recall that St. Elphege had been invoked by Becket at the St. Stephen's mass in October 1164 and that Elphege's martyrdom had been cited in discussions about Becket that same day.

137 Ep. 304, p. 723.

138 7:429–33; A. Duggan, *Actes . . . de Sédières*, ed. R. Foreville, p.33.

INDEX

CONTENTS OF
PREVIOUS VOLUMES

263